People of the Bays and Headlands:
Anthropological History and the Fate of
Communities in the Unknown Labrador

In July 1992 the Canadian government announced a moratorium on fishing for northern cod, closing the most important part of the New-foundland and Labrador fishery. Why had fish stocks disappeared and what would become of the people and communities long dependent on fishing? John C. Kennedy tells the story of some of these communities in Canada's newest and poorest province. He focuses on the European settlers of southeastern Labrador, the little-known region between Chateau and Sandwich bays. His is the first detailed examination of a region whose history resembles others on the margins of the North Atlantic rim.

Historically, families moved to barren headlands and islands each spring to harvest marine resources and returned each fall to their winter homesteads in sheltered bays. However, during the twentieth century new wage-labour opportunities and state-imposed regulations meant that most people abandoned this adaptive, dispersed settlement pattern and moved to new centres. Southeastern Labrador's twentieth-century history is one of rural centralization and growing dependence, and is thus similar to that of much of the formerly dispersed rural world.

The book breaks new ground in its critical discussion of the role of Inuit enclaves in early European settlement, the impact of the Grenfell Mission, the Labrador Development Company, and military base construction. In showing how settlers adjusted to some intrusive forces but not to others, the book increases our understanding of the growth and decline of peripheral areas.

JOHN C. KENNEDY is an associate professor in the Department of Anthropology, Memorial University of Newfoundland.

JOHN C. KENNEDY

People of the Bays and Headlands: Anthropological History and the Fate of Communities in the Unknown Labrador

UNIVERSITY OF TORONTO PRESS
Toronto Buffalo London

© University of Toronto Press Incorporated 1995
Toronto Buffalo London
Printed in Canada

ISBN 0-8020-0646-9 (cloth)
ISBN 0-8020-7600-9 (paper)

∞

Printed on acid-free paper

Canadian Cataloguing in Publication Data

Kennedy, John Charles
 People of the bays and headlands : anthropological
 history and the fate of communities in the unknown
 Labrador

 Includes bibliographical references and index.
 ISBN 0-8020-0646-9 (bound) ISBN 0-8020-7600-9 (pbk.)

 1. Labrador (Nfld.) – Social conditions.
 2. Labrador (Nfld.) – Economic conditions.
 3. Labrador (Nfld.) – History. I. Title.

 HN110.L3K4 1995   971.8′2   C95-930516-5

University of Toronto Press acknowledges the financial assistance to its
publishing program of the Canada Council and the Ontario Arts Council.

This book has been published with the help of a grant from the Social
Science Federation of Canada, using funds provided by the Social Sciences
and Humanities Research Council of Canada.

Contents

Preface

This book introduces the peoples of a region I call the 'unknown Labrador' – the coast, approximately three hundred kilometres long, south of Labrador's Groswater Bay (see Map 1). Completion of the book fulfils my promise to the people of southeastern Labrador to write a book about their history and way of life. Moreover, having specialized in Labrador studies since 1971 (and having taught a university course on this topic since the mid-1970s), I am aware that the southeastern Labrador coast is the last great unknown area of Canada's tenth province: Newfoundland and Labrador. And thus, this book attempts both to introduce the region and to stimulate further research.

In completing the book, I also have been inspired by other fortuitous, indeed primordial, ties to Labrador. As the grandson of Newfoundlanders (John James Kennedy and Margaret Elizabeth St John) who left Newfoundland late in the last century and emigrated to the 'Boston states,' I grew up hearing my late father (Joseph S. Kennedy) talk about Newfoundland and Labrador, and more specifically, about the Labrador coast, quite likely the region described here, where his 'mother's people' had traded. Coincidentally, the house where I was raised, in Medfield, Massachusetts, was surrounded by Americans with important links to Labrador. Across the street lived Joel Goldthwait, son of orthopaedic surgeon Dr Joel E. Goldthwait (a friend of my father who lived up the street), a friend of Dr Grenfell and fellow promoter of the role of diet in health. Dr Goldthwait's Grenfellian experimental 'Medfield Farms' was immediately west of my boyhood home. Next door lived our playmates Nat and Charlotte Goodhue, grandchildren of Dr Alexander Forbes, another Grenfell friend and a Labrador explorer. Like my father's stories about Labrador, these childhood coincidences of time and place enkindled my curiosity about Labrador long before I saw its forbidding grey coastline.

This book is based on a combination of ethnographic and archival research. I conducted fieldwork in the seasonal settlements of Lodge Bay and Cape Charles between February and August 1979, using standard ethnographic techniques: a household census, participant observation, random non-directed interviews, and more formal directed interviews. This was followed by a brief return to Cape Charles in the summer of 1980, three months in Port Hope Simpson in autumn 1982, three months in Cartwright in autumn 1983, and three weeks in Lodge Bay and Mary's Harbour in 1992.

Given the paucity of accessible sources on this little-known part of Labrador, I travelled to Lodge Bay in 1979 knowing little of what I would encounter. Furthermore, the oral tradition of the people of southeastern Labrador, which is their individual and collective memory, is limited to three generations. And even then, only a few older people were able to recall anything about life during their grandparents' era, around 1900. There are also very few local sources of written information, such as diaries, that might supplement oral tradition. Consequently, the book reconstructs history by piecing together the scraps of written records describing communities of the region, whenever possible coupling written and ethnographic sources.

I did my archival research between 1983 and 1989, the bulk of it during two unpaid leaves from the university during the winter terms of 1988 and 1989. I used a number of libraries and archives, particularly the Provincial Archives of Newfoundland and Labrador (PANL), the Centre for Newfoundland Studies (CNS) at Memorial University of Newfoundland's Queen Elizabeth II library, and several archives in the northeastern United States. However, the book's apparent reliance on archival documents is misleading. In fact, even sections based primarily on archival data – such as those chronicling southeast Labrador's twentieth-century whaling industry, its logging industries, and its modern umbrella of institutions – were enriched by discussions with local people. In short, I advocate combining field *and* archival research methods. This method gathers a wider range of data than is possible when only one methodology is used, and has consequences for theoretical questions related to this study.

Although production of this book has been primarily an individual labour of love, some persons and institutions have helped and deserve thanks. The Memorial University of Newfoundland's Institute of Social and Economic Research provided funds to conduct the ethnographic field research in 1979, 1980, and 1992. I also thank the federal SEED program, which funded university students to work with me on the manuscript. These students – Mark Dolomount in 1992, Leslie Tuff in 1993, and Greg White in 1994 – have been a tremendous help.

I also thank Rex Clark, Linda Epp, and David Macdonald for their helpful comments on earlier versions of specific chapters and my brother-in-law, Dan Bergeron, for his perceptive comments on an earlier version of the entire manuscript.

I appreciate the comments of my anonymous Social Science Federation of Canada and University of Toronto reviewers and, especially, the support of Executive Editor Virgil D. Duff.

I thank Doris Saunders of *Them Days* for copying from the magazine's extensive collection several photographs which appear in the book, and also several coastal Labradorians (whose names appear in the photo credits) who generously allowed me to copy their photos.

The people of southeastern Labrador deserve a special thanks; this book is for them.

Last but not least, I thank my wife, Karen Olsson, a former Grenfell nurse with an informed admiration for Labrador people. Karen has supported me throughout the writing of this book; she read and commented on several earlier versions of the manuscript, and allowed me the time necessary to complete the book. I dedicate the book to Karen, and to our two young sons, Alexander and Erik.

JOHN C. KENNEDY

Abbreviations

ACOA	Atlantic Canada Opportunities Agency
ADSF	*Among the Deep Sea Fishers*
CBC	Canadian Broadcasting Company
CLTEAC	Coastal Labrador Training and Education Advisory Committee
CNS	Centre for Newfoundland Studies (QE II Library, MUN)
CYC	Company of Young Canadians
DREE	Department of Regional Economic Expansion
ESLDA	East Shore Labrador Development Association
ET	*Evening Telegram (St John's)*
GRHS	Grenfell Regional Health Services
HBC	Hudson's Bay Company
IGA	International Grenfell Association
ISER	Institute for Social and Economic Research (MUN)
JHA	*Journal of the [Nfld] House of Assembly*
LCPA	Labrador Craft Producers Association
LDC	Labrador Development Company
LIA	Labrador Inuit Association
LINS	Labrador Institute of Northern Studies
LMA	Labrador Metis Association
LRAC	Labrador Resource Advisory Council
LSD	Labrador Services Division
MHA	Member of the House of Assembly (Newfoundland Legislature)
MUN	Memorial University of Newfoundland
NATO	North Atlantic Treaty Organization
NLRDC	Newfoundland and Labrador Rural Development Council

PANL   Provincial Archives of Newfoundland and Labrador
PC   Privy Council
RAND   Rural, Agricultural and Northern Development,
       Department of
RC   Resettlement Committee
RF   Resettlement Files
TD   *Them Days* Magazine

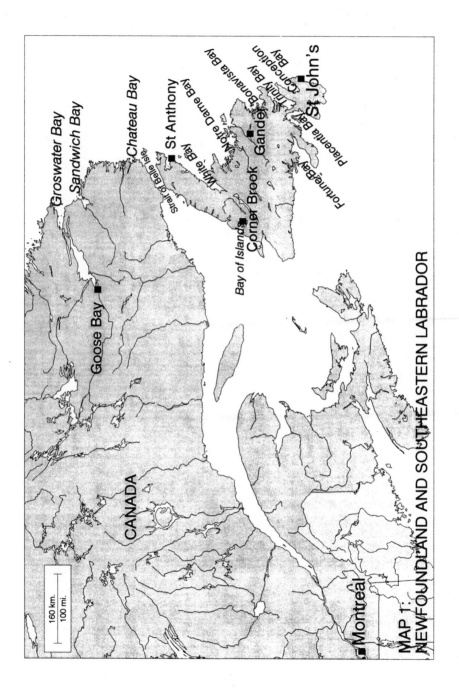

Groswater Bay
Sandwich Bay
Chateau Bay
St Anthony
Notre Dame Bay
Bonavista Bay
Trinity Bay
Conception Bay
St John's
Placentia Bay
Fortune Bay
White Bay
Strait of Belle Isle
Bay of Islands
Corner Brook
Gander
Goose Bay
CANADA
Montreal

160 km.
100 mi.

MAP 1:
NEWFOUNDLAND AND SOUTHEASTERN LABRADOR

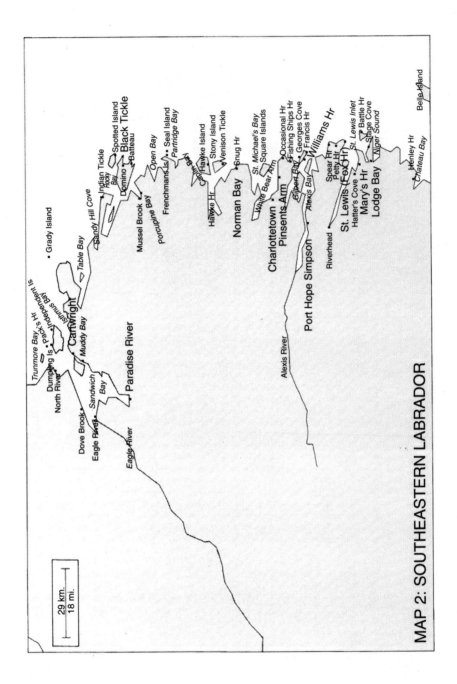

MAP 2: SOUTHEASTERN LABRADOR

Trunmore Bay · Pack's Hr
Dumpling Is · Independent Is
North River
Dove Brook
Eagle River
Eagle River
Sandwich Bay
Paradise River
Muddy Bay
Cartwright
Table Bay
Sandy Hill Cove
Grady Island
Indian Tickle
Rocky
Domino
Batteau
Spotted Island
Black Tickle
Mussel Brook
Open Bay
Porcupine Bay
Frenchmans Is.
Seal Island
Partridge Bay
Cape
Hawke Island
Hawke Hr
Stony Island
Venison Tickle
Snug Hr
Norman Bay
St. Michael's Bay
White Bear Arm
Square Islands
Charlottetown
Pinsents Arm
Occasional Hr
Fishing Ships Hr
Georges Cove
Francis Hr
Williams Hr
Gilbert Bay
Alexis Bay
Alexis River
Port Hope Simpson
Riverhead
Spear Hr
Petty Hr
St. Lewis (Fox Hr)
Hatter's Cove
Mary's Hr
St. Lewis Inlet
Battle Hr
Stage Cove
Niger Sound
Lodge Bay
Henley Hr
Chateau Bay
Belle Island

29 km.
18 mi.

Gready, Labrador, probably late nineteenth century, showing fish-drying flakes in foreground. (Provincial Archives of Newfoundland and Labrador)

Washing codfish at Battle Harbour, 1910. (*Them Days*)

Batteau, 1893. Note jack boat converted into salt house. (*Them Days*)

Man flenching whale at Hawke Harbour, ca 1930. (*Them Days*)

The John Kippenhuck family at George's Cove, ca 1940. (Courtesy
Celesta Acreman)

The Sam Burden family at George's Cove, ca 1940. (Courtesy
Celesta Acreman)

Campbell and Kippenhuck families after killing a polar bear at Charlottetown, 1939. (Courtesy Ben Powell)

Hauling up boat at Battle Harbour, ca 1950. (Courtesy Celesta Acreman)

LEFT: Cartwright settler with harpoon used to retrieve seals, autumn 1983.

RIGHT: Lodge Bay settler at Cape Charles, March 1979.

Abandoned radar base at Cartwright, 1983.

Mattie's Cove cod crew, 1979.

Cape Charles fisher with codfish, 1979.

Fish store (right), stage, and house, 1979.

Port Hope Simpson scene, showing stretched sealskin and woodpile,
autumn 1982.

Royal Orange Lodge Easter parade, 1979.

Saltboat at Earle Freighting Service stores, Frenchmen's Islands, 1979.

Wall's Tickle, Cape Charles, June 1992.

Indian Cove (near Battle Harbour), 1979.

Author cutting firewood at Port Hope Simpson, autumn 1982. (Courtesy
Karen Olsson)

People of the Bays and Headlands:
Anthropological History and the Fate of
Communities in the Unknown Labrador

1

Introduction

In July 1992 the Canadian government announced a moratorium on fishing for 'northern cod,' shutting down the most important part of Newfoundland's five-hundred-year-old cod fishery. The government paid fishers and plant workers not to work (a subsidy similar to those paid to prairie farmers not to farm), leaving over twenty thousand jobless. The moratorium was to last two years, but by then cod stocks had declined further. Consequently the area covered by the moratorium was expanded and the subsidy continued. More ominously, stocks of most other fish species off Canada's east coast had declined. The fishery crises became a national issue, with Canadian editorialists blaming idle fishers and the federal government attempting to curb foreign overfishing just beyond the 200-mile limit. Two questions became common in Newfoundland and Labrador: why had fish stocks disappeared, and what would become of the people and communities long dependent on fishing?

This book tells the largely untold story of communities in one region of Canada's newest and poorest province, Newfoundland and Labrador. This region, southeastern Labrador, now living under the northern cod moratorium, includes the sea coast and portions of the interior between Chateau and Sandwich bays (see Map 1).

In 1991, the *combined* population of the region's eleven tiny communities was 2962 – that of a small Canadian town (see Map 2). And although the populations of several of the smaller communities increased negligibly between 1986 and 1991, the population of Cartwright, the second-largest community, dropped almost 10 per cent, and consequently, the total regional population declined from 2983 (1986) to 2962 (1991), the first such decline in recent years.[1] My findings from the community of Lodge Bay suggest a similar decline (Kennedy, forthcoming). In 1979, the population of this old winter settlement peaked at 129, but by 1992 it had dropped to 98. Recent male emigration is troubling and historically unprecedented. Traditionally, young men remained home with the fishery while their sisters moved elsewhere to marry or work. Yet surprisingly, Lodge Bay folk are of two minds about the departure of their sons. On the one hand, the main cause of emigration – an imperilled fishery – worries them considerably, while on the other hand, people suppose that opportunities are better elsewhere. Community decline can also be inferred from attendance at the local school, which educated only half as many students in 1992 as in 1979. Older people blame the decline on unmarried youth not producing children but, to me, the decisions taken by single youth, many only in their twenties, seemed to be a manifestation of new, and unequalled, economic uncertainties overwhelming the community.

All eleven southeastern Labrador communities are accessible by boat in summer, by snowmobile in winter, and by small airplane year-round. They are remote, northern, and isolated. Until the beginning of the cod moratorium in 1992, people practised a nearly two-century-old migratory economy, harvesting the resources of the land and sea where they were most accessible. Until the early twentieth century, the environment and economy encouraged a dispersed and seasonally mobile settlement and exploitative pattern. Families moved seasonally to harvest available resources, congregating near other families at summer fishing stations and then dispersing each fall to their smaller, family-based winter homesteads. However, during the twentieth century new developments increasingly threatened this pattern. As with the eighteenth- and nineteenth-century transition from rural agrarian villages to commercial towns that occurred throughout much of the Western world, the decentralized Settler lifestyle was incompatible with emerging economic and institutional developments. Settlers were pressured to move to growing winter settlements, where wage employment and new services were to be provided. With some exceptions, the prospect of a regular income proved irresistible to people accustomed to the vicissitudes of the former lifestyle. Eventually various wage labour opportunities and, latterly, state-imposed regulations required that most people abandon their antiquated, although adaptive, dispersed settlement pattern and move to new centres. Phrased differently, the traditional and highly adaptive settlement pattern of the region was organized on centrifugal or decentralized principles. In this century this has been almost completely replaced by intrusive centripetal forces that have drawn people into larger communities for ever-greater portions of each year. One example of a centripetal force is the Grenfell Mission, which consolidated people near its services.

Historically, Settlers maintained and moved to two (and sometimes three) seasonal homes. The largest and most intense concentration of families occurred at summer fishing settlements, the social antithesis of isolated, family-based winter homesteads. Nowadays, people spend most of each year in large and relatively impersonal winter communities. Small wonder that many people still speak of outside fishing stations as 'home.' Survival once required resources near both summer and winter homes, whereas today, especially since the moratorium, only one home is necessary. Quite simply then, the story of southeastern Labrador is one of rural centralization and growing dependence, a movement similar to that of much of the formerly dispersed rural world during the past two centuries.

In 1990, prior to the moratorium, people wintering in the eleven winter communities travelled to one of forty-seven customarily used summer stations located along the bleak outer coast (Brice-Bennett 1992, 106). Although the number of summer stations has undoubtedly decreased during this century, the real change is the decline in the number of winter places. There were once perhaps three times as many winter communities as the present eleven, and this reduction is a large part of this book's focus. The 'continuity in change' (Sahlins 1994, 393) reported here is that summer fishing settlements persisted until recently, despite sweeping changes to winter settlements.

Since Newfoundland joined Canada, the people of southeastern Labrador have increasingly faced the dilemma of craving an expanding array of consumer goods and increased government services, notably education, health, social services, and the like, while rejecting the hidden long-term costs of such benefits: escalating dependence on government, community centralization, and now resource depletion. This trade-off, crystal clear in hindsight, is also part of the story.

Southeastern Labrador has a long, yet largely unknown history. My reason for telling the story of this region resembles the mountaineers' rationale: because it has not been told. Some anthropologists (Cohen 1980, 215; Whitaker 1988, 78–79) claim, with some justification, that Newfoundland and Labrador is the best-documented Canadian province. While this may be true of some parts of the province, like northern Labrador, other regions are virtual enigmas, and southeastern Labrador, what I call the *unknown Labrador*, is one of these.

In calling southeastern Labrador the *unknown* Labrador I am aware that other work has been published containing valuable information on the region. Such work includes George Cartwright's three-volume diary (1792); Bishop Feild's (1849; 1851) reports on his mid-nineteeth-century travels along the coast; De Boilieu's ([1861] 1969) recollections of St Lewis Inlet; Gosling's (1910) monumental and still unsurpassed history of Labrador; the Reverend Mr Gordon's (1972) journal of his decade (1915–25) in Sandwich Bay; portions of Tanner's (1944) classic overview, such as his portrait of Dove Brook (Sandwich Bay) Settlers; Jolin's study of Spotted Island fishing crews (1965); portions of the report of the Royal Commission on Labrador (Newfoundland 1974); *Them Days* magazine's invaluable booklet *Alluring Labrador* ([1975] 1982); Jackson's brief but eloquent *Bounty of a Barren Coast* (1982); the excellent theses of Southard (1982) on Port Hope Simpson and Schneider (1984) on Cartwright; relevant portions of Brice-Bennett's (1992) report on the fishery; and the recent work of Stopp and associates on archaeology (1991, 1992). Jackson's and Schneider's work is especially relevant to this study, although neither study examines the region as thoroughly as I do. Also, Abbott's (1988) pictorial essay on Quebec's Lower North Shore is a story very relevant to my own, and portions of McCloskey's *Fish Decks* (1990) are set in southeastern Labrador.

Yet despite the above, this study breaks new ground on a number of substantive issues: the role of Inuit enclaves in early European settlement; the relationship of early permanent settlement to the American fishery; the account of the nineteenth-century Settler adaptation and the reasons behind its disruption during this century; the critical account of the impact of the Grenfell Mission, the Labrador Development Company, and the construction of military bases on Settler communities; and others. Following Eric Wolf (1982) and others such as Kottak and Colson (1994), I attempt to expose *links* between southeastern Labrador and distant centres of control and capital. Even so, the attention to global linkages raises as many issues as it solves and I hope paves the way for future researchers. More generally, the story of southeastern Labrador communities is applicable to other regions. Indeed, I think that the general pattern of economic change, community growth, and decline is apropos for much of eastern Canada and that all familiar with particular Atlantic microregions will see 'their' bay or coastline in my work.

People of the Bays and Headlands seeks to fill a gap in our understanding of one part of Canada. My primary aim is descriptive, and the book is a baseline study repeatedly calling for further research. My focus is historical,[2] concentrating on social and economic history, chiefly since the early 1800s, when Europeans permanently settled the area. European Settlers[3] used aboriginal and European practices and knowledge to adapt to the rigorous subarctic Labrador environment. Examination of the region's long-term history reveals a pattern: some historical events and processes were compatible with the European Settlers' dispersed and migratory Labrador lifestyle, while others were not. Like the ocean waves that alternatively crash upon or caress Labrador's jagged shoreline, some developments originating from afar conformed to the Settler adaptation and others did not. I maintain that the Settlers' dispersed settlement pattern and family-based economy undermined their collective agency. Yet Settlers were not entirely passive recipients of global forces, an interpretative issue discussed in Chapter 12. The historical pattern whereby Settlers adjusted to some intrusive forces and were overwhelmed by others is the lesson of *People of the Bays and Headlands* and is, I believe, the source of its relevance to the present fishery crises.

REGIONS AND COMMUNITIES

How does one define the word 'region'? There are many answers, but here, following Matthews, a region is considered to be 'a distinctive type of social unit which can be located in territorial terms and which incorporates within it such smaller social units as communities, neighbourhoods, and cities' (1983, 14).[4] Among southeastern Labrador people, opinions are divided on whether *the* southeastern Labrador I am concerned with actually constitutes one region. As we will see in the overview of regional development associations in Chapter 11, some distinguish several smaller microregions. Most, however, would likely agree that the area between Chateau and Sandwich bays constitutes a region, and that broad sociocultural and historic characteristics distinguish it from other regions of Labrador.

My focus on the rise and fall of communities resembles the sociology of so-called boom towns, the rise and fall of (relatively) large industrial or smaller agricultural communities. One study of rural decline in the United States, for example, discusses the replacement of the family farm by corporate farms (Whiting 1974). In Canada, Lucas has written a well-known study of single-industry towns (1971). While there are similarities between the Labrador communities I discuss and Lucas's company towns, such as high rates of youth (especially female) out-migration, there are also significant differences, most attributable to scale and social composition. Thus, in one respect, Labrador communities are single-industry fishing communities; yet they are small and homogeneous compared to Lucas's milltowns and minetowns of thirty thousand people. Nevertheless, as does Lucas's study, this book demonstrates the vulnerability of single-industry communities to foreign control and global economic cycles.

My unit of analysis is communities, although of course communities are made up of individuals. Community studies have long been a method and community itself an object of empirical research by geographers, sociologists, and anthropologists (cf. Bell and Newby 1978; Arensberg and Kimball 1965; Clark 1973).[5]

Areas of common agreement emerge from the multitude of community definitions: area, common ties, and social interaction, and in a different vein, symbolic boundaries locally defined and communicated (Hillary 1955; Kaufman 1959; Lyon 1987; Cohen 1985). Commenting on the multitude of community definitions, Lyon observes that in the social sciences 'there seems to be an inverse relationship between the importance of a concept and the precision with which it is defined' (1987, 4). Here, I use 'community' as a social and cultural collectivity of people adapted to a locally defined geographic space. This older, more 'structural' meaning of community conforms to my longitudinal perspective. I reiterate that the communities I am talking about were seasonal: the historic winter communities were essentially family-based homesteads, although summer fishing stations tended to be larger.

CHAPTER OUTLINE

Chapter 2 briefly describes the environment of southeastern Labrador and its prehistoric and early European occupations to 1763, the beginning of the British era. Both during prehistory and more assuredly during the French regime, a seasonally mobile settlement pattern enabled adaptation to and productive use of this difficult environment. The details of seasonality are explained more completely in Chapter 3, and the era of early British colonialization and administration is illustrated here by the career of Captain George Cartwright. Although Cartwright's Labrador career preceded early permanent European settlement, his argument for year-round residency hastened its beginnings. The relative tranquillity of Cartwright's Labrador was shattered by the yearly arrival of thousands of visiting fishers, the subject of

Chapter 4. Foreign fisheries linked Labrador to the world markets and, I suggest, clandestine trade with local planters (petty merchant-fishers) enabled early settlement. More research, especially in American and British archives, is necessary to conclusively prove my connection between trade and early settlement, yet I believe that the circumstantial evidence presented here makes the case.

Chapter 5 describes early permanent settlement. This appears to have begun during the 1820s and 1830s, about the same time that visiting foreign fishers became more numerous. This chapter also argues for the first time that Inuit enclaves existed south of Groswater Bay during the late eighteenth and much of the nineteenth century. There are two consequences of these Inuit enclaves, one historic, the other contemporary. First, some first-generation Settlers found spouses among nearby Inuit. The availability of Inuit spouses means that permanent settlement could have occurred earlier, were it not for competition between rival merchants for labour and resources, competition which discouraged the transition from salaried servants to supplied Settlers. The second consequence is the recent politicization of ethnicity, specifically ethnogenesis of the Labrador Metis, as presented in Chapter 11, a saga to be played out during the next few years as the Labrador Metis Association attempts to amend the existing aboriginal map of Labrador.

Once Settlers acquired spouses and gained a foothold in Labrador, they set about developing a distinctive Labrador lifestyle, the topic of Chapter 6. This lifestyle resembled in its seasonal movements that of earlier peoples, such as the French, and drew both on aboriginal practices and beliefs and on those acquired from waves of Newfoundland (and other) transient fishers who arrived each summer. The historic Settler lifestyle, particularly its seasonal migrations, contains an obvious contemporary lesson: the more people abandon seasonality, the more it becomes necessary to embrace a fundamentally new economy. Given that such a new economy has failed to emerge, abandoning seasonality implies escalating dependence on the state.

Chapter 7 examines the nineteenth- and early twentieth-century extension of the state (the Newfoundland government) to its Labrador dependency. Most state policies were intended to serve the more numerous and politically powerful Newfoundland fishers who visited the Labrador coast to fish for three or four months each summer. Initially, the state had little effect on resident Settlers but this also changed, particularly in this century.

Chapter 8 discusses three twentieth-century industries (the herring, whale, and fur industries) congruous with the Settler lifestyle. Chapter 9 then discusses three developments inimical to it. These were the Grenfell Mission, the Labrador Development Company, and the construction of military bases; all were centripetal, attracting Settlers from their customary winter homesteads to new centres.

Following its entrance into the Canadian federation in 1949, the new province of Newfoundland and Labrador pondered the fate of its tiny rural 'outports,' leading to the ignominious resettlement program discussed in Chapter 10. Under this program, about three dozen southeastern Labrador winter settlements were reduced to eleven. While resettlement sounded the death-knell for many rural communities, the institutions discussed in Chapter 11, largely funded by the state, gave something back.

While I have lived with the people of the bays and headlands and support them in their current struggle, I am painfully aware that my interpretation of their past and predictions for the future, as presented in Chapter 12, are less optimistic than I would have liked. I hope, of course, that these predictions are wrong and, further, that *People of the Bays and Headlands* prompts further research and critical revision.

2

Environment, Prehistory, and European Exploitation to 1763

The periodic abundance of resources along the coast of Labrador has attracted human beings for several thousand years. This chapter describes the natural environment, paying particular attention to natural conditions important to people, and provides a summary of the prehistory and European exploration and exploitation of the region prior to the Treaty of Paris in 1763. Each of these three topics provides lessons relevant to the Settler communities discussed in subsequent chapters.

The lesson from the environment is elementary: this marginal, although occasionally abundant northern environment has definite limits. Human existence requires socio-economic practices responding to the seasonal availability of a finite number of natural resources. In Harris's words, 'the constraints of this environment precluded the kind of diversified production that allowed the development of a different society in New England and to a lesser extent in the Maritime provinces and determined the nature of the cultural and commercial patterns that were to control the lives and destinies of Newfoundlanders for centuries' (1990, 19). People who depart from dependence on seasonally available natural resources must either develop a new (and thus far unknown) economy, such as mining or forestry, or import necessities for living to the area.

Prehistory, although shrouded in the conundrums unavoidable in the study of archaeology, illustrates the necessity of a seasonal adaptation to the environment. Peoples inhabiting southeastern Labrador prior to recorded time unquestionably moved to exploit seasonally available resources, although their migrations may have occurred primarily along the outer coast (Stopp and Rutherford 1991, 32) unlike the historic transhumant pattern. When times were good, for instance after many animals, fish, or birds had been killed, prehistoric peoples probably congregated briefly in larger numbers, as if to test but quickly confirm the demographic limits of their hunting economy.

Two points are clear from early European involvement in the region, the first a rule, the other an exception. The rule is that early Europeans practised seasonal transhumance. The French migrated seasonally, just as English Settlers would later do. In fact, we know of cases where they inhabited the same places while exploiting the same resources! The exception is the exploitation of a single resource. Thus, Red Bay, Labrador's first single-industry boom town, specialized in whaling (Tuck and Grenier 1989). Similarly, the logging town of Port Hope Simpson cut spruce pit-props to the exclusion of other resources.

THE ENVIRONMENT

My account is brief, but I direct readers interested in environmental characteristics to relevant portions of Fitzhugh (1972), Jackson (1982), Kennedy (1982), Schneider (1984), Stopp and Rutherford (1991), Stopp and Reynolds (1992), Tanner (1944), and other works. Rather than listing an inventory of natural features and species as is conventional in most anthropological accounts, I will limit my remarks to four main environmental features that I think characterize the natural environment of the region; the last three are especially relevant to my argument. The four are: the consequences of ancient glaciers once covering Labrador, the Labrador current, Labrador's two coastlines, and the periodic scarcity and abundance of natural resources.

During the Pleistocene geological epoch, approximately ten thousand years before the present (BP), most of the Quebec-Labrador peninsula lay covered by glaciers – immense layers of snow and ice one or two kilometres thick. During this two- million-year-long epoch, snow and ice accumulated, reducing the amount of fresh water running into the sea in spring and summer. Brooks and rivers deposited less water into the sea, and consequently, sea levels, like temperatures, were lower than today's. The glaciers scraped the land bare of topsoil (depositing it well offshore), scattered huge boulders on barren uplands, and gouged the surface of Labrador's Precambrian geology (granites and gneisses almost as old as the earth itself), producing rivers, fjords, and lakes. In short, the Pleistocene period sculptured much of the present physiography, and its impact continues.

The second feature occurs in the form of an invisible yet dominating cold ocean current, the renowned Labrador current. The Labrador current includes waters from two cold arctic currents and from the warmer Irminger or West Greenland current; the three converge at Cape Chidley and flow south. The earth's rotation westward continuously deflects the current towards land, depositing its cargo of pack ice from the Canadian archipelago and towering icebergs which break off Greenland's ice-cap each year. Along with the climatic consequences of prevailing continental air masses that continually flow just south of the region, the Labrador current chills air temperatures, ensuring long and cold winters and short summers. The frigid effect of the icy (though technically subarctic) Labrador current on climate is underscored by comparison: Sandwich Bay shares the same north latitude as Manchester, England, and Chateau Bay bisects County Cork, Ireland, yet there is an enormous difference in their climates. The mixing of the cold and salty waters of the Labrador current with those of the warmer Gulf Stream (occurring off much of eastern Newfoundland and southern Labrador) has two other effects on the region: it enriches all marine life and causes considerable precipitation, notably fog during early summer.

As Dyke (1969, 128) correctly observed, Labrador has two coastlines – a relatively protected inner or mainland coast of bays and inlets and an exposed outer coast of capes and islands. The two coasts differ in climate, a point observed by Captain Cartwright and all others travelling to or living permanently along the coast. The climate of the exposed outer coast is marine – variable but generally raw and damp – and that of the inner coast is continental – stable, drier, and extreme, quite hot in summer and cold in winter. And the natural resources of both coasts differ dramatically. The outer coast has been the ocean bread basket, while the inner coast includes boreal forest flora and fauna. Local people and other observers have noted an essential symbiosis between these two coasts: people needed resources of the inner coast to procure those of the outer coast, and vice versa.[1]

Finally, the area is characterized at the same time by resource scarcity and abundance. Unlike more temperate and diverse environments, where a great many species inhabit an area for a greater portion of each year, the number of species found in southeastern Labrador is small and most are seasonal residents, only using the area for part of their annual cycle. Fortunately for people, not all of these transient species visit during the same time of year, and when visiting, most do so in great numbers. Both the strength and vulnerability of this small inventory of transient species continue to be its seasonal and cyclic availability: its periodic scarcity or abundance. I will speak more of seasonal availability but here is a brief and admittedly conjectural note on longer-term cycles. Many Labrador species are recognized to have long-term cycles of abundance or scarcity – varying hares, porcupine, fur-bearing animals, caribou, and others. I take another example, codfish.

The so-called northern codfish stocks (comprising the Northwest Atlantic Fisheries – NAFO divisions 2J3KL) have been of vital importance to Newfoundland and Labrador. Between 1845 and 1945, four-fifths of all fishers pursued northern cod (Smallwood 1981, 469), and more recently, 63 per cent of fishers and 69 per cent of plant workers, a minimum of 34,900 people, were employed in the northern cod fishery (Harris 1990, 40). The distinctive feature of this stock is its annual move from offshore spawning grounds towards Labrador coastal waters to feed in early summer (Pinhorn 1976, 5–6). These predictable (even if incompletely known) migrations facilitate human exploitation, traditionally inshore in summer and more recently well offshore, by modern draggers. Although it is a cold-water ground fish, temperatures affect the inshore movements and abundance of cod. Migrations towards shore are curtailed when the intermediate layer of ocean water is especially cold, creating a thermal barrier to cod movements (Harris 1990, 82–3). The occurrence of unusually cold water may also be cyclic. Thus, although focused primarily on Greenland, the work of Vibe (1967) and Dunbar (1951) documents a relationship between multi-year cold water cycles and the incidence of cod, leading Dunbar to conclude that the 'history of cod fishing ... is the history of water temperatures' (Dunbar 1951, 99). Although it is difficult to accurately access historic northern cod landings (Templeman 1966, 28; Harris 1990, 25–6), cycles of heavy ice and unusually cold water quite possibly explain the scarcities fishers encountered during the 1870s, during the second decade of this century, and today. The present, mysterious disappearance of cod and other fish species off Canada's east coast may ultimately be linked to a combination of complex environmental changes, such as cold water, or ozone depletions, and overfishing (Strauss 1993, D8). In any case, over the past thirty years, average water temperatures of the offshore spawning grounds have declined from about 0.5 to −1 degrees Celsius (ibid.) Cold water cycles also explain past scarcity.

Like cod, many other abundant species were short-term visitors to Labrador. One can use any group of species to illustrate the proportion of resident to migratory species. For example, Tanner (1944, 430) notes that only 10 per cent of the approximately 225 species of birds found in northern Labrador are year-round residents. This scarcity of resident species meant that one key to human adaptation was exploitation of the visitors. These passed by in great numbers seasonally, particularly in fall, spring, and summer. The October and November skies blackened with millions of the common eider, harlequin, and old-squaw ducks flying south. A little later, enormous herds of harp-seals also headed south to give birth, ideally passing southeastern Labrador just before the sea ice froze fast to the land and people retreated from the barren headlands and islands to the sheltered bays and coves of the inner coast. Spring brought the same visitors, waterfowl and seals, this time heading northward. Settlers travelled to the outer coast to harvest them, and soon thereafter the next transients, Atlantic salmon, made their appearance. Salmon were followed by three more transients: capelin, the diminutive ecological base of the marine ecosystem; cod, the economic mainstay; and then herring. Large and small marine mammals entered southeastern Labrador waters by late summer and some remained for several months. By late fall, the cycle of visitors began again.

If one key to human habitation lay in exploiting the transient resources of fall, spring, and summer, the other lay in taking advantage of boreal forest species during winter. Some of the latter were permanent residents, most obviously coniferous trees, such as the important black (and less important white) spruce and balsam fir comprising the boreal forest, as well as a handful of deciduous trees, such as birch. Other resident flora, some found on the outer coast, lay snow-covered in winter and were therefore gathered at other times of the year. I am thinking here of vascular plants, such as bog-bean (*Menyanthes trifoliata*), a green and sour-tasting marsh plant used as a medicine, as well as more commonly mentioned grasses, lichens, and berrying plants. Finally, a variety of other species found in or near the boreal forest, including caribou, bear, hares, ptarmigan, grouse, and various species of fur-bearing animals – to list but a few – were all important to humans.

PREHISTORY

Before early European explorers and adventurers began to describe Labrador in their historic accounts it was home to several kinds of prehistoric peoples, dating back to about nine thousand years before the present. Considerable archaeological research on these prehistoric peoples has taken place during the past two decades, mainly in the Strait of Belle Isle, Lake Melville, and northern Labrador. Until the recent

work of Stopp et al. (see below) southeastern Labrador was an archaeological enigma and glossed with generalizations such as Fitzhugh's
comment that 'the coast between Groswater Bay and Battle Harbour
appears less heavily settled in prehistoric times than was the coast north
of Makkovik' (1982, 53).

The surveys by Stopp and Rutherford (1991) and Stopp and Reynolds
(1992) were therefore much needed. In 1991 Stopp and Rutherford
surveyed the coast between Cape Charles and Seal Island and then in
1992 Stopp and Reynolds surveyed the coast between Frenchmen's
Island and Trunmore Bay. They surveyed both the inner and outer
coasts, although their exploration of the inner coast was hampered by
forest cover.

Archaeological research in other parts of Labrador reveals five major
prehistoric traditions, classified on the basis of surviving stone and bone
tools, radio-carbon dates, dwellings, burials, and the like. In chronologi-
cal order beginning with the earliest, these are Palaeo-Indian, Maritime
Archaic, Palaeo-Eskimo, Dorset (or Late Palaeo-Eskimo), and Thule (or
Neo-Eskimo). Archaeologists further subdivide some of these traditions
(i.e., Early, Middle, and Late Dorset) into smaller sequential stages.
Evidence of all but the oldest of the five major prehistoric traditions (the
Palaeo-Indian) has been found in southeastern Labrador, although some
traditions, such as the Dorset, are more common than others.

Around ten thousand years ago the glaciers began to melt. Rivers
flowed again, and forests and other vegetation began to grow. Along
the Labrador coast, sea levels rose at the rate of about 30 centimetres
per century. These and other climatic and ecological changes gradually
created an environment suitable for man.

The earliest people to inhabit Labrador arrived in the Strait of
Belle Isle around nine thousand years ago. Archaeologists call them
Palaeo-Indians. They did not remain in Labrador long, did not move
north of the Strait, and left few remains. About 8500 BP (Tuck 1982,
205), a second prehistoric Indian tradition emerged, the so-called Maritime Archaic. These peoples remained in Labrador for approximately
five thousand years, eventually moving as far north as the Saglek area.
Their tools included ground slate adzes and gouges, suggesting an
emphasis on woodworking. Other tools, such as bone harpoon heads,
suggest a dependence on marine resources, an assumption supported
by the discovery of seal and waterfowl bones at Maritime Archaic sites.
The presence of caribou bones also indicates that these early people
made use of interior resources. Stopp identifies two prehistoric 'Indian'

traditions which follow the Maritime Archaic and appear transitional to later, historic Innu.[2] In their 1992 survey, Stopp and Reynolds discovered seven of these intermediate and late prehistoric 'Indian' sites, all from the mouth of Sandwich Bay north to Porcupine Strand.

Around four thousand years ago, Maritime Archaic peoples who had moved north to Saglek Bay met and were gradually replaced by the first of two prehistoric Inuit-like peoples, whom archaeologists call the Early Palaeo (or old) Eskimos. Palaeo-Eskimos entered Labrador from the north, and at Saglek, where their cultural remains lie directly above those of the Maritime Archaic, there is some evidence of trade between these two cultures (Tuck 1975). During their two surveys of the southeastern coast, Stopp and her associates found a total of twelve Early-Palaeo-Eskimo sites, most in the northern part of the region.

Small or microlithic chert tools, probably hafted to wooden handles or arrow shafts, are common in Palaeo-Eskimo tool kits. In southeastern Labrador and across the Arctic, Early Palaeo-Eskimo sites are commonly located near the marine resources which constituted the focus of their adaptation.

A second, more recent prehistoric Eskimo-like tradition, referred to as the Late Palaeo-Eskimo or Dorset peoples, dates from approximately 2500 to 1800 BP in Labrador. Like the Early Palaeo-Eskimo tradition, the Dorset culture ranged across the entire Canadian Arctic and was also common in Newfoundland. Dorset artefact remains include small, delicate tools and sculptured animal figurines (perhaps used as ritual amulets). The large number of Dorset sites attests to their successful adaptation. Archaeologists recognize regional and temporal variants of the Dorset tradition, reflecting adjustments to the multitude of subtly different environments found in Labrador. Stopp and her associates found twenty-seven Dorset sites during their two summers; most were of the Middle Dorset period and found in the southern area.

Labrador's final prehistoric tradition, the so-called Thule or Neo-Eskimo, spans the horizon between history and prehistory. The Thule tradition originated in Alaska around 1000 AD. Sometime afterward, Thule peoples migrated eastward across the Canadian Arctic, reaching Labrador around 1400 AD, four centuries after Norse adventurers visited the region and only a century or so before the earliest European fishers and whalers. While the latter is the best known of the five traditions mentioned above, Stopp et al. were not able to positively identify any Thule sites, although they do list seven potential 'historic Inuit' sites in their 1991 report. As Stopp, Auger (1991), and other archaeologists agree, it is often difficult to differentiate Thule sod houses from those of early Europeans.

Like their prehistoric relatives, the Thule peoples spoke Inuktitut, the Inuit language, and referred to one another as Inuit, meaning the 'real' or 'true' people. Their nomadic hunting, foraging, and fishing economy focused on hunting marine animals, notably baleen whale species; on fishing for salmon and arctic char; and on foraging for a variety of foods, ranging from seaweeds to berries.

Inuit technology was both subtly intricate and portable, consistent with their flexible and nomadic lifestyle. They made clothing from seal and caribou skins; knives, harpoon heads, and arrow points from bone or stone; and lamps and cooking vessels from soapstone. Sealskin tents, whalebone and sod semi-subterranean houses, and snow houses provided shelter. Unlike the earlier Dorset peoples, Thule peoples used dogs to pull long wooden sleds and, in summer, skin-covered kayaks and umiaks ('women's boats') for sea transportation and hunting.

Thule social organization included small kin-based groups which customarily utilized particular regions of the coast. Several such groups commonly congregated in summer at a favourite bay or island. There, they exchanged news and renewed inter-group alliances through the mechanisms of marriage, trade, and ritual.

EARLY EUROPEAN HISTORY: 1000–1763 AD

Early European exploitation of what is now Newfoundland and Labrador dates from around the first millennium AD. Archaeological evidence clearly shows that the Norse colonized L'Anse aux Meadows in northern Newfoundland around 1000 AD. The Markland (Woodland) mentioned in Norse sagas is generally believed to be Labrador. But the problem of positively identifying places the Vikings mention in their sagas obscures their trail. Except in cases of unusual landmarks, such as the forty-kilometre-long sandy beach bisected by Cape Porcupine (just north of Sandwich Bay), which is believed to be the Wonderstrands of the sagas, whatever other use the Vikings may have made of Labrador is difficult to determine (Fitzhugh 1985, 27–9).

Four hundred years after arrival of the Norse, Toscaneli, an Italian physician, proposed the possibility of reaching the Orient by sailing westward (Gosling 1910). Toscaneli's theory influenced Italian explorers such as Columbus and Giovanni Caboto (John Cabot), and Cabot's first voyage (1497) led to the discovery of Newfoundland and, possibly, Labrador.[3]

Fifteenth-century navigational instruments were primitive, and the maps documenting visited places are open to various interpretations. The geographic relationship of Labrador to the island of Newfoundland remained unclear, and during the sixteenth century northern Labrador was often confused with or believed to be connected to Greenland. Slowly, the outline of southern Labrador began to emerge from successive European voyages of discovery, fishing, and whaling. Some local places received their names during this period.[4]

Cartier, who made his first voyage in 1534, is remembered for his famous condemnation of Labrador as the 'land God gave to Cain,' a characterization rivalling the equally unflattering note on the Ribero map of 1529 that there was 'nothing of much value' in Labrador (Gosling 1910, 96). Unlike many of his predecessors, Cartier left a record of his voyages and succeeded in systematically outlining the perimeters of the St Lawrence basin.

Some English, Portuguese, and French fishing and whaling took place during the first half of the sixteenth century, but the Basques were the first Europeans to exploit the 'newlands' in a sustained fashion. The Basque whale fishery in the Strait of Belle Isle was active between 1550 and 1600, but has only recently been studied.[5]

By the early 1600s, increasing financial difficulties, a decline in demand for whale-oil, possible plundering of whaling stations by Inuit during winter, and declining whale stocks led the Basques to decrease the size of their Labrador whale fishery. Meanwhile the fur trade and colonialization of New France continued during the seventeenth century, while to the north, Europeans continued the search for a northwest route to Asia. John Davis reached Hudson Strait in 1587 followed by George Weymouth in 1602. Eight years later Henry Hudson sailed into the bay which bears his name. In 1669, King Charles II of England granted a trading charter to the Hudson's Bay Company for exclusive trade rights to (Prince) Rupert's Land – all lands in which water bodies empty into either Hudson Strait or Hudson Bay – a land mass comprising roughly one-third of North America (Gosling 1910, 129).

By the beginning of the eighteenth century, the French controlled portions of Newfoundland (such as Placentia) and New France (Canada), including the Quebec North Shore, while the English controlled most of eastern Newfoundland (including St John's) and Rupert's Land, that is, much of what is now northern Quebec and Ontario. Because of wars and treaties, this picture was to change remarkably over the next two centuries. Throughout much of the seventeenth and early eighteenth century, the English limited their use of eastern Newfound-land to the migratory ship fishery, but brief and unsuccessful attempts at planned colonies were made at Cupids (1610-20) and, beginning in 1621, at Ferryland. Generally, however, the merchants of west England opposed year-round settlement in Newfoundland, opposition which lasted until the early nineteenth century.

Until the eighteenth century, Europeans considered Labrador an undisputed 'no-man's-land' (Gosling 1910, 129-30), an inhospitable coast inhabited by murderous Inuit. Inuit probably viewed each European (and American) ship as a source of exotic *things*; disputes between the two peoples were rooted in contradictory notions of property and exchange. Hostilities often resulted, but decreased after 1763 because of a number of peaceful overtures initiated under British rule.

Throughout this period (indeed, until the twentieth century), Labra-dor's other aboriginal people, the Innu (formerly called Montagnais-Naskapi Indians), continued to hunt in small, family-based bands throughout much of the Quebec-Labrador peninsula, visiting the coast each summer. The economic importance of maritime resources was greater for late prehistoric Innu (Loring 1992) but European occupation of the coast and the introduction of the fur trade would increasingly direct Innu attention to the resources of the interior.

THE FRENCH REGIME

Until the 1660s, most French colonialization took place in what is now Quebec. Much of this was in interior Quebec and undertaken by traders licensed by the French Crown. By the 1660s, the French had extended their seigneurial system eastward to the north shore of the Gulf of St Lawrence, the Strait of Belle Isle region, northern Newfoundland, and, ultimately, southeastern Labrador. Those holding seigneurial land concessions specialized in netting adolescent and adult harp-seals each fall and spring. The Crown also granted concessioners exclusive rights to hunt, fish, and trade with native peoples. The British Privy Council Boundary Documents list French grants to the Mingan area (1661), the Anticosti and St Lawrence area (1676), the Mingan Islands (1679), the Anticosti Islands (1680), Belle Isle (1689), Blanc Sablon, and portions of Newfoundland (1689). Some concessions were made 'in perpetuity' but most were restricted to nine or ten years, stipulating that the recipient continue to occupy and use the rights granted and to pay annual dues (rent), normally several beaver skins, to the Crown.

The first seigneurial concession to southeastern Labrador was awarded in 1702 to Augustin Le Gardeur de Courtemanche, usually known as Courtemanche. He obtained a ten-year trading grant from the governor of New France for the coast between the Kegaska River (near Anticosti Island) and the Kessessasskiou River (now Churchill River). Courtemanche established an impressive headquarters, ultimately numbering some two hundred buildings, at Bradore, Quebec. He employed between thirty and forty Innu families as well as French and Canadians as trappers or fishers (Gosling 1910, 150). Despite this large labour force and apparent capital expenditure, Courtemanche remained near Bradore, possibly fearing Inuit raids, which were common further north. In 1714, his lease was renewed and he was appointed commandant of the coast of Labrador, with authorization to settle fishery disputes between migratory French cod fishers who frequented the area each summer. When Courtemanche died in 1717, his concession and the office of commandant were passed to François Martel de Brouague, his stepson. Brouague maintained both until about 1795, restricting his fishing and trading to the area between Bradore Bay and West St Modeste. Gosling mentions that Brouague sent one vessel to Chateau Bay in 1742 to engage in the seal fishery and that peaceful trade with Inuit took place (1910, 154).

During Brouague's tenure, Charles de Beauharnois de La Boische, governor general of New France, granted several other concessions within territory originally assigned to Courtemanche. On 1 October 1736, Louis Bazil received a nine-year lease to establish a seal fishery at Chateau Bay and exclusive rights to hunt, fish, and conduct trade with Inuit. His tract was one-half league (one league equals approximately five kilometres) southwest and three and one-half leagues northeast of Chateau Bay, and included the interior, deemed necessary to maintain his operation. Bazil was obliged to pay customary dues of four winter beaver skins to the Crown each September. By May 1737, Bazil encountered financial difficulties and entered a partnership with François Havy and Louis Fornel. On 17 May 1737, King Louis XIV confirmed and ratified this new arrangement.

The year 1735 marked the beginning of a twenty-year association of the names Marsal and Cape Charles. That year, Governor Beauharnois and Gilles Hocquart, civil administrator of the colony, granted permission to Antoine Marsal, a Quebec City trader, to establish a sealing and trading post at Cape Charles. Marsal appears to have been an entrepreneur of some stature for he also obtained grants for a summer seal fishery at

Goelans Island (near present-day St Barbe Bay, Newfoundland) from 1736 to 1745 and Petit Harve (roughly Blanc Sablon, Quebec, to L'Anse au Clair, Labrador) from 1751 to 1760. Marsal's initial Cape Charles concession ran from 1735 to 1744 and extended from Cape Charles to the 'bay commonly called St. Alexis' (Beauharnois and Hocquart 1735), illustrating the antiquity of some contemporary place-names.

By 1742 Bazil's Chateau Bay post had fallen on hard times, probably because Bazil, the firm's senior partner, 'could not afford to develop' it (Fornel 1742). While still in partnership with Bazil, Fornel applied for a concession to Lake Melville and was told he would be given 'preference' as soon as he explored that area. In 1742, when Bazil's firm was in trouble, Fornel reminded the government minister of this and requested a nine-year concession at Chateau Bay so as to finance his exploration of Lake Melville. If awarded this concession, as well as trade goods and other effects for Inuit, Fornel promised to make the king's name known to these 'barbarians.' Fornel was not awarded the Chateau concession, possibly because of the 1742–8 war between England and France (PC 7 [1234]: 3188), but managed to make his way to Lake Melville. He established a post at North West River in 1743. With Chateau Bay abandoned, Gaultier was granted a nine-year lease to it in 1749.

Meanwhile, back at Cape Charles, hard times had also befallen Marsal. Inuit attacked his post in 1742, and heavy ice conditions during the unusually severe winter of 1742–3 had carried away all his seal nets. Fornel's (1742) description of the Inuit attack on Marsal's post states that some of Marsal's men had 'imprudently fired at [Inuit] in order to drive them away from an island where they had built huts.' This precipitated the attack, which occurred in the spring or early summer of 1742. Marsal's post was burned, sacked, and looted; the boats he had constructed were destroyed; and two of the three men who garrisoned the post were killed. Consequently, in 1743, Marsal could not obtain workers for the post and had to abandon some of his fishing gear near the Cape (Beauharnois and Hocquart 1743).

Following these setbacks, Marsal risked everything by borrowing money from friends and applying for and receiving a six-year extension to his Cape Charles concession. However, for unknown reasons, Marsal's affairs 'compelled him to return to France' (Duquesne and Bigot 1753) and he did not use his new lease to Cape Charles. The assumed economic potential of Cape Charles was not to be ignored for long. In 1749, a M. Baune (or de Bonne), described as a 'half-pay Captain' in the

Conde infantry regiment, applied for and received a nine-year lease (Lajonquiere and Bigot 1749). However, it appears that Captain Baune never sent anyone to operate the Cape Charles post and returned his patent. But Marsal soon returned. In 1751, his concession for Petit Havre (possibly Petty Harbour, north of St Lewis Harbour) took effect, and in 1753, he requested and received permission for 'another attempt' at Cape Charles (Duquesne and Bigot 1753).

Marsal's new grant for Cape Charles was to run from 1754 to 1763, and, even though he died in 1757, his name continued to be associated with Cape Charles. Thus, in 1758, Marsal's five creditors, united under the name of Tachet, applied for a nine-year lease to Marsal's Cape Charles post so as to recover the seven thousand livres they had advanced him. In their petition, Tachet and the others noted that Marsal had done a 'considerable amount of work in connection with that post and its fitting up' and, in using their funds, had 'so often held out the expectation of profits' (Tachet et al. 1758). While Marsal's creditors received permission to operate the post, it is not known whether they succeeded in recovering their losses.

The French were the first Europeans to systematically exploit the coast north of the Strait region (Trudel 1978). Whether the French system of exploitation – Crown-leased concessions – was the most efficient method is debatable, although repeated applications for locations such as Chateau Bay and Cape Charles suggest that the region's potential was considered tremendous. Thornton (1977, 155) and Stopp and Rutherford (1991, 32) mention another legacy of the French regime. In both in the Strait and southeastern Labrador regions, British adventurers and permanent Settlers reused locations discovered and used earlier by French concessioners. Thus, except for the brief and enigmatic period between 1775 and 1830, Cape Charles and several other places have been used continuously as whaling, sealing, and fishing sites, dating as far back as Marsal's initial grant in 1735. It is surprising that those using Cape Charles wintered at Lodge Bay, even though other, seemingly better sites for winter settlements exist nearby. Even so, the site of the contemporary winter community of Lodge Bay was utilized by Marsal, Nicholas Darby, Captain Cartwright, and the ancestors of contemporary Settlers. In sum, the French initiated European exploration of southeastern Labrador and established precedents followed after the fall of New France in 1763.

3

An Early British Adventure

The early British era, before the permanent European settlement of southeastern Labrador, was a time of anarchy, violence, and disorder (Jackson 1982). The British tried to enact policy and to bring order to their newly won Labrador amid older geopolitical and economic traditions in the territory. And then there were the transient Inuit traders, understandably unaware of the subtleties of European trade and of the ancient enmities Europeans brought with them to Labrador. Inuit were learning about both – often with bloody consequences.

Our journey through this turbulent period draws very largely on the experiences of several British adventurers, most notably a man named George Cartwright. His diary is unique, although his experiences with rival Europeans and aboriginal peoples may be representative.

Following the British conquest of New France in 1760 and the ensuing Treaty of Paris (1763), the administration of Labrador was based in St John's, Newfoundland (1763–74), then Quebec City (1774–1809), and, finally, St John's (1809–present). Commodore Hugh Palliser, the first governor of Newfoundland (1764–8) following the conquest, extended to the newly won Labrador British policies developed for insular Newfoundland: the fishery should continue to be a migratory ship fishery; no one should privately own fishing 'rooms,' stages, or other shore facilities; and year-round settlement should continue to be prohibited. This was the conservative practice of the powerful 'Western Adventurers,' as proposed in the Newfoundland Act of 1699 and applied with mixed success during much of the eighteenth century (Head 1976). Palliser wanted to extend the British fishery northward to exploit Labrador's rich fishing grounds and to train future seamen.

Many problems hindered Palliser's progress. Although the Treaty of

Paris (1763) terminated open hostilities between the English and French, French rights to erect temporary fishing premises along Newfoundland's 'French Shore' (Cape Bonavista to Point Riche), granted under the Treaty of Utrecht (1713), were renewed. As well, the islands of St Pierre and Miquelon became shelters for French fishing and illicit trade (Whitely 1969, 141–2). Feelings of alienation and rebellion were growing in the American colonies and an alliance was forming with France. All this meant that Newfoundland and southeastern Labrador were to become a stage on which broader, international disputes would be played.

Palliser moved quickly to promote British interests. He issued proclamations to French and New England fishers asserting British sovereignty over Newfoundland and Labrador, and corresponded with authorities in St Pierre and Boston. He tried to halt illegal trade between the French and the Americans and Newfoundland settlers. Along the Labrador coast, however, misunderstanding and violence between Inuit and Europeans stalled plans for a British ship fishery.

Enter the Moravians. The Moravians (or Unitas Fratrum), a European Protestant sect, established a mission among Greenlandic Inuit in the 1720s and unsuccessfully attempted a similar mission in Labrador in 1752. They were eager to try again. Following several years of negotiations between Palliser and the Moravians, British authorities permitted the Moravians to establish the first of an eventual chain of stations at Nain, in 1771.

Palliser recommended dividing coastal Labrador into three approximately three-hundred-mile-long districts, each with a garrisoned blockhouse and warship (Whitely 1969, 157). All that came of this proposal was Fort York. It was constructed at Pitt's Harbour, Chateau Bay, in the fall of 1766, by an engineer, a carpenter, and fifty seamen from the frigate *Niger*. The fort was equipped with light cannon and was garrisoned year-round by an officer and twenty seamen. The efficacy of the fort was questioned and it was abandoned in 1775, one year after Quebec assumed jurisdiction of the Labrador coast (Gosling 1910, 191; Whitely 1969, 159).

A final problem facing Palliser was that of Quebec merchants who had been granted Labrador concessions prior to the Treaty of Paris (1763). While geopolitical, this problem highlights contrasting interpretations of Labrador's environment, settlement pattern, and economic utility. The British assumed that Labrador could be treated like insular Newfoundland, that is, as a migratory cod fishery provisioned each spring from England. The Quebec merchants calculated Labrador's worth primarily in seal oil; years of experience had taught them that netting harp-seals required sedentary facilities and year-round residence.

Three examples illustrate different issues common during the early British era. The first two, those of Quebec-based British merchants William Brymer and Daniel Bayne, and of Nicholas Darby, illustrate residual problems from the seigneurial system predating the conquest. A third case, that of Jeremiah Coghlan, broadly resembles that of his partner, Captain Cartwright, insofar as Coghlan also faced continuous pressures from rival merchants for resources and for labour.

On 26 April 1763, one day after Labrador came under Newfoundland's jurisdiction (Rothney 1934, 267), Quebec governor Murray granted Messrs Brymer and Bayne land to establish a seal fishery at Cape Charles for a period of four years (PC 7 [1410]: 3671; Rothney 1934). On 8 April 1765, Palliser had unilaterally declared that the Crown owned all Labrador property (Rothney 1934, 268). This declaration, when added to British anxiety about illegal French trade to Labrador, set the stage for a British raid on Brymer's post. This occurred on 17 August 1765. One of Palliser's commanders 'raided the post, found French goods there, arrested Brymer's Agent, William Lead, together with his French-Canadian assistant, and brought them before the Governor at Pitt's Harbour (Chateau Bay)' (Whitely 1969, 156). Palliser's action against Brymer and Bayne was filled with misunderstanding; Palliser ultimately lost the £600 lawsuit filed by Brymer and Bayne (Rothney 1934, 275), but the Crown repaid Palliser the award plus legal expenses, suggesting that the British government condoned Palliser's overzealous actions (Whitely 1969, 160).

In summer, 1765, Captain Nicholas Darby, the second (following Bayne and Brymer) British adventurer to systematically exploit the Labrador fishery, sailed from England with a crew of 150 men. Darby established a whale, seal, cod, and salmon fishery on Seal Island, Cape Charles, with winter quarters at what is now Lodge Bay (Cartwright 1792, 1: 40). During the next four years, predatory raids by Inuit, often cases of mistaken revenge against New England whalers, led to Darby's downfall, much as had happened with Marsal some twenty-three years earlier. The threat of Inuit raids meant that, in 1765, Darby was unable to persuade any of his men to winter at the Cape. That winter Inuit looted and burned Darby's vacant premises. Considering Darby's losses, it is ironic that his original intention was to 'civilize' the Inuit by employing them as whalers. This plan had received 'great encouragement and promises of assistance' from Palliser, Lord Hillsborough, and other officials of the Crown (Gosling 1910, 200). The following year, Darby formed a partnership with Bristol merchant Michael Miller in order to raise capital; he sailed for Labrador with 180 English and Irish sailors and £8000 worth of equipment. Darby's 1766 voyage was so successful that he convinced some of his men to winter at Cape Charles. However, this winter crew lacked 'Canadians' experienced in the winter seal fisheries and thus enjoyed little success.

Darby and some 160 men returned to Cape Charles in the summer of 1767, only to have Inuit attack his station again that October. Inuit killed three of Darby's men and destroyed more than £4000 worth of boats and other equipment. Lieutenant Lucas of Fort York counter-attacked, killing twenty Inuit men and capturing nine women and children. Governor Palliser arranged for some of those captured to be taken to England. Among them was a fascinating woman, Mikak, who would later play an important role in the establishment of the Moravian Mission in northern Labrador (Gosling 1910, 201; Taylor 1983, 4–5).

Not dissuaded by his losses at Cape Charles, and with new financial backing from friends in London, Darby again sailed from London in May 1769, this time to pursue the cod fishery. By July, he had shipped a cargo of green (undried) fish and that winter he decided to net harp-seals. This attracted the attention of British troops at Fort York, particularly when they learned that three or four of his twelve sealers were 'Canadians' and that he planned to market seal oil through a Bradore, Quebec merchant.

On 11 August 1770, Lieutenant Samuel Davis, commander of Fort York, and twelve marines raided Darby's house at Forteau, ostensibly searching for contraband (i.e., French) goods. Finding none, they proceeded to Darby's warehouse, where they seized 145 casks of seal oil, 1500 seal skins, and other goods. Then the scene turned ugly. The bewildered Darby questioned whether Lieutenant Davis had Newfoundland governor Byron's authority for the seizure. Davis countered by calling Darby 'an impertinent puppy or to that effect' (PC 3 [310]: 1167), threatened to flog him and, the next day, sent a marine to Bradore Bay to retrieve thirty-nine casks of oil Darby had shipped. Cartwright's diary entry of 20 August 1770 suggests that this oil was indeed confiscated. Cartwright writes that he 'made an engagement with Lieutenant Davis to send the *Nimrod* to St. John's with some oil (which he had seized from Captain Darby)' (1792, 1: 26). Davis denied Darby's request for passage to St John's and again threatened to flog him for 'employing three Frenchmen' (ibid., 1168).

Darby left Labrador destitute (ibid.), although he continued visiting to trade and to fish, apparently in partnership with Lieutenant Lucas (Gosling 1910, 201–2; Cartwright 1792, 2: 48). The vindictive seizure of Darby's seal products was part of the ongoing jurisdictional dispute between English (and Newfoundland) and Quebec merchants, a dispute which would be addressed in the Quebec Act of 1774 (Whitely 1976).

The third example, illustrative of common problems in this era, is the case of Jeremiah Coghlan. He established a sealing post at Chateau Bay around 1765 (Gosling 1910, 203; Whitely 1976, 101). Like many British adventurers, Coghlan had previously established headquarters in New-foundland – at Fogo, which continued to be his summer headquarters, (Cartwright 1792, 1: 156) – and, like Darby, had received Palliser's encouragement to locate in Labrador. Wishing to expand to the coast north of Chateau, Coghlan formed a partnership with Thomas Perkins, Captain George Cartwright, and Lieutenant Lucas and established a 'settlement' at Cape Charles in 1769 (Coghlan 1777, 1270). Thus, Cogh-lan appears to have established a salmon fishery at Charles Brook (St Charles River) to which Cartwright refers (in July 1777, 1: 4). (Cart-wright [1792, 1: 1] dates the formation of this partnership to 30 March 1770). One of the partners, Lieutenant Lucas, drowned when the com-pany's schooner, the *Enterprise*, was lost at sea between Fogo and Oporto in October 1770 (Cartwright 1792, 1: 136). The partnership continued after Lucas's death, although Cartwright and Coghlan eventually separated. Coghlan claims that he and Cartwright applied for and received confir-mation from Lord Dartmouth, head of the Board of Trade, for Cartwright to control salmon rivers at Cape Charles and Sandwich Bay while Cogh-lan fished at a number of locations between Alexis and Porcupine bays (Coghlan 1777, 1270). During the following years, Coghlan expanded the size of his operations. By 1777, he employed one hundred men (on half-shares) in the seal and cod fisheries and forty men in the salmon fishing and fur-trapping business. That year, in accordance with ancient British policy and Governor Shuldham's proclamation of 1773, he had two ships 'cleared out of England' to replenish his operations (ibid.).

In addition to the constant threat posed by Inuit, competition and disorder prevailed among rival English merchants on the coast. As Whitely writes, 'the English merchants on the Labrador coast ceaselessly tried to undercut each other and continually lobbied the government for special favours' (1976, 93). As Coghlan and Cartwright complained, 'new-comers' were less apt to explore and locate new salmon and seal berths and more likely to seize established berths. So it was that in the summer of 1775 a Mr Baskomb, employed by a Mr Hooper of Poole, England, seized one of Coghlan's salmon rivers while the latter's men had 'gone to their store [house] for salt' (Coghlan 1777, 1270). Coghlan reported this infringement to Lord Shuldham and was awarded all the salmon Baskomb had netted. Two years later, however, in a letter dated 22 August 1777, Timothy Shea, Coghlan's agent at Spear Harbour, informed Coghlan that one of his salmon fishers, John Peaton (or Peyton), had absconded with the wages of four of Coghlan's salmon fishermen at Alexis and Black Bear rivers and hired them and three of Coghlan's sealers to accompany him to Coghlan's Sandy Hill Cove establishment. There, Peaton and his renegade crew wintered and followed the next summer's salmon fishery (Shea 1777, 3: 1271).

Coghlan reported these defections to Newfoundland governor Montagu, who, while sympathetic, could offer little help because administration of the coast had shifted to Quebec authorities. However, Montagu did dispatch Lieutenant Schomberg and the schooner *Labrador* to investigate Coghlan's complaint. In his report, dated 19 September 1777, Schomberg supports Coghlan's allegations and ordered Peaton and others to honour Coghlan's rights to all fishing properties that he had discovered (Schomberg 1777, 3: 1275). Coghlan went bankrupt in 1782 (Whitely 1976, 102) but was, along with Cartwright, the first English merchant to operate a chain of trapping and fishing establishments north of Cape Charles, a stretch of coast that had previously been considered dangerous Inuit territory.

Coghlan's case illustrates the confusing nature of administration on the coast following the transfer of Labrador's administration to Quebec (ibid., 101–2). Such confusion is exemplified by Newfoundland governor Montagu's dispatch of Lieutenant Schomberg to investigate Coghlan's problem with Peaton. Moreover, during the American War of Independence, confusion and ineffectiveness gave way to military vulnerability, and Labrador merchants such as Coghlan's former partner, George Cartwright, would pay dearly.

CAPTAIN GEORGE CARTWRIGHT

Captain George Cartwright is the best known of all Labrador merchants of this period, and his story is one of bitter competition between rival merchants, of the impact of the American Revolution, and of cracks in the armour of British colonial policy in Labrador. I present an extended version of Cartwright's saga because it reveals much of what we know about southeastern Labrador during the early British era. But the story of George Cartwright is in many ways a sad one. The tribulations he suffered at the hands of merchant rivals are well known. A combination of generosity and poor business sense often left Cartwright holding an empty purse. His relations with aboriginal peoples are also sad, and their consequences were often lethal. Yet sad stories are often captivating. Indeed the ongoing attraction of this two-century-old saga is evidenced by Steffler's (1992) acclaimed resurrection – *The Afterlife of George Cartwright*, a fictitious continuation of Cartwright's Labrador adventures.

Cartwright's notoriety is attributable to his three-volume diary, entitled *A Journal of Transactions and Events during a Residence of Nearly Sixteen Years on the Coast of Labrador*, published in 1792, six years after he left the coast. Newfoundland historian D.W. Prowse (1895, 599) called the *Journal* 'one of the most remarkable books ever written.' And Samuel Coleridge applauded its 'strange simplicity' (Townsend 1907, 228). The *Journal*'s style has been described as 'somewhat tedious to read' (Gosling 1910, 224) and compared to that of a ship's log (Story 1981). To me, the diary is indispensable, yet frustrating. In recounting daily events, Cartwright frequently assumes that the reader has detailed knowledge of the persons, places, circumstances, and situations mentioned. He either fails to be specific or assumes common knowledge of places where his adventures took place. He also has a rather annoying penchant for giving the same place-name to locations separated by hundreds of kilometres (e.g., Hoop-pole, Sandwich Bay district, and Hoop-pole, St Lewis Bay). Yet unlike others who have used Cartwright's diary, I bring to it some knowledge of the country in which it is set, allowing me to clarify a few of the *Journal*'s many ambiguities.

George Cartwright was born on 12 February 1738 at Marnham, Nottinghamshire, England. Following a rather undistinguished academic career at Newark, Randall's Academy, and the Royal Military Academy at Woolwich, he joined the army and saw service in India and Germany, ultimately advancing to the rank of captain. When he returned to England after the Seven Years' War, he was unhappy about not being promoted and decided to retire on half-pay to Scotland. By the spring of 1765, he discovered that two shillings and four pence a day was insufficient to sustain a mistress, two servants, two horses, and six dogs! Cartwright and his 'family' depended mainly on the fish and game he bagged, and the scarcity of these resources forced him to auction his furniture and return with mistress and dogs to London in the fall of 1765.

The next spring he decided to accompany his brother John, newly appointed first lieutenant of Governor-Designate Hugh Palliser's flagship *Guernsey*, to Newfoundland. In the summer of 1767, he rejoined the army as captain of the company of the Thirty-seventh Regiment of Footsoldiers on the Mediterranean Island of Minorca, contracted malaria, and returned to England. In the spring of 1768, Cartwright made a second voyage to Newfoundland in order to restore his health. The highlight of this second trip was Cartwright's participation in his brother John's unsuccessful attempt to contact and establish friendly relations with insular Newfoundland's mysterious indigenous people, the Beothuks.

Cartwright returned to England and again retired from the army on half-pay. On 30 March 1770, he entered partnership with Lieutenant Francis Lucas, Mr Thomas Perkins, and Jeremiah Coghlan. Cartwright spent about three weeks in Newfoundland during which he and his brother John led a second party intending to contact the Beothuks. He then hired men and on 24 July 1770 sailed for Labrador aboard the company schooner *Enterprise*, commanded by Lieutenant Lucas. The first stop was Fort York, where Cartwright met his friend and old shipmate Lieutenant Davis. They then sailed north of Cape Charles, where Cartwright claimed possession of Darby's headquarters on 'Seal Island.' The following day (30 July), they sailed into Charles River, as far as a boat can go, to the site of Darby's winter house, on the north side of the river.[1] The house was in good condition and, in early August, Cartwright's carpenters began converting Darby's workshop (measuring some thirty-seven by fourteen feet) into a dwelling-house. Darby's house and the servants' house became Cartwright's storehouses. On 22 September 1770, even before these renovations were completed, Cartwright christened his house 'Ranger Lodge,' in honour of His Majesty's schooner *Ranger*, which happened to be moored before its door (1792, 1: 38). ,

Ranger Lodge, along with two ancillary buildings, served as both home and centre of Cartwright's operations until they were destroyed by fire in 1772. During the Ranger Lodge period, Cartwright was both excited and optimistic about his new adventure, even though his salmon post on the Charles River was first raided in June 1772 by the rival firm of Noble and Pinson.

Cartwright's trapping and hunting necessitated frequent travel by boat during the open water season and by foot after freeze-up. During his first voyage (1770–2), such travel was limited to the coast between

Chateau Bay and St Lewis Inlet. He also visited his crews stationed seasonally at several outposts. These included a sealing station at Seal Island (Cape Charles); his salmon post at Ranger Lodge, trapping posts, and a sawmill at the 'Colleroon River' (St Lewis River); his cooperage at 'Hoop-pole' Cove (Hatter's Cove); a hunting and trapping tilt (cabin) on 'Eyre' (Azzizes) Island; and a sealing post at Stage Cove.

Cartwright's partners (Perkins, Coghlan, and Lucas, who was lost at sea in October 1770) failed to provide him with much logistical support (Coghlan withdrew from the partnership early because of heavy losses [1777, 1270]), but competition with Noble and Pinson became Cartwright's main problem. Competition between merchants was common (Whitely 1977) and was increasingly caused by the irrelevance of Palliser's 1765 regulations, favouring the migratory cod fishery. Cartwright's two years' experience had taught him the value of the seal and salmon fisheries, both of which required the preparation of nets, barrels, and other technologies. Thus, while in England, Cartwright submitted on 6 January 1773 a formal protest against the seizure by Noble and Pinson of his salmon post on Charles River and his sealing post on Seal Island. Cartwright's decisive protest cogently argued that Labrador's environment (specifically, for example, the persistence of land-fast ice) necessitated year-round residence and individual ownership of fishing premises (Cartwright 1773). On 29 January 1773, Mr J. Pownall of the Board of Trade wrote Andrew Pinson requesting his company's explanation of Cartwright's allegations (PC 3 [269]: 1067). In their response (undated, but apparently drafted in early February, 1773) to the Board of Trade, Noble and Pinson toed the official line – alleging that every adventurer should be allowed to take 'quiet possession' of any salmon or sealing post provided that they man such posts with crews leaving England each year (PC 3 [270]: 1068–9). Noble and Pinson also reminded the board that their 1771 application for a grant to their headquarters in Lance Cove (Chateau Bay) had been returned on a technicality and that they had nevertheless carried on, successfully drying fish in Labrador, a practice then thought impracticable (ibid.). Their cod-fishing company had expanded into the salmon and seal fisheries and, since it annually supplied its posts with new British and Irish crews, the acquisition of new posts, such as at Seal Island (Cape Charles), was within existing regulations.

All this amounted to a standoff. On 18 February 1773 the Board of Trade resolved the dispute. The board's resolution (contained in a document entitled 'A Representation of the Lords of Trade to the King,' dated 2 March 1773) confirmed Cartwright's rights to Charles River, but awarded Noble and Pinson Cartwright's Cape Charles sealing post (Cartwright 1792, 1: 267). More important, the board accepted Cartwright's argument that actual residence was essential to the salmon and seal fisheries and that persons conducting such fisheries should enjoy continued possession of their establishments, providing they supplied them annually from Great Britain. This compromise between Palliser's ideal of a migratory ship fishery and Cartwright's plea for year-round residence changed British policy towards Labrador and inadvertently cleared the way for eventual permanent settlement. Lord Dartmouth, head of the Board of Trade, wrote Newfoundland governor Shuldham on 9 March 1773 advising him of the new policy. The governor's proclamation of 21 August 1773 expressed the government's new position and, like Palliser's regulations of 1765, its policy predecessor, was delivered at Chateau Bay.

Returning from England for his second voyage in August 1773, Cartwright divided his base of operations between Charles River, where some of his buildings remained, and Stage Cove, on Charles Harbour, about ten kilometres west of Wall's Island.

As early as Cartwright's first voyage, the harassment of Noble and Pinson had forced Cartwright to expand north into St Lewis Bay. But there too, Noble and Pinson's larger and more powerful crews followed, seizing Cartwright's Colleroon River (St Lewis River) salmon post in the spring of 1773, and compelling Cartwright's men to establish posts at Port Marnham (near present-day St Lewis) and at nearby Deer Harbour, in the summer of 1773. By fall, Noble and Pinson operated a sealing post at St Lewis (Fox Harbour) (Cartwright 1792, 1: 284).

Lacking the shipping connections enjoyed during his former partnership, Cartwright sent goods to Stage Cove through a Mr Adam Lymburner of Quebec. Ironically, Cartwright also records shipping forty-five tierces of salmon through his adversary, Mr Pinson of Lance Cove (1792, 1: 282).

In September 1773, Cartwright reported seeing a sealing crew of the Slades, who had expanded from Twillingate to Chateau, heading north from Charles Harbour. This is the first reference to the Slades, subsequently important Battle Harbour merchants.

Cartwright spent the winter of 1773–4 in England. He then entered a partnership with brothers John and Robert Scott, on half-shares, and sailed to Labrador for his third voyage, on 16 May 1774. His carpenters expanded his Stage Cove post, a post which would now serve as his new winter headquarters.[2] That September Cartwright sent his shallop

Otter north to the Alexis River, where four coopers were to winter. Then, further north, the shallop left three trappers to winter at Sandwich Bay and to prepare for the summer salmon fishery.

Several new English 'planters' were now operating in the area but Cartwright provides few details about them. For example, on 18 September 1774 he records that skiffs belonging to Mr Hooper and Mr Coghlan visited Stage Cove. Some of Mr Hooper's men wintered on an island near Cape Charles, in 1774–5, and the following summer Cartwright passed two of Hooper's shallops en route from St Michael's Bay. Cartwright also observes that a 'planter's shallop' from Chateau visited Stage Cove on 6 October 1774, and in an entry on 6 November implies that there was a planter living on Seal Island, Cape Charles (1792, 2: 33). Similarly, on 4 February 1775, he speaks of a planter from Lodge Bay (perhaps John Hayes – 1792, 2: 49) visiting Stage Cove (2: 48). Several other entries are even more perplexing. For example, on 31 January 1775, Cartwright writes that 'a man belonging to Captain Darby came here today' (2: 48), and on 20 May, that he receives a letter from Mr Darby (2: 69). These references confirm that Darby continued to fish and trade in Labrador after his 1770 bankruptcy, although little more is known.

On 4 June 1775 Cartwright sailed north to Alexis and Sandwich bays. Proceeding to Longstretch, Sandwich Bay, he entered the house built by the 1774 trapping party and found a note dated 23 May 1775. It told a sad tale of starvation. Its authors had eaten their dogs and then, in desperation, headed to the outer coast in search of sea-bird eggs and ducks (2: 83). Their remains were never found.

On the brighter side, Cartwright was excited about the apparent fishing, hunting, and trapping potential of Sandwich Bay. He selected a winter house site near Merlin Point in a harbour he named Cartwright Harbour, within the modern community of Cartwright.[3] In September 1775, he returned to Stage Cove, collected his 'housekeeper' Mrs Selby and his Inuit servants, and returned to Cartwright Harbour, naming his new house 'Caribou Castle' on 23 October 1775.

That fall and winter Cartwright and his crews enjoyed moderately good hunting and trapping in this new and comparatively untouched country. In the spring of 1776 Cartwright constructed new salmon posts on the Dykes and Eagle rivers. That summer his Sandwich Bay salmon fishery yielded 381 tierces, compared with the 150 tieces produced at his three 'Charles Harbour' posts (presumably on Charles River, Port Marnham, and St Lewis River).

On 5 September 1776, Cartwright purchased 50 per cent of the shares in his company belonging to the Scott brothers for £1200 (2: 204–5). Later that month, he sailed for Charles Harbour and then on to Temple Bay, where he stayed the night of 30 September with Mr Pinson. The next day a rather extraordinary incident occurred, illustrating the kind of bad business deal to which Cartwright was prone. Nobel and Pinson's supply ship had been lost en route from Ireland and Mr Pinson asked John Scott, one of Cartwright's (former) partners, to lend him some supplies until more could be obtained. Scott agreed to the loan, which consequently left Cartwright's Sandwich Bay crews short of provisions. When Cartwright asked Pinson for a temporary loan of basic supplies to replace those Scott had loaned Pinson, Pinson would only agree to sell them at what Cartwright considered an 'exorbitant price.' With few other options available, Cartwright gave in (2: 211).

After selecting John Bruce as his agent at Stage Cove, Cartwright sailed for England in November 1776. When he returned to Labrador for his fourth voyage, in the spring of 1777, the American War of Independence was in progress and American privateers were active off the Newfoundland coast.

Following a mediocre summer fishery, Cartwright and his crews prepared for fall trapping and sealing activities. Sealing had not proved successful in Sandwich Bay, so on 26 September 1777, Cartwright sent his sealers to Sutton Bay (now Trunmore Bay). However, by 24 December, his men had not even sighted any seals.

During his second year at Sandwich Bay, Cartwright and his crews had contact with several new English planters. For example, on 29 July 1777, Cartwright reports going to 'Cartwright River' (now North River) in search of 'the planter' who is later said to have returned from Ivucktoke Bay (Hamilton Inlet) on 8 August (2: 243). Cartwright is more specific about the identity of the planters John Wrixon (a trapper Cartwright met in August 1771 [1: 156]) and William Phippard, two of Jeremiah Coghlan's four salmon fishers who quit working for him in August 1777, yet continued to fish at his Black Bear and Porcupine Bay posts. Before Wrixon was lost on an ice pan, apparently in July 1778, he or one of his crews wintered at Table Bay. Phippard wintered at Lake Melville (perhaps at English River; see Zimmerly 1975, 55) and Cartwright regularly saw Phippard and his crew travelling between Lake Melville and Sandhill Cove.

At his cod-fishing station on Great Island (now Cartwright Island) Cartwright was suddenly awakened at 1:00 a.m., 27 August 1778, by

John Grimes, Boston privateer and commander of the *Minerva*. Grimes and his 160 men had raided a number of posts along the coast, including Cartwright's Stage Cove post, and had learned of Cartwright's Great Island location from four of Cartwright's former servants. Over the next four days, Grimes plundered and/or took possession of most of Cartwright's property. When the *Minerva* sailed from Great Island on 30 August, she carried four of Cartwright's Inuit servants and thirty-two of his men, who had defected to Grimes after the privateer's promise (ultimately not kept) of part of the booty. Cartwright estimated his losses at £14,000 and predicted that the raid would 'prove [his] ruin' (2: 367).

The raid left Cartwright short of men and provisions; thirty-six men remained at Sandwich Bay and only one at Ranger Lodge. After 29 October, when the contracts of thirteen of the men expired, Cartwright's labour force dwindled to fewer than two dozen (2: 383). On 3 September, with winter approaching, Cartwright sent Mr. Daubeny and four men to Stage Cove, and then on to Newfoundland to purchase provisions. Meanwhile, Captain Kinlock sailed the *Wolvering* to St John's in an attempt to obtain a vessel to carry the remaining salmon and cod to market (2: 368). Aside from the prospect of marketing these fish, Cartwright's financial situation was abysmal, and it remains unclear what collateral Daubeny offered to obtain a vessel and necessary provisions. But when Daubeny returned to Sandwich Bay on 4 November 1778, he was sailing one of Mr Seydes's shallops, and later Cartwright and Seydes established a partnership. Seydes and Company maintained a room across from Stage Cove, possibly at Wolf Cove or Man of War Cove (2: 486).

In the fall of 1778, following the ransacking of Caribou Castle by Grimes, Cartwright erected a new winter house at Isthmus Bay, only a few kilometres from his fishing post on Great Island and about one kilometre from his coopers' house at Southwest Cove, Isthmus Bay (2: 369, 2: 390, 3: 67). He spent his last two Labrador winters (1778–9, 1785–6) at Isthmus Bay, but also developed a very substantial post at Paradise River. The Paradise post included several large buildings and gardens, probably near Raspberry Point, on the southwest side of the river (see 3: 9, and the M. Lane map, in Cartwright). Archaeologists Stopp and Reynolds (1992) surveyed Isthmus Bay and Paradise River but the sites they found could not be positively attributed to Cartwright.

The 1778–9 trapping season was poor. Fox fur was of poor quality and, because Grimes had taken Cartwright's best traps, many foxes escaped or their fur was mangled. Moreover, there were many mice that winter, so the foxes were not hungry for trap bait (2: 420; Elton 1942).

Fortunately, the peninsula between Isthmus Bay and Cape North was good caribou habitat, allowing Cartwright and his men to kill enough caribou to survive. By 1 March 1779, they could again enjoy three meals daily, although Cartwright admitted that his men had been close to mutiny several times since the Grimes raid (2: 445).

June meant open water and renewed communication with the outside world. Cartwright received news that another American privateer had raided Twillingate and Battle Harbour that spring. At the latter locale, the privateer had taken some twenty-two tons of Slade's seal oil (2: 459). This would confirm that the Slades had a sealing post at Battle Harbour by 1778, if one can assume that the oil taken by the Americans in the spring of 1779 was rendered from seals taken in the late autumn harp fishery. This predates Browne's (1909, 240) claim that the Slade Brothers arrived in Battle Harbour in 1795.

Cartwright also learned that John Baskem, his former boat-builder, had seized Cartwright's Port Marnham salmon post and that all of the 'English crews in that neighbourhood' had plundered Cartwright's houses in or near Stage Cove (Cartwright 1792, 2: 460). However, when Cartwright visited Stage Cove on 14 September 1779, he found 'all my houses shut up and nothing missing of what had been left this spring' (2: 485).

Given the threat of additional American attacks, Cartwright planted some young trees to conceal his Isthmus Bay house, hid two barrels of furs in the woods, and, on 22 August 1779, accepted arms and ammunition from the Newfoundland governor for protection against privateers. Before departing for Stage Cove in September, Cartwright issued the guns and instructions to his men at Paradise, promising monetary rewards to those first sighting the enemy (2: 482).

Cartwright travelled to Stage Cove in September 1779 in order to check his posts, reclaim Port Marnham, and acquire supplies. He visited Mr Forsythe, Coghlan's agent at St Francis Harbour and Spear Harbour, Mr George March, Mr Thomas's agent at Cape Charles, and officers of His Majesty's sloop *Cygnet*, then patrolling Labrador waters. Finding Mr Baskem's wife and children destitute at Port Marnham, the beneficent Cartwright formally ceded Port Marnham and some gear to the absent Baskem. At Spear Harbour, Cartwright's indefatigable trust (or naïvety) got the better of him. He arranged to loan Mr Forsythe some fishery salt in exchange for provisions he would later collect at Sandhill Cove. The next month Cartwright sent his trusted servant Mr Robert Collingham to collect the provisions. Cartwright learned that Forsythe had deceived him; he did not have the supplies he had promised, and was himself forced to borrow provisions from the *Cygnet* (2: 498).

Rumours of marauding privateers compelled Cartwright to return to Isthmus Bay. His men had caught 390 tierces of salmon during the 1779 season. In late October, Cartwright sailed for St John's and then England, leaving his servant, Mr Collingham, to manage his affairs.

Cartwright spent the period between 1779 and 1783 in England, attempting to consolidate his financial affairs and to convince his creditors to give him more time to pay his debts. Cartwright's father died in December 1781, leaving George's brother John as chief beneficiary. To add to his problems, Cartwright's ship, the *Countess of Essingham*, was lost at sea in the spring of 1781 and a new schooner was built at Paradise River that same year. However, the Americans seized the new schooner in 1782. Loss of these vessels prevented Mr Collingham from marketing the company's fish and furs.

Back in England in June 1783, Cartwright's spirits were lifted with news from Labrador that Mr Collingham had discovered a twenty-inch-wide vein of ore, thought to be gold. Cartwright hired a Derbyshire miner named Samuel Mather and departed for Labrador on 7 July 1783, on what was to be a short fifth voyage.

Cartwright and Mather sailed aboard a brig belonging to Mr Lester of Poole and thus stopped at Trinity Harbour to visit Mr Stone, Lester's partner. Stone informed Cartwright that the former's vessel had sailed to Labrador that summer and collected all of Cartwright's catch, including 560 tierces of salmon, 504 quintals of cod, and 15 hogsheads of seal oil (Cartwright 1792, 3: 5). Most of this had been caught in 1782; the 1783 salmon catch dropped to 71 tierces. Cartwright also learned that the ore discovered the year before was worthless. He wrote: I 'foresaw inevitable ruin waiting my return to England' (3: 9).

Following an exceptionally stormy crossing to England in December 1783 and January 1784, Cartwright learned that the *John*, a vessel carrying his furs and baleen (which he had purchased from Inuit in September 1783), had foundered at sea and sunk, shortly after departing Trinity, Newfoundland (3: 37). In London, he learned that he now owed £7000. By 1785 he was bankrupt, his assets sold at a Poole auction to Robert Hunter, a London merchant who dealt extensively with Noble and Pinson! Hunter then sold Cartwright's former Sandwich Bay salmon posts to Noble and Pinson for one-quarter of what Cartwright believed was their value (3: 72–3).

By his forty-sixth birthday (12 February 1784), Cartwright was increasingly afflicted with sciatica and periodically experienced great difficulty walking. Nonetheless, the following year his undiminished sense of obligation to former creditors, and the realization that he could not earn money to repay them in England, compelled him to attempt another voyage. His plan was to employ a small labour force for trapping during winter and concentrate on the trade with Inuit during summer. He accepted the suggestion that he take four convicts to Labrador as workers. (Prior to the American revolutionary war, the British deported criminals to the American colony of Georgia, but during and after the war sought new destinations. This practice is well known in relation to the colonization of Australia.)

Cartwright and his convict-workers sailed for Labrador on 29 April 1785 and arrived at Mr Lester's house at Trinity on 31 May. There, Cartwright hired a former employee, John Tilsed, as boatsmaster for two summers and a winter. Tilsed was paid £37, including passage home (3: 46–7). On 4 June, Cartwright auctioned a shallop and other possessions which had been sent from Labrador for the bankruptcy sale. He ordered his men to repair another shallop (he does not explain how he acquired it), the *Martin*, renamed it the *Fox*, and, following an ice-delayed voyage, arrived at Isthmus Bay on 11 August (3: 67). That summer cod were scarce in northern Newfoundland waters and Cartwright records encountering a number of Newfoundland vessels at Englee and Quirpon, which were bound for Labrador.

On returning to Isthmus Bay, Cartwright was bothered by severe sciatic pains and limited mobility. On 15 August, for example, he was not able to walk more than ten yards and 'crawled upon the hill' near his house (3: 68). Again, there was contact with Noble and Pinson's men. The following day, a Mr William Dier, master of Noble and Pinson's brig *Mary*, stopped at Isthmus Bay en route from Paradise to Temple Bay. Dier lamented the poor salmon fishery – Cartwright's former posts on the Paradise and Eagle Rivers had only produced 390 tierces of salmon.

On 8 September, Mr Dier 'forcibly seized' Mr Collingham's baleen, seal oil, and furs, together with what belonged to Cartwright and his assignees, and sent all to Mr Pinson's son William at Temple Bay. Cartwright sent the *Fox* to Paradise to collect Mr and Mrs Collingham and their belongings.

On 15 September 1785, Cartwright and his trusted employee Mr Collingham entered a partnership, which was to last until 10 September

1788. Days after the initial agreement, on 14 September, Collingham and three men sailed to Temple Bay to seek restitution for goods Mr Dier had seized at Paradise River. Collingham returned to Isthmus Bay on 28 September with the seized goods.

On 5 October 1785, Quebec merchant Pierre Marcoux arrived at Isthmus Bay en route to Ivucktoke Bay (Lake Melville), where he planned to winter (Cartwright 1792, 3: 81; Zimmerly 1975, 53–4). Another party of Quebec merchants arrived on 20 October. This included Nicholas Gabourite, an old Montagnais (Innu) man, his daughter, and four of her children. Unfortunately, Gabourite's vessel ran aground near 'Gready's sealing tilt' (at Indian Island) and his party was apprehensive about venturing further north (Cartwright 1792, 3: 86). Gabourite asked Cartwright where his party might winter and Cartwright suggested Muddy Bay (3: 88). During the following winter, Cartwright received occasional visits from Gabourite's party and, to a lesser extent, from Noble and Pinson's Paradise River crew.

Springtime and open water brought a shallop belonging to a Mr Domoetie (Dumontier) and his partner. They had wintered at North West River (Zimmerly 1975, 54) and like their winter neighbour, Mr Marcoux, reported a poor trapping season (3: 178–9, 198). Perhaps spurred by reports from Dumontier, Collingham sailed to Ivucktoke Bay on 19 June and purchased a small amount of baleen, seal oil, and fur from Inuit (3: 181). Collingham learned that in addition to Marcoux and Dumontier, two Englishmen, probably William Phippard and John Nooks, had wintered in Lake Melville (Zimmerly 1975, 52–4).

Cartwright's relations with Noble and Pinson became increasingly vitriolic during his final summer in Labrador. On 12 July 1786, Noble and Pinson's brig *Mary* arrived at Isthmus Bay carrying an officer of His Majesty's *Merlin*, whom Newfoundland governor Elliot had sent to collect the arms issued British merchants during the American War of Independence. The *Mary* also carried a letter from Noble and Pinson accusing Cartwright and Collingham of embezzling part of Cartwright's father's estate (Cartwright 1792 3: 186). Cartwright immediately decided to return to England to 'confute their villainies and recover the goods' (ibid.). Later in July, Cartwright resolved that he would have 'as little connection with them [Noble and Pinson's men] as possible' and, at one point, refused to pilot the *Mary* out of Isthmus Bay (3: 193).

Cartwright left Isthmus Bay for the last time on 30 July 1786. His journal provides no indication that he realized the finality of this departure. Indeed, his partnership with Mr Collingham had over two years remaining and the Collinghams, in addition to several servants, remained at the post.

Cartwright's description of his journey south reveals the many changes which had occurred along the southeastern Labrador coast since his arrival in 1770. He mentions Pierre Marcoux's sealing post near Seal Islands and a new sealing house and fishing room built by the crews of a Mr Hyde of Poole, at Hawke Island. At Square Islands (where Cartwright had once operated a cod-fishing room), he encountered a brig belonging to Mr Tory. Tory had built there after the creation of the French Shore had forced him from White Bay, Newfoundland. At Temple Bay, Cartwright accepted passage on the *Merlin*, which continued south through the Strait. He mentions Noble and Pinson's post at L'Anse au Loup, Jersey companies, and several planters at Forteau and Blanc Sablon, and American whalers at Isle de Bois. In short, travelling the coast for the last time, Cartwright leaves the impression that he was leaving a region far more developed than when he first arrived.

CARTWRIGHT: RELATIONS WITH ABORIGINAL PEOPLES

Anthropologists and historians commonly credit Cartwright with establishing amicable relations with Inuit. This may be true, although I believe that the transition from Inuit-European hostility to harmony that occurred during Cartwright's tenure must also be attributed to other changes occurring in Labrador, including the Moravian and British government's efforts to stop Inuit from travelling south to trade, and the introduction of European diseases. Cartwright's relations with Inuit (Eskimos) were far more extensive than with Innu (Montagnais-Naskapi Indians), chiefly because Inuit possessed the baleen and other local products which Europeans valued.

Most of Cartwright's contact with Inuit occurred during his first voyage, between 1770 and 1772. Like other Europeans of the time, Cartwright wanted to trade, and toward that end, he attempted to increase his understanding of the Inuit. Several consequences resulted from Cartwright's relations with Inuit. These consequences include Cartwright's valuable descriptions of 'traditional' Inuit culture and of the middleman trade, both then on the wane; his well-intended although lethal exportation of Inuit to England; his exploitation (including sexual) of Inuit; and subsequently, several children from unions between Inuit women and Cartwright's men.

Cartwright's relations with Labrador Inuit began less than three months after his arrival in Labrador. On 5 October 1770, his partner, Lieutenant Lucas, returned from 'Auchbucktoke,' likely Avertok, or the Moravians' Hopedale (Taylor 1977, 51; 1983, 13), having convinced the Inuk Attuiock (whom Cartwright described as the 'chief of Auchbucktoke') and his family to winter near Cartwright. Lucas had learned Inuktitut a couple of years before, when he escorted Mikak and several other Inuit to England, following the 1767 raid on Darby's whaling post, and he provided Cartwright with an Inuktitut vocabulary enabling some communication (1792, 1: 66). Cartwright's purpose was 'to give me an opportunity, of laying a foundation for a friendly intercourse with them' (1: 41). In his 1773 memorial to the Earl of Dartmouth, Cartwright (the Memorialist) cast himself as a useful British mediator with Inuit and cited his relations with Attuiock and his family as an illustration: 'The two successive seasons (1770–72) he [Cartwright] ventured to pitch his tent in their camp; having never more than a single attendant, and being sometimes alone. He [Cartwright] lived amongst them in this manner for some weeks, and very frequently entertained large parties of them at his own house; by means of which he at length obtained such an ascendancy over them that they became entirely observant of his commands' (1064). Cartwright claimed to have gained the confidence of Inuit and that they sided with him in his dispute with Noble and Pinson.

Cartwright's descriptions of Inuit culture before it was extensively altered by European contact have lasting ethnographic value. Although related to trade, Cartwright's interest in Inuit culture was also caused by curiosity. Like the European settlers who would later establish homesteads in Labrador, he was learning about Labrador life. Thus, we learn about building snow houses, archery games, shamanistic rites, values, and a host of other things. We also learn about the impact of trade on marriage. Cartwright writes that in October 1770, Attuiock's extended family included two wives, three young children, Attuiock's seventeen-year-old brother Tooklavina, Etuiock, his fifteen-year-old nephew, and a 'maid servant.' Attuiock benefited from his association with Cartwright and two years later expressed his new-found affluence in the Inuit manner by adding two more wives (1792 1: 262).

Although Attuiock and most of the Inuit Cartwright encountered each summer were middlemen traders, they hunted throughout the remainder of the year. Cartwright describes this mixed trading and hunting economy. In 1770, for example, Attuiock's family was to winter at 'Cape

Cove' (possibly now 'Indian Cove', Cape Charles), but on 23 October 1770, they complained that they 'could kill no provisions there.' Cartwright then ordered his men to repair an 'old Canadian house' about one-half mile down river from Ranger Lodge (1792, 1: 48). There, Attuiock's family lived until 10 February 1771, when they moved to 'Lyon Head' (a peninsula near Kyer Cove). Here they built a snow house and hunted ringed seals basking on the spring sea ice (1: 92, 96). By April, they had moved into a skin tent near Seal Island. Here, in early July, they were joined by five other families, totalling thirty-two people. These new arrivals wintered at one of the three 'southernmost (Inuit) settlements, where no whales are killed,' and traded baleen with more northern Inuit groups (1: 143–4). On 9 July, following two days of trade with Cartwright, the Inuit traders demonstrated their advertising techniques, probably overlooking what is now Wall's Tickle (Cape Charles). The Inuit 'chief' Shuglawina (possibly the influential Tug-lavina; see Taylor 1983 and 1984) solemnly led a suspicious Cartwright up the hill behind Cartwright's tent to a place overlooking the Strait of Belle Isle. The Inuit had gathered wood for a gigantic fire (upon which Cartwright initially feared that he was to be 'sacrificed') to attract vessels at sea (1: 143).

One week later, on 16 July 1771, the traders moved south to Camp Islands, and on 25 July they were joined by five more shallops of Inuit (1: 151). The following July (1772), Cartwright again visited and traded with a large party of Inuit traders at Camp Islands, a location favoured by Inuit middlemen-traders because of its proximity to Chateau Bay and its view of the Strait.

Inuit traders recognized differences among Europeans, and these sometimes affected the outcome of trade. Thus, on 2 July 1772, Cartwright and the Inuit observed a ship and several smaller vessels sail from Quirpon, Newfoundland, to Chateau, Labrador. The following day, two shallops of Inuit left Camp Islands for Chateau to trade with the newcomers. They returned the following day, claiming to be 'very much dissatisfied with the reception they met there,' and immediately resumed trade with Cartwright (1: 237–8).

Cartwright also exploited Inuit. Once, for example, he describes bartering 'a stick of whale bone (baleen) and two ranger (seal) skins for a few beads' (1: 231). Similarly, in 1773, he purchased Tweegock, a fourteen-year-old Inuk girl, for one bait skiff (small wooden boat). On many other occasions, Cartwright visits Inuit women at their camps, possibly for sexual encounters.

No Inuit wintered with Cartwright during 1771–2 but the following winter Cartwright decided to take Attuiock, Ickcongoque (the youngest of four wives), Ickeuma (her daughter), Tooklavina (Attuiock's brother), and Caubvick, Tooklavina's wife, to England. Cartwright's description of the Inuit reaction to England is one of the best examples of European-native contact in the Labrador literature, illustrating a broad range of transcultural themes, including the distinction between nature and culture. For example, Cartwright expressed surprise when the Inuit did not comment on passing through London Bridge, a structure which they took to be a 'natural rock which extended across the river' (1: 266). Likewise, after two months in London, Cartwright took his weary and homesick visitors to his father's country home at Marnham. There, the Inuit astutely observed that the cultivated meadows and fields were 'all made' by man (1: 266).

The unexpected price which four of the five Inuit were to pay for our cross-cultural insight was their lives. Shortly after embarking for Labrador, in May 1773, all except Caubvick fell ill and died of smallpox. Worse still, Cartwright later learned that Caubvick had unintentionally introduced smallpox to Ivucktoke (Groswater) Bay Inuit, leading to many more deaths (1792, 2: 424).

Cartwright was heartbroken by the deaths of Attuiock and the others. His poignant description of Caubvick's reunion with approximately five hundred Inuit ('almost the whole of the three southern-most tribes') at Lodge Bay in late August 1773 is most distressing. The women beat their heads and faces with stones, Cartwright wept, and as the scene unfolded, Inuit pressed forward to console Cartwright and assure him that they did not hold him responsible for the four deaths (1: 274–5). Sadly, three months later, Cartwright repeated his mistake. In November 1773, he took Noozelliack, a twelve-year-old Inuk boy, to England, where he hoped to train the youth as an interpreter. Through Noozelliack, Cartwright hoped to gain 'full information on their (Inuit) religion, customs and manners' (1: 287). Noozelliack died in England three days after being inoculated for smallpox.

Finally, Cartwright's relations with Inuit – or those of his men – produced several physically mixed offspring. These include twin girls born to Nooquashock and David Scully and a daughter (who died as an infant) born to Tweegock and James Gready (Stopp and Rutherford 1991, 15). Unfortunately, the names of these children are unknown, as is whether they are the mixed Inuit who marry the first generation of permanent settlers in the early nineteenth century.

Cartwright's relations with Labrador Innu (Indians), though sporadic and short-lived, continued periodically throughout his tenure on the coast. During Cartwright's first five years in Labrador, he saw many more signs (usually the remains of 'whigwhams') of Innu than Innu themselves. A partial list of the locations and dates of these sightings includes: the Gilbert River on 25 August 1770; Beaver Brook, Alexis Bay, and Gilbert narrows on 26 August 1770; 'Nescaupick Ridge' (near Lodge Bay) on 14 November 1770; Mary's Harbour on 29 May 1771; St Lewis River on 7 June 1771; Haines Harbour, Granby Island, on 5 September 1771; and Deer Harbour, St Lewis Bay, on 14 October 1771. Judging from the wary and reluctant manner in which the Innu later approached Cartwright, Innu were well aware of his presence but hesitant to make themselves known.

Cartwright first met Innu on 18 June 1774 when 'two canoes of Nascaupick Indians' came to Lodge Bay and made him a present of a beaver and marten skin for which he gave them some gunpowder and rum (2: 9). Two days later, Cartwright introduced the Innu to Inuit who had wintered near Stage Cove during 1773–4. Given the suspicion and distrust characteristic of Innu-Inuit relations (Taylor 1979), one wonders how this meeting went. Later in August of the same year, Cartwright saw the same group of Innu at Gilbert Bay.

Cartwright purchased furs from Innu on 18–19 September 1774 and 9 March 1775 at Stage Cove. On 13 April 1775, two Innu brought Cartwright a sledful of caribou meat, while their families remained near Fox Harbour (St Lewis) (2: 62–3). On his July 1775 trip north, Cartwright travelled part of the way from the St Lewis River to Sandwich Bay with two Innu families, totalling thirteen people. However, according to Cartwright, the Innu would accompany him no further than Venison Island because he had refused to give 'Captain Jack' (one of the Innu) rum the night before (2: 93). As he did with Inuit, Cartwright contributed to the already developed Innu taste for alcohol. Rum or brandy was offered in exchange for furs. This was done, for example, on 11–12 September 1776, at Caribou Castle (Cartwright). There, seven Innu arrived in two canoes and, according to Cartwright, 'gave me four beaver skins, and afterwards stole them again and sold them to me. They continued to drink brandy, until they were quite drunk' (2: 206). Innu consumption of alcohol while trading may have had a ritual dimension. This is suggested by Winterbotham's description of leadership and ceremony surrounding mid-eighteenth-century trade between the Hudson's Bay Company and Quebec Indians. Winterbotham

(1795, 4: 31–7) notes that brandy and, especially, tobacco were consumed in a highly ritualistic fashion before trading transpired.

Four Innu also came to Caribou Castle during the summer of 1776 and visited Cartwright's Isthmus Bay house in October 1778, promising to return with the rest of their band. In the interim, Cartwright spotted three Innu on Berry Hill, near Isthmus Bay, and invited them to his house. The three were a family, including Pere Barecack, his wife Concofish, and their daughter, Catherine Ooquioo. They stayed the night, got drunk, and were, Cartwright complained, 'very troublesome' (2: 377). The remainder of the band did not visit Isthmus Bay but were met by Mr Collingham at Longstretch, Sandwich Bay, on 12 October. The band numbered approximately forty Innu and travelled in eight canoes; they were heading for Paradise River. Mr Collingham purchased forty-eight beaver, eleven otter, and three black bear skins. Two weeks later they disappeared up either the Paradise or White Bear River into the interior.

Just as Cartwright experimented with some Inuit technology, such as dog team traction, 'snoweyes' or snow goggles, sealskin boots, and kayaks, so too he tried Innu toboggans, snowshoes, and canoes. Cartwright described the Innu as excellent marksmen, even when inebriated (2: 206), and he was impressed with their rapid-fire method of shooting caribou (ibid.).

Finally, like many other early Europeans, Cartwright preferred Inuit to Innu, calling the former people the 'best tempered people I ever met' (3: 232). He praised Innu adaptive skills, but was less complimentary about what he termed their 'morals.' He complained that they were addicted to 'drunkenness and theft' (3: 231), neglecting to acknowledge his role in contributing to the former vice.

CARTWRIGHT'S LEGACY

Cartwright's legacy is twofold: his *Journal* and his blueprint for Labrador living. As we have seen, his *Journal* provides an astonishingly complete account of southeastern Labrador just before initial permanent European settlement. Along with other, lesser-known British adventurers, Cartwright applies the fundamental lesson of the French regime: survival in Labrador requires year-round residence and a seasonally mobile settlement pattern. Early permanent Settlers would follow and expand upon Cartwright's blueprint.

4

Visiting Fishers

Although Cartwright's adventure helped convince British authorities that survival in Labrador required year-round residence, he should not be called an early settler. He left Labrador forever in 1786 and died in England in 1819. Nevertheless, a causal relationship does exist between foreign fishers and early settlement. And while this relationship has never been advanced in the Labrador literature, others, like Gosling (1910, 1911), have recognized in a more general sense the monumental impact of these fisheries on Labrador. Thus, this chapter discusses the social impact of the many thousands of American, French, and Newfoundland fishers who visited Labrador each summer for much of the nineteenth century (and, in the case of Newfoundlanders, into this century). Such a discussion sets the stage for the argument of chapter 5, that American trade with early planters fostered permanent settlement.

THE AMERICAN FISHERY IN LABRADOR

America's Labrador fishery is a neglected but crucial chapter of Labrador history. Its origins derive from the American whale fishery in Labrador and New England fishing and trade in Newfoundland (see Gosling 1910, 318–19). New Englanders fished in Newfoundland waters as early as 1645, but they also traded American, European, and West Indian products (Gosling 1910, 318). A 1756 petition by Boston Selectmen to the Massachusetts governor gives some idea of the magnitude and importance of this trade, centred in Boston, and of new competition which threatened it. At an 11 February 1756 Boston town meeting, residents protested their shrinking monopoly over the distilling of molasses and refining of sugar. Until then, Bostonians had processed these West Indian products and supplied Newfoundland, Nova Scotia, New Hampshire, Rhode Island, Connecticut, New York, the Jerseys, Maryland, Virginia, and North and South Carolina. In exchange, Boston merchants received 'wheat, flour, peas, pork, beef, fish train oil, pitch, tar, turpentine, furs, hides, skins, tallow and many other valuable commodities' (Boston Board of Selectmen 1756). Between 1736 and 1756, however, competition from distilling houses in Rhode Island, Connecticut, New York, Pennsylvania, and Nova Scotia eroded Boston's control over this trade, leading to suffering among the town's 'lower sorts,' who presumably lost their jobs (ibid.).

American trade also took place along the Labrador coast. Gosling mentions the trading expeditions of Captain Atkins (of Boston) to Labrador in 1729 and 1758. For example, near latitude 53°40' (possibly near Spotted Island), Atkins traded £120 worth (Boston value) of whalebone (baleen) with 'Indians' (Inuit) for ten shillings worth of 'trifles' (Gosling 1910, 322).

Prior to the American War of Independence, American whalers conducted an extensive fishery in the Gulf of St Lawrence and Strait of Belle Isle. The British authorities largely ignored American whaling until after the Treaty of Paris (1763), when coastal Labrador came under Newfoundland's jurisdiction. Nantucket, Massachusetts, and New London, Connecticut, were the major home ports for this industry. Descriptions of the American whale fishery come from American (e.g., Goode 1887) and British (e.g., Gosling 1910, 1911) scholars. For example, Gosling writes: 'Prior to the war with France, which culminated in the conquest of Canada, the adventurous New Englanders had carried on a whale fishery in the Gulf of St. Lawrence to the mouth of the Strait of Bell [sic] Isle: and as soon as peace was declared, and the Coast of Labrador thus thrown open to their operations, they flocked thither in great numbers. Their vessels were fitted both for whale and cod-fishing, so that if unsuccessful in the former they might make a saving voyage by the latter means' (1911, 6).

Newfoundland governor Hugh Palliser began a number of efforts to curb depredations against Inuit by American whalers, to prevent American fishers from selling codfish to French on the French Shore, and to stop the destruction of British premises by the New Englanders (Gosling 1910, 329–30). A 1773 narrative claims that each spring several New England whaling vessels came to the Strait of Belle Isle to intercept migrating whales and that, if unsuccessful with whales, they proceeded north along the coast to fish (Anonymous 1773, 1087). Gosling also claims that the near monopoly the Americans enjoyed in Labrador waters motivated Governor Palliser's attempts to extend the British ship fishery there (1911, 6–7).

During the American revolutionary war, many 'erstwhile [American] fishermen turned privateers and returned to their former haunts' (Gosling 1910, 332), now enemy territory. I have already described the destruction of Captain Cartwright's premises by Boston privateer John Grimes. The only related point here is that several years of American privateering in Newfoundland and Labrador undoubtedly increased American familiarity with the potential of the area's fishery.

Peace talks beginning in 1779 carefully considered the fisheries, and the Treaty of Paris (1783) confirmed the American right to fish on the Grand Banks and their liberty to take fish in the parts of Newfoundland used by British fishers, including Labrador, and to dry and cure fish ashore in unsettled harbours (Gosling 1910, 333–4). The Americans were not, however, permitted to purchase fish from locals (ibid., 344). Moreover, the Americans made a treaty with their French allies during the War of Independence, agreeing not to interfere with France's North American (i.e., French shore) fisheries (Gosling 1911, 10–11). This agreement confined the early American fishery to the Labrador coast.

Each May, the American fleet embarked from ports such as Newburyport, Massachusetts, sailed through the Canso Straits, around Bay Chaleur to the Magdalen Islands, and then on to Labrador (Gosling 1911, 11). Americans fished along the Quebec North Shore and southeastern Labrador coasts until late August (Gosling 1910, 365). Given that the Canso Straits and Newfoundland's west coast were normally ice-free, the Americans reached Labrador before the Newfoundland vessels (ibid., 352).

Geopolitical factors influence estimations of the size of the American fishery. Because the American presence interfered with British colonial control of Newfoundland and Labrador, British estimations of the American fishery may be inflated. Rowe reviews some of the British estimates:

Captain Innes of the Royal Navy estimated that 2500 American brigs, schooners and sloops, each carrying 10 to 15 men, fished on the Labrador coast in 1806. In 1813, Governor Keats estimated that there were about 1500 American vessels on the Labrador coast and three to four hundred on the Newfoundland Banks. In 1820, Captain Robinson of the Royal Navy estimated 530 American vessels on the (Labrador) coast, carrying 5830 men. That year the Americans took

530,000 quintals of fish, compared with the 134,000 quintals taken by the New-foundland and English ships. (1980, 469)

The British claimed the American fleet was large, aggressive, lawless, and effective. Captain Innes considered the Americans 'more numerous, active and successful' than their Newfoundland or English counterparts (Whitely 1977, 24). Evidence collected by Captain James Northey during his 1805 patrol attributes the greater success of the Americans more to industry than to lawlessness (ibid.), although, by 1820, British Captain Robinson claimed that the quality of fish produced by American fishers was inferior to that produced by English or Newfoundland fishers (Gosling 1910, 370).

American estimates of the size of their Labrador fishery are smaller. The first American vessel to participate in the Labrador cod fishery sailed from Newburyport, Massachusetts, about 1794 (Plummer, quoted in Goode 1887, 145). From then until 'the year 1879 there was scarcely a year when one or more Newburyport vessels have not visited the Labrador coast. In 1806 this fleet numbered 45 sail; in 1817, 65 sail; in 1860, 60 sail; in 1874, 2 sail; in 1876, 2 sail; 1879, none; in 1880, one vessel' (ibid.). The northern Massachusetts town of Newburyport was the major home port for the Labrador fishery. Other important ports included Gloucester, Provincetown, and Boston in Massachusetts and Westport and Booth Bay in Maine (ibid., 146).

The discrepancy between British and American assessments is obvious when one compares the Royal Navy's Captain Innes's estimation that 2500 American vessels fished along coastal Labrador in 1806 with Mr Plummer's claim that forty-five Labrador-bound vessels sailed from Newburyport, Massachusetts that same year. In sum, while estimates of the scale of the American fishery must be treated with caution, the fact remains that annually many hundreds of fishers descended on the Labrador coast south of Groswater Bay.

PRODUCTION METHODS OF AMERICAN FISHERS

A variety of American smacks (small, thirty-ton vessels rigged as sloops), sloops, brigs, and schooners used a number of fishing methods in the Labrador fishery. Labrador-bound vessels ranged between 45 and 140 tons, 100 being average (Goode 1887, 146). Each vessel carried one to four small boats used in fishing or obtaining bait. Crews averaged ten to fifteen men per vessel.

Methods used for codfish, the main species, were varied and changed over time. Until the mid-nineteenth century, hooks baited with capelin predominated, followed later by the cod seine. Captain Atwood, who sailed from Provincetown, Massachusetts, on 6 June 1820 to Groswater Bay, describes his fishing methods as follows:

Our mode of fishing then was to let the vessel lie in the harbor and send the boats out. At that time Provincetown had not a single vessel on the Grand Bank, and had two or three small vessels which went to the Gulf of St. Lawrence for mackerel. All the fishing vessels were on the coast of Labrador. We carried four boats. We used one to get capelin for bait when capelin were plenty during the capelin school. The bait boat would seldom go fishing. The fishing boats were baited out of her. We had one of the crew to throat, one to head, and one to split, and a salter in the hold of the vessel salting them as they came down. On our arrival on the coast of Labrador very few could be caught until the capelin came in, and then the capelin schools of cod came in also. The capelin school lasted about three weeks. After they went away we picked up fish very slowly. After the capelin had finished spawning the fish slacked off, and we used to say that the cod were 'capelin sick.' (Quoted in Goode 1887, 140–1)

Until capelin arrived in inshore waters, there were few local sources of bait. Consequently, American fishers often brought clams with them, caught mackerel in the Gulf of St Lawrence or caught lance or herring in Labrador (ibid., 140–2).

I am uncertain precisely when fishers began to use movable cod seines but Mr Plummer claims Newburyport Captain Sandborn used seines that were 'flat knit and gathered at the sides' during his first voyage to Labrador, in 1833 (quoted in Goode 1887, 144). More generally, Goode later claims that Americans had used seines on the Labrador coast for thirty years (i.e., since about 1854) and that they were especially popular among Newburyport fishers (1887, 142). Mr Wilcox describes both the structure and use of seines: 'A small boat is first sent to look over the ground [i.e., bottom], a water telescope being used – this being a small box 8 by 10 inches square, with a glass bottom. By the use of the water telescope the cod school may be seen moving through the water. When the fish are discovered the seine is set around them; the length of the seine is usually about 100 fathoms; its depth, 55 to 75 feet, the mesh ranging from 3 1/4 to 4 1/2 inches. From 2,000 to 12,000 codfish have been taken at a haul' (quoted in Goode 1887, 142).

An important auxiliary technology used with cod seines was the 'net bag.' Net bags permitted storage of part of a large catch of fish until it could be collected by small boat and transported to the main vessel. Captain Sandborn explains both the use of net bags and smaller-mesh nets used to catch capelin: 'Sometimes they used large bags made of nets, which they would fill with fish and anchor them until the boats could return for them. The vessels carried fine-mesh nets in which to catch caplin for bait' (quoted in Goode 1887, 144). None of these descriptions of cod seines mentions 'cod knockers.' Elderly Cape Charles fishers told me that when using cod seines, early twentieth-century Settler fishers bounced cod knockers off the bottom in order to scare codfish into seines.

American fishers brought most of their codfish 'green' to the United States for drying. If time and weather conditions permitted, however, they might split some of the fish, stack it in bulks, and 'make' it on shore. Hallock states that after the splitter had split the fish, they were passed to the salter, who

piles them in 'kenches', head and tail, salting profusely between the layers. After remaining thus for three weeks the water and 'gurry' (slime) are absorbed, and they are then placed on the 'flakes' to dry. At the end of three days they are said to be 'made.' After this they are piled in 'kenches' again for a day to 'sweat them' – that is, to remove remaining moisture – and are again thrown upon the flake for a day. They are then ready to be stowed in bulk in the vessel. Thus cured they bring from $2 to $3.50 per quintal. (Quoted in Goode 1887, 140)

Alternatively, the crew might attempt to dry the fish during the home voyage. Captain Atwood describes his 1821 voyage and his unsuccessful attempt to cure fish on the passage home:

We got about 1,200 quintals of fish (at Indian Harbour), which was considered a good fare. Then we came down into the Straits of Belle Isle and went to a place called Pinware, where we washed our fish out and took them ashore to dry them on the rocks. We had to turn and dry them on both sides. I think we staid [sic] here about four weeks. We then took our fish aboard for home. On our arrival here, the fish were not dry enough for market and we went to Gloucester and took them out and dried them over again, and then carried them to Boston where we sold them. My share of the voyage amounted to $83. (Quoted in Goode 1887, 141)

Captain Sandborn describes the excitement in home ports such as Newburyport on the return of the Labrador fleet and the employment generated in the curing of their catch: 'We used to have great times here [Newburyport] when the vessels came in from Labrador. All the men and boys we could scare up were employed in washing, hauling, drying, and packing the fish, and shipping them to market. The [fish] oil was shipped mostly to Philadelphia, and the vessels usually brought back coal, corn, sugar, and molasses' (quoted in Goode 1887, 144). Mr Sayward of Gloucester provides more particulars on Massachusetts locations used to cure the Labrador catch and on the production process itself:

Several of this class of vessels (topsail schooners), belonging at Newburyport and Provincetown, resorted to Cape Ann [Gloucester, Massachusetts area] during the first half of the present century, to cure their fares of fish, which had been caught at Labrador. At first the favourite locality for curing was at Wheeler's Point, on Squam River, but afterwards some of the schooners visited Gloucester Harbor for this purpose. The vessels generally arrived home from Labrador about September. A flake yard was hired, and the crew, who remained on board, 'handled' the fish and prepared them for market. The time necessary for the proper curing of a Labrador trip was usually about five to six weeks. (Quoted in Goode 1887, 141)

American fishers shipped most of their fish in wooden casks to Bilbao, Spain (Gosling 1910, 374), or, secondarily, to the West Indies. While cod (and associated bait species, including mackerel) were the principal quarry, some salmon fishing also occurred. The diary of Newburyport fisher John Woodwell (1809), aboard the schooner *Phoenix*, describes what may have been a typical voyage. The *Phoenix* left Newburyport on 20 May 1809, sailed through Canso Strait, and arrived at Indian Tickle, Labrador, on 11 June. There, the crew went to the islands to gather eggs. On 13 June they went to 'Hadlock's Cove' in Sandwich Bay and on 20 June to 'Coles Birth' (possibly 'berth'), both defunct place-names. They fished for salmon from 22 June to 19 July, taking some 2073 salmon. On 20 July they took up their salmon nets and sailed to Horse Chops. By 31 July they had caught ninety-six thousand codfish, but had exhausted their supply of salt. They headed south, passing many vessels, and arrived back at Davenporte Wharf, Newburyport.

American vessels returning to the United States were required by the government to file customs reports on their voyages, listing the owners, skippers and crews, amount caught, and method of remuneration. A copy of one of these relating to the 1866 voyage of the schooner *Native American* may be viewed in the Essex Institute, in Salem, Massachusetts. The voyage lasted over three and one-half months. The schooner, her skipper (Thomas Tobin), and her crew of fifteen (including one 'dresser' and one 'salter') caught 600 quintals of codfish, divided equally between the vessel's owner and the skipper and his men. We know from the 1864 journal (also at the Essex Institute) of the same vessel that she fished between the Quebec North Shore and Cape Charles, using baited hooks, seines, and trawls.[1]

After the mid-nineteenth century and principally between 1860 and 1880 (Gosling 1910, 425–6), the herring fishery became increasingly important. Gosling writes that Labrador herring were 'larger and fatter than any other known variety, and were marketed at good prices in Canada and Western America' (ibid.). This fishery was concentrated in the southern portion of southeastern Labrador, primarily between St Francis Harbour and Battle Harbour. Maxwell writes: 'The herring fishery begins in September, and is prosecuted principally from Azzizes Harbour, which is crowded with vessels at this time, which hope to compensate for a bad cod fishery by a plentiful catch of herrings' (1887, 383).

The Americans both fished for herring and purchased it, the latter practice contrary to treaty rights (Gosling 1910, 344). The herring fishery attracted fishers from Nova Scotia, Prince Edward Island, the United States, Newfoundland, and local Settlers. There were many disputes between competing fishers, particularly over the 'barring' of herring. Barring refers to pounding or enclosing herring in a seine. Gosling writes that an 1862 Newfoundland government regulation outlawed this wasteful practice but adds that the Nova Scotians and Americans 'resisted the enforcement of this ordinance, the latter claiming that it could not be enforced against them as it was not the law before 1854, when the last Reciprocity Treaty had been made' (ibid., 411–12).

Captain Hamilton describes the lawlessness associated with the herring fishery around Battle Harbour, which he claimed 'retains its reputation of being the most lawless and disorderly place on the whole (Labrador) coast' (1863, 399). Hamilton continues: 'In Battle Harbour numerous thefts of herring nets occurred; another robbery was by a Southerner (as those who return to Newfoundland are called) who went up Lewis Inlet and broke open and took everything from the winter house of one of the residents. Fortunately it was discovered and the things were returned before he [presumably the Newfoundlander] sailed; unfortunately for the furtherance of justice, the aggrieved man would not complain to me' (ibid.).

Judge Pinsent describes nearby Azzize's ('Size's') Harbour as a 'boom town':

In the locality extending from Size's Harbour to St. Francis Bight; where, in the short and exciting period when the herrings struck in, there was much violent interference with the Seines employed in that fishery, and taking away by force the herrings hauled. In most of these cases the herrings were barred, which is illegal; but of course that does not justify people in violently taking them out of the Seines of those who had hauled and barred them. I am of [the] opinion that the presence of a ship-of-war in that locality during the period of the herring fishery would be the best and most effectual means of preventing in future such turbulent and unlawful conduct. (1869, 659)

By the 1870s, fishers increasingly used nets rather than seines to catch herring, reducing the lawlessness and enabling more fishers, including local Settlers, to participate. Thus, in 1873, Judge Pinsent writes: 'The herring fishery was good; the fish come in early and steadily, and were principally caught in nets, which is preferable to seine hauling, as it gives the poorer class of fishermen a fairer opportunity of catching their share; and the condition of the fish is better for curing' (1874, 869).

But the end of America's Labrador fishery came quickly. Writing in 1867, Pinsent states that 'very few vessels from the United States of America now come to Labrador for any purpose' (1868, 549D). One year later, Pinsent writes: 'The Americans appear to have discontinued the fishery, which they formerly carried on there to a considerable extent' (1869, 660). By 1871, Captain Brown reports that there were 'no American or Nova Scotia fishermen in the [Cape Charles] neighbourhood, and consequently no disputes about "barring herring"' (1872, 663). Two years later, during the excellent fishery of 1873, Pinsent writes that the 'people of the United States seem to have given up, as a fishing station, that part of Labrador comprised within the limits of the Newfoundland Government' (1874, 869).[2]

Goode lists two reasons for the decline of America's Labrador fishery: a demand for larger codfish and the introduction of offshore trawling (1887, 145). During the 1860s, a decade or so before the Americans vacated the Labrador coast, they began frequenting the south coast of Newfoundland, trading with local planters for bait, and engaging in an offshore trawl fishery (Macdonald 1988, 69–73, 184–6).

THE FRENCH FISHERY

French fishing rights to portions of Newfoundland were delineated in Article 13 of the Treaty of Utrecht (1713) following the War of Spanish Succession (1701–14) (Neary 1980). Fishers were permitted to catch fish and dry them along the 'French Shore,' between Cape Bonavista and Point Riche. The Treaty of Paris (1763) confirmed the provisions of the previous treaty and ceded the islands of St Pierre and Miquelon to France as havens for French fishers. The Treaty of Versailles (1783) redefined the French Shore to include the coast between Cape St John and Cape Ray.

By the late eighteenth and early nineteenth century, St John's 'rising mercantile elite' assumed control of the Newfoundland fishery from West Country merchants (Neary 1980, 97). Between then and the signing of the Anglo-French Convention in 1904, Newfoundland governments often used French (and American and Nova Scotian) fishers as scapegoats for recurrent economic problems (Neary 1980; Smallwood 1984, 617).

Between 1834 and 1855 the 'French problem' consisted of alleged violations of treaty privileges, overfishing, and prevention of British subjects from fishing. Customs collector Elias Rendell's report from 1841 is typical: 'The encroachment of the French on the rights of our Fisheries on the coast of Labrador is also a subject of just complaint. From Blanc Sublons [sic] in the Straits of Belle Isle to Henley Harbor – the shore is literally lined with French boats; protected by their numbers, it is useless for the inhabitants to order them off or show the least resistance; nothing but a ship of war will intimidate them, or can protect the interests of British Fishermen' (43). Many suspected collusion between French and Settler fishers. Merchant Matthew Warren wrote: 'Pinware, Lance-au-Loup, and San [sic] Modeste are the principal harbours to which they [the French] resort. The inhabitants of these harbours, or rather some of them, receive from the French the [cod] liver for the use of their stages, and the liberty of fishing' (1851, 157).

Although smaller than the American fishery, the French fishery was sizeable, with twelve to fifteen hundred fishers fishing on the Labrador side of the Strait annually (White 1852, 113). The French were said to fish on Sunday (March 1866, 179) and to 'take possession of all the good fishing grounds, and keep our own fishermen off' (White 1852, 113). In General Superintendent March's report from 1865, he reports that French fishers 'disguised their batteaux by rubbing out their names, and by making them look, as much as possible, like yachts or pleasure boats' (1866, 178–9).

Between about 1860 and 1870, the focus of the 'French problem' shifted to French procurement of bait fish in Labrador and to related use of *bultows* or baited trawls in the Strait of Belle Isle. Local 'English fishermen' (presumably Settlers and Newfoundland fishers) were divided over the legality and impact of selling bait (principally capelin) to the French. One group favoured selling bait and another opposed it on the grounds of decreased Labrador cod catches (Hood 1866, 169–70).

Like the American fishery, the French fishery in Labrador declined after about 1870, about the same time that the Newfoundland government began complaining about French and American encroachment on the Bank fishery off Newfoundland (Smallwood 1984, 609).

NEWFOUNDLAND'S LABRADOR FISHERY AND THE IRISH CONNECTION

While the American and French fisheries and trade are not well-known chapters of Labrador history, the story of Newfoundland's Labrador fishery is. However, my account of this latter fishery begins with events far from Newfoundland.

Beginning in the late 1720s, periodic crop failures and trade depressions ushered in over a century of famine and economic distress in Ireland, causing hungry and unemployed rural people to flee to cities or emigrate in search of work (Brody [1973] 1982; Head 1976, 93–4). Work and imported American food were to be found in Newfoundland, attracting a steady influx of Irish immigrants in the eighteenth and early nineteenth century. Many settled in Conception Bay and along the southern shore of the Avalon peninsula. Following the prosperous times Newfoundland enjoyed during the American revolutionary war, the years leading up to the Napoleonic Wars were characterized by poor fishing returns and high costs of living and production. These caused extreme poverty for the approximately twenty thousand people wintering in Newfoundland. By the late eighteenth century, this led to new pressures on formerly under-utilized resources and regions. The conjuncture of these events and conditions – Irish immigration and resource depletion in inshore waters between St John's and Trinity Bay – increased the numbers of Newfoundlanders who began to follow the spring seal hunt and northern fishery (Head 1976, 221–6). Thus, we see the origin of Newfoundland's Labrador fishery.

According to Gosling, Newfoundland fishers disregarded Governor Palliser's 'Regulations for Labrador Fishery 1765.' Although the first regulation specifically prohibited any inhabitant of Newfoundland from going to Labrador (1910, 381), Newfoundland-based vessels fished the Labrador coast as early as 1766. Gosling writes that the first of these vessels were probably British ship-fishers stationed in Newfoundland but adds that, by about 1800, they were 'Newfoundland vessels pure and simple, manned by residents of Newfoundland' (ibid., 387). Some of the fishers were planters, petty merchant-fishers, supplied by larger merchants from Harbour Grace. In 1792, the Harbour Grace merchants petitioned Chief Justice Reeves claiming that the planters they supplied were hiring servants and enjoying too much independence (ibid., 389).

By 1806, the repeated failure of the Conception Bay fishery pressured more Newfoundland fishers to go to Labrador, and by 1813 the number of vessels had 'doubled,' presumably from the previous summer (ibid., 390; Ryan 1983, 52). Regulations prohibiting Newfoundland fishers from using the French Shore compelled them to fish in Labrador. Thus, in 1864, Packard encountered Newfoundlanders at Square Islands who explained that the creation of the French Shore had forced them to fish in Labrador. Packard's informants claimed this had begun seventy years earlier, about 1794 (Packard 1891, 146).

In addition, the end of the Napoleonic Wars in 1815 greatly accelerated Newfoundland's Labrador fishery. MacKay writes that 'after the Napoleonic Wars the French returned to the Banks and to the Treaty Shore which included the northern and all the west coasts, and many Newfoundland fishermen who had moved in during the period of war were compelled to move out. They found an alternative fishing area on the Labrador coast, to which Newfoundland fishing vessels began to make annual voyages, as formerly British fishing vessels had done to Newfoundland' (1946, 271). And Gosling provides an idea of the scope of this fishery: 'Owing to the Newfoundland fishermen being driven from the French shore, they were compelled to go further afield, and on this account the Labrador fishery was said to have increased sixfold between 1814 and 1829' (1910, 405).

By 1825, 60 vessels from St John's and another 200 from Conception Bay, totalling approximately five thousand men, sailed to the Labrador fishery (Gosling 1910, 402). Another estimate of the size of Newfoundland's Labrador fishery occurs in a petition presented to the Newfoundland House of Assembly on 3 April 1845 by Newfoundland-based planters and ship owners trading and supplying the Labrador fishery

(Gordon et al. 1845, 100–1). The petition claimed that a minimum of 200 Newfoundland ships fished annually off Labrador, carrying at least five thousand men. The petitioners accused the French of treaty violations at Belle Isle and Labrador's 'winter residents' (i.e., Settlers) of burning and destroying 'stages, flakes and houses' erected by the petitioners.[3] The petitioners lamented the cessation (in 1834) of the Labrador Court and recommended that a British warship patrol Labrador.

It is very important to emphasize that until the mid-nineteenth century, Newfoundland's Labrador fishers, like the Americans, primarily fished between the Strait and Hamilton Inlet. However, after the 1850s and especially the 1860s (Kleivan 1966, 118), the Newfoundland fishery sailed north into Moravian Labrador.

While American fishers relied primarily on cod seines, Newfoundland fishers fished by hook and line. These competing technologies caused frequent disputes among fishers from both countries. The disputes prompted calls for the establishment of courts for Labrador. The more numerous Americans held the upper hand until about 1840, when Newfoundlanders began to outnumber the Americans. The Americans, Gosling adds, may have 'found the Labrador a little *warm* for them, which may account for the rapid decline of their fishery after 1840' (1910, 405).

Gosling's description of a 1826 court case provides an idea of how Newfoundland fishers conducted the early Labrador fishery. Newfoundland schooners sailed for Labrador in early June, carrying a crew of six as well as ten fishers employed in curing fish ashore. Once in Labrador, fishers divided into three fishing crews. The schooner was moored and actual fishing took place from smaller open boats or skiffs. Fish were brought ashore, split, and salted at the skipper's 'room.' Once the schooner was filled, some of the men sailed it to St John's, unloaded it, and returned for a second voyage, finally returning from Labrador about mid-October. Remuneration was paid either in wages or in shares of the catch, after the skipper had calculated the costs of supplies furnished to the men (Gosling 1910, 401–2). The average yearly Newfoundland catch in Labrador was approximately one million quintals (ibid., 406).

Until the 1992 moratorium prohibiting fishing for 'northern cod' mentioned at the beginning of this book, southeastern Labrador waters continued to be fished by Newfoundland fishers each summer. Newfoundland fishers traditionally practised three kinds of fisheries; these have been labelled differently by different people (Tanner 1944, 748), but here will be called by their most common names: the *floater*, *stationer*, and *banker* fisheries. Floater fishers normally fished from schooners, generally using the cod trap and salting their catches in the ship's hold.

Stationers travelled to Labrador aboard large passenger-mail ships such as the legendary *Kyle*; they either brought their fishing boats and gear with them or stored these over the winter in Labrador. They fished from 'rooms' or 'premises' along the coast, and normally dried their fish ashore. There were many similarities and considerable interaction between Newfoundland stationer and Labrador Settler fisheries.

The third type, the banker fishery, is the least known, perhaps because the scale of this fishery was dwarfed by the other two. Banking schooners were larger than those used by floater fishers. Bankers fished from dories, using baited trawls. The mobility of the bankers and the trawls themselves caused resentment towards the bankers among more sedentary Settler fishers, much as happened during the nineteenth century regarding the French bultow. According to Judge Morris:

Another matter of very serious import to the local fishermen from Battle Harbour to Indian Harbour was brought before the court by the fishermen at Batteau. It appears that during recent years, early in the month of September, a large number of American, Canadian and Newfoundland bankers come in from the Grand Banks. They anchor in the different harbours at night, and sail out in the mornings to the near fishing grounds and set out huge fleets of trawls, covering every available fishery berth, to the exclusion of the local fishermen. (1909, 469–70)

Morris continues that the minister of fisheries promised regulations to prohibit use of trawls until after the first of October. What irritated Settler fishers about the banker fishery was also its greatest asset: mobility. Like recent longliner fishers, bankers moved their trawls to large concentrations of fish, which by early autumn were well offshore (Tanner 1944, 761).

On 4 September 1916, during a Labrador visit, Governor Davidson observed 'many Burin and Fortune Bankers off Indian Tickle and Venison; I am told that these boats sometimes have as much as 20 miles of net [sic] out. They are the aristocrat of the Coast' (1916, 24). On his September 1920 visit to Labrador, Governor Harris describes two bankers at Batteau which had come in to chop up their bait and were preparing their lines for the next day (1920, 6).

Dr Grenfell describes a dispute between mobile bankers and local trap fishers. Fish were plentiful in the summer of 1926 around Spotted

Island but were not approaching inshore waters; the Settler trap fishery was a failure. In contrast, Grenfell writes: 'The banking vessels with their dories, running in and out from the same [as the trap fishers] harbours daily and going only a few miles to sea, come home every night with a big haul' (1927, 36). Dyson describes how the banker dory fishers fished: 'They'd have maybe four tubs of gear with maybe ten lines in a tub ... They'd go in the morning, sometimes in the night, and have their day catchin' fish, come back and clear away a deck load of fish, and then they'd bait up their trawls for the next day' (1980, 55).

Other references to the banker fishery are rare, although Hussey (1981, 30) notes that bankers frequented the Batteau area and commonly returned to Newfoundland around mid-October. Ranger Christian mentions seven banking schooners fishing near Battle Harbour in August 1941 and observes that their catch was small because of a shortage of bait (Christian 1941b). Finally, Stevenson mentions a Lunenburg, Nova Scotia, banker at Hawke Harbour on 9 October 1950 (1950–1, 16).

Participants in each of these three fisheries came from different parts of Newfoundland. Most stationers came from Conception Bay outports, from Carbonear south to Brigus. Many of the floaters wintered at Conception Bay, but also came from various Trinity, Bonavista, and Notre Dame Bay communities. Bankers came from Newfoundland's south coast, primarily from larger settlements in Fortune and Placentia bays.

The fishing season of each fishery also differed. Stationer and floater fishers departed for Labrador in June, but the stationers stopped fishing in August or early September (Tanner 1944, 752), and floaters stopped about one month later. Bankers usually did not arrive in Labrador until mid-August to September and fished for a month or so.

The involvement of women differed with each fishery. Brothers or fathers and sons generally formed the core of stationer crews, although female family members performed essential duties ranging from helping at the fishing stages to cooking and cleaning. Floater crews employed girls or women as cooks. Banker crews were exclusively male, numbering up to fourteen men (Hussey 1981, 30).

State support for Newfoundland's Labrador fishery increased greatly during the period 1900–49. Beginning in the late nineteenth century, the Newfoundland government initiated a number of measures to support its Labrador fishers and merchants. These included subsidies to mail/passenger steamers, expansion of the Marconi wireless communication system, and seasonal medical and educational services. For example, in 1909, Judge Morris recommended a new Marconi station for

Ford's Harbour (near Nain), explaining that it would be 'immensely more valuable to Newfoundland trade and the fishermen on the Labrador coast for fishery news and information than is the present chain' (1909, 464). Three years later, Postmaster Woods, whose office administered wireless operations, noted that 'the 300 miles of coastal Labrador served by Marconi... while navigation is open ... have been erected for the benefit of the Newfoundland fishermen who go North in large numbers ... thus enabling them to communicate with each other during the fortnightly periods of waiting for the Mail Steamer in summer time. They are also used by merchants in various parts of the Island to communicate with their Agents on the Labrador Coast, there being no other telegraph system available' (1913, 328). By 1923, Newfoundland's Labrador fishery was served by Marconi wireless stations at Battle Harbour, Venison Island, Domino, and Grady (Abbott 1990, 6).

The same purpose justified the short-lived addition of a second Labrador steamer to serve northern Labrador, from Ailik (near Makkovik) 'nearly to Cape Chidley' (Woods 1912, 551–2). The Newfoundland House of Assembly also passed legislation prohibiting the use of steam vessels in the Labrador fishery and regulating conditions in which stationer women travelled aboard Labrador-bound vessels.

Preparations for the floater and stationer fisheries occurred in Newfoundland during winter. Stationers left for Labrador in June, usually travelling to and from Labrador aboard government-subsidized coastal steamers. Floaters travelled aboard privately owned schooners to and from Labrador.

There can be little doubt that floater and stationer fishers faced 'substandard' (Black 1960) living conditions, and, as explained below, it was initially the needs of these people that attracted the British missionary doctor Grenfell. Grenfell describes the 'good humour and forbearance' of Newfoundland fishers returning to the island in one cramped schooner. The vessel's hold was 'chalked into partitions, six feet in length, with the name of the family that was to rest opposite each section ... A man with 6 children was trying to fit into his space with his trap net, barrels, bedding, cooking gear, winter fish, and odds and ends of supplies in barrels. The next man's gear trespassed on his domain about 8 inches ... "You'll have to move closer up, Uncle Abe, as us can't get in ..." "Right you are, boy" said the veteran, "Tis only the bedding what got shaken down ..."' (Grenfell 1906, 12).

Muir accompanied West Coast Newfoundland stationers travelling to Labrador and writes: 'On the steamer 'Home' on our way from the Bay of Islands to the Labrador coast, we noticed a fisherman and his family who were going to the fishing grounds north of Red Bay. A more distressed looking family I hope never to see ... the wife of this fisherman wore a thin ragged muslin gown, and had no coat or wrap of any kind ... they were steerage passengers, but the baby of the family was ill ... ' (1910, 38–9). Many similar descriptions exist.

Newfoundland floater fishers used 'heavy-ballast, deep-draught vessel[s] built of spruce' (Black 1960, 277); 85 per cent were built in Newfoundland (ibid., 276) at a cost ranging from nine to fifteen thousand dollars (ibid., 291). Both to and from Labrador, floaters normally towed or were accompanied by a trap (or motor) boat. Once on the Labrador fishing grounds, schooners lay anchored much of the time, essentially serving as 'floating stages.' Crews used the trap boat (and perhaps a smaller boat) in their two or three daily trips to the trap(s). Floater fishers split and salted their fish aboard their schooners and piled fish in bulks in the ship's hold. Stationers either left their boats in Labrador over winter (Hussey 1981, 34) or transported them with the vessel carrying them to Labrador.

Floater crews numbered at least three men; four or five was a common number (Dyson 1980, 58). A significant percentage (37 per cent) included nine or ten men (Black 1960, 286), presumably divided into two or three trap crews. Black states that two-thirds of the Labrador floater fleet fished with two or three cod traps (ibid., 286). All crew members had a named status (for example, 'header,' 'splitter,' or 'salter') depending on their duties in fish processing (ibid., 278). Hussey (1981, 34) notes that there were five men in his father's stationer crew and that women performed vital support services, such as working at fishing stages, cooking, and cleaning. The *Lear* crew fished with 'two cod traps, a couple of salmon nets, and a fishing stage in which we could salt six hundred quintals of fish' (ibid.).

Floater fishers claimed cod trap berths on a first-come, first-served basis (Black 1960, 273). Most berths were located close to shore. They were graded according to their productivity and named for some distinctive characteristic (for example, the 'Crack in the Wall' [ibid., 274]). Considerable competition among floaters for prime berths resulted in the annual race of Newfoundland schooners for the Labrador coast.

Stationers more commonly claimed usufruct rights to particular berths that were generally respected locally (Hussey 1981, 34–5). Stationers often owned legal title to their Labrador 'rooms,' and there are many examples of these rooms being purchased by stationers or Settlers.

Black explains that the main cod runs lasted two to six weeks and that the local timing of such runs varied along the coast (1960, 273). Some salmon fishing occasionally preceded the trap fishery. Salmon might be consumed that day, salted for domestic use by the fishers, or sold fresh to local buyers.

There were numerous methods for sharing the catch. All took into consideration the costs of production and treated the vessel as if it were an independent corporate entity. Several of these distribution systems are explained by Black (1960, 284). When applied to a hypothetical catch of a thousand quintals, made by an eleven-member crew whose skipper owned the vessel and paid all expenses, the distribution system worked as follows: 'The skipper-owner received a full share of 80 quintals, and from each shareman he also received a half-share, giving him a total of 400 quintals. From this amount the skipper paid all operating expenses. Each of the 10 crewmen received a half-share or 40 quintals. The trap boat was charged with a half-share, and the vessel was given a full share of 80 quintals' (ibid.). The vessel was considered an independent entity; it was both charged a half-share and given a full share. Such transfers presumably accounted for long-term depreciation of the vessel itself. Similarly, when Labrador floater fishers worked for large fishing merchants, the costs of outfitting the vessel were 'maintained separately from the fishermen's accounts' (ibid.).

Catches and prices varied. One hundred quintals per crew member was considered a good voyage (Hussey 1981, 34). Black agrees and explains that, for floaters, catch-per-crew-member decreased as the size of crew increased (1960, 289); optimal efficiency occurred with the ten-man crew using three traps (ibid., 290).

Although relatively immutable, Newfoundland's Labrador fishery witnessed occasional technological changes. For example, in 1904, merchants Baine and Grieve of Battle Harbour erected a bait freezer. Previously, without bait supplies, thousands of quintals of each year's potential catch swam free. Still, unpredictable supplies of bait remained a problem, and by 1923 Abbott recommended refrigerated bait depots at Domino and Venison Island, and one at Emily Harbour, just north of the study area (1990, 7).

Other technological changes affected the production of cod-liver oil, an important by-product of the fishery. In 1904 Grenfell describes a new (Norwegian) method of producing cod-liver oil: 'The oil is made by passing steam directly into the livers under pressure from a small boiler. The whole outfit is inexpensive, takes infinitely less time, is said to make much better oil and seems bound to replace the old and tedious method of having men to stir the cooking livers for five hours on a stretch' (18). Hussey mentions that Fraser Sellers and Sons of Western Bay operated a cod-liver oil refining factory at Batteau (1981, 21), and Dyson (1980, 56) claims that Fraser's brother operated a small liver factory at nearby Salmon Bight.

Technological changes sometimes produced unexpected consequences. Thus, the open motor (or trap) boat replaced the nineteenth-century decked 'bully' or 'jack' boat, powered by sail (Grenfell 1927, 36), a change enhancing the mobility of fishers (Tanner 1944, 752). And whereas in earlier times only two jack boat fishers were needed to fish using long lines far off shore, their sons or grandsons who adopted cod traps required crews of three or more. These increased labour requirements almost certainly encouraged the concentration of people into larger summer fishing settlements and, consequently, the cessation of some smaller summer stations. Grenfell considered this change in boat and gear very important, as he explained in 1930: 'One of the most important changes that my 38 years in Labrador have witnessed is the decline of the inshore fishing, with motor boats replacing the old sailing boats and the consequent abandoning of the outer shoals miles off the land. There hardy old salts used to venture before the trap net replaced the long line and the hand line' (150). Given that the best time for trapping cod is in July and August and that the best time for longlining and trawling is September, I suspect the transition Grenfell describes also changed the season when most fishing effort was made. And while the effectiveness of expensive cod traps (Grenfell estimates the cost of a cod trap at about $400 in 1926 [Grenfell 1927, 36; 1929; also see Tanner 1944, 757]) is unquestioned, they required that fish approach inshore waters, something that did not always happen.

THE DECLINE OF NEWFOUNDLAND'S LABRADOR FISHERIES

Initial signs of trouble in Newfoundland's Labrador fishery came in August 1914 with news of the First World War. British steamers were ordered to remain in port, telegraph stations closed, fish prices fell, flour prices rose, and alarm and depression spread through the population (Luther 1915, 8; Grenfell 1914). Even after the war, Grenfell observed: 'Our main customers in the Mediterranean cannot pay the prices for fish that we must obtain in order to live, for our supplies are still at war prices, owing to the heavy duties levied to meet a public debt the country cannot afford' (1921b, 76). The direct impact of the war on Newfoundland's Labrador fishery is obviously apparent in an anonymous author's observation that 'the number of schooners now engaged in cod trapping is less than half that of twenty years ago' (1920a, 135). The scale of this reduction may be calculated using figures this person provides – eighty-five schooners in port at Batteau and between sixty and eighty at Indian Harbour, all with their related motor boats. The decline continued, and by the 1929 crash of the stock market, fish prices had fallen 50 per cent (Tanner 1944, 763). That year, Dr Paddon reported a 60 per cent reduction in the floater fishery and a 75 per cent reduction in stationers at Indian Harbour (1929, 108–9). Paddon's estimate is supported by Grenfell's observation that the 'islands at the entrance of Hamilton Inlet, once the rendezvous for countless fishing schooners and the scene of large annual summer shore fisheries, have at any rate, temporarily, become more and more abandoned' (1929, 36).

While war and depression caused the Labrador cod fishery to stagnate, there were also problems of quality control and foreign competition as early as 1912. That year, a government report noted that: 'In view of the better handling, curing and packing of the Iceland and Norwegian products competing with Labrador, which is yearly becoming more and more noticeable, a policy which permits irregular salting, careless splitting, and dirty shipments, is, to say the least, suicidal, and that all parties interested should awake to the very serious results of its being permitted to continue' (Piccott 1913, 570). The European development of steam trawlers and drifters had led to the overproduction of fish in Europe and, consequently, to a decrease in the price and value of 'Labrador cure,' that is, heavily salted, sun-dried cod fish. (Lodge 1939). Black (1960) attributes the decline in the Labrador fishery after the 1930s to foreign competition, the rise in state-structured European fisheries, and shrinking markets for the heavily salted Labrador cure. Following confederation with Canada in 1949, unprecedented economic benefits from the Canadian welfare state decreased dependence on merchants, improved what Black considered the 'substandard' living conditions of floater fishers, and may have discouraged some fishers from making the arduous journey to Labrador.

It is clear that southeastern Labrador was a very busy place during much of the nineteenth and early twentieth centuries. The large fleets of American, French, Nova Scotian, and Newfoundland fishers overwhelmed the region's nascent Settler population. The character of 'international' relations among these visiting fishers ranged from harmony to competition. Although not much is known about relations between Settlers and French or American fishers, we do know that considerable trade between them occurred. Packard describes one example of good relations between Newfoundland and American fishers. Packard was ice-bound at Square Islands on 4 July 1864. While the Yankees saluted their flag and cheered, a captain of one of the Newfoundland vessels 'politely' launched rockets and roman candles. The celebrations lasted until eleven o'clock and presented, Packard concludes, a scene never before witnessed by what he calls 'Labradorians' (1891, 149).[4]

With regard to relations between these 'Labradorians' and Newfoundland fishers, we know that many Settler males met and married Newfoundland women who accompanied the fleet to Labrador to work as servants or cooks. We also know that many Newfoundlanders (Powell 1979 and Poole 1987) ventured to the Labrador fishery and remained forever.

5

A New World

Cartwright's saga contains occasional references to men who ceased working for their former merchant employers and attempted to fish or net seals on their own. Such a shift was fundamental, involving a change from being salaried workers to being supplied by merchants on credit. This change was essential to early permanent settlement. Unlike island Newfoundland and the Labrador Strait, an indigenous source of wives for early Settlers existed in southeastern Labrador. Thus, the timing of permanent settlement was not delayed by an absence of women; instead the timing appears related to two other factors: an apparent reduction in merchant opposition to settlement after around 1800 and an influx of thousands of visiting fisher/traders. Indigenous women and illicit trade figure prominently in the history of early permanent settlement.

Three assumptions pervade this explanation of early permanent settlement. *First*, our examination must be regional. In a general sense, there are many likenesses in history and culture throughout all of English-speaking Newfoundland and Labrador. At another level, however, there are very real although often subtle differences between regions. Consequently, while some relevant lessons may be drawn from other parts of Newfoundland or Labrador, the historical and socio-economic character of each region is unique. Some similarities (such as the fact that founding Settlers often married Inuit) exist between early settlement in northern and southeastern Labrador, as well as important differences, such as the enormous institutional influence of the Moravian missions on northern Labrador. Consequently, caution must be used in making comparisons.

My second assumption concerns the quality of relations between rival merchants, between merchants and the servants they employed, and between merchants and the planters (or settlers) they supplied. My understanding of these three types of relationships is characterized more by words like 'domination' and 'competition' than 'interdependence' and 'reciprocity,' as would appear to be the case in the Newfoundland model. I am not simply saying Settlers or fishers were helpless victims of mercantile capitalism, only that they faced horrendous obstacles limiting their ability to shape their own history.

However, one possibility long available to fishers is leakage, essentially an act of resistance, whereby planters or Settlers simultaneously and covertly dealt with traders other than their supplying merchant. I maintain that leakage has been a continuous feature of merchant-fisher relations, even though the vigilant eye of supplying merchants made such surreptitious trade difficult to conduct. As Macdonald states, this view of leakage concludes that reciprocity, 'the obligation of a fisherman to remit his catch to the merchant who supplied him' (1989, 142), has always been incomplete.

Finally, and consistent with the position taken here, I do not believe that regions or peoples can be viewed as isolates but, instead, are always linked to global forces. In this case, I maintain that intrusive forces, chiefly foreign fisheries, engendered conditions which facilitated the transition from salaried servants to provisioned permanent Settlers.

PROBLEMS OF RECONSTRUCTING EARLY SETTLEMENT IN SOUTH-EASTERN LABRADOR

Regrettably, the story of early permanent settlement in southeastern Labrador will never be completely known. Yet a great deal is known about early settlement in the Labrador Strait and in northern and central Labrador. Why is this so? Since their arrival in northern Labrador in 1771, European Moravian missionaries meticulously chronicled local events in their diaries and other writings. They made detailed records of births, marriages, and deaths, and their 'supplementary catalogues' recorded the movements of people between mission settlements. Consequently, both in the Moravian *Periodical Accounts,* and in the tremendous corpus of other Moravian writings, we learn a great deal about the arrival and early years of European Settlers in northern Labrador. Similarly, although to a lesser extent, in central Labrador, the records of the Hudson's Bay Company after its arrival in the 1830s, as well as written published accounts of famous early Settlers, such as Lydia Campbell or Margaret Baikie, describe early settlement in that region (cf. Plaice 1990). In contrast, very little documentary material exists describing early permanent settlement in southeastern Labrador.

The Anglican church established a mission at Battle Harbour in 1850, twenty or more years after permanent settlement began. Although adequate, the Anglican records lack the detail and antiquity of the Moravians' and only record the arrival of a second 'wave' of Settlers. I know all this first-hand. In 1979 and 1980, I hand-recorded all the Anglican baptismal, marriage, and death data between 1880 and 1980 at Mary's Harbour, now headquarters of the old Battle Harbour mission. These were later supplemented with copies of marriage and birth data between 1850 and 1880, contained in the Provincial Archives, and with tombstone entries which I collected from most of the cemeteries between Chateau Bay and Sandwich Bay. These church and gravestone data were entered in a computer as data for this and another study (Bear 1984). Computerization made the data more accessible but raised more questions than it gave answers. Few marriages occurring before 1850 are listed, and the earliest individuals appear to be the sons and daughters of first-generation Settlers. Thus the Battle Harbour data are of some, but limited, use.

Another source of data on early settlement in other parts of Labrador is the 'voluntary statements' and affidavits gathered during the first two decades of this century, as evidence for the Labrador Boundary Case. Beginning in the late nineteenth century, central Labrador Settlers trapped extensively in the Labrador interior, and this explains why Newfoundland government officials interviewed many of them to build a legal case showing the importance of the interior to the coast. Consequently, there are many such statements from northern and central Labrador people, containing valuable information about social history. But there are only two written statements from southeastern Labrador. The first is that of William Collingham, the British-born (1842) clerk for Slades and later Baine Johnston at Battle Harbour, and the second is that of former Cartwright Hudson's Bay Company post manager W.E. Swaffield. He signed an affidavit, at Montreal in 1926, but it, like Collingham's, says little about settlement.

Personal diaries are also rare, although we do have the so-called Moss diary (1832) from Battle Harbour. In Cape Charles I heard about several diaries that are believed to exist. These include the so-called Pye-Bellows diary, said to have mysteriously disappeared on the death of its last caretaker, near Corner Brook, Newfoundland. Several people claimed to have seen it and said that it described the earliest Cape

Charles Pyes. I was able to examine an anonymous diary describing Cape Charles in 1857 which was locally believed to be associated with a man named George Buckingham, thought to have been a petty merchant. In time period, style, and content, this anonymous 'Buckingham' diary resembles the older Moss diary.

Another potential documentary source, Newfoundland fishery or customs reports contained in the *Journal of the House of Assembly*, begins in 1833, yet these reports contain little of value until the 1840s and 1850s, and say little about permanent settlement. Finally, except for Bishop Edward Feild's excellent 1849 account and shorter accounts by Methodists Hickson and Knight, the handful of relevant first-hand accounts (e.g., Chappell 1818; Moss 1832; Tucker 1839; and De Boilieu [1861] 1969) are either vague or silent about early permanent settlement.

Local people kindly allowed me to copy the genealogical information commonly written in family bibles, yet few ancestors prior to about 1850 are listed. Likewise, local memories are limited to about three generations, extending back to around 1900. In short, while I will date the first permanent settlement of southeastern Labrador to the years between 1830 and 1870, few of the particulars will likely ever be known.[1]

THE NEWFOUNDLAND MODEL OF EARLY PERMANENT SETTLEMENT

What I will call the Newfoundland model of early permanent settlement attempts to explain how settlement occurred, at what time, and why. The important question is: What conditions led to the transition from a migratory fishery conducted by seasonal servants to a resident fishery in which planters or settlers drew most of their provisions on credit from local merchants?

Matthews (1968, 1988), the pioneering historical researcher, emphasizes the unique importance of the fishery in the political debate over permanent settlement, and the long-term geopolitical relevance of colonial America and New France in questions relating to early Newfoundland. The many geographers (Head 1976; Handcock 1989; Mannion 1977; Thornton 1977, 1979; and others) working on early settlement emphasize space, specifically the adaptations necessary for transient fishing servants to become permanent residents, and the locations and conditions fostering their move from England.

The debate over settlement centred on whether Newfoundland should remain only a destination for the migratory ship fishery or become a home. In the Labrador context, after the fall of New France in 1763, opposing sides of this debate were advanced by Governor Palliser, whose 1765 Labrador regulations prohibited permanent settlement, and by Captain Cartwright, whose 1773 petition advocated year-round residency. However, as Matthews, the geographers, and others conclude, efforts to curb permanent settlement were futile.

Before settlement began, the general pattern of the migratory ship fishery, dating from the early 1500s to around 1800 in Newfoundland and from after 1763 in Labrador, was as follows. Each January and February ships' agents recruited single young men for the fishery in the fairs and markets of interior west England (Matthews 1988; Handcock 1989, 63). Ships embarked for Newfoundland in early spring, fished during the summer, and returned to England in fall. However, as this migratory fishery developed, companies left some men to overwinter; some of these 'winter men' eventually became permanent settlers. Also, British mercantile firms established headquarters in Newfoundland or Labrador, bringing new crews of servants and supplies from England each spring to fish for cod, salmon, seal, and so on.

Describing Newfoundland society in the late eighteenth and early nineteenth century, Head observes that 'almost every man in Newfoundland in these years could be described as either merchant, boat keeper, or servant' (1976, 142, 230). Head is referring to the period prior to settlement, and to a historic mode of production which Sider (1986) calls the servant fishery. Cartwright's *Journal* suggests that such a three-tiered status system also existed in late eighteenth-century southeastern Labrador. Servants worked for wages, serving either from spring to fall or for two summers and a winter. The status of boat keeper or by-boat keeper was roughly synonymous with that of planter, an equally ambiguous category with at least four meanings in Newfoundland and Labrador (Story et al. 1982, 382–3). Generally, however, a planter was a more or less permanent Settler or fisher who, as boat keeper, normally owned a fishing boat and provisioned himself through a merchant, who then claimed the man's catch.

Excluding the short-lived planned colonies of the early seventeenth century, early permanent settlement in Newfoundland began around the mid-eighteenth century and was, Head (1976, 93) contends, tied to several coincidental external forces, including trade with the American colonies for bread and other foodstuffs necessary to survive in Newfoundland. Handcock shows how wars during the second half of the eighteenth century decreased the importance of the migratory fishery (1989, 75) relative to the resident fishery. Matthews (1988, 145) and Handcock (1989, 75) explain how the Napoleonic Wars (1802–15) marked the crucial turning point, after which resident fishers predominated, now supplied by merchants based in Newfoundland rather than England.

Referring to the Newfoundland model, scholars of early settlement emphasize two key points I have not yet mentioned: a) that merchants voluntarily began supplying former servants with supplies, on credit, and b) that the timing of permanent settlement depended on the availability of women as wives for potential Settlers. Thornton makes both points, and given that her work occurred just south of our study area, it is pertinent here.

Thornton's (1977, 1979) work on early settlement on the Newfoundland and Labrador sides of the Strait of Belle Isle pinpoints the beginnings of permanent settlement there to 1830–50. Since no 'indigenous source of wives was available' on the Labrador side of the Strait, the phasing of settlement awaited the immigration of females from Newfoundland (1979, 75). The second determinant in Thornton's explanation was the sudden recognition by merchants that it was more 'flexible and efficient' (ibid., 78) to supply Settlers with provisions on credit and later purchase the seal, salmon, and fur they produced than to employ them on wages. Just why this recognition occurred when Thornton claims it did (after 1830) is not entirely obvious. What is also unclear is why merchants relinquished control of essential means of production, such as salmon or sealing posts, to local planters, when, as Thornton admits, doing so created a leak which ultimately brought about the demise of the migratory ship fishery (ibid.) and its replacement by resident merchants supplying local Settlers.

Although data show similar turnovers at Battle Harbour, voluntary turnovers appear to contradict a theme of nineteenth- and early twentieth-century history, which claims that merchants maintained control of fishing berths and other valued property but allowed Settlers to use them in exchange for rent or to fish them on shares. Frankly I cannot resolve these contrasting views of allocations of merchant property – one stating that property rights were voluntarily relinquished, the other that they were vigorously maintained.

Thornton is a leading authority on early settlement. Yet, as rich and convincing as her work is on the Strait of Belle Isle, her version of early settlement, based as it is on the Newfoundland model, requires, I believe, an amendment if it is to be applied to southeastern Labrador.

This amendment involves three factors, factors which make the south-eastern Labrador case different from that of the Labrador Strait and island Newfoundland. These three factors are: a) the disorder and competition which characterize the early British era; b) the transient trade, especially with the American traders; and c) the presence of Inuit women as potential spouses.

THE MERCANTILE BACKGROUND OF EARLY PERMANENT SETTLEMENT

Fierce competition over resources and labour characterized relations between rival Labrador merchants during the late eighteenth century. Sabotage, arson, and other cutthroat tactics were common. One case of rivalry between John Slade and Company and Noble and Pinson was resolved by a formal truce, witnessed by a British naval officer. The truce's concluding statement is indicative of the monopolistic power of mercantile capitalism: both parties agree to 'prevent any strangers coming on the Caribou [Great Caribou Island, Battle Harbour] to the prejudice of our settlements at Battle Harbour or Cape Charles' (Slade Ledgers 1793). Although they do not specify what kind of 'strangers' they seek to prevent, I assume they are talking about other merchants or even planters who would threaten their newly bounded territories.

While pacts were possible between large and equally powerful rivals, large firms commonly used bullying and ultimatums to intimidate weaker merchants, planters, and servants. Remarks appended to a 1792 report vividly describe how merchants treated planters:

The coast of Labrador, in the Straits of Belle Isle, is much in want of some attention from Government. The planters and furriers, who are numerous, (although I cannot return how many), are entirely subject to the oppression of the merchants, who impose whatever price they please, and upon any debt however small being incurred and not being paid upon immediate demand, the boats and other effects of the debted are seized (without any authority for so doing), sold, and purchased by the creditors for sometimes one-sixth of their value. (Gosling 1910, 386)

Merchants reacted swiftly and mercilessly to any leakage from the planters they supplied. In the 1780s, for example, two Camp Island planters, Mr Macy and Mr Dean, leaked their salmon and cod to Net-lam Tory, the merchant based in White Bay, Newfoundland, who was forced to relocate to Labrador after extension of the French Shore in 1783.[2] Macy and Dean had been supplied by the powerful merchant William Pinson, who in the autumn of 1786 told Macy he would 'ruin him' if Macy continued to sell to Tory. In Whitely's words: 'Pinson charged extortionate prices on all articles sold to Macy and Dean and ordered a crew to be got ready to take over their salmon river. Faced with such ruthlessness, Macy was forced to sign without even being able to consult his partner' (1977, 19). Merchants also attempted to prevent servants from defecting to other merchants, and to prevent them from marrying (Thornton 1990, 108).

Labrador's lack of government meant that anarchy and disorder were common and, following 1763, the regulations of successive governors did little to alleviate the situation. Between 1774 and 1809, coastal Labrador was nominally administered by Quebec, but its distance from Quebec City and the fact that authorities there lacked both naval forces and the political will to provide regular patrols meant that injustice and disorder prevailed (Whitely 1977). British authorities received with incredulity George Cartwright's 1787 petition for a separate government for Labrador, with himself as principal justice of the peace (Whitely 1977, 19–20). By 1793, Newfoundland chief justice Reeves concluded that: 'The coast of Labrador is under the government of Canada [i.e., Quebec]; but the influence it feels from a centre so far removed is very small. In truth there is no government whatsoever on the Coast of Labrador ... It is very much to be wished that some plan be devised for affording to that deserted coast something like the effect of civil government (quoted in Jackson 1982, 13). Given this lawless backdrop and assuming strong and well-capitalized merchant monopolies, replenished by constant supplies of inexpensive imported servant labour, the mercantile system seemed incompatible with permanent settlement. Newcomers (the 'strangers' whom the Pinson/Slade truce sought to exclude) threatened merchant monopolies. Similarly, the arrival of new merchants or transient traders endangered merchant domination since these newcomers allowed planters supplied by one merchant to leak a portion of their catch to another.

Yet we do have evidence, albeit piecemeal, that after about 1800, the Battle Harbour firm of John Slade advanced productive technology and/or berths to former servants – including Alex Hutchings, William Holloway, John Grant, Thomas Peckham, and John Rumbolt – in exchange for some of the seal oil or cod produced. While some of these men may have became permanent settlers, they are not (excepting

Rumbolt, Holloway, and perhaps Akerman) ancestral to contemporary Settlers. This places the timing of permanent settlement – which Thornton ties to merchants divesting property to planters and having women to marry – in question.

So when did the ancestors of today's settlers arrive? If we limit our consideration to the Battle Harbour area and recall that Rumbolt is one of the few ancestors appearing in the Slade Ledgers, we can obtain a tentative answer by comparing the Slade documents from two later time periods, 1832 and 1871. The Moss (1832) diary from 9 February to 7 September contains roughly the same number of familiar Settler names (e.g., Rumbolt, 'Pole' [possibly later Poole], Russell, Allen, Pye) and unknown names. A more recent body of Slade documents, from 1871, reveals an increased number of familiar names. These Slade documents include three lists of Slade planters and servants from 1871. The first list contains the names of twenty-four resident planters supplied to fish cod, most with names associated with the Battle Harbour area. Those appearing on the second, twenty-four 'southern' planters, were Conception Bay men supplied to fish cod, while on a third list, nine Fox Harbour area men, were supplied to fish salmon. This third list mainly contains names associated with the Fox Harbour area. Comparison of these three time periods suggests that most early permanent settlement, at least in the southern portion of southeastern Labrador, occurred between 1830 and 1870. I believe that the chances of planters surviving were increased through trade with transient traders, a subject to which I now turn.

TRANSIENT AMERICAN TRADERS AND EARLY SETTLEMENT

Although distant from many centres of power and affluence, southeastern Labrador was influenced by broader, international forces; one of these was transient trade. Atlantic Canadian regional studies mentioning transient traders often fail to analyse their role adequately. Fortunately, there are studies (e.g., Gosling 1910, 1911; Innis [1940] 1978; and Whitely [1977]) that discuss transient trade. Head (1976) links trade to permanent settlement and Macdonald (1989) shows how the bait trade influenced settlement of the northeast corner of Fortune Bay.

I maintain that in the case of southeastern Labrador, sufficient evidence exists to make the trade/settlement connection. While I admit that this interpretation (or any other) cannot be proved conclusively, there is circumstantial evidence that transient trade undermined the trade monopoly of local merchants. It provided the incipient Settler population with less-expensive goods necessary for survival and thus allowed them some degree of independence from local merchants. Although the French and Newfoundlanders conducted trade along the Labrador coast, the transient American trade is more important to the early settlement of southeastern Labrador.

Newfoundland trade with the American colonies dates to the early seventeenth century. Americans used Newfoundland as a commodities clearing-house, an entrepôt for illegal trade with Europe. Davis explains that:

Sugar and tobacco, both enumerated commodities, were carried by New Englanders to Boston; thence to Newfoundland; thence to Holland or Scotland. Foreign manufactures returned by the same route. With no settled government in Newfoundland smuggling could not be stopped; a vice-admiralty court was set up there in 1708 but failed to curb what was by then a strong vested interest. Another complaint by the mother country was the spiriting away of colonists and fishermen to New England – headed up in casts to escape discovery – impairing both England's economy and recruitment for her navy. (1974, 167)

Such trade increased greatly during the second half of the century, primarily because Newfoundland lacked a customs arrangement with other colonies of the British Empire (Head 1976, 111–12). During the decades immediately preceding the American War of Independence, Newfoundland became an increasingly attractive market in which Americans could trade their surplus foodstuffs, replacing western adventurers as suppliers of Newfoundland's growing resident population (ibid., 102; Kerr 1941, 71).

During the early years of the American fishery, Labrador merchants repeatedly accused American fishers of illegal, aggressive, and disruptive behaviour (such as burning forests, drying fish ashore in settled harbours, seizing cod and salmon berths, and polluting bait grounds with fish offal). Whitely (1977) explains that such complaints were one reason why British officials in St John's re-annexed the administration of Labrador. However, as Whitely also notes, British authorities were probably more concerned with illicit trade than with other offences allegedly committed by the Americans. After 1809, Labrador merchants (then based in Newfoundland) continued to protest what they considered inadequate British protection against American fishers. Complaints about illicit trade intensified after the Anglo-American Convention of 1818, which created the American Shore (which included Newfound-

land's west coast and the Labrador Coast, from Mt Joly, Quebec, north
to Cape Chidley [see Neary 1980, 102]) and confirmed American rights
to land and dry fish in unsettled places along the Labrador coast. The
American fishery in Labrador grew until about 1840 (Gosling 1910,
373–4) and declined after 1870.

The Americans practised two forms of illicit trade. Newfoundland
governor Holloway describes the first form, 'transhipment,' in a 1807
letter to the Privy Council: 'The Americans that fish on the coast of
Labrador have long been suspected, and upon good information, of
carrying great quantities of provisions as well as other contraband
articles, which they sell and barter to the British merchants, who with
great facility tranship them in small quantities to this Island [Newfound-
land]' (quoted in Gosling 1910, 342). Transhipment required complicity
between American fishers and the Labrador merchants who benefited
from it. Royal Navy captain James Northey reported that 'when he did
try to check the Americans he was often asked to desist by British
fishers, who had their own tacit understanding with the Yankees'
(Whitely 1977, 24). That the Americans were convenient scapegoats for
Labrador fishers is evident in Northey's disclosure: 'If you meet a
(British fishing) boat (though scarcely able to swim with the quantity of
fish on board) and ask, is fish plenty? The constant answer is sure to be,
"oh no Sir, very scarce indeed, the Americans will soon ruin us, they
take all the fish"' (quoted in Whitely 1977, 24). The second, and for
present purposes more important form of trade, which I call 'planter
trade,' undercut Labrador merchants and was, I submit, beneficial to the
economic survival of the emerging Settler population. American fishers
covertly traded goods duty free with early Settlers. This trade permitted
early Settlers to exchange a portion of their catch actually owed a supplying merchant and to enjoy a modicum of economic sustenance which
was otherwise difficult to realize. Planter trade occurred throughout the
duration of the American fishery (ca. 1783– 1870) but especially from
the 1830s to the 1860s.

Governor Keats described the clandestine nature of the American
trade:

They [the Americans] are also in the habit of sending Light Ships [i.e., vessels
equipped with warning devices] from America to some of the harbours on the
Labrador, particularly Labrador Harbour [Quebec North Shore], Red Bay, and
Cape Charles, which receive the fish caught and prepared by them on the coast,
and take it with what they procure clandestinely from our Boat keepers by

Purchase or Barter, for they come prepared with money and goods for that purpose, and thus become the Carriers of a proportion of our own fish to the Market. (quoted in Gosling 1910, 353)

The American trade circumvented duties and offered Settlers staples as well as liquor (Rendell 1841). Around 1840, several Labrador merchants, including B. and J. Slade, of Battle Harbour, Francis Harbour, and Grady, presented a memorial to the British secretary of state for the colonies, bemoaning their loss through illicit trade and requesting an exemption from Newfoundland duties. There are many examples of this, of which two are representative. In one, Superintendent of Fisheries Tobin writes: 'Owing to the hitherto neglected state of the Labrador coast, Americans have so far encroached on the rights permitted to them by treaty, as to occupy many of the harbors, and become the vendors of all sorts of wares, free of duty, collect fish, oils, and furs, etc., return to the United States with their British exchanges of produce, free of all duties, and thus, in every way undersell the British trader' (1853, 133). Similarly, J. Finlay adds: 'The resident population upon these coasts (the French Shore and Labrador coast), amount to several thousands, and from the traders the chief part of the supplies are drawn, whilst the transient fishermen have an opportunity to dispose of their surplus produce with great advantage to themselves. These adventurers have now monopolized the entire trading business, especially upon the coast of Labrador; they pay neither duties nor taxes of any description, although they unquestionably come within the jurisdiction of this government' (1853, 139–40).

Although we have few accounts from the American perspective, Sabine commented on British allegations that following the War of 1812:

Fifteen hundred American vessels had been engaged in the Labrador fishery alone, in a single season; that these vessels carried and dealt out teas, coffee, spirits, and other articles, on which no duty was paid; that these smugglers and interlopers exercised a ruinous influence upon the British fishery and the morals of British fishermen; that men, provisions, and outfits were cheaper in the United States than elsewhere, and that of consequence British fishermen on the coast could buy what they needed on better terms of the American vessels than on the colonial merchants. (1853, 214–15)

By the mid-nineteenth century, government revenues lost through this 'free trade' led Bowen (1854, 333) and Hamilton (1863, 400–1) to call for a customs house to tax American traders. Hamilton makes intriguing reference to plans apparently underway for an American Consul at Salmon Bay, Quebec, but suggested instead Cape Harrison, Battle Harbour, or Salt Ponds (north of St Lewis) as these locations were more 'frequented by American schooners' (1863, 401).

Lest there be any confusion about the importance of American trade to southeastern Labrador, I reiterate the American presence between 1783 and about 1850 was heaviest in southeastern Labrador. Only after the mid-nineteenth century did the Americans push further north (Gosling 1910, 413).

Although this evidence demonstrates that Settlers were trading with hundreds of Americans visiting each summer, it is still difficult to access the impact of planter trade. My conjecture that such trade encouraged early settlement requires further research and is rooted both in my perception of inter-merchant rivalry and my view that 'leakage' has been a continuous feature of merchant-fisher relations. In southeastern Labrador, the Americans (and to a lesser extent the French, Nova Scotians, and Newfoundlanders) offered early Settlers the chance to trade part of their catch on the side, behind their main supplier's back, greatly enhancing survival possibilities. I am not suggesting that Settlers ceased dealing with resident merchants – we know they did not – only that they also dealt with transients. In short, American traders created a 'free market' economy which allowed many small planters and former servants to gain some measure of independence and security in their new homeland.

THE FIRST SETTLERS: WHAT IS KNOWN

The greatest historical enigma for southeastern Labrador people (and interested scholars) involves the origin, identity, and circumstances of the earliest permanent settlers. Interest in this topic is shared by old and young alike. When visiting households in the region, I was occasionally handed the cherished family bible containing a few scribbled names and dates, all that remains of the family's genealogy.

Local interest in the past is also reflected in attention given to annual patterns of seasons and events.[3] People remember years when the freeze-up occurred unusually early or late, when salmon or cod were plentiful or scarce, or when bakeapples were exceptionally abundant. The local custom of recording significant events (the first coastal boat of the year, the date the bay ice froze, and so on) on the household calendar also illustrates local interest in past and current events. Indeed household calendars may serve as evidence summoned to resolve lively spats about when this or that event occurred. Regrettably, however, few calendars survive more than a few years; most suffer the fate of other household waste and are eventually 'fired [thrown] in the stove.'

One source of information on early settlement is the collection of ledgers from the Slade company at Battle Harbour. They cover about two decades, spanning the late eighteenth and early nineteenth century. Although inconclusive on most questions, some of the ledgers contain tantalizing clues which can be related to other sources of information. The Ledgers record that some tradesmen were transitory labourers, remaining in the area and working for successive companies. One example is John Tilsed, listed in the 1793 ledger. Tilsed worked for Cartwright at Ranger Lodge and then for Cartwright's friend Mr Lester at Trinity, Newfoundland, and was re-hired by Cartwright in late May 1785, as a boatsmaster for two summers and a winter at a wage of £37.

Other workers listed in the ledgers may have attempted to fish on their own, but failed. For example, Mr James Macy appears in the 1793 ledger. In 1786 Macy, along with a partner named Dean, suffered ruthless coercion from Noble and Pinson and was eventually forced out of business. Macy's career illustrates the view that the survival prospects of relatively independent former servants and planters were at best difficult.

Then there are those like Samuel Akerman, who may possibly be ancestral to contemporary Settlers. Akerman is among the forty-one men employed by Slades in the fall of 1793. Now Whitely (1977, 21) claims that many of the surnames (Blake, Broomfield, Clark, Ford, Hilliar, Rumbold, Yeatman, and others) found in the ledgers represent the founders of families still in the area. Whitely may be correct but he fails to cite his evidence, and frankly, my computerized data are inconclusive on this question.[4]

By 1794 Samuel Akerman's stint with the Company had lasted some seven summers and six winters; it was to end in the fall of 1796. Also employed for the 1793–4 year was John Rumbold; his year ended 10 October 1794. By 1802, Akerman and Rumbold are no longer listed as salaried Slade employees. The following year, Rumbold is listed with former Slade employee William Holloway in what appears to be a joint venture supplied by Slades. Holloway had worked at Slade's Hawke's Island sealing post as early as 1793 and was a veteran Labrador sealer. (Another Holloway, perhaps William's son or even brother, Benjamin

[1784–1872], is buried at the Catholic cemetery at Cat Gulch, Matthew's Cove.)

William Holloway and Rumbold purchased shovels, nails, and other building materials from the Slades and rented one of the company's fishing rooms at Fox Harbour (St Lewis). The partners appear to be striking out on their own, supplied with essentials by the Slades. By 1804–5, their supplies include two pairs of women's shoes, suggesting that one or both had acquired a female companion. However, by 1806, their partnership had ended, with each man in debt to the Slades. Rumbold fished on his own in 1809 and also conducted a seal fishery at Square Islands. However, the following year he and Holloway again entered into a joint venture with the Slades; Rumbold and Holloway realized half the income from the 249 seals they netted and the Slades received the other half.

Holloway and Rumbold's on-again/off-again joint venture illustrates the difficult transition from salaried employee to supplied Settler. But their case also raises many questions. We know little about the relationship Rumbold and Holloway had with their former employer or what, if any, trade relations the two men had with American or Newfoundland fishers. We also learn that their many years of experience alone did not ensure success. These two experienced Labrador hands teetered on the brink of failure, making it easy to imagine how selling several casks of seal oil or quintals of codfish to some transient buyer might have made the difference. While the antiquity of family names such as Rumbolt indicates that John Rumbold (or another Rumbold) eventually obtained some measure of independence and success, it appears that many other incipient planters fell deeper into debt and eventually left the region. Their case also leads us to ask whether the two men were lineal ancestors of subsequent Rumbolts and Holloways appearing in the computer data, and who the women for whom they purchased shoes were.

One can only make educated guesses about these questions. However, it seems probable that both were related to later Rumbolts and Holloways. After all, a scant seventeen years separates John Rumbolt from Robert Rumbolt (born about 1826), the earliest Rumbolt listed in my computerized Anglican records. However, to again illustrate the difficulties of reconstructing early settlement, the Moss diary entry from 11 June 1832 records that a 'Robert Rumbold came down from his winter quarters' (1832, 13). While this (and the 17 June 1832 entry – 'all the planters arrived this evening [a Saturday] from their winter quarters' [ibid.]) clearly establishes that a Settler population was wintering near Battle Harbour by the 1830s, it also raises the question of whether *this* Robert Rumbold was an uncle of the Robert born in 1826 or, perhaps, John Rumbold's brother.

And to return to William Holloway, it is probable that he was the father of Robert Holloway, born near Battle Harbour in 1828 and the earliest Holloway baptized by the Battle Harbour mission. It should also be noted that unlike the surname Rumbolt, that of Holloway disappears from the Anglican records in the late nineteenth century, illustrating another common theme of southeastern Labrador history: individuals and surnames appear in the records, perhaps to fish for a season or more, make their contribution to the region's social and genetic history, and then disappear, either through 'accidents' of marriage or emigration.

And what of the women who wore new shoes in the autumn of 1804? Some possibility exists they were European, but they were more likely Inuit. Inuit in southeastern Labrador? Such a claim challenges conventional notions of Labrador's aboriginal map, which generally shows no Inuit living south of Groswater Bay. And existing aboriginal maps appear to be backed by archaeological findings. Thus, the archaeologist M.P. Stopp and her associates (1991, 1992) report very few potential Thule (late prehistoric to early historic) Inuit sites. Similarly, a 1980 issue of the journal *Inuit Studies* devoted to the question of the southern range of the Thule or Neo-Eskimo shows scholars divided.

On the one hand, proponents of the view that Inuit resided as far south as Quebec's North Shore, primarily during the French regime, including Clermont and Martijn, cite tantalizing historic, linguistic, and cartographic evidence suggesting that historic Inuit did, in fact, residue as far west as Mingan. Their plea is for more study of the question of southern range, and particularly for greater attention to extant French texts. On the other hand, ethnohistorian J.G. Taylor (1980) counters with the view that Inuit wintered along the northern Labrador coast and only ventured south to trade or plunder European posts. At one point Taylor briefly acknowledges that southern Inuit (such as those De Boileau visited at St Lewis) engendered the region's contemporary mixed-blood population, but immediately drops this vital admission and retreats to an earlier time period and to data supporting his position. Strangely absent in the papers of this 1980 collection, even those supporting a southern Labrador Inuit population, is reference to many other sources (such as the reports of Bishop Feild), sources which very clearly show that Inuit enclaves existed as far south as St Lewis throughout the nineteenth century.

How and when did these enclaves begin? The few Thule sites found by Stopp, and Captain Cartwright's failure to mention a permanent Inuit population, lead me to conclude that these enclaves were not established until the final decades of the eighteenth century. Who were the Inuit who founded them? Quite possibly, founders may have been Inuit banished from Moravian mission stations for diverse moral infractions; enclaves may have been started by Inuit who voluntarily ventured south from central or northern Labrador to populate the region; or they may have been established by northern Inuit middlemen involved with trade with Europeans who decided to remain in southeastern Labrador.

But there definitely were Inuit. An early reference to Inuit comes from an 'Indian Account' (at the time, Indian usually meant Inuit) which appears in the 1798 Slade ledger from Battle Harbour. In it are unmistakably Inuit names (e.g., Shilmuck, Eteweooke, Oglucock) listed beside references to seal skins and oil sold to the company (Slade Ledger 1798). Next, is the Reverend Mr Hickson's 1824 description of Inuit and part-Inuit at Dumpling Island, Tub Harbour (Esquimaux Bay–Groswater Bay), and in Lake Melville – where the majority of the estimated 326 people were Inuit – (41) clearly establishing that in the northern part of southeastern and central Labrador, Inuit were both numerous and still living a relatively traditional lifestyle. Less than a decade later, the Moss diary contains several references to 'Indians' or 'Esquime [sic] Indians,' some living at St Francis Harbour, who visited Battle Harbour in February 1832 asking for harp-seal carcasses to eat. One Inuit party had a 'Comatic and 13 dogs' and included Thomas Paul, an Inuk probably related to the contemporary Paul family (Pollo or Paulo) of Port Hope Simpson, whose aboriginal roots are locally thought to be Indian (Innu or Mi'kmaq). The Anglican bishop Feild's mid-nineteenth-century travels between Forteau and Dumpling (outside Sandwich Bay) leave little doubt that the vast majority of women on the coast were either Inuit, mixed (Inuit-European), or Indian, in that order. In 1848, European men outnumbered women 'eight or nine to one' (Feild 1851, 47) and in the bishop's words. 'all the females are either Esquimaux [Inuit] or mountaineer Indians [Innu], or descended from them' (1849, 17). Feild was explicit on exceptions to this generalization. For example, on 8 August 1848 he visited Mr Saunders, who had served as agent for Messrs Hunt and Company for some twenty-one years, at St Francis

Harbour. Feild described Mr Saunders as the 'first lady who ever visited this coast, and, as far as I know, the only female who has come from England to dwell on the Labrador' (1851, 52).

Feild described a large Inuit population at Sandwich Bay, a population more 'intelligent' and 'hardy' than those living further south. Feild attributed this to 'longer acquaintance' and more 'familiar intercourse' with Europeans (1851, 67–8). Once again, Feild observed the effects of acculturation and praised the agent for Hunt and Company for taking 'considerable pains' to 'instruct and civilize the natives' (ibid., 68). According to Feild, the only element of traditional Inuit clothing still worn was skin boots. This can be compared with Hickson's (in Windsor n.d., 37–8) descriptions in 1824 of Inuit between Batteau and Groswater Bay (Esquimaux Bay), where Inuit wore cassocks of purchased swanskin (heavy woollen flannel, akin to the 'Grenfell' cloth of recent times [Story 1982, 548–9]) during summer, and sealskin clothing in winter.

Another reference to Inuit comes from the Reverend Mr Noble's description of an 'exhibition of the kayak' at St Lewis (Fox Harbour) on 11 July 1859: 'It [the kayak] was light and tight, and ringy as a drum, and floated on the water like a bubble. Under the strokes of the kayaker, it darted forward over low swells with a grace and fleetness unknown to the birch bark canoe' (1861, 195). And W.A. Stearns, visiting St Lewis on 12 August 1882, writes: 'Our men returned to the vessel loaded with spears, bows and arrows, komatik whips, sealskin boots and mittens, and several finely spotted skins. One of the party procured the tusks of a young walrus, two of these animals have been killed by the natives the previous winter' (1884, 289). A few years later Maxwell described southeastern Labrador's Inuit population as follows: 'At various places along the coast north of Battle Harbour, Eskimo halfbreeds have established themselves, but there is no large settlement of them till as far north as Cartwright harbour, where a great number are congregated about a post of the North West Company' (1887, 379).

What became of the Inuit of these nineteenth-century Inuit enclaves? We don't know, but there are at least two possibilities: first, they fell prey to disease, and second, they became assimilated. First, as with Lake Melville Inuit, disease could have reduced the size of these nineteenth-century Inuit enclaves, which, I suspect, were never very big. By the fall of 1915, the Reverend Mr Gordon describes old Aunt Nancy Williams, of North River, Sandwich Bay, as being a 'pure-bred Eskimo ... the only one of her race in the whole Bay' (1972, 33). Second, southeastern Labrador people were overhelmed by each summer's arrival of Newfoundland's Labrador fishers. This fishery enabled marital unions between Newfoundlanders and Labrador folk and, consequently, diluted the physical expression of Inuit traits. At the same time, the part-Inuit ancestry of many southeastern Labrador people survives and, as we will see in Chapter 11, has acquired new significance.

The preceding accounts clearly establish that Inuit enclaves existed along the southeastern coast during the nineteenth century. This fact, together with the absence of European women during the early part of that century, leads me to conclude that, as in more northerly parts of Labrador, Inuit women became wives of many first-generation Settler males. Kleivan supports this view when in referring to northern Labrador Settlers, he remarks: 'Down to the middle of the last century a number of people, who had earlier lived for a while around or south of Hamilton Inlet, came north. In some instances these were children of European-Eskimo marriages, which occurred considerably earlier down there than within the [Moravian] mission area' (1966, 92). Bishop Feild's 1848 expedition along the southeastern coast provides a rare glimpse of the ethnic mosaic (which he would later gloss as a 'race of mixed blood, or Anglo-Esquimaux' [1851, 68]) and the mixed marriages of the day. On 9 August 1848, for example, Feild baptized five children at St Francis Harbour. Three of these were described as offspring of an 'Indian' (likely Inuit, as Feild generally referred to Indians as 'moun-taineers') mother and an English father (Feild 1851, 54). Three days later, Feild visited two families at Venison Islands. These included a man named Green, the son of a Ringwood (England) attorney. Green 'married' a half-breed woman named Bourne, whose father was an Englishman and mother an Inuk (ibid., 59). This could have been John Green, born about 1824 and the earliest Green listed in the computer-ized data. That John Green married a woman named Elizabeth, also born 1824. The first of their four children was born in 1844, at Venison Tickle. Unfortunately, my data show no Elizabeth Bourne, although other Bournes, the earliest born about 1817, were then living in the Venison Island area. The surname Bourne disappears from the coast in the late nineteenth century, while the surname Green is still found in the communities of Charlottetown and Cartwright.

Feild visited another ethnically mixed Venison Island family, that of an Englishman named Stevens, who described his wife as 'sort of a half Indian.' Stevens married the woman in 1831 and Archdeacon Wix baptized two of their children the same year. There are several Stevens (or Stephens) in my computer data. All were born around 1837 in the Venison Islands area, of unknown parents.

At the Hunt and Company post at Seal Islands Bishop Feild encountered five Englishmen; the other residents were 'Indians' (Inuit) and 'half Indians' (mixed persons), crowded into two small huts. One Englishman (apparently not associated with Hunt and Company) had taken a mixed women as his wife. On visiting one of the two native huts, Feild found it was occupied by twenty-three people. The bishop's remarks show that considerable acculturation had taken place; most of the Inuit spoke English without any trace of Inuktitut and had ('cast aside or forgotten their old superstitions' and 'expressed a desire to be properly baptized and married' (Feild 1849, 64).

The Reverend Mr Disney also comments on ethnically mixed unions: 'the number of Englishmen who have married Esquimaux women, from time to time, is very considerable, and this also produces a good feeling between us and the Esquimaux' (1851, 4). Similarly, following his summer cruise between Battle Harbour and Cape Harrison, Commander Preston writes that 'the permanent settlers [of Labrador] are gradually increasing in number, I was astonished to find so many of the English ones married to Indians or Esquimeaux women' (1864, 631).

A penultimate point about unions between European Settlers and aboriginal people. The computer data include a number of persons whose surnames are suspicious. These may have been given by missionaries to native people at baptism or marriage or are Anglicized phonetic versions of aboriginal names. For example, the data record that Thomas Elishoc, born about 1830, married a woman named Harriet, born about the same year. George Ittiock, born about 1838, married a woman named Eliza, also born about 1838. William Russell, born about 1836, married Nancy Tuccolk, born about the same year. An unknown male, born about 1853, married Jane Toumishey, also born about 1853, and another unknown male married Jane Kibenock; both were born about 1837. All that can be said about this partial list is that the surnames Russell, Toomashie (Toumishey), and Kippenhuck (Kipenock) survive today, primarily in the communities of Williams Harbour, Cartwright, and Port Hope Simpson, respectively. Contemporary representatives of these surnames exhibit 'native' physical characteristics, as do those with other possibly aboriginal surnames. The Russell-Tocculk marriage is of particular interest insofar as two of the couple's four children (Thomas, born 1859, and James, born 1866) were born at William's Harbour, where the majority of the Russells of southeastern Labrador now reside. The computer data permit the tracing of some of James Russell's descendants to the present day.

On the other hand, surnames resembling Elishock and Ittiock no longer exist in the region. Their loss may be due to out-migration, genetic drift, or a change of surname encouraged either by missionaries or by individual attempts to assimilate. However, I assume that Elishoc, Ittiock, and/or Tuccolk were Inuit, and made their genetic and cultural contribution to the region.

Finally, possible motivations for and consequences of European-aboriginal unions warrant some attention. The previously explained shortage of European women was clearly the primary reason why Settler males acquired native spouses. Feild's rather moralistic and enigmatic account of the Englishman (or men – Feild ambiguously alternates between singular and plural) who had taken a mixed woman for his wife at Seal Islands implies that the man (or men) felt guilty about doing so. (Kleivan [1966, 100] provides similar historical evidence from northern Labrador of Settlers who felt ashamed for marrying Inuit.) Feild wrote that the (English) 'men confessed that they had only taken the women to live with them as wives, without any form of marriage; but they well knew, they said, the propriety and necessity of the religious service and sanction' (1851, 64). Loneliness and a desire to settle permanently in Labrador probably also explain why Settler males sought aboriginal wives.

This chapter reconstructs the beginnings of early European settlement. Significant differences exist between regions such as southeastern Labrador, the Labrador Strait, or part of Newfoundland. Consequently, arguments imported from other regions may not apply. While arguing that an indigenous source of wives distinguishes southeastern Labrador from island Newfoundland and even the Labrador Strait, it is not advisable to view southeastern Labrador as an isolate. Indeed, my argument for the importance of illicit trade links settlement of the region with broader, global forces. Yet, I also (and regrettably) conclude that many details of early settlement of the region may never be known. This last point is more than an insignificant historical detail: a major concern of many contemporary Settlers is to prove their aboriginal ancestry so as to join the Labrador Metis Association, a new native organization. This chapter shows that miscegenation occurred. My hope is that further research will both reveal additional details and critically evaluate the settlement scenario I have advanced.

6

Life in the Bays and on the Headlands

Once Settlers struck out on their own and acquired spouses, they also set about acquiring the practices and beliefs necessary to live in Labrador. Some of these adaptations were indigenous and others imported from the Settlers' former English or Irish homelands. A number of writers (Anderson 1984; Thornton 1979; Jackson 1982) rightly emphasize that the Settler adaptation had to exploit all useful resources. As noted in Chapter 2, key to this was the practice which A.P. Dyke (1969) called *seasonal transhumance*, whereby people move between two or more seasonal habitations located near available resources. Seasonal transhumance enabled a generalized, seasonally based ecological adaptation, allowing families to harvest usable resources, including those with subsistence and market value. Fish, sea mammals, migratory waterfowl, berries, fur-bearing animals, and forest products were all taken when most abundant or marketable. This pattern of 'residential dualism' was once widespread throughout Newfoundland and Labrador (Smith 1987) and the Quebec North Shore (Bowen 1854); it survives today only in southeastern Labrador, where its practice is now reduced by the fishery crises.

This chapter describes selected elements of Settler economy, society, and culture – evoking images of an earlier Settler life. The time period spans the nineteenth and early twentieth century, the period prior to the sweeping changes accompanying the Second World War. My intent is to set the stage for subsequent discussions of how Settler communities were affected by intrusive changes.

The dearth of relevant information limits what will likely ever be known about the historic Settler lifestyle (especially that of the winter season). What I present draws on the handful of extant sources, supplemented by my interviews with older Settlers. This is necessary because few early travellers say much about the early Settlers, especially about life during the long Labrador winters. Put differently, history (at least 'academic' history, for 'lay' history, as it appears in the pages of *Them Days* magazine, is helpful) is silent about the Settlers. Once families left the outer coast each fall for their winter quarters, it is as if they became invisible, truly people without a history. No de Tocqueville wandered among the Settlers; they wintered beyond the fringes of literature or time. We have only glimpses of the Settler winter lifestyle, as sketched out on the coast by lettered summertime visitors, such as Walsh (1896) and Durgin (1908), who jotted a few lines about Labrador's permanent residents. After all, compared to the transient fishers who crowded the coast each summer, the Settlers were an insignificant minority, a few families whose pioneering lifestyle was an anachronism, even to nineteenth-century American fishers, who were themselves only a few generations removed from a frontier lifestyle.

We do not even know how many Settlers were living along the coast during the nineteenth and early twentieth century. Labrador's population data, especially those of southeastern Labrador, are notoriously unreliable (Newfoundland 1974) and only become worthwhile after Newfoundland's Confederation in 1949. One of the better early censuses, taken by Judge Sweetland (1865) during the summer of 1864, illustrates this problem. Judge Sweetland counted 1261 'residents' between Chateau and Sandwich bays. Yet he lumped Settlers with passing Newfoundland fishers and made no effort to separate the two categories. In making no mention of winter quarters, and by lumping transients with residents, Judge Sweetland and virtually all enumerators until Confederation nullified the Settlers. Hence, we know something about Settler fisheries along the outer coast, but little about their hunting or trapping practices or life in their winter homes.

SEASONAL TRANSHUMANCE

As anthropologist Julian Steward's work demonstrates, human social arrangements conform to economic realities. Comparison of historic Settler seasonal settlements reveals that the social organization of winter settlements was, as Zimmerly (1975) emphasized for Lake Melville

Settlers, confined to the family level of integration, reflecting the minimal labour requirements of relatively individualistic endeavours like trapping, hunting, and cutting wood. Winter settlements were spaced far enough apart to permit families easy access to renewable resources. With the relatively recent exceptions of trapped furs and handicrafts, families consumed commodities produced during winter as part of their domestic economy. In summer communities located along the outer coast, however, several families normally lived near one another because many hands were necessary to haul cod seines and seal nets, or cooperatively hunt migratory waterfowl. The cod and seal jointly produced were convertible, albeit on credit, into imported necessities such as fishing salt, flour, molasses, tea, and pork. The joint production units or crews of summer and fall epitomized a more complex division of labour than was necessary during winter. Unlike the social organization of winter homesteads, that of the summer stations was also more differentiated: merchants supplied fishers, and fishing crews included skippers and sharemen. The extent to which such differentiation influenced social action is not known, but if we can extrapolate from the present, we would expect that egalitarian values continuously undermined class distinctions.

An early reference to seasonal transhumance is the Reverend Mr Hickson's observation at Grady in 1824 that 'those who stay on the coast, go up the Bays, where they are a little more sheltered from the wintry blasts, and have a means of procuring something towards their support' (in Windsor n.d., 42). Similarly, Walsh's description of the Pyes of Cape Charles records that 'in the winter time the people literally take to the woods – that is, they retire into winter quarters in some woods (i.e. Lodge Bay) about nine miles away' (1896, 33).

Following Tanner (1944), who distinguishes between two types of Settler adaptations – illustrated by the specialized Grand River trappers and the more generalized Dove Brook people – three types of adaptations may be discerned in southeastern Labrador. On one end of a continuum were communities such as Paradise River, whose economy was focused primarily on trapping to the exclusion of 'outside' resources. At the other end, were 'outside' communities like Indian Cove and Battle Harbour, located near seals, sea birds, and fish and who consequently only travelled into St Lewis Inlet to cut firewood. Between these two extremes were most other communities. Historically, for example, although Cape Charles people relied more heavily on 'outside' resources like fish, seals, and migratory waterfowl than on 'inside' resources, they did spend two or three months at their winter home, Lodge Bay. Like the people who wintered at Mussel Brook (Dyson 1982, 52) and fished at Batteau, Lodge Bay people moved to their outside settlements on the sea ice and returned to Lodge Bay in fall, when the ice had frozen again. In short, adaptations varied considerably, depending on the local environmental and economic possibilities.

Local residents told me that there was once a tendency for some families to 'winter' in one place one year and in a new place the next. My experience suggests that poorer Settlers or those newly resident in Labrador were the ones most likely to change winter quarters; yet some experimentation was probably common, as families searched for a more productive winter place (Baikie 1976, 2). This pattern of shifting winter settlements each year continued well into the twentieth century and arose because of a variety of unforeseen circumstances: the sudden loss or availability of work, the offer of a house which would otherwise be vacant that winter, an illness in the family, requiring residence near a Grenfell station, and so on. An unfortunate consequence of shifting winter settlements is that it is impossible to quantify exactly how many winter settlements were occupied at any given time.

SETTLER HOUSING

De Boilieu provides the most complete description of nineteenth-century winter houses, focusing on the intriguing notion of wooden chimneys:

The Settler, in fixing his home, selects a square plot of growing trees, say about eighteen feet; he then cuts down the centre ones, and leaves the four corner ones, denuded of their branches to a height of about nine feet. On these four trees the 'wall-plate' is laid, and upright timbers are placed side by side until the whole is enclosed, save a place for the doorway and the fireplace – the latter also answering their purpose of a window, as there are none in the sides of the house. The whole of the sides are caulked, or cinched, with a species of moss called on the coast 'moldow.' This caulking or filling-up of the crevices makes the house all but air-tight. Next to the outer walls are the sleeping cabins, built precisely in the same manner as on board ship. The fireplace which, as I say, also admits light, is built inside, or square with building, and is about nine feet long and four feet wide. The chimney being built entirely of wood, a 'household engine' – that is, a bucket of water – is kept at hand, and a ladder kept stationed at the back in case of fire. It generally happens that the chimney catches fire two or three times a night. ([1861] 1969, 52-3)

Along with Stearns (1884, 285), one wonders that the house didn't burn down or at least how they got any sleep! People today claim that their forefathers' winter homes were located in dense woods, because, they say, early Settlers sought to 'hide away' in the woods. This may have been true in some cases, but a more logical explanation is that of Lake Melville Settler Lydia Campbell, who told her daughter, Margaret Baikie, that Settlers built winter houses in the woods to be near firewood (Baikie 1976, 8).

Stearns observes that summer houses grew 'smaller and smaller the farther north' of Fox Harbour one went (1884, 281). He describes summer houses at Square Islands: 'The houses here looked more like the nests of an army of cliff swallows than anything else that I can imagine; they were perched everywhere on the high rocks close to the cliffs, and looked as if glued to them, so closely did they stand; and so near the color of the rocks were the weathered boards and boughs of which they were composed, while so snug was the harbor, that one might have hunted for weeks for the location' (290). Stearns also observes that summer houses were more modest than winter houses and that differences in housing existed, a probable reference to relative prosperity.

BETWEEN POCKETS OF PLENTY

At any given time and over time, economic abundance was unevenly distributed throughout Settler society. One hundred years ago, a visitor to Ephraim Pye's summer fishing station at Cape Charles might be impressed by Pye's stately two-storey house and large fishing stores. Such properties contrasted sharply with the summer hovels of Settlers from Battle Harbour northward. Pye's estate was the Labrador equivalent of the ante-bellum plantations of the Old South, while the hovels further north were mere frontier cabins. Yet there were, then and since, poor Pyes. Like the fate of whole communities, family fortunes rose and fell over time.

Passing visitors sometimes commented on such economic differences.

Compare, for example, Packard's 1864 description of Settler Charles Stone,[1] of Henley Harbour, with that of poorer Square Islands Settlers.

I interviewed a Mr. Stone, one of the Settlers, regarding the fisheries and hunting at this point, and he gave me the following facts: At the height of the herring fishery in August – and it should be borne in mind that this fish is only a summer visitant, not spawning on the Labrador coast, but passes up, as Hind in his work on the Labrador peninsula states, as far as Hudson's Strait – Stone has caught 200 barrels in a season. He has to pay twelve barrels for a hogshead of salt, the price of which is now very high. He secures 800 quintals of fish at 18s. a quintal, which amounts to £720 for a successful season's work. He can cure the fish on this coast during the short summer, and is now building a shed for this purpose. (1891, 132)

In contrast, at Square Islands, 'The "longshoremen" [Settlers], of whom there are here seven families, are sadly improvident, often giving up fishing towards the last of the season and idling; hence as the result, when the trader [sic] have failed them, they are reduced as happened last winter, to actual starvation. Owing to the lack of fresh meat and vegetables they are afflicted with the scurvy' (146). Packard's explanation of poverty centres on 'industry,' the amount of 'get up and go' a person had. Presumably, industry was inversely related to poverty and both were unevenly distributed. It may well be that some Settlers were, as Packard describes the Square Islands folk, 'thriftless,' yet I question the probability of survival in Labrador if idleness, improvidence, and thriftlessness were common economic characteristics.

Packard's comparison needs to be placed in context: throughout the history of the region, from the mid-nineteenth century to relocation in the 1960s, we find brief but repeated references to an area of periodic poverty, specifically between St Lewis Inlet and Spotted Island. Visitors considered economic conditions to be more favourable in communities north and south of this long coastline, that is, in Sandwich Bay and from around Battle Harbour south to Mr Stone's home of Pitt's Arm/Henley Harbour.

Moreover, the economic scarcity experienced by people living along this long coastline was especially grave during cycles of poverty, notably in the 1870s, the 1930s, and today. I illustrate such cycles here first by reference to a little-known cycle occurring from about 1905 to 1915 and then to the better-known 1930s.

The former 'mini' depression appears to have been caused by natural conditions, specifically unusually heavy ice conditions (even though the timing does not coincide with Vibe's [1967] fluctuations), probably colder water, and more certainly poor fishing seasons. We learn about this difficult decade from people associated with the Grenfell Mission (e.g., Mayou 1910, 12; Grieve 1911) and we must, therefore, treat their reports with caution, given that mission personnel (particularly Grenfell himself) sometimes magnified the severity of economic adversity for fund-raising purposes. Yet Dr Grieve's report appears believable. During the winter of 1911, Grieve toured winter communities between his headquarters at Battle Harbour and Indian Harbour. He used fur returns as an index of tough times and reported difficult conditions for many families between Fox Harbour and Reed's Pond (Porcupine Bay). Conversely, and predictably, Cape Charles and winter communities in Sandwich Bay fared better. Grieve notes that families who had trapped few furs were either on government relief or on 'government work' (1911).

Two reports dating from the global depression of the mid-1930s paint a similar picture. Writing in November 1935, Constable Jillett reports on the 'worst year for some time' for the sixteen settlements between Battle Harbour and Black Tickle, where many families required government assistance during winter (1935, 1). He continues: 'All the families at Bolter's Rock, Seal Islands, Black Tickle, Spotted Islands, Batteau and Indian Tickles [sic] had to be relieved, as the codfishery was very poor and the suppliers [merchants] were not prepared in any way to advance them food.' Again, people living in Sandwich Bay and from Cape Charles south were better off.

Also reporting on the winter of 1935–6 but looking south from Cartwright, Ranger Martin (1936) notes a 'marked difference in the people of Sandwich Bay and the people in the southern part of the District' (i.e., from Black Tickle south). Ranger Martin explains the differences between Sandwich Bay and southern Settlers according to the degree of economic diversification practised in the two areas. Presaging Tanner's (1944) classic portrait of the generalized economic adaptation of Dove Brook (Sandwich Bay) Settlers, Ranger Martin observes that Sandwich Bay Settlers relied on furs, fish, gardening, and the like, whereas Settlers from Black Tickle south to Battle specialized in fishing.

How does one explain economic differences within historic Settler society? We must first distinguish between kinds of difference: those between families, those between communities, and those arising during cycles of privation. We will discuss the last of these first. Although remote, Labrador was and is part of the world outside; most cycles of poverty were local manifestations of global economic slow-downs. Inter-family differences are much more complicated. My field research suggests that 'successful' Settlers like Charles Stone or Eiphraim Pye often gained control and made good use of crucial productive technologies, such as one or more cod traps, a prime cod trap berth, or a good trapping territory. Finally, how can we explain the poverty so often described in settlements from St Lewis Inlet north to Spotted Island? First, examination of the Sandwich Bay area and that south of Battle Harbour suggests that environmental possibilities were not equal in the two areas. The mighty rivers (notably the Eagle and White Bear) emptying into Sandwich Bay once teemed with salmon; each winter, these rivers became frozen highways to interior trap lines; after the salmon season, cod were once plentiful at Grady and nearby outside fishing places. The environmental possibilities south of Battle Harbour resulted from the funnel leading south into the Strait of Belle Isle; seals, whales, and other migratory sea mammals had to travel through this funnel and did so relatively close to land. While I would not want to overstate the environmental possibilities in interpreting economic differences, such possibilities should be considered. Related to these environmental differences is Ranger Martin's (1936) endorsement of economic diversification, a view as valid then as it is now.

Finally, I believe that the poverty so often described between St Lewis Inlet and the Spotted Island area may have resulted from isolation from important institutions, an interpretation similar to Harold Innis's staples theory, which focuses on the institutions founded to produce staple products and sees them as important, and even generating influences on patterns of economic growth, settlement, and culture. People living along the coastline between St Lewis Inlet and the Spotted Island were too far from vital institutions – merchants, churches, schools – and thus were unable to take advantage of the ever-changing opportunities provided by such institutions. For example, we shall see that Settlers living too far south of Battle Harbour were unable to enjoy the economic benefits of selling their salmon fresh and therefore fell behind Settlers fishing closer to Battle Harbour. Similarly, during the early twentieth century, the coastal boats from Corner Brook, Newfoundland, often travelled only as far north as Battle Harbour. People living along the more 'isolated' stretch of coast north of Battle Harbour were less able to travel to the Corner Brook area to participate in the short but lucrative fall herring fishery and to return to Labrador with coins jingling in their pockets. In this case, then, institutions servicing Battle Harbour afforded Settlers living from that point southwards the chance to earn several weeks' wages, placing them ahead of their counterparts further north.

MERCHANT-SETTLER RELATIONS

Settlers dealt with merchants on the basis of credit or barter, obtaining promissory notes for the amount of fish or oil they produced for their supplying merchant and presenting these to obtain food and other necessities in exchange (De Boilieu [1861] 1969, 18). Cash rarely changed hands and as Walsh observed, the 'general medium of exchange throughout Labrador is trade; money is seldom used, and its value is but dimly appreciated' (1896, 37).[2]

Middlebury College (Vermont) president (and son of Grenfell's spiritual mentor, Rev. Dwight Moody) W.R. Moody spent two weeks with Dr Grenfell aboard the *Strathcona* in the summer of 1905. His insightful description of the merchant-fisher relationship in *Among the Deep Sea Fishers* illuminates many of its significant features and, in many ways, is timeless:

The relationship between the average fisherman and his merchant still further tends to place him [the fisher] at a disadvantage. In the spring of the year he purchases his supplies and fishing outfit on credit. This debt is really a first lien upon all his summer's work and he must sell his 'catch' to the merchant who has supplied him. Early in the season the merchants determine the 'current price' to be paid for fish, and this remains fixed. To an unscrupulous merchant such a system offers temptations to defraud with impunity, for the keeping of accounts to an illiterate fisherman is an unfathomable mystery. Thus it often happens that some of these men are in debt all their lives and never seem to get ahead in spite of seasons of plenty. (1906, 11)

Merchants asserted their claim to the fish and trade from the fishers they supplied. Thus, Moody also explains the pricing tactics supplying merchants used to systematically exploit 'their' fishers.

The (Labrador) fishermen sold their summer's catch at a uniform price of $3.40

per quintal (112 pounds); the same goods were sold in St. John's at $6.50 per quintal. But this was not all, for in many instances the dealers to whom the fishermen sold their 'catch' were also the dealers from whom they purchased their supplies. Thus a dealer would purchase flour at $4.85 a barrel (in large quantities) in St. John's, sell it to the fishermen on the Labrador for $7.50 and debit his account for the full retail price while paying in exchange about half the actual wholesale price of fish in Newfoundland. That large fortunes are amassed by a score of firms in St. John's, who in turn control the island both commercially and politically, is not surprising. (1906, 10)

Yet, as argued above, fishers continuously attempted leakage, that is, to quietly deal at least part of their catch with traders other than their supplying merchant. The result was a 'cat and mouse' game and the cat was always watching. This point is obvious in a 1932 letter I read at Henley Harbour, to a fisher from his supplying merchant in Battle Harbour:

July 23, 1932

Dear Sir,

It has come to our hearing that you are curing a quantity, if not all of your fish light salted, and evidently intended for sale elsewhere. We wish to state again that we do not supply salt to any of our fishermen with the idea that they can do what they wish with their catch. If we take the necessary trouble and means to supply salt it is with the understanding that we are to get at least 5 to 6 quintals of Labrador heavy salted fish to every hogshead of salt used. We notice that beside the salt you only have had one item of any other goods viz. a pair of rubber boots. We take this opportunity also to inform you that we will not be in the market this year to pay any cash for fish, nor can we afford to supply salt only especially at such a distance without additional trade. No other business firm is prepared to do this kind of business and if our firm is prepared to do this from year to year, especially in such times as present, we expect the people to appreciate it to a greater extent and help us out by having further business with us, and we also again state that our salt is not given out so that other firms can get the benefit of it in getting the fish. I consider it both in your interest and ours that I should inform you as above, so that you may again know our mind on the matter and that it will not be necessary to further advise you.

Yours very truly,
Baine Johnston, & Co. Ltd
per Stephen Loveridge

Clearly the 'mouse' provoked two criticisms from his supplier, Baine Johnston and Company. The company thought the fisher was preparing fish for another buyer and complained at the same time that he had only purchased one pair of boots! Perhaps the Henley Harbour fisher availed himself of better prices elsewhere. One wonders how Baine Johnston and Company learned of this leakage. If, as I suspect, the merchant learned about it through gossip, then the case suggests that Settler society was, like all egalitarian societies, subtly competitive.

There were many other dimensions to merchant-fisher relations but I will limit discussion to two: the question of quality and changes in ownership of merchant houses within the region.

Differences of opinion between fishers (and other fishers) and merchants about the quality of fish produced sometimes led to heated arguments and threats of violence. Throughout the period described here, fish were either culled and graded according to size and quality when shipped or, earlier in this century (see Black 1960, 270–1) sold *tal qual*, that is, ungraded. Since fishers gained meaning and self-worth from the quality of codfish they produced, they abhorred selling tal qual. By mingling fish of various qualities and paying a common price, the tal qual method removed an important source of pride among fishers and a means by which they evaluated themselves in relation to their peers. When fish were not bought tal qual, fishers often disagreed with grades or prices offered. Older informants recalled angry incidents at stage heads between fishers and merchant's agents. Some even spoke of covert resistance and of crews who deliberately mishandled their fish, or urinated in stages where green fish was stored, to protest low prices.

Mercantile establishments had an important institutional influence on nearby Settlers. Mercantile establishments, such as at Battle Harbour or Cartwright, attracted transient visitors and other institutions, such as churches or schools. My analysis of mercantile establishments during the nineteenth and early twentieth century produces two conclusions. First, two large firms dominated trade throughout most of nineteenth-century southeastern Labrador, just as Noble and Pinson had a century before. Hunt and Henley dominated the northern part of the region, particularly from Seal Islands north, while in the south, the Slades continued to operate at Battle Harbour and Venison Tickle. Second, during the 1860s and 1870s, many older firms sold their Labrador properties. For example, in 1867, Ridley and Sons purchased the Slade premises (apparently derelict for a couple of years) at Venison Tickle; in 1871, Baine Johnston purchased the old Slade property at Battle

Harbour; and in 1873, the Hudson's Bay Company purchased the Hunt property at Cartwright.

What circumstances explain this concentration of turnovers? First and foremost, there were several poor fisheries during the 1860s and 1870s, such as in 1868 (Smallwood 1984, 147). Colder water over several successive seasons produced repeated poor fisheries. For example, writing about the 1870 season, Judge Pinsent notes: 'This season the quantity of field ice on the coast of Labrador was unprecedented ... [and] most injurious to the fisheries ... [with the result that] voyages of cod and herring were the most unsuccessful perhaps ever known on the coast of Labrador' (1871, 705). But 1870 wasn't the only poor year. Following it, several poor years led to some Settler out-migration, and this may have caused old mercantile firms to reconsider the profitability of their Labrador trade (Collingham 1922, 1569).

Another contributing factor to the turnovers may have been the Newfoundland Customs Act of 1863 and determined efforts by revenue agents to collect duties on goods entering Labrador from places other than Newfoundland. Gosling notes how Hunt and Henley 'vigorously resisted the payment of duties,' arguing (among other things) that they were not represented by the Newfoundland House of Assembly and 'that the duties collected were not spent for the advantage of Labrador' (1910, 417–18). By the 1870s, some large firms had had enough. In one case we know of, Slade and later Baine Johnston employee William Collingham claims that the Slades were 'so incensed (by Newfoundland customs collectors) that they sold the Venison Island property to Ridley's of Harbour Grace' (1922, 1569).

Whatever the cause, the large number of mercantile turnovers in the 1860s and 1870s changed the suppliers Settlers now depended upon. Two companies – the Hudson's Bay Company and Baine Johnston – moved into the region during this difficult time and lost little time in exerting control over local resources. The transfer of older mercantile firms to new ones did not improve prospects for local Settlers.

Another challenge Settlers faced was gaining access to the means of production (land, fishing 'rooms,' and berths) which had been appropriated and maintained by local merchants or transient Newfoundland fishers. It is ironic that many Settlers had to lease the property needed for fishing from transient Newfoundland fishers or local merchants. Yet during the nineteenth- and early twentieth-century, other Settlers were able to purchase the means of production necessary for the fishery.

Fishing rooms included stages, 'bawns' (carpets of flat stones, arranged side by side, on which fish are spread to dry), storehouses, dwelling quarters, and other buildings. Reconstruction of fishing stages was required after violent storms, a problem especially acute at exposed coastal locations. Construction and maintenance of such properties was facilitated by the longer (than today) stay at outside fishing stations. People today describe the more elaborate and well-maintained stages once characteristic of fishing communities and complain that the short time now spent 'outside' does not allow time for maintenance.

Maintenance of stages took place before fishing started in spring or during occasional slack periods. Bawns were used to dry fish in places where wooden stages were not feasible. The importance of bawns as capital equipment necessary for the fishery is illustrated by a dispute Dr Grenfell adjudicated in September 1905, apparently at Indian Harbour. Two parties claimed ownership of one bawn; upon hearing the evidence, Grenfell divided use of it between the disputants (1906, 9).

As mentioned above, merchants leased or sold berths (the favoured locations where nets were placed) and gear to Settlers or employed them to fish them on shares. The Slade accounts of resident planters from 1871 imply that the company rented cod seines and boats to Settlers living near Battle Harbour. One example of this practice (occurring after the Slade company withdrew) concerns Edmund Pye of Cape Charles, who leased the rights to fish for cod and salmon between Soldier's Cove and Rock Point (Cape Charles), from the Baine Johnston Company of Battle Harbour, for an annual rent of $4. Baine Johnston likely acquired 'ownership' of these properties as payment for an unpaid loan.

In Sandwich Bay, the Hudson's Bay Company ran its lucrative salmon fishery on a share system, just as it did its fisheries in northern Labrador (Anonymous 1939, 2). As a result, the company maintained control of the means of production, asserting an 'unfounded claim to certain good fishing berths' (ibid.). Bird explains further: 'The Hudson [sic] Bay Company just about controlled the whole area around this bay. They had little places put around, fishin' places, ya know, with little houses built and a dory and so many nets. People used to fish those places on the thirds. Thirds meant that the person doin' the fishin' got a third of the catch and the rest went for the hire of the equipment and the place' (1980, 44).

In the historical period described here, fewer boats were built and owned than at present. Some fishers leased boats from merchants, while others were eventually able to purchase boats from visiting fishers. For example, the Moss diary makes reference to a Settler purchasing a boat from Nova Scotia fishers for 600 quintals of salmon (1832, 21). De Boilieu ([1861] 1969, 54) vaguely mentions a British 'premium' to encourage boat building. Admittedly, there were some places in southeastern Labrador where boats were built, such as in Sandwich Bay (cf. J.C. Davis 1976, 11–13). But exceptions aside, southeastern Labrador Settlers claimed that their fathers and grandfathers did not know how to build boats and obtained them instead from Newfoundlanders.

Fishing gear was expensive. In 1926 cod traps and trawls cost about $400 and $40 to $50, respectively (Grenfell 1927, 36). Leaden jiggers, killicks, and grapelines were less expensive and sometimes manufactured locally.

Vacant fishing berths could be taken over on a first-come/first-served basis. If all the better berths near a fishing settlement were being used, younger fishers and their families sometimes moved to other, less-populated summer stations. Such moves undoubtedly took place all along the coast as they did at Cape Charles during the 1940s and 1950s; a scarcity of berths led several Cape Charles families to establish new fishing stations at Pleasure Harbour and Carrol's Cove.

Inheritance of fishing and other property was normally agnatic, with occasional female links. Inheritance reveals moral evaluations, in this case that males should inherit fishing berths. An inheritance might be criticized if one son inherited too much or if the 'wrong' person inherited something. Ideally, ultimogeniture prevailed, with the youngest son remaining with his ageing parents and inheriting the winter home. Yet death and emigration sometimes required that fishing property go to females, as the following case illustrates.

A Sandwich Bay Settler described the circuitous route by which he acquired ownership of a salmon berth at Indian Harbour, Huntington Island (Sandwich Bay). My informant, Harry, was nine years old at the time of the 1918 flu epidemic and living at his family's winter homestead at Jackey's Point, North River. Both his father, Jim, and mother were killed in the epidemic and he and his sister were each sent to different relatives. He was raised by his mother's brother's family. When his father's father, Bill, died, he left a will, leaving the Indian Harbour salmon post to his son, Jim. However, because Jim had died in 1918, the berth went to Jim's sister Jane, who fished it for several years. The berth would have gone to Jane's son but he left Sandwich Bay in the 1940s to work in Goose Bay. This permitted Harry, Jane's brother's son, to inherit it. He used it for a number of years before passing it to his son, who continues to use it today. (Another case of women inheriting fishing property is described by Davis [1981, 12].)

SEASONAL ADAPTATIONS

Spring and Summer

By the time the land-fast ice had broken up, Settlers were already at their 'outside' stations although they might occasionally return to winter homes by boat to retrieve or store various items. May and June were months for netting harp-seals and shooting waterfowl migrating north. Families harvested and sometimes preserved waterfowl and sea-bird eggs.

Some Settlers defied Labrador's acidic soils, vexatious sled dogs, and short growing season by attempting to raise a few vegetables or domesticated animals. Experimentation with plant domestication had begun with Captain Cartwright and was continued by other 'outsiders' during the nineteenth and early twentieth century. Townsend (1907, 211) described kitchen gardens of turnip and cabbage at Cape Charles, and Durgin (1908, 62) made similar observations further north. The 1874 Census listed thirty-two swine and seventeen goats at communities between Chateau and Cape Charles, and by 1891, Settlers as far north as Sandwich Bay kept sheep, swine and poultry. Without a doubt the region's agricultural potential suffered from the scarcity of seeds and preoccupation with the fishery.

Salmon

Preparations for the Settler salmon fishery, the first species fished, began as early as March, depending on the nature and extent of tasks faced by individual fishers. Salmon appear in inshore waters in mid-June, migrate north, and ultimately ascend their natal rivers to spawn. Natural factors, such as ice and tides, influence the movement and numbers of salmon. Salmon nets were set near the surface of the water and at a right angle to the shore at particular locations, or berths, so as to intercept the surface (or pelagic) swimming salmon. Chappell (1818) and De Boilieu ([1861] 1969) describe the two common methods for netting salmon. Merchant houses powerful enough to control salmon rivers used one method, catching them 'by means of a net extended quite across the river, into which salmon run their heads, when going up the stream to deposit their spawn' (Chappell 1818, 159). The other method, used first by merchant houses and later by Settlers, involved enclosing salmon in a pound. 'The mode of catching these is with a 'fleet' of three nets, which are fastened to each other so as to form a pound [see Story et al (1982, 382) for a correction of Bredin's misinterpretation of De Boilieu]; the fish in striking the first and even the second of these may not be meshed, but he cannot escape the third, as, when once there, it is impossible for it to retrace its swim' (De Boilieu [1861] 1969, 16).

Older Cape Charles fishers remembered when salmon were pounded. Settlers used hemp gill-styled nets, measuring fifty fathoms in length (300 feet) by about two fathoms deep. These resembled contemporary nylon nets except that the hemp had to be 'barked' (darkened) periodically. Fishers employed 'fleets' of three such nets with fifty linear fathoms equalling one fleet. Informants spoke of a 'hook' at the outer end of a salmon net, forming a V. Any salmon that did not initially become meshed in the net and, instead, followed it offshore would likely be meshed in the inside of this hook.

The nineteenth- and early twentieth-century salmon fishery illustrates both continuity and change. With the exception of preservation by canning, discussed below, until the 1920s all salmon were preserved by salt, just as they had been in Captain Cartwright's time. Bird describes the 'old-fashioned' method of splitting salmon for salting:

The old fashioned way to cure a salmon was to split 'en down the back. Rip 'en right down the centre of the back, same as you'd split a trout. Those fish had to be cleaned perfect, all the blood out of the veins and everything. They had to be perfect to get a number one fish them days. But the old people really knew how to do it. When they had it all done, you'd see their salmon with nare drop of blood to be seen anywhere. Then they salted 'um ... Fishermen had to make sure that their barrels were perfectly tight, to hold the pickle as well as the salt, so the salmon was right down in the salt and pickle. You dare not let your salmon come above the pickle, because then he was a spoiled salmon. (1980, 45)

Freshly pickled salmon were stored and sold in either barrels or tierces (300 pounds), and shipped each fall.

The canning of salmon began in the 1860s. Plaice (1990, 33) credits Donald Smith, factor of the Hudson's Bay Company's post at North West River between 1848 and 1869, with the introduction of this practice to Labrador. The earliest mention of salmon canning in southeastern Labrador occurs in Captain Hood's 1865 report. He reports that thirty-four thousand pounds of 'preserved' salmon were produced at Sandwich Bay and adds that 'the preserved salmon is to be sent to Australia, the (salted) tierces principally to the Mediterranean' (Hood 1865, 175). Pinsent explains that 'salmon caught on the open sea coast are usually salted in casks for exportation' (1868, 549D). By about 1873 salmon were canned at St Francis Harbour, Venison Island, and Sandwich Bay. However, the tinning of salmon appears to have stopped some years after it began; Gordon states that by 1917 no canning facilities existed in Sandwich Bay (1972, 98).

During the height of the salmon fishery organized by the Hudson's Bay Company in Sandwich Bay, Settlers participating in it used 'the company's nets, and fish on the shares' (Newfoundland 1876). The company used three collecting boats, for the Eagle River, for Paradise River, and for Earle's Island. This fishery was compatible with the dispersed, seasonally occupied, Settler salmon camps.

During the 1920s salmon began to be purchased fresh, for freezing.[3] According to Davis (1981, 20–1), a British steamer first purchased fresh salmon outside Cartwright in 1921; during the next several years a number of Newfoundland firms followed suit. However, in Sandwich Bay between the 1920s and 1940s, the uncertainty of buyers meant that salmon processing fluctuated between fresh-frozen and salted. For their part, Settler fishers preferred to sell salmon fresh because it involved less work and because the price was good.

Further south along the coast, in this same time period, competition between salmon buyers reigned, at least during some years. Older Cape Charles informants recalled that a buyer named George Allen began buying fresh salmon there about 1930, for three cents per pound. Competition between rival buyers over the next decade caused variable prices until, eventually, all competing buyers harmonized their price. Some information suggests that the buying of fresh salmon made smaller summer stations more isolated, and, consequently, more vulnerable. One Lodge Bay man told me about Camp Islands during the 1930s and 1940s:

Them times they wouldn't trouble so much about salmon as they do now because there wasn't much of a price ... [we were] mostly after [cod]fish. We only got five cents a pound [for salmon] ... and there was thousands of 'em. Even then, you had a job to sell 'em for five cents a pound. They had collectors. There was only Baine Johnston then, at Battle Harbour and there was a fellow named Herb Porter from Corner Brook at Cape Charles. There was enough [fishers] down at the Cape [Charles] and Battle Harbour to keep 'em busy so we had to salt a lot of ours down.

Thus, with the exception of Sandwich Bay, where the HBC collecting system was well organized, outlying summer stations further south could not always take advantage of the fresh salmon revolution. In some ways, then, buying fresh salmon encouraged centralization because the collecting system had not developed sufficiently (some say it still has not) to guarantee buyers for more 'isolated' fishers. Conversely, the buying of fresh salmon in or near larger summer stations meant greater competition, steadily rising prices for fishers, and increased fishing pressure on local salmon stocks.

As today, there has always been disagreement between those who saw salmon stocks as inexhaustible and those concerned about their preservation. In 1865 Commissioner March predicted the end of the salmon fishery if river mouths continued to be blocked; he recommended a system of private ownership and protection of salmon rivers, as he claimed existed in Quebec (1866, 182). However, as late as Governor MacGregor's 1905 visit to Labrador, people were netting salmon in rivers and considering it their right to do so (1909, 74).

Cod

Codfish has long been the staple species along the coast. Settlers 'jigged' (hooked) codfish using hooks attached to long lines baited with capelin or lance, or if bait was unavailable, they used leaden jiggers. Settlers of the Battle Harbour area were using cod seines as early as 1832 (Moss 1832), and in some instances such cooperative technologies may have encouraged several families to summer near each other. Seine technology resembled that used by the Americans, as discussed in Chapter 4. Older informants remembered several gadgets associated with cod seines: a 'glass' with which to stare into the water to determine what direction the fish were swimming, and a 'douser' or 'knocker,' essentially weights on ropes, lowered to the sea floor and bounced, to freighten cod into the seine.

Movable cod seines were eventually replaced by stationary cod traps, an 1866 invention ordinarily attributed to Bonne Esperance (Quebec) merchant W.H. Whitely. Cod traps are box-shaped netted enclosures set alongside and perpendicular to the shore. Whitely's invention was almost certainly based on the more mobile cod seine, which American fishers had been using in the area for several decades. The cod trap increased cod landings, some believed dangerously so and, consequently, there were political efforts to ban its use (Smallwood 1984, 612-13).

Fishers set their cod traps as soon as the first signs of cod appeared, normally in July. Traps were 'hauled' (emptied) two or three times daily. The trap season was short, but days were long; crews worked by lantern-light late into the night to salt the last catch of the day. Crews arriving in from each fishing trip used a two-pronged fork to place each fish onto the stage head. The fish were next put into the rectangular 'throat' box located at one end of the splitting table (Davis 1980, 60). From there the crew or family members dressed each fish by removing the head and internal organs. Cod livers were thrown into 'punchen' tubs, where they were stored during the summer for later sale to produce cod-liver oil. Crews washed each split fish in a large tub, then pushed loaded wheelbarrows full of fish to the 'bulk,' where they were stacked atop earlier catches, belly up, head-to-tail, and heavily salted in tiered layers called 'bulks.' Codfish absorbed salt in bulk for a minimum of twenty-one days, after which they were 'struck.' Struck fish were washed, scrubbed, and stacked in faggots or 'waterhorses' to press out any remaining water. When dry (but not too sunny) weather occurred, fish were laid head-to-tail, on either wooden flakes or cobbled bawn, to dry. Each night, crews or their families gathered the drying fish, piled them in faggots, and covered them with canvas to reduce exposure to dampness. This process of drying salted codfish continued for a week or so, depending on drying conditions.

Older people fondly remember the traditional salt-cod fishery. Women and children played important roles, helping to spread and stack drying fish and to cut of fish at the splitting tables. For wives and mothers otherwise confined to tedious household duties, the time spent in spreading codfish on 'flakes' or bawns was a welcome outdoor relief from household drudgery.

Codfish began moving offshore following the short cod trapping season, and were caught by baited trawls. Capelin, herring, and lance were commonly used as bait fish. If bait species were too plentiful or remained inshore too long, cod might be glutted, making the use of trawls and jiggers ineffective (Guzzwell 1941b). More commonly a scarcity of bait species reduced the fall fishery.

Herring
By 1890, Labrador's herring fishery was increasingly important to Settler

fishers. Thus, Inspector Moore from Pickled Fish writes: 'Year after year it is becoming apparent that people on the Labrador are trusting more and more to herring, as this fishery relieves somewhat the markets to which cod-fish is sent. The Labrador herring is the same auxiliary to the cod-fishery as agriculture is on the island' (1890, 439). Settlers caught herring in gill-type nets. Herring were pickled or smoked and used as bait for codfish, as dog food, and as a major part of the winter diet.

Fall and Winter

The freezing of sea ice (or land-fast ice) in December or January enabled movement to winter homes located in sheltered bays and inlets. There, wood cutting, fur-trapping, and hunting were the main occupations of males, while females remained busy with a variety of household and family tasks. Sealskin boots were made during long winter nights. Men usually made sealskin boots south of Fox Harbour (St Lewis), while either men or women made them from there north. Settlers used a curvilinear, Inuit-style knife as well as other knives to clean fat from seal skins. Sealskin boots were made until the 1950s. Sealskin was also used to make dog-team traces and covers for felt mittens. Indeed the entire dog-team complex, including dog-team commands, 'uuk' for right and 'utter' for left, along with whalebone komatik shoes, finds its roots in Inuit culture. However, the older people I interviewed claimed uncertainty about the cultural origins of skin bootmaking or the dog-team complex. They smiled uneasily when telling me about it, as if to distance themselves from their part-aboriginal ancestry.

Sealing
Seals were netted in the fall and spring. In early December, for example, the netting of harp-seals occurred at 'tickles' (channels) and islands on the outer coast. De Boilieu described two kinds of seal nets used at Battle Harbour: the more common gill-type net, forty fathoms long by two deep and submerged by 'killicks' (weights), and a second type, the 'stopper-net,' used in tickles. Stopper nets required a more active type of hunting than submerged nets. One net was permanently set at one end of the tickle, while a second, which could be raised by a capstan, was placed across the other end of the tickle. Once a large pod of seals had passed over the suspended net and entered the tickle, this net was raised, entrapping the seals.

Settlers cached frozen seal carcasses over winter in storehouses for skinning the following spring. Seals were skinned at the rate of about fifteen skins per man each day, and 'rands' of fat were then 'rendered out' or reduced to oil in large iron boilers (De Boilieu [1861] 1969, 71–2). The oil was casked for shipment to England (ibid., 72).

The importance of sealing may be illustrated by a specific example. December 1941 was an exceptionally good month for seals in the Battle Harbour district, when 2150 harp-seals were taken. This large catch was fortunate in several respects. Few herring had been caught in the summer of 1941 and therefore many people lacked sufficient dog food for the winter of 1941–2 (Dwyer 1941b). The netting of these seals saved 'a great number of people from killing their dogs,' their only means of getting around in winter (Christian 1942). Approximately two hundred of the total were used for dog food and for making skin boots. The rest were bartered with Baine Johnston for $2 per quintal (25 cents more than paid in 1941), permitting local Settlers to purchase food and clothing (ibid.).

During the early decades of this century, the economy in certain parts of the coast diversified; some men concentrated on trapping and, later, others on logging (see Chapter 9). For example, in the Alexis River system and in Sandwich Bay, natural conditions favoured the development of fur-trapping, while along other parts of the coast the local ecology favoured the maintenance of a more generalized pattern. Since it is impossible to net seals out on the coast and at the same time trap fur-bearing animals inland, economic diversification affected transhumant patterns. Generally, communities in the southern part of the region, nearest the Strait of Belle Isle, maintained their orientation towards 'outside' activities – fishing, sealing, and duck hunting. As noted above, the same environmental possibilities that enabled sealing explain why the Slades and later Baine Johnston at Battle Harbour were the only merchants who consistently purchased seal products.

Hunting
Hunting for migratory waterfowl was an extremely important fall and spring pursuit. According to Walsh, 'eider-ducks abound, as do guillemots, puffin, murres, and auks' (1896, 37). De Boilieu describes strategic methods of hunting waterfowl used by the Slade crews at Battle Harbour. Crews erected a 'gaze,' or blind, from which waterfowl were shot. In May, De Boilieu continues, such crews commonly killed twenty-five to thirty ducks per man each morning ([1861] 1969, 73). Nineteenth- and

twentieth-century Settlers used similar tactics. Dressed in white canvas clothes, they drifted in white boats amidst spring pack ice awaiting a shot. They preserved slain waterfowl for later consumption by salting or freezing them in casks.

The hunting of migratory waterfowl continued into November, when it gradually blended with preparations for the fall seal hunt and, more generally, for winter. Harp-seals were the most important of the several seal species (i.e., harbour, ringed, bearded, hooded, and grey) pursued by Settlers. Harps make predictable migrations along the coast in fall and spring, travelling south each November or December and north each April or May. Predictable migrations lead to strategic hunting, in this case using nets.

Although Settlers hunted big game like caribou and bear, most of the animals killed for meat were small, such as rabbits, ptarmigan, spruce partridges, and porcupines (Walsh 1896, 33-4). These food resources were often killed while men worked in the forest, obtaining wood.

Wooding

Along most parts of the coast, wood cutting was the most important winter pursuit, since without an adequate supply of firewood and lumber, families would be unable to live at outside fishing settlements and consequently unable to repay merchants for necessities taken on credit the previous fall.

Settlers used local wood for fuel and construction, primarily spruce, fir, juniper, and birch. Cutting of wood for summer use began in January and, by late in the month, Settlers were hauling wood by dog teams to outside fishing settlements or collecting it in places from whence it could be rafted out at open-water season. An anonymous author of an 1888 diary from Lodge Bay writes: 'January 26, 1888. In the evening I went in the woods and cut a [wood] slide load of wood. We finished cutting 1080 burns [logs] of wood. Fine and frosty today. Pretty well all the wood is cut. Non [no one?] in the Lodge now. January 31, 1888. A fine day. Every one is hauling wood out today. We have 600 and 48 [648?] out' (Anonymous, 1888).

Settlers once rafted wood for heating fuel and construction to outside fishing stations in huge tiered rafts which informants said measured about twenty feet wide by forty feet long and often held one thousand to fifteen hundred turns or 'sticks' (logs) of wood. This practice may not have been followed in all southeastern Labrador communities. In years when rafting was practised, wood was rafted immediately after the fast ice disappeared. Rafting was often a cooperative venture in which men pooled the labour necessary to assemble and tow several rafts of wood.

All year round people used local plants (and less frequently, animals) for medicinal purposes. As elsewhere in Labrador (Goudie 1973, 11) spring tonics were made from boiled spruce or juniper boughs, along with other ingredients. The Moss diary entry for 9 May records travelling to Caribou Island for 'spruce to brew with' (1832, 9). Beer was made by boiling black spruce branches and then draining the liquid into a jar. Molasses or sugar and yeast were then added and the resulting concoction brewed for ten to twelve days. Spruce beer served as a purgative, to 'clean the blood' and to prevent colds after the long winter. More recently spruce beer has been used as an intoxicant.

Tonics were also made from other plants. Colds, stomach pains, and menstrual cramps were treated with a tonic made from ground juniper. Boiled ground juniper was also given to babies, 'to make them healthy.' Another blood-cleaning medicine was a spoonful of molasses and one of sulphur.

Balsam fir 'bladders' (whose contents consisted of 'turpentine') were used as astringents, being placed on bleeding cuts or wounds, bandaged, and left for several days. The bitter roots and beans of a green marsh plant (*Menyanthes trifoliata*) called bog-bean, buck bean, or duck plant (Herbe au canard) bean (Peter Scott, conversation with author, 31 July 1992) were used for flu or to increase the appetite of those suffering from cancer. Settlers regularly consumed cod-liver oil to prevent tuberculosis.

Settlers made lozenges from molasses and kerosene. One spoonful of kerosene was added to about two cups of molasses and the mixture heated to the soft-boil stage, kneaded, and cut into small squares. These lozenges were used to treat sore throats, as was a mixture of friar's balsam and sugar.

'Gatherings' were customarily treated with poultices. (A 'gathering' is a boil under the skin, filled with pus.) Bread poultices were most common. Soft bread, excluding the crust, was boiled in water, placed over the gathering, and a bandage applied. An older woman recalled once applying such a poultice to her husband just before the unexpected arrival of the Grenfell ship. The doctor aboard said that the poultice was as good as any treatment he might have provided. Less commonly, a poultice was made from a small bird, such as a sparrow. The bird was split open and, while still warm, placed on the 'gathering' in order to bring it to a head.

Another kind of poultice was used for chest colds. A mixture of kerosene, butter, and Miner's Liniment was heated on the stove and then rubbed on the patient's chest, which was then covered with a warm flannel cloth. This remedy was also applied to loosen a chest which had 'tighten[ed] up' – that is, was not able to cough up phlegm.

The foregoing discussion of historic Settler adaptations sketches the seasonal nature of the economy and social arrangements. It is safe to conclude, with Jackson, that the Settlers enjoyed a 'meagre independence' and that fluctuations in 'catch and price' and of good and bad luck were persistent realities (1982, 17–18). Settlers were able to harvest much of what they needed to survive from local resources, and in many ways this relative self-sufficiency stands in stark contrast to their life today. While most Settlers were poor, some were better off; indeed there appear to have been pockets of poverty as well as areas of relative plenty.

7

The Impact of the State: 1832–1949

Residents of the island of Newfoundland were entitled to elect representatives to the House of Assembly during the periods of both representative (1832–55) and responsible government (1855–1934). However, even though the Newfoundland Act (1809) returned sovereignty over Labrador to Newfoundland, Labrador residents were not allowed to vote until 1946. Yet the issue of representation remained important throughout the nineteenth century. The progressive Scottish-born Newfoundland governor William MacGregor strongly encouraged extension of the franchise to the Labrador 'dependency,' as had the secretary of state in 1863 (MacGregor 1909, 125). If enabling Labrador people to vote was going to be impossible, MacGregor suggested that a minister of the Crown responsible to Labrador should be appointed (126). That he understood the importance of viewing Labrador regionally (and culturally) was evidenced by his 1909 indication that the franchise would soon be extended to southern Labrador (188). But the Newfoundland government failed to follow MacGregor's advice and also ignored a much more stinging, anonymous critique (probably authored by Dr H.L. Paddon in 1920) (Anonymous 1920c). This four-page critique records systemic injustices inflicted on Labrador Settlers by visiting Newfoundland fishers and by the 'little army of Government officials' visiting Labrador each summer. Lacking the vote and living within a system weighted to favour Newfoundlanders, Settlers continued to suffer injustices up until recent years.[1]

The 1825 British North America Act partitioned Labrador, re-annexing the coast west of Blanc Sablon and the fifty-second degree parallel to Lower Canada (Budgel and Stavely 1987). The British Privy Council decision of 1927 essentially upheld this one-hundred-year-old southern boundary and established the interior boundary at the height of land, or continental divide. Ambiguities surrounding Labrador's place as a 'dependency' (*JHA* 1863, 628) within the Dominion of Newfoundland did not slow the passage of acts and the implementation of treaties which had important consequences for Labrador. A description of several of these follows, focusing on their jurisdiction, administration, revenue, communication, and services.

Between 1811 and 1826 surrogate courts operated in Labrador with naval officers or local men as judges (Gosling 1910, 390). Labrador circuit courts of civil jurisdiction replaced surrogate courts in 1826. These were discontinued in 1834 because the small 'amount of work ... was not considered commensurate to the cost' (ibid., 400). In 1840 Elias Rendell was appointed to collect duties in Labrador but experienced so much resistance from contumacious merchants that he recommended re-establishing a court and introducing police protection of the coast (ibid., 408).

Customs collectors visited Labrador yearly, and the circuit court, dissolved in 1833, operated again between 1863 and 1874 (Gosling 1910, 419). Statistics of cases brought before this court (primarily) in southeastern Labrador between 1867 and 1874 provide some insight into the social problems common during this tumultuous era. The highest percentage of cases (32 of 104, or 30 per cent) involved fishers' debts and may be attributed to problems of the fishery during this era, as discussed elsewhere in relation to environmental and economic difficulties. Existing debt laws compounded the problem. Travelling judge Pinsent complained that existing laws demanded that guilty debtors pay creditors all existing debts. This demand placed the court in a legal straitjacket and decreased its discretionary powers to reach compromise judgments. Pinsent recommended legal changes so as to reduce the economic impact of insolvency, both on indebted fishers and on creditor merchants. Such changes would allow the merchant to recover 'his fair claim upon the assets of his debtor' (Pinsent 1868, 549B) without forcing fishers into bankruptcy. Judge Pinsent repeated this recommendation in 1870, using more informal language (1871, 703).

Excluding offences in the cumulative category 'other,' the second most frequent offence was assault (11.5 per cent, or 12 of 104 cases). Many assaults resulted from the barring of herring and Judge Pinsent went so far as to recommend a 'ship-of-war' to quell such 'turbulent and unlawful conduct' (Pinsent 1869, 659). The 'boom town' atmosphere of the region's herring fishery probably also contributed to larceny, perhaps in relation to allegations of barring herring, which was the third most frequent offence (10.5 per cent, or 11 of 104 cases).

Although the circuit court was discontinued in 1874, Judge Pinsent believed that it had an 'important moral effect of preventing offences against the law, and in causing private settlements of accounts between parties engaged in the fisheries and trade' (1868, 549B). Pinsent's opinion would appear justified when one considers the large size and international composition of the fisheries. Contemporary with the circuit court system, respected local men (such as Mr Goodridge, agent for Hunt and Henley, of Cartwright) were appointed as justices of the peace. They were empowered to conduct marriages, but their other duties are unknown.

In addition to the administration of justice, the state administration also collected of duties and other revenues, particularly after about 1840 (the Moravian Missions of northern Labrador and the Deep Sea Mission [later the Grenfell Mission] were exempt from duties [MacGregor 1909, 85]). Revenue officers, who often travelled aboard the same vessels that carried the circuit court judge, encountered stiff opposition to the payment of Newfoundland duties, from both resident mercantile firms and foreign fishers. Gosling summarizes the reasons behind merchant opposition to payment: 'They (merchants) claimed that they carried on their business from England, and had very little communication with Newfoundland, that they were not represented in the Newfoundland legislature, and that the duties collected were not spent for the advantage of Labrador' (1910, 418). The resistance that revenue officers met originated in the head offices of the mercantile firms. For example, when Newfoundland revenue officer Winter attempted to collect duties from Battle Harbour merchants T. and D. Slade (of Poole), local agent Mr Bendell told Winter that 'he had positive instructions not to pay any duties' (Winter 1864, 620; Collingham 1922, 1569). Under Winter's threat to seize store goods, Bendell eventually paid the duties, albeit under protest. A common objection to duties was that Labrador was politically a part of Newfoundland, yet had no elected representation (Packard 1891, 219). In 1863, the Newfoundland House of Assembly passed a Customs Act affirming its jurisdictional authority in Labrador, and thereby it hoped to end merchant opposition to taxation.

Successful herring seasons attracted transient traders who bartered for herring using goods subject to duty (principally tea, molasses, spirits, etc.). In those years when the herring fishery was poor, such as 1864, fewer traders were attracted and thus the revenues collected were reduced (Winter 1865, 703).

Both merchants and foreign fishers occasionally used local ambiguities surrounding the precise location of Labrador's southern boundary with Canada to avoid paying Newfoundland duties. One of the numerous examples occurred in 1863, when Blanc Sablon merchants argued that they were outside Newfoundland jurisdiction (Winter 1864, 618). Similarly, the previous year, Newfoundland fishery officer Hamilton encountered American fishers who were 'not aware that the principal part of the Labrador coast is under the Newfoundland Government' (Hamilton 1863, 401).

Revenue collection was sometimes violent. The case involving Revenue Collector Winter and a Nova Scotia trader named Green illustrates this. In the summer of 1867 Winter, while at Cartwright, learned about Green from Mr Goodridge, agent for Hunt and Henley. Goodridge complained that Green would purchase much of the salmon normally purchased by Hunt and Henley. Goodridge warned Winter that Hunt and Henley would withhold their duties unless Green was apprehended. Winter caught up with Green and in the verbal and physical confrontation that followed, Green knocked Winter unconscious with an oar! Green escaped but was apprehended in Red Bay by Judge Pinsent in late September 1867 and taken to St John's for trial.

In a similar incident in 1863 on Grady Island, employees of local merchants King and Larmour fired a cannon at Officer Winter for over an hour. Winter writes that King and Larmour's men did so 'evidently for the purpose of intimidating me in the discharge of my duty' (1864, 622).

As did appointed justices of the peace, revenue officers appointed local men as 'preventative officers' or 'sub-collectors.' These local officers were apparently intended to provide a more continuous state presence in coastal Labrador than would be possible with transient revenue officers alone. Those appointed were often local agents for mercantile firms and thus the same persons who had once opposed payment of duties. By instituting this system, government may have sought to co-opt those opposing revenue collection. For example, following Revenue Officer Winter's confrontation with Slade agent Bendell, Winter writes that he 'then gave Mr Bendell a commission as Sub-Collector, to collect from Traders' (1864, 621).

SOCIAL SERVICES

Although Labrador merchants were generally correct in claiming that Labrador received few services from the Newfoundland government, some services were extended to the region, increasingly after the mid-nineteenth century. These included education, health, welfare, and communication. While services were intended primarily to serve Newfoundlanders fishing along the Labrador coast, they increased the infrastructure of some fishing ports that would later become communities.

Education

In March 1857, a group of Harbour Grace residents petitioned the House of Assembly for a small sum of money to support a school at Battle Harbour, Labrador (*JHA* 1857, 118). By the summer of 1864, Circuit Judge B. Sweetland reported a day-school at Battle Harbour, held in the house of the Reverend Mr Hutchinson, the Anglican minister (1865, 708). The following summer, Judge Sweetland reported summer schools at Cape Charles and Venison Tickle, both with female teachers from Conception Bay. Their students included both local Settlers and the children of transient Newfoundland fishers (Sweetland 1866, 197). The data presented in Table 1 for the period of the mid-1860s to the mid-1870s indicate a changeable, yet gradually expanding, school system operating in the southern half of southeastern Labrador.

The state paid teachers' salaries and supplied books. Children were expected to pay a small fee, normally 2s 6d, per school season. Such fees were exorbitant for some, however. In 1898, Square Islands folk – then numbering some eight families with a total of forty-five children – were described as too poor to support a school; instead, Dr Willway recommended relocating them 'off the coast' (Willway 1898, 330).

Most pupils were young, ranging between four and twelve years. The curriculum was basic, focusing on simple arithmetic, writing on slates, and reading the Scriptures (*JHA* 1875, 930–42).

Most students within the area covered by the Battle Harbour mission were Anglican although some families were Roman Catholic or Methodist. For example, in 1868, two of the eighteen children studying at Cape Charles were listed as 'Wesleyan Methodists,' while two of the thirteen at Venison Tickle were Roman Catholic (Young 1869, 774; Pike 1869, 776).

Table 1 shows that the total number of pupils increased from 51 in 1868 to 132 in 1873. Also, it may be noted that throughout most of the years summarized therein, school operated only in summer, normally between June and early October. This period coincided with the fishing season and represented an adaptation both to the Newfoundland sta-

TABLE 1
Schools operating within study area: 1864–76

Year	Cape Charles	Battle Harbour	Matthews Cove	Venison Tickle	Little Harbour	Total Students
1864		S only		S only		
1865	S only					
1866						
1867	S only	S only		S only		
1868	S only (18)	S only (20)		S only (13)		51
1869	S only (25)	S & W (23) (13)	S only (15)			76
1870	S only (25)	Combined (59)	S only*			84
1871	S only (30)	Combined (59)	S only*			89
1872	S only (25)	S & W (31)	S only (70)			126
1873	S & W (26)	S & W ? (36)	S only (70)			132
1874	S & W (20)†	S & W	S & W	W only	S & W	
1875						
1876	S only	S & W				

SOURCE: *JHA* for years reported, excepting 1874.
NOTES: S & W means summer and winter. Numbers in parenthesis are numbers of students.
*In 1870–1 Battle Harbour and Matthews Cove offered school in summer only with a *combined* enrolment of 59 students between the two settlements.
†Mews 1922, 1597.

tioner fishery and to local seasonal transhumance, since summer was the season with the largest concentration of population assembled at 'outside' fishing stations. The school year and pupil lists varied annually, probably in relation to the local labour requirements of the fishery. Thus, in 1868 the Reverend Mr Wilson, the Anglican minister of Battle Harbour, explains that 'in winter many boys who are employed in the fishing season attend school and in winter there is also a night school for adults' (1869, 775). As flexible as the system was, some argued for a more decentralized approach, which eventually would became known as the itinerant system. Foremost among advocates of this system was Judge Pinsent. In 1869 he explained that 'Labrador is not a favourable country for the establishment of schools; the people there are so scattered that, with very few exceptions, it is impracticable to get a sufficient number of them together for that purpose. The general and most effective mode of instruction is by supplying books to the isolated inhabitants, and thus enabling them to learn at home by their own firesides, where they teach one another' (1870, 506). Judge Sweetland also argued that the economy and settlement pattern of the northern half of the region, particularly Sandwich Bay, did not permit the establishment of schools. He noted that 'In Sandwich and Esquimaux (L. Melville) Bays the inhabitants disperse themselves for the sake of furring in the winter and catching salmon in summer; very little can be done in the way of an established School' (1865, 708). Consequently, children in the northern half of the region did not have schools until the latter part of the nineteenth century. Instead, instruction was offered by itinerant teachers who travelled from one Settler homestead to another.

By the winter of 1883 a schoolteacher was given the formidable task of serving both Sandwich and Groswater bays! The next year we read that 'an itinerant schoolmaster has for the fishing season kept school on the most important centres on the coast [outside of Sandwich Bay], and in the winter followed the settlers and kept school in their winter quarters up the Bay' (Department of Education 1884). This itinerant system of education continued into the early twentieth century, when it was replaced by centralized boarding-schools, which would have disastrous consequences for dispersed Settler settlements.

Medical Services

It is popularly believed in Newfoundland and Labrador that medical services were non-existent in Labrador until the arrival of the Grenfell

Mission. But actually, this is not true. As early as 1867, Judge Pinsent mentioned dispensing medicines and drugs provided by the government, and noted that the surgeon aboard the HMS *Fawn* made two short visits between the Labrador Strait and Hopedale in 1867 (1868, 549F). The following summer, Pinsent declared that the health of Labrador people was generally good, but added that no doctor was resident there. By 1873, Pinsent recommended that a doctor accompany the circuit court vessel (1874, 868). In 1875 Harbour Grace interests petitioned the government for a doctor for their fishers.

Between July and October 1886 Dr F.J. White travelled the southeastern Labrador coast, treating Newfoundland fishers and Settlers (1887). Similar visits by government medical officers occurred throughout the 1880s and 1890s, and the physicians tended seven to eight hundred patients each summer (Smallwood 1984, 877). Government medical officers concentrated on the majority population, transient Newfoundland fishers. Newfoundlanders brought many new diseases to Labrador, including scarlet fever in 1867 and diphtheria in 1890.

Welfare

During the 1860s the Newfoundland government increased expenditures for 'poor relief' from an average of £6,150 in 1855–60 to an average of £14,600 in 1861–5 (Smallwood 1984, 605). In 1865 Judge Sweetland reported giving assistance to two families in 'great distress' (1866, 196). Two years later, Judge Pinsent reported that 'although the amount of pauperism is comparatively small at Labrador, yet a few cases will occur, in which the resident mercantile agents, or other principal inhabitants, may have to give assistance to destitute persons having no special claims on them; and in such cases they (the merchants) look to the Government for reimbursement' (1868, 549E).

Government also responded to damage caused by the hurricane which ravaged southeastern Labrador on 9 October 1867 by leasing the Baine Johnston and Company steamer *Panther* for ten days and immediately sending it to Labrador to provide aid and free passage for the survivors, many of whom were Newfoundland fishers. Over forty people and about the same number of vessels were lost in this storm; the government spent $1944.45 on storm-related aid (Shea 1869, 128).

Judge Pinsent's description of the case of Bay Roberts fisher Edward Mercer illustrates the negative aspect of relying on local merchants to dispense relief. Mercer fished at Pack's Harbour for several years but in the winter of 1868–9 he, his wife, five sons, and a daughter decided to overwinter in Labrador, at North River, Sandwich Bay. They had exhausted their supplies by mid-January and there was 'no supply to be had at the Merchant stores [i.e., Hunt and Co.] in Sandwich Bay.' They struggled on through the winter, relying largely on mussels and on the aid provided them by an Inuk (one of the Inuit) at Pack's Harbour. By April, four of the five sons had died, and when Pinsent met Mercer in August 1869 he was 'greatly debilitated and unable to work.' Judge Pinsent noted that excepting the Slades at Battle Harbour, no mercantile establishments stocked provisions for poor relief and recommended that henceforth a stock of 50 to 100 barrels of Indian corn be left at each establishment for that purpose (1870, 501–2).

Poor fishing seasons and the resulting increase in government poor relief during the 1860s led confederates to urge that Newfoundland and Labrador join Canada, as provided for under Section 146 of the British North America Act (1867). However, this move to confederate was defeated in the election of 13 November 1869, which ended the administration of Frederick Carter (Smallwood 1984, 606–7).

Communication and Transportation

In 1867 Judge Pinsent observed that it would be 'gratifying to all those engaged in business at Labrador to have postal communication with St John's' (1868, 549G). Those working or living in Labrador felt they were entitled to such a service, Pinsent continued, particularly since they contributed to the state revenue yet received few benefits. Few of Judge Pinsent's recommendations to government were implemented so quickly. The *Ariel* was dispatched to Labrador on 5 August 1867 with mail, although its service was intended primarily to serve the 'commercial body' (Bemister 1867). The Newfoundland government appointed Patrick Furlong as mail officer in 1870 and he sailed north on the steam packet *Walrus* (Furlong 1871, 706). By 1871, Judge Pinsent observed, 'the Mail Service for Labrador, introduced by the Government last summer, was doubtless of great utility and convenience generally to the merchants and fishermen engaged in the trade and fisheries of that coast' (1872, 875). That the mail service was restricted primarily to the Strait and southeastern Labrador coast is evident from Pinsent's observation: 'I know that the mercantile houses at Blanc Sablon, the Southern extremity of our territory, and the Hudson's Bay Company at Rigoulette, Hamilton Inlet, in the north, are dissatisfied that the Postal Steamer does not call at those places, as they are thus practically excluded from the advantages enjoyed by the rest of the mercantile community' (ibid.).

By 1874 there were thirty-one postal harbours within the study area, each with a way officer (Prendergast 1875, 952). The mail officer for the Labrador service worked under the supervision of Newfoundland's postmaster general. Gosling writes that the Labrador Steam Mail Service 'has been gradually extended until now (1910) a comfortable steamer makes fortnightly trips during the season' (1910, 420).

Occasional requests for improvements to transportation came from Newfoundland fishers or merchants. For example, in a letter written on 15 November 1911 to Mr Pickett, minister of Marine and Fisheries, fisher James Noseworthy (1911) asked that a lighthouse be built at Copper Island, Azzize's Harbour. Noseworthy justified the need for a lighthouse by explaining that Azzize's Harbour (near Battle Harbour) was 'a great bring up' popular with the (Newfoundland) fishing schooners and the coastal steamers, and 'a perfectly safe harbour from storms from all points on the compass.' But Noseworthy went further, offering the government his own building materials for the construction, which could be purchased at a 'great bargain at the present time' (Noseworthy 1911).

Grenfell commented on the insensitivity of the Newfoundland government to the need for lighthouses along the coast. However, once Grenfell had raised money from 'outside friends' for a lighthouse near the Battle Harbour hospital, the government denied permission for a private light, and erected Labrador's first lighthouse, at Double Island. Then the government erected another near the Indian Harbour hospital, Groswater Bay (Grenfell 1932, 183–4).

Like lighthouses, wireless stations were to serve the Newfoundland fishing fleet. The Newfoundland government took over the Canadian Marconi wireless stations in Labrador about 1907. A heavy gale that year destroyed a number of vessels and killed or marooned many people; wireless communication of this information was immediately appreciated (Woods 1907, 148).

During the period 1900–49, the Newfoundland government attempted several times to lease or sell the Labrador territory, such as one year after the British Privy Council decision of 1927, which defined Labrador's boundaries and officially placed interior Labrador under Newfoundland's jurisdiction (Budgel and Stavely 1987, 11). However, Labrador was to remain under Newfoundland's ægis, and during the twentieth century that government passed a number of laws and agreements which had a significant impact the on southeastern area which is the focus of this study.

The major influence of Robert Bond's Liberal government (1900–9) was through a reciprocity draft agreement reached with American secretary of state John Hay on 8 November 1902, the so-called Bond-Hay Convention. The history of this agreement dates to 1783; it reconciled conflicting interpretations of American rights to the fishery and Newfoundland's access to American markets. Pressure from New England fishers caused the United States Senate to reject the Bond-Hay Convention, leading Britain to seek arbitration at the International Tribunal at the Hague (1910). The tribunal settled seven questions regarding Newfoundland's rights to control its fishery and, in general, increased its rights to do so (Smallwood 1984, 774–5).

The administration of Edward Morris (1909–17) passed several acts relevant to the region, including a 1911 amendment to the Crown Lands Act (1903) making it easier for timber speculators to acquire Crown lands (Smallwood 1984, 619). This led to a flurry of timber concessions, some in southeastern Labrador. In 1921 the first Squire administration passed additional legislation regarding the cutting and exporting of timber (ibid., 622).

The Monroe administration (1924–8) established the Newfoundland Cold Storage Corporation for the developing frozen-fish industry. Monroe's administration is also remembered for events leading to the 1927 Privy Council boundary decision. Following this decision, the Newfoundland government passed the 'Labrador Act,' Act 18, George V, Chapter II, 'An Act to Govern the Granting of Lands and Rights in Labrador,' which sought to keep Labrador (relatively) free from new development and hence ready for sale. The crash of the New York stock market in 1929 decreased fish prices, and thus new loans were required to bolster Newfoundland's sagging economy.

The second Alderdice administration (1932–4), Newfoundland's last elected government until Confederation, secretly and unsuccessfully attempted to lease Labrador to British financiers (Smallwood 1984, 627). The government's inability to meet loan payments led Alderdice to agree to a royal commission on Newfoundland's future, composed of Scotsman William W. Mackenzie, the Lord Baron Amulree, and two Canadian bankers (Noel 1971, 217). The royal commission recommended that until Newfoundland was economically self-supporting, it should be run by a commission responsible to and controlled by the British government. As for Labrador, Amulree considered various options, such as leasing or selling the territory to a trading company. If, however, such a company could not be found, Lord Amulree concluded: 'We think that Newfoundland should retain the territory and administer it. The general opinion is that the territory is capable of great possibilities. Hitherto these possibilities have only been guessed at' (Great Britain 1933, 186).

THE ROAD TO CANADA

In many ways, the administration of Labrador was more effective during the dictatorial commission of government than during responsible government, even though neither form of government allowed the people of Labrador to vote. The mandate of the six commissioners who took office on 16 February 1934 was to rehabilitate Newfoundland's economic, social, and political life, and some of the commission's development initiatives were more enlightened than those since Confederation.

In autumn 1935 John Hope Simpson, commissioner of Natural Resources, proposed repealing the Labrador Act (1927) and applying Newfoundland Crown lands legislation to Labrador. The same year, the commission reorganized the magistracy. Labrador was administered by the district magistrate in St Anthony, although in 1938, Commissioner for Justice L.E. Emerson recommended a separate magistrate for the Labrador territory and that Labrador Inuit become wards of the government (Emerson 1938). So far as I know, nothing came of these suggestions.

Magistrates administered public policy in rural Newfoundland and were ably assisted by a new rural police, the Newfoundland Rangers. The rangers provided a wider range of economic and social services than rural residents had ever known (Horwood 1986). As is evident from the many references from rangers cited throughout this book, the rangers chronicled rural social and economic life to an extent not equalled until the academic studies of the 1960s and 1970s. Less obvious was the rangers' intelligence-gathering function, channelling information and complaints from the hinterland to the commissioner of justice. An example of this occurred in 1947 when the chief ranger in St John's sent confidential letters to all rangers requesting the views of people in their district regarding union with Canada, the return of responsible government, or continuation of the commission of government. The Southeastern Labrador rangers reported that most people favoured union with Canada.

The rangers collected this information in the context of the national convention then considering Newfoundland's political future, and this requires some comment. Following the economic prosperity generated in Newfoundland and Labrador by military-base construction during the Second World War, British prime minister Attlee announced in December 1945 that a national convention would be assembled to consider Newfoundland's future (Noel 1971, 245). The following June, residents of Newfoundland voted for the first time since 1932, electing forty-five delegates to the convention which was held in St John's between September 1946 and January 1948. This election of delegates marked the first time Labrador residents (excepting those in Moravian communities) had voted.

The convention's mandate was twofold: to examine the economic and financial situation and to propose to the British government alternative forms of government. Delegates soon split into two groups, one favouring a return to the responsible government suspended in 1934, and led by Major Peter Cashin, and another favouring confederation with Canada, led by Joseph R. Smallwood. The convention proceedings were a media event, broadcast nightly on the radio. There is much that can be said about the proceedings of the convention but I limit my comments to one point: the fishery. Pro-responsible leader Cashin warned of the negative impact confederation would have on Newfoundland's small industries, such as agriculture (a point even Smallwood acknowledged), and on the fishery. Significantly, Section 3 of the Terms of Union placed the fishery under Canadian jurisdiction (BNA Act, Section 91[12]): a marine resource administered by inland bureaucrats. During the past two decades, Newfoundland has repeatedly tried without success to regain control of the fishery and, failing that, to implement joint management.

Advocates of confederation paraded social benefits guaranteed under the then-emerging Canadian welfare state, such as family allowances. Although confederation does not appear to have been the will of the convention, skilful political manoeuvring by pro-confederates eventually placed confederation on the first of the two referenda necessary to secure a majority vote.

The pace of change affecting southeastern Labrador accelerated during the second half of the nineteenth century. Most of the services the Newfoundland government extended to Labrador were intended to serve primarily Newfoundland fishers and only secondarily the region's permanent Settlers. The impact of externally initiated change trickled down to the Settlers. Consequently, while Settlers were not entirely passive victims of those controlling state policies, neither were they masters of their own destiny. Romantic notions to the contrary, the Settlers occupied the periphery rather than centre stage; they played supporting rather than leading roles, and their ability to modify events and policies was not great compared to forces such as the state.

8

Compatible Developments

This chapter and the next describe six of the many developments and events occurring in southeastern Labrador during the first half of the twentieth century, subdivided into two broad types: developments compatible with the Settlers' dispersed and mobile lifestyle and those which were not. Thus, the first type of development, discussed in this chapter, appears to have had relatively little impact on the dispersed and transhumant Settler lifestyle, while those described in the next chapter have had a major impact on the Settlers.

The period between 1900 and 1949 is of immense importance in understanding communities of today because it constitutes the 'before' that has been irrevocably changed since Newfoundland and Labrador became Canada's tenth province in 1949. It is also a period of many significant events – the tragic influenza epidemic of 1918–19, the Labrador boundary decision of 1927, the international depression of the 1930s, two world wars, confederation with Canada, and more. Yet despite the many significant changes of this period, 1900–49 was also the twilight of the traditional Settler lifestyle, the era romanticized by contemporary Labradorians in song and story (cf. *Them Days* magazine).

Before discussing three resource-based industries which essentially dovetailed with the traditional Settler lifestyle, I briefly discuss several massive developments once planned for southeastern Labrador. These failed to occur but set the stage for the future by opening our imaginations to the range of possibilities.

FORGOTTEN DREAMS

In 1909 the Labrador Syndicate Ltd, a group of London capitalists, proposed a little-known development which would have dramatically changed southeastern Labrador. The syndicate applied to the Newfoundland government for permission to build a railway from central Canada to the Labrador coast and to construct harbour facilities (Labrador Syndicate 1909–30).

A related component of the syndicate's version of this grandiose scheme, also proposed at about the same time, involved the construction of a ten-mile-long dam across the Strait of Belle Isle. Atop the dam would be a rail causeway facilitating rail lines to St John's. The dam would also deflect the cold Labrador current back into the Arctic, thereby enabling the Gulf Stream to warm the climate of Newfoundland, the maritimes, and the northeastern United States (Burns 1921). Clearly the syndicate's megaprojects would change the lives of many more people than the handful of Settler families scattered along the southeastern Labrador coast.

The Labrador Syndicate also applied for, and received, exclusive two-year rights to explore five hundred square miles at Sandwich Bay for minerals (Watson 1910). About the same time, the syndicate applied for exclusive rights for oil exploration along the coast between St Lewis Inlet and Pinware (it may be added that this is the first reference to petroleum exploration in Labrador known by the writer).

The syndicate's development intentions for areas outside southeastern Labrador were equally impressive and included plans to harness Muskrat Falls (on what is now the lower Churchill River) in order to manufacture 'nitrates from the atmosphere and Soda and bleaching powder from salt by means of electric power generated at Muskrat Falls' (Owen 1911). However, by 1911, the Newfoundland government became uncharacteristically cautious about the syndicate's proposals. That year, the Newfoundland minister of agriculture and mines wrote Britain's colonial secretary Robert Watson suggesting that before mineral rights to Sandwich Bay were approved, the prospective mine sites should be examined. The government also qualified its permission to harness Muskrat Falls, allowing the syndicate only one-third of its hydro potential (ibid.).

Even though the syndicate's proposed rail link and harbour south of Battle Harbour were not constructed, the idea survived for some years, as the following wartime quote from Dr Grenfell suggests:

Consultations which I had in Ottawa showed that the authorities there are seriously considering a railway line from Quebec to the Atlantic coast near

Battle Harbour. It would have been invaluable at this time when tonnage is scarce, food queues so long in London, and while supplies are still plentiful on this side. It would involve only two nights at sea, for a steamer going twenty-five knots, from land to land; and in time of peace would shorten the mail service to Chicago by twenty-four hours. The untold water power available from the big, rapid rivers crossed would supply all power possibly needed; and although the mineral and industrial expansion possibly attendant is not immediately apparent, without any question new remunerative openings for constructive labour would be discovered. We have afforded all the information we could give and firmly believe in the project for the world as well as for the Empire. Dr. Grieve, so long resident at Battle Harbour, believes that a winter harbour could be maintained near Cape Charles. (1918, 122)

Grenfell may have been referring to the proposal of a Quebec firm. Later, in the 1920s, a railway was proposed between the Lake St John region of Quebec and the Labrador coast near Cape Charles. Then, following the Labrador boundary decision of 1927, Reginald Saunders Meredith, a Briton, along with several Quebec partners of the Quebec firm of Quebec Labrador Railway Company (QLRC), sought to renew the approval to build such a railway, apparently first granted in 1913 to the Canadian North American Corporation (CNAC) Ltd. Meredith and his associates sought to use this latter firm as a 'parent company' which would negotiate on behalf of the QLRC to buy Labrador (and solve Newfoundland's financial difficulties), construct docks, a town site, and airport at Cape Charles, and then construct an east–west railway (Meredith 1934). Meredith argued that the railway and new port would enable a three-day Atlantic crossing between Europe and Canada, but British and Newfoundland authorities were openly sceptical of the scheme. Remarkably, the proposal lingered for about a decade and, apparently, was ultimately rejected on a technicality. P.A. Clutterbuck (1945) explains that the Newfoundland government passed an act in 1913, granting the Corporation (CNAC) certain rights and facilities, subject to the condition that the act would lapse if the corporation did not commence construction of the railway within four years from the date of the passing of the act and did not complete it within ten years. Although Newfoundland Act 14 of 1916 and 5 of 1924 subsequently extended this time limit, the corporation ultimately failed to start construction of the railway within four years and the rights granted to them finally lapsed in 1928 (ibid.).

However bizarre these projects seem today, they were probably no more outrageous than others proposed or completed within what is now the province of Newfoundland and Labrador. Nevertheless, some of the developments and events which did occur in southeastern Labrador were to have relatively few consequences for the dispersed Settler communities.

THE MODERN HERRING FISHERY

Herring has long been important to Settlers and non-residents as bait for codfish, as dog food, and as a part of the winter diet. In addition to the Settlers' subsistence fishery, southeastern Labrador has experienced two commercial herring bonanzas since the mid-nineteenth century. The first occurred during the last four decades of the century (especially from 1860 to 1880), while the second began during the 1930s.

In 1923 Abbott noted the twentieth-century potential of this fishery but added that there was little interest in it at that time. He recommended it be developed in much the same way as the herring fishery of Norway (1990, 14). However, nothing appears to have come of this recommendation. During his 1937 visit to Labrador, Tanner was impressed by the number, size, and high fat content of Labrador herring. He mentioned the nineteenth-century commercial fishery (even though, following Gosling, he abbreviated its actual duration by about fifteen years) and observed that herring fishing aroused little commercial interest, even though fishers took some herring for bait (1944, 761). Tanner was right about the high quality of Labrador herring, and if his visit had occurred a year or so later (or had he visited Cape Charles), he would have observed a small but vibrant herring industry. Newfoundland capital financed this industry, which began in the late 1930s and lasted until the late 1950s. It was an important, although part-time and seasonal, source of employment for many Labrador people who worked as herring fishers and processors.

Cape Charles informants described a herring plant which operated first from Wall's Island, Cape Charles, and later at nearby Banikhin's Island. Francis Banikhin, whom informants characterized as a 'Russian Jew from St John's,' started this plant about 1937.

Informants appreciated the employment Banikhin provided. Herring fishing occurred from August onward, but most locals worked for herring producers in the fall, from late September to late October, after the catching (and most of the making) of cod. At Cape Charles, fishers often worked for Banikhin part-time, during the afternoons, leaving them the morning to fish or work at other jobs. Pay was hourly, 15 cents per hour in 1938. Some men only sold herring to Banikhin, while others produced pickled herring. Those working at producing herring worked at 'gibbing' the fish, that is, at removing the gills and entrails.

Fishers usually caught herring in gill-type nets with about a two-and-one-half-inch mesh size, though they also used seines. Banikhin furnished those selling herring to him with nets and employed fishers on shares; they initially received $2.50 per tub of herring. Word of Banikhin's plant spread, attracting some twenty-five L'Anse au Loup men to work at Cape Charles in 1941 (Guzzwell 1941a, 1). Improved market conditions led Banikhin to raise his price to $5 in 1945, competing favourably with the $3 offered fishers using their own nets at Red Bay (Delaney 1945, 19). Banikhin's son Wilfred managed a herring plant at Matthew's Cove (near Battle Harbour), which operated until about 1954. The Banikhin Island plant burned in 1957 or 1958, leading Banikhin to purchase an abandoned herring facility from Curling Fisheries of Newfoundland, at Azzize's Harbour.

Demand for herring was high during and following the Second World War (Smallwood 1984, 924). In the fall of 1941, herring plants were opened at Comfort Bight and Rocky Bay for the production of herring meal and oil (Dwyer 1941c, 1). Describing why the Rocky Bay herring plant, complete with its 'forty thousand dollars worth of machinery,' was being 'rushed to completion' for the summer of the 1941 herring fishery, Port Hope Simpson ranger Dwyer notes that the herring oil 'is needed for the war to make explosives' (1941a, 1).

Just why this twentieth-century herring fishery ceased is not known. Some suggest that local herring stocks were unpredictable; market conditions, particularly during the war, may have also played a role. When one considers times such as the summer of 1944, when herring were especially plentiful, it is hard to imagine such a vibrant industry failing. That year, herring compensated for a poor cod fishery and constituted roughly 13 per cent ($31,500.30 of $233,549.44) of all goods exported from Battle Harbour (Christian 1945a, 2).

Finally, during the period described here, some Settlers from the area from Battle Harbour south travelled to the Corner Brook and Bay of Islands area to work in the fall herring fishery. Scheduled steamer service between Battle Harbour and Humber Mouth (Corner Brook) facilitated travel to and from Corner Brook. Labrador men probably learned about the fall herring fishery from those Battle Harbour/Cape Charles area men who worked seasonally in the Corner Brook pulp and paper mill beginning in the late 1920s. A number of marriage and kin connections continue to link this part of Labrador with the Corner Brook area, which explains why many families relocated there during the resettlement era (see Chapter 10).

THE MODERN WHALING INDUSTRY

Most of the whaling that has occurred in Labrador, perhaps with the exception of the sixteenth-century Basque whaling industry in the Labrador Strait, took place along the southeastern coast during the first half of the twentieth century.

In 1840 the Newfoundland government passed an act to encourage the whale fishery (Smallwood 1984, 597). This appears to have had little effect on whaling in southeastern Labrador, although in 1876, the government mail officer, James Prendergast, observed two schooners involved in the whale fishery. One was said to have manufactured its oil near Punch Bowl (near Hawke Harbour), but Prendergast adds that their whaling had not been very successful (1877, 1114).

The invention of the explosive harpoon gun by the Norwegian Svend Foyn, the depletion of Norwegian whale stocks, and the promotional efforts by Adolphe Neilson, the Newfoundland government's fishery adviser, led to the expansion of whaling in Newfoundland, beginning in 1897–8 (Murphy 1903, 131). Initial interest in, and profits from, the industry were high. The realization that Norway had nearly depleted its whale resources in just fourteen years led the Newfoundland government to pass the Whaling Act (1902; amended in 1927). This required licences from the state, and stipulated that whaling stations be located at least fifty miles apart, that flensed whale carcasses be towed 50 miles from shore and that each factory be charged licence fees of $1500 (Sergeant 1953, 687). By 1903, at least fifteen applications had been submitted for whaling stations along the Labrador coast. One of these stations (at Antle's Cove, near Cape Charles) opened in 1904. The Hawke Harbour station opened in 1905 (Dawe 1906, 149). Catches and profits dropped after that and by 1913 only Hawke Harbour remained. However, Grady opened in 1927 (Bird 1977, 8; Mallalieu 1929, 26) and operated until 1934 (Sergeant 1953, 691).[1] Pomphrey visited Grady in 1931 and reports that the station was closed for one year because of an 'overproduction of oil' (1932, 174). Hawke Harbour closed permanently in 1959 when a fire destroyed the plant; it was probably not rebuilt because of declining demand for whale products.

Organization of the Whale Fishery

Norwegians owned (in whole or part) all southeastern Labrador whaling stations. However, Newfoundland companies operated some stations and there were many turnovers in ownership and operation. The St John's firm Bowring Brothers, which supplied the Carbonear-based Labrador fishing fleet bound for nearby Cape Charles, operated a whaling station at Antle's Cove during its short life (ca. 1904–12). Bowring Brothers hunted the coast from Barge Point (south of Cape Charles) north to Ship Harbour (Bowring Brothers 1903). Further north, at Hawke Harbour, a Labrador informant said that a 'Norwegian company owned [the Polar Whaling Company] Hawke Harbour ... They got permission from the Newfoundland government to build there but they had to have a Newfoundland crew [working] on the land.' Similarly, Stevenson mentions that the St John's firm A.H. Murray was the Newfoundland agent for the Polar Whaling Company (1951, 21). Grady was a joint British-Norwegian company. Its management and one-third of its workers were Norwegian.

An economic division of labour between Norwegian and Newfoundland workers existed at all stations throughout the approximately fifty-year history of whaling in southeastern Labrador. Governor MacGregor noted this on his 7 August 1905 visit to Antle's Cove. He observed that the station employed fifty men ashore, all 'natives of Newfoundland,' and paid them a monthly salary. Norwegians working on shares manned one steam whaling vessel (MacGregor 1909, 72). Generally, Newfoundlanders (and a few Labrador Settlers) worked at the less desirable shore jobs while the Norwegians worked offshore. For example, during the 1944 season, 160 Newfoundlanders and 4 Labradorians worked for the Polar Whaling Company at Hawke Harbour, the latter group presumably doing manual jobs (Christian 1945a, 2).

In 1981 I interviewed a Newfoundlander who had worked at the Grady Island whaling station in the early 1930s. He claimed that Norwegians 'always got the best jobs.' And when discussing Hawke Harbour in the 1950s, a Labrador informant explained that Norwegians always manned the 'killing ships.' When Newfoundlanders (like Isaac Smith, who worked at Hawke Harbour in the 1950s) were allowed to work on the whaleboats, it was usually as temporary replacements for Norwegian crewmen, and the 'gunner [harpooner] was always a Norwegian' (Smith 1988). The hierarchy that saw Norwegians, Newfoundlanders, and finally 'Labradormen' in a descending order of socio-economic status does not appear to have generated the kind of antipathy and dissent that we might expect. In fact the Norwegians seem to have been well regarded, probably because they brought some of the first wage labour to the region and exemplified the local ethos of hard work.

Labrador men who worked at the whaling stations usually did so after completion of the summer fishery, although Stevenson reports that during the exceptionally busy July of 1951, efforts were made to hire local workers from Venison Islands and other nearby localities. Normally, however, Labrador Settlers replaced Newfoundland whale factory employees in the fall, when, as one Labrador informant put it, the Newfoundlanders got 'homesick' and returned to the island. The stations could, and occasionally did, operate throughout mild winters, but were usually forced to close in autumn, when the winches (used to hoist whales onto slipways for butchering) and hoses (used for supplying fresh water) froze. Just before the stations closed for winter, employers might give Settler workmen potatoes and other remaining foodstuffs, in tacit recognition for, as an informant put it, 'coming [to work] when they wanted us.' Even when deserted for the winter, the factories occasionally attracted Settlers who came for whale meat for their sledge dogs. Some whaling stations hired Settlers as winter caretakers. For example, the brothers Albert and William Pye of Cape Charles worked as winter caretakers at Antle's Cove.

Whaling crews (numbering twelve men – Pendergast 1981, 11) left the whaling stations Monday morning and, Smith (1988) claims, were not permitted to return until Friday, unless to tow in whales or to obtain supplies. Stevenson's unpublished diary covers the 1950 and 1951 seasons and describes whaling boats returning to Hawke Harbour fairly regularly to deposit whale carcasses. Whaleboats used at Grady were powerful vessels, measuring between seventy and eighty feet, which cruised at about twenty knots but were capable of much faster speeds (Davis 1977, 4).

Whales might be encountered anywhere, but generally there was some pattern to the hunt, depending on season, location, and species. The range of area hunted expanded throughout the history of the Labrador hunt, probably reflecting improving technology and decreasing whale stocks. By the late 1940s, Hawke Harbour whaling boats headed south in June to the Strait of Belle Isle and Gulf region. There, large pods of blue (sulphur-bottom) and, later, fin whales congregated to feed on krill (Stevenson 1951, 3). Even so, by 1951, Stevenson reports a dramatic decline in the Strait blue whale kill. This decline was from forty-eight (1948) to twenty-eight (1949) to sixteen (1950) to ten (1951) and was almost certainly caused by hunting pressures from Hawkes Harbour and from the Olsen Whaling Company, in Northern New-foundland (ibid., 3). By July, whaling for a broader range of species took place closer to Hawke Harbour. Crews killed some whales close to shore, where they had followed spawning capelin, and killed others about one hundred and sixty kilometres offshore, at the edge of the continental shelf.

A Labrador informant provided a complete description of the hunt:

They had these whalers, see, what we call 'gun boats.' They'd go out now and they had the harpoons ... we say harpoons, that's what they fire [with the] big line on 'em. They fire at the whale and stick it into 'em, well the whale'l go on. Then they fire the dumb harpoons with no lines on 'em to kill 'en. Yeh, they kill 'en. Now they had a big boat [i.e., mother ship] there for towin 'em in. Used to tow eighteen or nineteen to a tow. That's what she used to tow, she was a great big boat. You'd kill the whales, they was blowed up with a steam pump from the whaler. Then they were flagged. Now you [the whaler's skipper] was talkin to this big one [the mother ship] all the time, tellin' how many you had and what position the whale was into, because she [the mother ship] had five whalers see to look after. Now when she'd get her tow, she pick 'em up see, she'd go on to Hawke Harbour. Now you'd kill away at the whales, kill away at 'em, and they'd pick 'em up.

Killing whales was unpleasant business. Stevenson reports that approximately one-quarter of the whales killed during summer were pregnant. One of three fin-backs killed on 14 July 1950 was a lactating female, separated from its calf while nursing. In another gripping case that occurred on 31 July 1951, an overzealous gunner harpooned a young humpback which had leaped on its mother's back when she was harpooned. Inspector Stevenson makes little attempt to conceal his disgust with such violations of the International Whaling Act, which prohibited killing lactating and undersized whales.

While the Norwegian-designed, four-barbed exploding harpoon heads were obviously more effective than earlier harpoons, Smith (1988) claims that even these harpoons missed their target seven out of ten times! Sperm whales were especially dangerous, even vindictive, and might turn on the whaleboat that had harpooned them. In one of many stories about killing sperm whales, Newfoundlander Pendergast, a veteran of many summers at Hawke Harbour, recalled: 'One time we killed a sperm, and he come back, well, the feller to the wheel, rung ahead instead of ringin' back and it blew our midship, and the whale's tail swung and beat up our lifeboat and the whole lot. We had to go in, but we got the whale' (1981, 10). Crews flagged slain and inflated whales with bamboo poles with flags on top. Prendergast explained that these could be detected 'with the radar for miles.' Killer whales sometimes consumed flagged whales (Stevenson 1951, 7).

Once towed to the factories, crews temporarily tied slain whales to buoys to await processing. Time was important, since the longer the time between the killing and butchering of a whale, the poorer the quality of the whale products produced. For example, on 23 July 1951 Stevenson reports a large number of kills and production slow-downs, resulting in 'rotten whales and no. 4 (grade) oil' (1951, 10). Whales had to be butchered within thirty-three hours after being killed to produce the best (number 1) oil (ibid., 2).

The main work of Newfoundlanders and Labradorians began once the whales were towed to the stations. The stations themselves were enormous complexes, which all agree were smelly, smoke-filled, and dirty. All consisted of 'An ugly square box-like building, several smaller buildings, great tanks for steaming, boiling, and settling, a black cylindrical chimney and a slip or inclined plane, very slippery in sooth, on which the bodies of the whales are drawn up' (Townsend 1907, 93–4). The landing slip at Grady inclined upward from the water about ninety feet to the huge rectangular flensing platform, capable of holding six whales at a time (Kent 1928).

Davis describes the butchering procedure at Grady: 'Well, when they'd get a whale, the first thing they'd do was to haul 'er up on the top-slip, that's where I used to work. They cut 'en up there, cut 'en right up altogether, bones and all. The whales was just level with the top of the boiler. They'd just shove the pieces of whale over and it'd run down in the boiler, and when they'd get 'en full, they'd screw down the cover, right tight, put the steam on, hundreds of pounds of pressure' (1977, 7). During the pressure cooking, the crew rendered the whale fat and pumped it to holding tanks, where it was stored until shipped. Then they removed the remaining bones and meat through a hatch in the bottom of the boiler (Bird 1977, 9) and transported it by conveyer belt to the drier. From then on, the possibility of spontaneous combustion increased, particularly if the guano was not properly dried or contained too much fat. Workers dried guano in iron cylindric driers (two of these survive at Antle's Cove). Guano produced from this process was 'finer than flour' and was later bagged in fine 'brin sacks' each holding 100 pounds of guano fertilizer.

Whale-oil was the main product. Davis (1977, 6) describes getting seven or eight forty-five-gallon drums of 'pure oil' from a whale's head, and Smith (1988) claims that one sperm whale could render up to 125 barrels of oil. Some species produced more oil than others. Stevenson mentions that the relatively rare humpbacks produced more oil than blue whales (sulphur-bottoms) (1951, 6).

According to Joel C. Goldthwait (conversion with author, 14 April 1988), Hawke Harbour exported large amounts of whale meat to Norway to be used as food for the Norwegian silver fox industry. Finally, an informant claimed that the Hawke Harbour plant manufactured soap, and W.A. Paddon reports eating a locally 'tinned whale beef' there (1947, 52).

My analysis of the number of whales killed at Cape Charles (Antle's Cove) and Hawke Harbour between 1904 and 1915 reveals that the highest percentage of whales killed were fin (85 per cent), followed by humpbacks (12 per cent), sulphur-bottoms or blues (2 per cent), and sperm (1 per cent) (JHA for all data except 1904 and 1905, taken from MacGregor 1909, 72). Inexplicably, the number of whales recorded in official data is far lower than mentioned by Pendergast and later Stevenson at Hawke Harbour. For example, Pendergast claims: 'we'd get anywhere from 200 to 500 whales' each summer at Hawke Harbour (1981, 9), ten to fifteen per day (Smallwood 1984, 854). Pendergast's estimates are supported by Stevenson's counts from 1949, 1950, and 1951. Stevenson claims that 349, 330, and 378 whales were killed in these years (respectively) and that the last number (378) was a record for the Hawke Harbour station. One reason for the discrepancy is that by mid-century, the technique for killing whales had become even more deadly.

The Impact of the Whaling Industry

Opinions about wages are usually relative and difficult to compare, but the local economic impact of whaling appears to have been beneficial. Although some controversy existed about pollution from whaling, Labrador people generally welcomed the industry even though few actually worked in it. One who did claimed that 'we used to almost live on that' (seasonal work at Hawke Harbour). Ironically, this same man complained of the pay of $70 per month or, as he calculated, about 11 cents per hour. Newfoundlander Pendergast reports earning $16 per month working full-time as an 'oil rat' (i.e., a person who works on the oil boilers) at Hawke Harbour, in the 1920s (1981, 6). Pendergast recalls that his lowest net pay for a summer's work at Hawke Harbour was $123 while his highest was $1775 (ibid., 12). Stevenson states that workers were non-unionized and implies that their 50-cent hourly wages (75 cents on Sundays) were low, compared to unionized 1950 wages (1950, 7).

However, most men praised the pay. For example, describing his part-time work ('landin' coal, helpin' the firemen, draggin' around whales from boiler to boiler') at Grady during the summer of 1928, Bird boasts that his 25 cents per hour was 'big money them times' (1977, 8). Likewise Edward Pardy earned $45 per month one winter 'cookin' for the Newfoundlanders' at Grady and considered that 'Good money!!' (1977, 10). Pardy also applauded the fact that in addition to their wages, everything from clothing to cigarettes was 'found' (provided) to workers (ibid., 11).

A negative impact of the whaling industry was its alleged environmental impact on the cod fishery. For example, we read in the 1904 *Journal of the House of Assembly* that 'many people believe that the destruction of these great animals would injure the cod fishery' (Murphy 1903, 131). Laracy reports such fears at Cape Charles in 1904 but adds that four fishers enjoyed their best catch in years from a cod trap located a few hundred yards from the Antle's Cove whale station (1973, 13). However, Stevenson describes whale intestines being dumped into Hawke Harbour during peak periods of production in 1950 and 1951. He feared the practice would either foul fishing gear or boat propellers and warned the factory manager of the possibility of a lawsuit against the company.

Such contamination is illustrated by the legal case launched by Harbour Grace merchant John McRae, whose company R.D. McRae and Sons had supplied Newfoundland fishers and Labrador Settlers at Big Grady Island for almost one hundred years prior to the establishment of the whaling station there in 1927 (Kent 1928). The British Norwegian Whaling Company established their factory during that summer near fresh water at Waterin' Cove, about nine hundred metres from Mc-Crae's fishing premises (Kent 1928; Noseworthy 1977, 11). The cod-fishing season was nearly over before whaling began in September, yet McRae complained about several kinds of pollution, such as whale grease on nets and traps (Davis 1977, 8), and took the whaling company to court. In his judgment, Supreme Court judge James Kent found the whaling company guilty of polluting the public waters off the Labrador coast and restrained them from further operations. The company dismantled its factory and sold it to the Polar Whaling Company at Hawke Harbour.[2]

Because few Settlers worked at the whaling stations, and since those who did worked only after the summer fishery or during winter, southeastern Labrador's fifty-year-long whaling industry had relatively little impact on the region's communities. Settler families continued to practise their traditional lifestyle almost as if the busy whaling plant nearby did not exist. Given the seasonal or short-term involvement of local Settlers with whaling, the industry supplemented, rather than replaced, the fishery and therefore did not foster centralization.

Other social effects on southeastern Labrador people may only be hinted at. As noted, relations among Settlers and the Newfoundlanders and Norwegians appear to have been good, even if asymmetrical. Some marriages undoubtedly occurred, although I have proof of only one case, the marriage between Amelia (Millie) Pye of Cape Charles and Newfoundlander Ira Kennedy, a worker at the Antle's Cove factory. As noted above, both Amelia's father (William) and her father's brother (Albert) worked as winter caretakers at Antle's Cove.

The Demise of Whaling

The major reason for the demise of southeastern Labrador's modern whaling industry was the gradual decline in the demand for whale products, especially whale-oil. One Labrador informant claims that the fate of Hawke Harbour was apparent several years before its closure and that its workforce dwindled from 260 men working on shore to about two dozen. However, Stevenson estimates that approximately 250 men worked at Hawke Harbour in 1950 and, as stated, a record of 378 whales were taken there in 1957. The same Labrador informant implies that the fire which destroyed the station had suspicious origins. In contrast, Mr von B. Neuhauser, who visited Hawke Harbour in August 1959, reports that the station had been closed for several years because of the low price of whale products but that the plant was still owned by a Captain Burgenson, of St John's (1959, 71). Little evidence remains today of a once-flourishing industry.

THE FUR INDUSTRY

Fur-trapping has been an important fall and winter economic activity in the region since the French regime. De Boilieu ([1861] 1969) devotes

a chapter to 'Fur Animals and Seals' and describes several mid-nineteenth-century trapping methods, some of which are still used. I discuss
the fur industry here because of the high demand for furs, particularly
foxes, during the early decades of this century. A new element that
emerged during this period was the controversy about the trapping and
farming of fur- bearing animals.

History

Until the beginning of this century, the Hudson's Bay Company's
Cartwright post was the most important one in Labrador. Baine Johnston operated further south, at Battle Harbour. These were the main
(and in some years, only) suppliers of provisions during winter. Around
1900, thirty-year-old Samuel Butler Russell Fequet, a native of Old Fort
on the Quebec North Shore, moved to Paradise River and opened a fur-
trading post (Bourque 1975, 2–3). Shortly after 1906–8, Fequet bought
Hunt and Henley's store and fish plant at Pack's Harbour (ibid., 4), and
Gordon notes that Fequet relocated his business to Cartwright in the
summer of 1918 (1972, 128). Before that, in the fall of 1915, Fequet
opened a small power-driven sawmill at Red Island Brook, near Paradise Arm (Gordon 1972, 36; J.C. Davis 1976, 14), which operated inter-
mittently at least until 1925 (ibid., 246). Fequet also opened a store at
North West River, in the 1930s (Bourque 1975, 7), which was still operating in the fall of 1941 (Elson 1981, 38). In short, during the time period
discussed here, the locally popular Fequet offered competition to the
Hudson's Bay Company.

About 1907, the French-owned Revillon Frères Trading Company Ltd
opened a fur-trading post at Muddy Bay, about ten kilometres west of
Cartwright. This operated until around 1912. It was one of several
Revillon posts opened during the first decade of the twentieth century;
a longer-operating and better-known Revillon post was located at North
West River, across the river from the Hudson's Bay Company's post
(Zimmerly 1975, 175).

In and near Sandwich Bay there was keen competition for the skins
of trapped animals among Fequet's, the HBC and for a short time, the
Revillon company. By spring 1913, however, a new ingredient was
introduced when Dr Grenfell persuaded a biologist-turned-fur-farmer
from Brooklyn, New York, Clarence Birdseye, to come to Labrador and
investigate the possibilities of establishing a commercial fox farm.
Birdseye spent the winter of 1912–13 travelling in Lake Melville and

purchased the short-lived Revillon post at Muddy Bay in spring 1913 (McClure 1975). Birdseye returned permanently to the United States in 1917, but during his four years in Labrador, he introduced fur farming, thereby engendering a debate about trapping versus raising foxes.

Organization of Trapping

Southeastern Labrador trappers pursued many species of fur-bearing animals, including varieties of the coloured fox, the lynx, and marten and riverine species such as beaver, otter, muskrat, and mink. The availability of species, fluctuating demand, and the varying importance of trapping within the region meant that trappers pursued some fur species more than others. Throughout the first three decades of this century, international markets favoured silver fox, and after that, lynx and otter became popular.

As noted, each community's adaptation to local conditions meant that trapping effort within the region varied considerably. Because of the fur habitat along the several large rivers draining into Sandwich Bay, it is hardly surprising that trapping was more important in this bay than along the outer coast. Indeed, communities such as Paradise River were largely dependent on trapping. Far south of Sandwich Bay, however, outside communities such as George's Cove relied very little on trapping (Gordon 1972, 113). Likewise, at Green Bay (just south of the study area) a former resident recalled that men cut firewood in fall but might occasionally do a little trapping, in order to 'give 'em a spell from the woods.' For the majority of communities in the region, the importance of trapping lay between these two extremes. Men trapped within a radius of twenty-five to thirty kilometres from their winter homes for periods ranging from a day to a week. In short, except in Paradise River, trapping in southeastern Labrador never reached the 'florescence' Zimmerly (1975) describes for central Labrador during the early decades of this century.

It must be noted that variations in trapping effort between communities are not based solely on proximity to good trapping grounds. Dove Brook is only about twenty-five kilometres from Paradise River, yet many Dove Brook men trapped within twenty kilometres of their community for periods of a week or so. In contrast, the trips of Paradise River trappers lasted between seven weeks and three months, taking them as far as the headwaters of the St Augustine River (Lethbridge 1979, 35). Given the extent of such trap lines and the high prices paid for furs, it is not surprising that in the years preceding the flu epidemic of 1918, Paradise River was the largest settlement in Sandwich Bay, consisting of 'some twelve homesteads' (Gordon 1972, 36). As explained below, events beyond local control, specifically the influenza epidemic of 1918, decimated Paradise River and began the chain of events leading to the ascendancy of Cartwright.

Two other variables affected the trapping effort: fur prices and competing economic activities, particularly sealing. Individuals and whole communities trapped more in some years than others because of high fur prices. As an older Norman Bay informant explained, 'if you goes trapping, fits right out for trapping, you can't go sealing.' He went on to explain that netting harp-seals in the fall competed with furs during their best season, that you had to go 'outside' for harps, and that this implied that you 'neglect the fur.' Moreover, in his father's time (the first half of this century), his community's distance from Battle Harbour meant that seals had little value except for dog food. Marketing other seal products (such as skins and oil) was impossible because 'it would cost you a fortune now if you had to haul 'em to Battle Harbour, and that was the only company (Baine Johnston) was buyin' 'em, them times.' Thus, for extensive trapping effort to occur, such as at Paradise River, trappers needed access to both trapping grounds and markets. Conversely, communities near Battle Harbour were more dependent on sealing because of both resource availability and a local market for seal skins. In both instances, the emphasis on sealing or trapping profoundly affected a community's seasonal economic round and the timing of its transhumant migrations.

An older informant explained how Otter Bay trappers transported their equipment to the trapping grounds:

They'd go in back [along the Hawke River] ... to the intersection of the three forks. Every man would branch off on his own quarters, hey. From Otter Bay ... you can travel right up to Pinsent's Arm and they used to have a little boat ther' an' just 'cross the Arm ... Only an hour from that and you're on the river ... They had these canvas camps [tents], and their big wooden camp was in Pinsent's Arm, that's where they had he [the wooden camp] at. Well, they could go from our [Otter] Bay to Pinsent's Arm in one day to the wooden camp. Next day they'd go in on the river. Now they'd have probably a week in there in their canvas camp, they used to lug. There was two or three of them, see, in a crowd. Well, some would have the camp, more the grub and traps, one thing or the other. Once you was trappin' in there, your traps was buried in there, see. You'd only have to carry them once a year.

Trappers would usually walk to their trapping grounds in fall and would use 'rackets' (snowshoes) when sufficient snow accumulated. They sometimes used one or two dogs to haul a short (two-metre) komatik and several informants also mentioned that later in the winter, trappers used dog teams to travel to trapping grounds, particularly on short excursions to check traps (see Gordon 1972, 94). In autumn, trappers used canoes to reach trapping grounds.

Marketing

Demand for furs during much of the first half of this century was high and competition was keen. During most of this time, the Hudson's Bay Company post in Cartwright and Baine Johnston of Battle Harbour were the only suppliers of provisions during winter. Both outfitted Settler trappers and fishers on credit. As noted above, however, the monopoly of these two firms was challenged a number of times. Thus, Fequet's and Porter's challenged the Hudson's Bay Company's Sandwich Bay monopoly while the Campbells opened a store in St Michael's Bay in the early 1900s. This was the first store between Battle Harbour and Cartwright (Campbell 1984, 55). By (but probably before) January 1938, the Hubson's Bay Company operated a post at Frenchman's Island (Clark 1981, 18; Tanner 1944, 735).

Competition also came from transient fur buyers, who paid cash. An informant described the first three decades of this century by noting: 'There was all kinds of fur buyers goin' round then, English fur buyers, United States fur buyers. They was payin' the biggest kind of licence for comin' over buying furs, see.' The Reverend Mr Gordon encountered one such fur buyer, Mr Dave Borenstein, of Montreal, at Long Harbour (near Hawke Harbour) in late January 1918. After approximately two and one-half years in Labrador, Gordon had developed strong personal contacts with the employees of resident firms, particularly the Hudson's Bay Company, and this probably explains his negative reaction to Borenstein: 'Much as one desired the trapper to get the best price possible for his fur, I couldn't help but feel that our visitor [i.e., Borenstein] was taking an unfair advantage of the resident trading companies, for whereas a pirate trader could buy for cash, and then clear off, the local firms had to carry large stocks of food and materials, and more or less husband the trappers when fur returns were scarce' (1972, 113). Although initially wary of Borenstein, Gordon eventually found him a 'likeable chap.' He noted that the 'arrival of my companion (in Cartwright) was not greeted with much favour' by the 'two trading companies' (apparently Fequets and the Hudson's Bay Company) (ibid., 114).

Competition from transient traders such as Borenstein, as well as among resident traders, forced the latter to begin travelling the coast buying furs. Both Sam Fequet and, later, his right-hand man and nephew Steve MacDonald (Sam's sister's son) travelled the coast for this reason. Likewise, Cartwright Hudson's Bay Company employees travelled north and south of that community buying furs. Such competition increased fur prices, and Gordon notes that in 1917 a good silver fox sold for $1000 (1972, 92).

Clarence Birdseye's short-lived Muddy Bay fox farm created a seller's market for live foxes. Both Sandwich Bay Settlers and the Reverend Mr Gordon were wary of Birdseye's experiment, yet Birdseye continued to tour the coast seeking breeding stock and by March 1917 had a dozen or so mating pairs (Gordon 1972, 93). Birdseye purchased breeding stock from Settler trappers unable to resist the high prices he offered even though all knew the potential impact of a market flooded with farmed foxes. This contradiction is obvious from a conversation said to have taken place between one informant's father (Joe) and buyer Sam Fequet, at Otter Bay. Joe had caught a live silver fox and was apparently intending to sell it to Birdseye. My informant said that Fequet warned: 'Joe, you're ruinin' your own self for sellin' t' Birdseye ... live foxes ... you'll see the day that silver fox'll be down to five or six dollars. Sell 'en ner one, kill' en or sell 'en to me.'

As events unfolded, Birdseye left the coast in the fall of 1917, either because of the entrance of the United States into the First World War (McClure 1975, 6), because of orders from his company in New York to close down (Gordon 1972, 105), or because of some combination of the two. Birdseye's short-lived success may have influenced the establishment of the Hudson's Bay Company's fur farm, which operated during the early 1930s, also at Muddy Bay (Beare 1983, 23). Moreover, Birdseye's connections with New York City financiers and furriers may explain why the New York company of Charles S. Porter erected a fur-trading post at Cartwright, either in 1916 (Swaffield 1926) or in 1918 (Gordon 1972, 128).

The production of animal furs during the first half of this century did little to alter traditional Settler community patterns. Seasonal trapping was perfectly suited to the dispersed settlement pattern and to seasonal transhumance, because Settler homesteads and trapping territories were sufficiently spaced along the coast. Since trappers could successfully prepare, store, and transport furs for market, the potentially centralizing role markets played in other, heavier staples, such as fish or seals, was negated. And as Tanner (1944) showed in his illuminating comparison of Dove Brook (Sandwich Bay) Settlers, with their generalized economy, and the highly specialized Grand River (Lake Melville) trappers, trapping never became the focus of the southeastern Labrador economy. Some competition over trapping grounds undoubtedly occurred, although my impression is that this never reached the proportions of the more frenzied trapping 'florescence' of central Labrador. Had fur farming become an established industry, as buyers like Fequet warned, it could have removed trapping as an important fall and winter pursuit.

Similarly, neither the herring nor the whale fisheries affected the Settlers, for they also were compatible with the seasonal cycle of activities. Thus, it is not necessarily the scale of a development which explains its impact on, or compatibility with, the 'traditional' Settler lifestyle, but instead factors such as the labour requirement and seasonality of work. The developments which least influenced Labrador Settlers were those which dovetailed rather than competed with the annual Settler socio-economic cycle.

9

From Homesteads to Centres

Neither the modern herring fishery, whaling, nor the fur industry drew Settlers from their winter homesteads, whereas, three twentieth-century economic and institutional developments did. The first of these, the Grenfell Mission, actually began in the late nineteenth century and would eventually become the *de facto* government in southeastern Labrador. The second is the Labrador Development Company's timber-cutting operations in Alexis and St Lewis and St Michael bays. Timber cutting began in 1934 and produced Port Hope Simpson, Labrador's first modern company town. The third is the construction of various military installations during and after the Second World War. These, and other more recent centripetal policies and events, undermined many small and dispersed family homesteads, causing Settlers to move to growing centres.

THE GRENFELL MISSION

The Early Years

In 1891, Francis J. Hopwood, a member of the British Board of Trade and of the council of the Royal National Mission to Deep Sea Fishermen, travelled to St John's, Newfoundland, for a week-long business trip. Hopwood learned a great deal, and upon returning to England wrote a scathing six-thousand-word letter to the Royal National Mission's magazine, *Toilers of the Sea*, poignantly describing the horrifying conditions endured by Newfoundlanders fishing along the Labrador coast. He recommended that someone be sent to Newfoundland and Labrador to investigate the need for the Royal Mission's services (Kerr 1959, 50–7).

The following year, Wilfred Grenfell, a twenty-seven-year-old Royal National Mission doctor, journeyed to Newfoundland and Labrador and treated nine hundred people. The next year (1893), Baine Johnston and Company, St John's and Battle Harbour merchants, donated money for the first Grenfell hospital at Battle Harbour. The Grenfell mission had begun.

Since much has been written on Grenfell (cf. Berton 1978; Evans 1954; Kerr 1959; Kober 1979; Moore 1980; Porter 1975; Rompkey 1991; and others) only a few biographical points need be made here. First, Grenfell was one of those fascinating and contradictory products of Victorian England. An avid admirer of heroes, an athlete, and an indifferent medical student (during his second year, he attended only four of sixty lectures on medicine [Kerr 1959, 16]), Grenfell was 'saved' during a sermon by American evangelist Dwight Moody in 1885. Porter writes that Grenfell followed family friend Charles Kingsley by embracing the dual and interrelated doctrines of the 'new imperialism' and an impulsive version of 'muscular Christianity' (1975, 3). Muscular Christianity characterized the ideal Christian as a man of vigour and vitality. Grenfell approached his Labrador mission first as an evangelistic Christian, second as a phenomenal and often charismatic fund raiser, and finally, when called upon by patients, as an impetuous and impatient physician.

As Berton (1978) has written, Grenfell knew everyone and everyone knew Grenfell. His connections were instrumental in drawing a variety of influential and affluent people to Labrador, and for this alone Grenfell's contribution to the territory is unequalled.[1]

Grenfell chose Battle Harbour and, later, Indian Harbour, the site of the mission's second hospital, because both were then centres of Newfoundland's Labrador fishery, which he sought to serve. This is important because popular misconceptions (later fostered by Grenfell himself) of Grenfell's labouring amidst Labrador natives fail to recognize that northern Labrador Inuit were primarily left to the care of the Moravians, and Labrador Innu (Indians) spent most of their year as nomadic hunters in the Labrador interior. Thus, the choice of Battle Harbour and Indian Harbour was tied to the realities of Newfoundland's seasonal Labrador fishery. Had larger numbers of Newfoundland fishers congregated at Square Islands, Chateau, or some other harbour, Grenfell and what would become his mission would have followed. In 1905 Grenfell wrote that 'the only way for a Doctor to do justice to the sick and especially surgical cases, [is] to *centralize* them at a hospital on an extended coast like Labrador where travelling is so difficult' (1905a, my emphasis).

Grenfell's choice for his third hospital and eventual winter headquarters, the tiny northern Newfoundland village of St Anthony, was based on that community's location midway between the Newfoundland winter homes of Newfoundland's Labrador fishers and their summer fishing grounds along the Labrador coast, and the fact that the fishing fleet often stopped there en route to or from Labrador. But stationary hospitals could not serve all the medical needs of such fishers, or of Labrador's dispersed Settler population; more mobile hospital ships were needed. The first of these, the motor vessel *Sir Donald*, was donated in 1894 by Lord Strathcona (Sir Donald Smith, former innovative factor of the North West River Hudson's Bay Company's post), then president of the Bank of Montreal, the Hudson's Bay Company, and the Canadian Pacific Railway (Houghton 1966, 34). The *Sir Donald* would later be replaced by larger hospital ships, three of which were named *Strathcona*. When the Royal National Mission complained that it could not support Grenfell's plans for expansion, he turned instead to prominent philanthropists. He established committees in many Canadian, American, and British cities and began spending most winters on fund-raising tours. Consequently, Grenfell never wintered in Labrador.

Although highly principled and idealistic, Grenfell was realistic enough to accept occasional financial support for his mission from government, but he clearly opposed governmental administration. As he wrote in 1902, 'hospitals are best run, we believe, everywhere, not by government departments, but by philanthropic bodies' (119). In 1912, the Royal Mission supported an arrangement under which its Newfoundland and Labrador property would be held in trust by Grenfell, and, with participation from the international committees he had formed, Grenfell established the International Grenfell Association (IGA) (Kerr 1959, 53). By 1914, the medical facilities of the newly incorporated IGA included four hospitals and six nursing stations; Grenfell's mission treated over six thousand patients that year (Kerr 1959, 201).

Although the IGA sought to offer the entire range of health care, two health problems were especially acute during the early years: various 'deficiency diseases' (scurvy, rickets, beri-beri, etc.) and tuberculosis. The mission's agricultural program sought to decrease the causes of these deficiency diseases while various public health measures targeted tuberculosis. Some of the prophylactic and convalescent measures to reduce tuberculosis included Nurse Bailey's valiant attempts to implement Grenfell's 'no spitting' campaign at Forteau, persistent steps to encourage open windows and ventilation, and the eventual establishment of the region's sanatorium at Cartwright.[2]

The Development and Expansion of the Grenfell Mission

As word of Grenfell's mission spread, many physicians and nurses flocked to Labrador as salaried workers or volunteers. Among these was a former Royal Mission doctor, Harry Paddon, who took charge of the Indian Harbour hospital in 1912 and became central Labrador's main physician and the IGA's main ideologue. It was Paddon who would later describe the mission's 'fourfold' mandate as medical, educational, industrial, and agricultural (1930, 157).

Many American college students came for the adventure as 'WOPS' (workers without pay, IGA volunteers). Prominent American colleges and medical schools established traditions of serving the medical, educational, and other needs of particular fishing stations. For example, beginning in 1914, students from Columbia University's College of Physicians and Surgeons served at Spotted Island for a decade or so. By the summer of 1922, the Reverend Mr Gordon (1972, 203) observes that there were three Yale medical students at Spotted Island. Johns Hopkins students claimed Battle Harbour, Harvard students St Anthony, and so on. Working for Dr Grenfell's mission was clearly the fashionable thing to do.

Among Newfoundland's small wealthy class, however, involvement with Grenfell was less common. During his 1905 visit to Labrador, Governor MacGregor observed that although private individuals, churches, or schools had endowed the beds at the Indian Harbour hospital, no endowments had come from Newfoundland. The governor's sanguine prediction that endowments would come from wealthy Newfoundlanders if people only knew about the mission is, however, debatable. Opinion among Newfoundland's small gentry class was always divided about Grenfell and his work. For example, although Newfoundland's governor Harris was chairman of the Board of Directors of the Grenfell Association of Newfoundland, Prime Minister Squires and others in the business community bitterly opposed his involvement. The gentry opposed Grenfell because, with some justification, they believed he exaggerated the poverty of the colony's social and economic conditions so as to raise more money during his winter fundraising tours in the United States, England, and Canada. To the gentry, however, this was, quite simply, bad for business. The publicity Grenfell brought to Newfoundland also exposed class divisions popularly thought to be non-existent and piqued the inferiority complex of highly placed Newfoundlanders.

Grenfell's fervent, yet ecumenical, religiosity led him to oppose Newfoundland's denominational educational system (Grenfell 1913) because he correctly believed it exacerbated schisms within and between communities. Paradoxically, Grenfell praised the educational accomplishments of the Moravian missionaries among northern Labrador Inuit, and once contrasted the illiteracy of Newfoundland fishers generally with the case of an Inuk (singular of Inuit) who was 'called in to read and write a letter for a Newfoundland fisherman' (ibid. 175).

The Grenfell Mission and Centralization

The tragic influenza epidemic which struck Labrador in the fall and early winter of 1918–19 claimed sixty-nine of the three hundred people of Sandwich Bay (Gordon 1972, 142). The epidemic left many orphans, and the mission opened its first boarding-school at Muddy Bay to provide for their future. The Reverend Mr H. Kirby, predecessor to long-time Anglican minister Henry Gordon at Cartwright, as well as Gordon himself, had advocated such a school long before the epidemic (Gordon 1972, 107). Dr Harry Paddon vigorously supported the school which opened on 1 November 1920 with a staff of ten and forty orphan-pupils (ibid., 173).

It might be argued that the Grenfell Mission was as much an opportunistic follower of the events which shaped southeastern Labrador history as a catalyst for change. In much the same way as an intelligent scavenger would, the mission continuously surveyed the land and sea, looking for its next prospect. Thus, following the epidemic leading to Muddy Bay's boarding-school, Grenfell writes of plans to start 'a new nursing station at Cartwright with the money supplied by the Hudson Bay Company' (1920, 81). The Cartwright nursing station (later a regional hospital) joined a growing gravitational pull, which included relocation of the Muddy Bay school to Cartwright, and began to transform that community into a population centre.

Thus, the opening of the Muddy Bay boarding-school began a new and decisive chapter in the history of southeastern Labrador. Another boarding-school was established at Mary's Harbour, and both schools recruited children from nearby bays and coves. Eventually, families followed their children to Mary's Harbour and Cartwright, sounding the death-knell to the dispersed way of life that IGA planners considered obsolete.

In part, this movement of the population to 'inside' centres responded to the needs of the Grenfell Mission's increasing Settler clientele and a corresponding decrease in its focus on transient Newfoundland fishers. Thus, in 1929, Dr Paddon (108–9) reported a 60 per cent reduction in the Newfoundland floater fishery and a 75 per cent reduction in stationers. The centralization of Settlers to Cartwright and Mary's Harbour also signalled the beginning of the end of the 'outside' hospitals and the decline of the mobile medical services which had characterized the mission's first quarter-century (Kennedy 1988a).

Yet the growth of 'inside' centres did not cause the mission's involvement with 'outside' communities to cease altogether. In 1940, for example, the mission sent a nurse and a summer-school teacher to George's Cove, to serve the 150 people fishing nearby (Lewis 1940, 82). The George's Cove mission house was closed for the next eight years, but reopened in the summer of 1949 (Robbins 1949, 73). This pattern of intermittent, yet gradually decreasing involvement with outside communities continued to the 1960s. Thus, the mission operated its Spotted Island station, which began around 1926, during the summer of 1963 (Williams 1964).

Another branch of the mission's educational program utilized the energies of IGA WOPs and salaried staff, and included activities which the mission would call 'social development.' These included founding local chapters of Boy Scouts or Girl Guides, offering night classes, and hosting 'social evenings.' At these social evenings, Grenfell staff advertised that they would be 'at home' and welcomed local guests. Visiting nurse Anna Jones's description of one such evening at Battle Harbour illustrates the cultural distance between the affluent, educated, and probably boisterous Grenfell staff and the shy and subdued local population. Jones writes: 'We found the people had no idea of "taking part" in any games. The first half of the evening was spent by the staff's strenuous and solitary participation in games, such as "going to Jerusalem," and "Throw the Towel," to the silent and solemn astonishment of the audience. After considerable urging and actual shoving and pulling a small group were persuaded to take part; and to our joy, and probably for the first time in their lives, lost themselves completely with hilarious laughter in the game' (1921, 161). Appreciating the reticence and timidity still characteristic of many Settlers, I suspect the 'hilarious laughter' Jones triumphantly witnessed was prompted by the nervous tension and social ambiguities of such a staged spectacle rather than by the games themselves.

Another author explains that social evenings at the mission hall provided the locals with an opportunity to 'amuse themselves by playing the "gramophone" and such games as they knew' (Anonymous 1920b, 112–113). However, the author adds, 'things would not 'go,' unless there was someone to organize games and keep things moving' (ibid.). Near the end of the evening, the locals were allowed their traditional dances and the pace and character of the evening changed dramatically. Our author reports: 'Instantly sets would be organized for the native reel and the floor would fairly rock under the impact of forty-eight shuffling feet. As often as we saw this dance we never got over our bewilderment at its intricacies or at the marvellous ability of the fishermen to clog in high rubber boots' (ibid., 113).

These accounts provide some insight into the essentially colonial or interventionist (Rompkey 1991) character of the Grenfell Mission, the well-intentioned, though patronizing, perspective of Grenfell staff, and the ability of Settlers to accommodate each summer's influx of these educated, energetic yet impatient representatives of what sociologist Ferdinand Tonnies called *Gesellschaft* (society). Though materially poor, Settlers had a rich and valued sense of place and kin, and they must have felt grateful to their Grenfell patrons, yet intimidated and overwhelmed by their annual invasions. One might also consider the controlled and intricate dances, which awed our anonymous informant, as a metaphor for all that was complex and hidden in the *Gemeinschaft* (community) which Grenfell staff could observe but never fully comprehend.

Older locals remember the inflexible, patronizing manner of many mission personnel. Mission land was fenced, separating it from local communities. Grenfell staff did not hesitate to tell families where to move, both within communities and to other places. Some former residents of Battle Harbour remembered a poor man and his family who came expecting to winter at Gin Cove (near Mary's Harbour) but were denied permission to land by the autocratic Dr Moret, who, in the locals' memory, 'thought he owned Mary's Harbour.' The mission had its rules, such as that sled dogs must be penned or tied up after the 14th of May each year. One person opined that it 'seems like they [the mission] had the rule of the place.' A Settler told Schneider that, 'Grenfell was a dictator; they (the mission) told you what to do. He took sick people away. He tried to take Nellie's eye out because she was having trouble, but her mother wouldn't let him' (1984, 419).

Some mission staff are remembered as eccentric. Dr Helen Hosmer, for example, is remembered for dressing like a man, for her greying and short hair, and for wearing riding britches in a horseless land. Locals put it succinctly: it was a 'job to please her.' In sum, although Settlers said little, they remembered much; their accommodation to a mission which in so many ways they appreciated was also tinged with resentment.

More Social Engineering

Despite Grenfell's pessimism about the prospect of domesticating plants and animals in Labrador, he encouraged experimentation. One of his earliest (and, ultimately, unsuccessful) experiments involved domesticated reindeer. Although cautious, he also supported horticultural experimentation for what it would bring to Settlers: greater self-sufficiency, reduced dependence on merchants, and fewer deficiency diseases. The IGA's foremost proponent of horticulture was Grenfell's friend Fred C. Sears, professor of pomology (fruit cultivation) at Massachusetts Agricultural College. For a decade or so, beginning about 1928, Sears visited the Labrador coast most summers, investigating and implementing practical solutions to the natural impediments to horticulture (soil conditions, pest control, and so on [see Sears 1929]). The disjunction between official and Settler perspectives is suggested by the fact that all that older informants could remember about Professor Sears is that he was continuously taking pictures.

Another of Grenfell's many American friends and colleagues, Boston orthopaedic surgeon Dr Joel E. Goldthwait, also advocated agricultural development (cf. Goldthwait 1932, 36–7). Goldthwait proposed increasing protein intake through the consumption of dairy products and stressed the importance of good posture and diet for the maintenance of good health. Like his friend Grenfell in Labrador, Goldthwait explored the relationship between diet and health at his experimental 'Medfield Farms' in Massachusetts. Goldthwait's donation of the sixty-eight-foot pleasure yacht the *Jessie Goldthwait* (built for and named after Goldthwait's first wife, Jessie Sophia Rand Goldthwait) to the Grenfell mission in 1932, and its subsequent sale by the mission, meant that Goldthwait indirectly funded the Jessie Goldthwait dairy farm in St Anthony.

Probably because of his long tenure at the relatively temperate Lake Melville, Dr Harry Paddon's outlook for agriculture in Labrador was more favourable than Grenfell's. It is significant that Paddon's plan implied major sociocultural changes for the Settlers, whom he encouraged to grow crops. He reasoned that seasonal transhumance (and the mission's annual move between North West River and Indian Harbour) caused agricultural development in Lake Melville to stagnate. He argued that Settlers relied too heavily on fishing and trapping and on the merchants who purchased their catch. Increased gardening could lessen government relief and promote self-sufficiency (Paddon 1933). By implication, Paddon's agricultural plan envisioned large community gardens, such as those eventually planted at Cartwright, North West River, and Mary's Harbour. Much like his promotion of boarding-schools, Paddon's agricultural plan required greater population central-ization and the resulting termination of the dispersed Settler settlement pattern and lifestyle.

The social engineering inherent in the mission's educational and agricultural programs is evident in the IGA's role in the creation of a new Grenfell community at Mary's Harbour. As early as about 1915, Battle Harbour hospital staff sought a mainland winter location for the hospital, largely because of the occasional inaccessibility of Battle Har-bour in fall and spring. Their first winter site may have been Ships Harbour, on the south side of St Lewis Inlet, not far from Mary's Har-bour. Although I could not find any mention of Ships Harbour in written documents, some older people (opinions are divided on this) remember a Grenfell nursing station and wharf at Ships Harbour brook. The next winter site for Battle Harbour was picturesque Hatter's Cove (Cartwright's Hoop-pole Cove), a few kilometres west of Ships Harbour. Hatter's Cove appears in the written documentation. Grenfell wrote, 'we were able to influence a small lumber mill to start St Lewis Bay Nursing Station in the long, well-wooded bay that runs in 30 miles from the seaboard' (1921a, 58).

Just who owned this mill is unclear from written sources. Paddon implies that it was privately operated, perhaps by Labrador Stores Limited (Dohme 1921, 59). Labrador Stores Limited was a company begun in 1916 by Dr Grieve, a mission doctor, as a cooperative at Cape Charles (Grenfell 1917, 66); the cooperative became a company in 1919. Locals remember that George Sellers (later member of the House of Assembly for southern Labrador) operated a sawmill and store at Hat-ter's Cove, as did another man, Gerry Thoms. Nurse Dohme states that 174 people settled for the winter around the mill in the autumn of 1920

(1921, 60). Dr Knapp (1924) describes Hatter's Cove as a busy community during the winter of 1922–3. The community then numbered 188. During the winter of 1923, ten new houses were built, others were renovated, and some were rebuilt closer to the fenced IGA compound. Despite the poor fishery of 1922, the mission offered Settlers construction or industrial work, paying them in food (such as wholewheat flour) and clothing; other Settlers earned government relief by cutting timber (ibid., 7). The mission also organized a Christmas dinner, dances throughout the winter, and a spring sports day. Older Settlers remember Hatter's Cove as a larger community than this, perhaps with as many as four hundred people and one which included most of the families who fished at Battle Harbour, Indian Cove, Trap Cove, and Mattie's Cove. One informant added that there were 'even people from Fox Harbour.' In any event, Hatter's Cove was very clearly the major winter community of the early 1920s. But its days were numbered; the mission would soon establish a new winter community for Battle Harbour, and the Settlers would eventually follow.

Locals remember that Hatter's Cove was abandoned in 1928, probably because Mary's Harbour, Battle Harbour's new winter headquarters, was considered preferable (Gilmour 1931). As usual, Grenfell is vague about the move. He cryptically observes: 'we decided to abandon Hatter's Cove nursing station, as all the people had moved away' (1932, 282).

I consider it important to note that until the spring of 1929, Mary's Harbour (St Mary's River) was only one of many sparsely inhabited coves in St Lewis Bay (Forsyth 1936, 60). Grenfell staff were unquestionably attracted to Mary's Harbour's lagoon-like harbour, its proximity to St Mary's River, and the fact that its sole resident, trapper-horticulturalist Peter Blanchard, had a prolific garden (Sears 1929, 145). Moreover, Grenfell's agricultural adviser, Professor Sears, had tested the soil acidity in Blanchard's garden and found it acceptable (ibid.).[3] Although I do not have specific evidence of Sear's role in the choice of Mary's Harbour, I strongly suspect that his account of the agricultural possibilities of the Mary's Harbour was important.

Construction of the Mary's Harbour mission began in summer 1930 under the stern supervision of Battle Harbour's Dr Moret. The coincidental burning of the thirty-eight-year-old Battle Harbour hospital on 4 November 1930, the eve of the Guy Fawkes's bonfire, assured Mary's Harbour's future as a centre (Grenfell 1931, 40). However, the real cause of the fire remains unknown, and events during it reveal a previously unreported resistance to the mission. At the time, Dr Moret was at

Cartwright and Nurse Cornelius and all patients had already moved to Mary's Harbour, which Grenfell later called the 'new Battle Harbour at St Mary's River' (1932, 282). Grenfell claimed that the fire was not preventable, having started from a cigarette butt in the nearby Baine Johnston store. His description of the fire is tinged more with relief than remorse at the loss of his first hospital. He presumed that the former hospital's $6000 insurance coverage would be collected and then acknowledged the help of the Hudson's Bay Company and Newfoundland government in building a new 'central station for the whole east coast of Labrador 200 miles farther north at Cartwright' (Grenfell 1931, 40–1).

Not mentioned in the written accounts of the fire but remembered by locals was the looting which took place as the hospital burnt. In the words of one person, 'some were trying to save [the contents] while some were trying to steal.' Local looters made off with towels, bedding, and other items, even carrying some away by boat. This image of Settlers looting Grenfell's first hospital is at odds with the popular, even the academic Grenfell legend, one in which Grenfell and his mission are deified. Yet interpreted more critically, the looting of the burning hospital must be placed within the context of the colonial, often imperious manner of the mission, against which the looting may have been a long-awaited act of resistance.

During the 1930s, horticultural and livestock production at Mary's Harbour, Cartwright, North West River, and St Anthony increased. Vegetables and animal products were needed to feed the many patients, students, and others dependent on the increased services of these increasingly important communities. Dr Paddon's North West River operation included the only greenhouse north of the Strait of Belle Isle; the mission sold cabbage seedlings to locals in June for one cent each (Paddon 1933, 71). Between the late 1930s and Confederation in 1949, agricultural productivity declined. Of course the Second World War disrupted many IGA activities, but there are also signs that the agricultural promise of centres like Mary's Harbour had waned. Dr Forsyth states that the horticultural yields at Mary's Harbour dropped in the late 1930s and, in 1941, Dr Hosmer complained of the loss of the station's 'outdoor man' and of problems posed by swarms of biting blackflies (Forsyth 1937, 13; Hosmer 1941, 10). Meanwhile, gardens at Cartwright and North West River continued supplying local needs. At St Anthony, the Jessie Goldthwait dairy farm was opened in 1939. Its twenty-four holsteins provided the hospital's one hundred patients with fresh milk daily (McNeill 1956).

The Industrial Department of the IGA was the broadest and in many ways the most ambiguous of the fourfold mission Dr Harry Paddon had described. Grenfell initiated this department soon after he arrived in Newfoundland because of the causal relationship he observed between poverty and the merchant-controlled credit system. The department's emphasis varied regionally and changed over time in response to changes affecting the mission area.

For example, Grenfell's attack on the merchant credit system involved the introduction of cooperative stores (Porter 1975, 27). His most successful co-op was at Red Bay, just south of the study area. Short-lived cooperatives were also established at Cape Charles and West St Modeste. According to Grenfell, the Cape Charles Co-op (the only Grenfell cooperative within the study area) was condemned by the local merchant (presumably G. Soper and Sons, who operated there for several years) as a threat to trade and, as happened repeatedly, the Newfoundland government appointed a commission to investigate the mission. The commission exonerated the mission.

For Dr Harry Paddon, development meant large-scale industrial *developments* (Rompkey 1991, 292) offering employment to replace the trapping and fishing economy, which, I believe, he only tolerated. While Paddon supported efforts to increase what he (and Grenfell) called self-sufficiency, his notion of development was ultimately centralist and incompatible with the centrifugal nature of a lifestyle which, while meagre, was more self-sufficient than that which followed. At the same time, Paddon travelled the coast more than any 'outsider,' spending a considerable amount of time with Labrador folk. While it may seem paradoxical that he would proffer developments which were antithetical to the Settler lifestyle, it must be remembered that he served during very difficult and different times, marked as he once put it by the D-quartet – disease, dole, death, and despair (Paddon 1939, 85). Paddon witnessed the privation and uncertainty Settlers experienced and he did what he thought best to alleviate them.

An important part of the mission's industrial department was handicraft production. An early as 1908, Durgin refers to Grenfell handicrafts in southeastern Labrador, remarking that 'the women do beautiful embroideries in silk on caribou skins and moccasins, which the Grenfell Mission sends abroad for sale and offers to the few tourists who venture into these wilds' (51). Greater organization of craft production under the tutelage of two Industrial Department stalwarts, Miss Luther and Mrs Keddie, stimulated knitting, rug hooking, and carving. The mission paid Settler (primarily women) craft producers for the items they produced in either money or clothing.

The content of the crafts, in the spirit of so many of the Grenfell organization's initiatives, was intrusive. For instance, many northern Newfoundland and southeastern Labrador women, having little familiarity with Inuit culture, hooked rugs depicting brightly coloured Inuit kayaks or snow houses on pre-stencilled burlap provided by the mission. Readily identifiable Inuit idioms attracted the attention of southern buyers in Grenfell handicraft shops established in Canada and the United States. The fact that the craft producers knew little more about Inuit than those buying the crafts made little difference. It is important to note that the only surviving mission-inspired industrial development in southeastern Labrador is commercial handicraft production, the 'cottage industry' that was entirely compatible with the dispersed Settler settlement pattern.

THE LABRADOR DEVELOPMENT COMPANY

By the late 1920s and early 1930s Newfoundland and its newly bounded Labrador territory were on the verge of bankruptcy. The quality and market value of salt codfish exports had declined during the 1920s and these trends increased with the beginning of the interwar depression (Alexander 1977). Labrador fisher George Poole remembers that around 1930 codfish prices dropped from $5.00 to $1.50 a quintal (1987, 23). By 1933 fish prices dropped to their lowest level since 1913 (Gillespie 1986, 55) and Southard reports that by 1934, prices fell to 85 cents per quintal, down from $2 the previous year (1982, 17).

Steadily declining fish prices made life very difficult for the people of southeastern Labrador. Grenfell nurse Berthelsen visited all houses between Cartwright and St Mary's, during the winter of 1932. She found, for example, that at Fox Harbour, most houses were in darkness because of a lack of lamp oil, and conditions were said to be even worse north of St Michael's Bay (Berthelsen 1933, 88).

Late in 1932, Newfoundland's Alderdice government established a royal commission to study Newfoundland's economic prospects (Smallwood 1981, 43). Among the many recommendations of the Amulree Royal Commission (see Great Britain 1933) was that the responsible government which Newfoundland had enjoyed since 1855 be replaced by a six-man commission of government controlled by and responsible to the British government, and charged with developing measures to improve the Newfoundland economy. When the commission of government took office on 16 February 1934 one of its six commissioners was Sir John Hope Simpson, who headed the commission's Department of Natural Resources until 1936. This department's role in stabilizing the Newfoundland economy included a variety of innovations in the fisheries, in forestry, in economic cooperatives, and so on. One of these developments was the establishment of a large timber-cutting operation – the Labrador Development Company (LDC) – in southeastern Labrador.

J.O. Williams and the Early Years of the LDC

Throughout the twentieth century, few Newfoundland governments have been able to resist the glitter and promise of foreign capitalists who offer to come and develop the economy. One of the things which makes the little-known story of J.O. Williams and his Labrador Development Company so current is its similarity to those of recent economic saviours such as John Sheheen, John C. Doyle, and Phillip Sprung, men who have offered Newfoundland 'quick fix' economic solutions at bargain-basement prices.

Unless otherwise noted, much of the following biography of Williams and description of his operations is taken from Supreme Court judge Brian Dunfield's 1945 inquiry. The description of living and working conditions in Port Hope Simpson, Labrador's first modern company town and headquarters of the Labrador Development Company, makes critical use of Frank Southard's study of this community, as well as my own field notes and other published sources.

John Osborn (J.O.) Williams was born in or near Cardiff, Wales, either in 1886 or 1887. He left school in 1900 and entered the timber importing business. In 1908, at age twenty-two, Williams went to work for Evans and Reid, Ltd of Cardiff, exporters of coal and importers of the pit-props used to reinforce subterranean coalmines. This company opened a pit-prop cutting operation in Finland, and young Williams spent much of 1909–14 either there or with the company's Baltic operations. When the first World War broke out in 1914, the Baltic operations closed and Williams decided to come to Canada to seek new sources of pit-props. He travelled to Montreal in August 1914 and spent September to December in Newfoundland.

Around 1921 Williams obtained £10 thousand of financial backing from Franklin Thomas and Company Ltd, Cardiff coal importers who sought to enter the pit-prop business and helped Williams form J.O. Williams and Company, Ltd. Williams took one-third shares in the company bearing his name. Sometime after forming J.O. Williams and Company, Ltd, Williams and Thomas travelled to Newfoundland and formed the British North American Trading Company Ltd to export pit-props to England. J.O. Williams and Company, Ltd owned one-third of this new company (meaning Williams owned one-ninth interest). Because of high production costs, the British North American Trading Company went into liquidation in 1925, owing $43 thousand and taking down with it the first J.O. Williams and Company Ltd.

Back in Cardiff, and with the backing of a larger firm, the Powell Duffryn Steam Coal Company Ltd, Williams formed J.O. Williams and Company (1926) Ltd (otherwise known as the 'Cardiff Company') in 1926. Williams's brother Hiram was made company director. Until the outbreak of the Second World War in 1939, this company successfully competed in the Baltic and Biscay pit-prop trade.

Early in 1934, Williams travelled to New York for a holiday, visiting Newfoundland in February. Coincidentally, he travelled from Halifax to St John's aboard the vessel carrying John Hope Simpson and Thomas Lodge (although he did not meet them at this time), en route to St John's to become commissioners of Newfoundland's caretaker government.

When on holiday, Williams decided to form a new company to export pit-props to England. He began negotiations with Japp Hatch and Company of London, to purchase two unused Labrador timber licences, containing 1160 square miles between St Lewis River and Hawke Bay, Labrador. Both J.O. and his brother Hiram were familiar with the Hatch properties because J.O. owned part interest in one (the former Jardine property) and he and Hiram had interests in the other (the Galway licence) (Summers 1935). The two properties had each changed hands ten or more times during the twenty years before the Labrador Development Company bought them in 1934.

The Labrador Development Company Ltd (LDC) was registered under the Newfoundland Companies Act on 29 April 1934, followed by the purchase (for £20 thousand) of the two timber licences on 15 May 1934. The LDC began with capital of $1 million, divided into 200,000 shares of $5 each. The LDC became a 'majority owner of the Cardiff Company, and vice versa' (Dunfield 1945, 17) in a complex and leveraged transfer of share capital between J.O. Williams and Company Ltd and the LDC, a transaction which would later become a major bone of contention.

The LDC established headquarters at a site on the south side of Alexis Bay in June 1934, two months after registration of the company. The speed with which five hundred Newfoundland and Labrador men rushed to the work site that summer attests both to the desperate economic conditions of 1934 and to the effectiveness of wireless and oral communication. Only four hundred men were needed and this labour surplus (and probably other, unknown problems) led to a strike in June 1934. The strike cost the company $15 thousand, most of it spent returning workers who were not needed to Newfoundland.

Except for the strike, the 1934 season was successful, and the company's honeymoon with government lasted through much of the 1934–35 season. Indeed, while informing his fellow commissioners about potential revenues lost through derelict Labrador timber licences, Natural Resources Commissioner (and then Acting Commissioner of Justice) John Hope Simpson praised the LDC as 'the class of operation which we are most interested in seeing developed' (1935).[4] As of March 1935, there were '150 single men and 90 families supported by that Company, who would otherwise probably be on the dole, and it is anticipated that in the Spring provision will be made there for 200 more families and for a total labour force in excess of 500' (ibid.).

Both Williams and the government clearly envisioned a permanent town site, 'so as to have family labour regularly at hand' and thereby cut down on transient labour (Williams 1945, 11–12). In the fall of 1934, Williams moved to obtain additional concessions from the government. In late October, he wrote Commissioner of Justice Howley suggesting certain changes in a proposed agreement between LDC and the government and the improvement of the LDC town site. Among the improvements, Williams expressed the need for land to build two or three hundred 'houses, [plus] schools and churches,' a grant of one square mile along the north shore of the bay for Williams's private home, a customs officer and permanent policeman, and mail delivery (Williams 1934).

Grenfell has written that the simultaneous establishment of Port Hope Simpson and of the Commission of Government in 1934 was not coincidental. Until then, a law existed that prevented the export of unmanufactured forest timber from Labrador. This law was repealed, Grenfell writes, and 'one result of this is that for the first time a permanent logging camp had been established at Alexis River' (1935, 46).

Judge Dunfield states that by 1936 Port Hope Simpson had a population of 500, including 250 working men. That some of Williams's promises to develop the town site had been kept is clear in Dunfield's statement that by 1936 the LDC had 'erected 14 houses, a staff house and mess room, a hospital, a community hall, a store and offices, warehouses, a bunk house, a sawmill, forges, stables, barns and some piers and wharves, with their equipment' (1945, 31). An informant recalled that during its peak there were twenty-seven people on the administrative staff alone, and Southard notes that the company had its own cook, blacksmith, telegraph operator, store clerk, medical personnel, harbour pilots, woods manager, and Newfoundland ranger (1982, 18). Jupp notes that the majority of the workforce were Newfoundlanders and that during summer local Settlers moved 'outside' to fish (1971, 24). Moreover, she states that local Settlers wintered 'across the Bay' from Port Hope Simpson at the 'permanent Settlement of Blackwater Brook' (ibid.). Jupp adds that in 1938 there were 'about 200–300 people in Alexis Bay, and 300–350 in Lewis Bay' (ibid.).

Temporarily poor Welsh coal and pit-prop prices, Newfoundland's 25 cents-per-cord export tax, and the funding necessary for Williams's town site development led to negotiations in October 1934 between Williams and the two commissioners of government (John Hope Simpson and Thomas Lodge), most supportive of LDC. These talks eventually led to revisions in the terms of agreement between the government and the LDC and to a British Colonial Development Fund loan to Newfoundland, ultimately advanced to the LDC in the amount of £40 thousand (then about $193.6 thousand). Williams agreed to a ten-year mortgage, using the LDC's Labrador properties and Cardiff Company as collateral (Dunfield 1945, 19). To secure the use of the Cardiff Company as collateral, the government, through the then commissioner of natural resources John Hope Simpson, received 970 ordinary shares of £1 each in J.O. Williams and Company Ltd. This arrangement for the security on the loan made the government the major corporate shareholder of LDC and a significant owner of the Cardiff Company. The commission held 67,600 of the 80,005 shares then issued in LDC and could vote and/or sell all or any of these without reference to J.O. Williams and Company Ltd. (Assistant Secretary for Justice 1942). This loan guarantee was dated 29 April 1935, and the $193.6 thousand loan constituted a major turning point in the history of LDC.

Government Begins to Question the LDC

The government had ventured the loan to the LDC encouraged by the initial success of the company and the jobs it offered. Commissioners

Lodge and Simpson realized that Williams required additional capital to construct houses and other town site infrastructure. The terms of the loan required the Williams practise modern forestry techniques and that a forestry officer be stationed in Labrador.

Sometime after the 1935 loan, however, an 'outside investor' paid $50 thousand to purchase LDC shares. On 31 July 1935, Williams used this money, plus an additional $6 thousand, to buy two unused Labrador timber properties. These included the Dickey properties in Sandwich Bay ($6 thousand) and the nearby Macaulay-Riordan properties ($50 thousand). Together these lands totalled 2400 square miles adjacent to the property LDC had purchased in 1934 (Cook [written for Williams] 1944, 18–19; Dunfield 1945, 17). In 1936 the LDC entered into a three-year agreement to supply the Newfoundland railway annually with a minimum of forty thousand tons of Rhymney Valley (just east of Cardiff) coal, to be purchased from Powell Duffryn Steam Coal Co. Ltd who, in return, agreed to purchase eighty thousand tons (one cord pit-props equalled approximately two tons) of pit-props.

In the spring of 1936, the government director of the LDC arranged for a temporary loan of $75 thousand to be used as working capital (Dunfield 1945, 32). But 1936 also brought bad news for LDC. On 10 June, the estate of the late J.J. Tobin, owners of a 2434-square-mile, rectangularly-shaped, ambiguously bounded and unused timber concession on the southern periphery of the LDC property, brought suit in the Newfoundland Supreme Court against LDC, alleging its workers had trespassed and logged the Tobin property since 1934. Tobin's estate sought $50 thousand in damages, but after an inconclusive court case (for example, the presiding judge was unable to determine the true boundaries of Tobin's concession [Dunfield 1945, 27]), the LDC (with approval from Government Commissioner Ewbank) purchased the Tobin lands for $112 thousand in May 1937 (Cook [written for Williams] 1944, 22).

By (or before) 1937 the Newfoundland government and business community were beginning to sour on J.O. Williams. Memories of the 1926 insolvency of Williams's British North American Trading Company persisted. And, we always have, as Judge Dunfield writes, those 'politically-minded persons to whom the mere fact that an enterprise is being assisted by the Government is reason enough for talking against it' (1945, 33). Between February and March 1937, Williams suffered from what his lawyer Cook called a 'severe mental breakdown' (Cook [writing for Williams] 1944, 22). He was, Judge Dunfield reports, 'incapacitated by illness for several months' (1945, 35).

By January 1938, the LDC had met virtually all its financial obliga-
tions to government, although in November it obtained its second
temporary loan of $75 thousand as working capital to pay merchant
creditors and meet other payments and royalties. In the fall of that year,
Williams hinted that he might have to close down his Labrador operation unless he was awarded the coal contract for the Newfoundland
railway. However, instead of remaining in St John's and discussing this
with Mr Chesman (LDC's St John's office manager) and Government
Commissioner Ewbank, who was responsible for the LDC, the erratic
Williams returned to England. This increased suspicions within the
government that Williams was using government loans to increase 'his
stocks in Finnish wood as a speculation against the early out-break of
war' (Dunfield 1945, 45). However, Judge Dunfield found no supporting
evidence and explained that people wrongly considered the Cardiff
Company as a 'hostile rival entity' rather than 'an indispensable subsidiary of the Labrador Company' which, along with the LDC and Williams
himself, the Newfoundland government controlled 'very completely'
(ibid., 38, 45).

The outbreak of war between Great Britain and Germany on 3 September 1939 signalled further difficulties for the LDC, and some of these
difficulties reverberated to Labrador. The Second World War increased
the risk of shipping everything, including pit-props, now in the hands
of the United Kingdom Timber Control. Under the Timber Control,
Newfoundland and Labrador pit-props received lower prices than their
Canadian counterparts (Dunfield 1945, 63). In the fall of 1939, the crew
of the ship *Benwood*, freshly loaded with pit-props, refused to cross the
Atlantic and sailed instead to Halifax. There, the pit-props remained
over winter and were shipped to Cardiff at a loss in the spring of 1940
(ibid., 64).

The government's concern with the management of the company
persisted, and with it came the decision that there could be no further
managerial appointments without government approval (Dunfield 1945,
46). Around June 1939, however, J.O. Williams sent his son Eric to Port
Hope Simpson to oversee his interests. Friction soon developed between
the junior Williams and Keith Yonge, the company's young, adventurous, and well-educated Labrador manager (ibid., 53). But ultimately this
disagreement was of little consequence; in late January 1940, Eric
Williams lost his life in a mysterious house fire at Port Hope Simpson.[5]

In June 1940 government director Fraser informed the LDC that all
rentals must be paid at once, and later that month the government

pressured J.O. Williams to resign as managing director. The company owed approximately $110.5 thousand (Dunfield 1945, 62).

All company business ceased in the summer of 1941, and that fall some staff and Settlers left Port Hope Simpson (Dunfield 1945, 66). By the fall of 1942 there were only about fifteen men cutting railway ties near Port Hope Simpson and in St Lewis Inlet (ibid., 67). In November, Commissioner of Natural Resources Dunn informed J.O. Williams that it would be impossible to compete for labour with contractors building the Goose Bay aerodrome (ibid.). Williams retorted that the LDC had had no problems obtaining labour until the fall of 1940 and that men would not have gone to Goose Bay for 'temporary employment' if permanent work had been available at Port Hope Simpson (Cook [written for Williams] 1944, 57). Throughout 1942 and 1943, the government continued to regret its association with J.O. Williams, who was now considered an unmitigated nuisance. Even though the government had removed Williams as managing director, he customarily 'acted as chairman at meetings at which he is present' and by 1942 had succeeded in having his brother Hiram made a company director (Assistant Secretary for Justice 1942).

In May 1943 the government accused the LDC of defaulting on payments and interests, but no action seems to have been taken (Dunfield 1945, 67). The next month, Williams urged the British secretary of state for dominion affairs to hold an inquiry to vindicate his business reputation and to save the LDC (ibid., 2). In 1944 the government decided to hold an inquiry (not necessarily on Williams's terms). Supreme court judge Brian Dunfield conducted the inquiry, which studied the management, operation, and finances of the LDC. Much of the twenty-one-day (20 November 1944 to 13 January 1945) inquiry focused on the relationship between the LDC and J.O. Williams and Company and on Williams's temperamental character.

In his report dated 13 May 1945, Judge Dunfield concluded that both Williams and the government were to blame for the problems of the LDC. What had begun with a spirit of optimism and trust had degenerated to cynicism and vitriol. Williams was 'primarily responsible'; it was his company – the purchase of the additional timber properties eliminated necessary working capital. Finally, the coincidentally poor timing of the Second World War greatly hurt pit-prop exports.

But Dunfield reserved his harshest criticisms for the government. It had failed to appreciate the costs and benefits of the founding of Port Hope Simpson. For an investment of approximately $344 thousand ($194 thousand plus the two $75 thousand loans), $800 thousand in wages had been earned between 1935 and 1939, thus saving dole expenditures. The LDC had exported $1 million thousand worth of wood (Dunfield 1945, 71–2).

Judge Dunfield recommended that J.O. Williams be given another chance. Countering local concerns about Williams's honesty, the judge called him an 'optimistic and speculative operator' who had displayed 'considerable assiduity and resource' in conducting the 'twin companies, the Labrador producer and the Cardiff outlet' (Dunfield 1945, 81–4). The judge concluded that any future dealings with Williams should be approached by government with a 'friendly attitude' (ibid., 84).

The months following the release of Judge Dunfield's report were filled with three developments. The first involved sabre-rattling by Williams's British lawyers, who claimed he should be compensated for the 'mental agony and damage to his reputation' caused by the Dunfield Enquiry (Brown, Turner, Compton Carr & Co. 1945). In the second, Williams badgered government for permission to resume logging operations immediately, adding that royalties on wood shipped from Labrador should be forgiven. Third, the government gave permission to log, but in accordance with a twenty-two-condition agreement, dated 28 June 1945 and effective from 1 June 1945 to 31 December 1946.

Although the LDC commenced logging under terms of the 28 June 1945 agreement, Williams and his lawyers relentlessly sought compensation from the government, which finally came in terms of a settlement between the LDC and the government, reached on 20 March 1946. During the winter of 1946 the LDC obtained a contract with the Timber Control to supply eight to twelve thousand fathoms of wood, at $38 per fathom, and requested the Dominions Office to issue securities totalling $200 thousand, to fulfil this contract (Flinn 1946). Apparently, nothing came of this contract, for in May 1946 the British Treasury refused Williams's request to convert sterling into dollars, citing Williams's failure to fulfil a 1945–6 contract (British Secretary of State for Dominion Affairs 1947).

Even though Williams's possibilities were clearly dwindling, he refused to give up. In July 1947, he asked the Newfoundland government for a $500 thousand loan to undertake further operations in Labrador. Williams planned to cut thirty thousand cords of wood at Alexis Bay, St Lewis Bay, St Michael's Bay, and Hawke Bay, an operation which he claimed would take 'care of the bulk of the Labrador families between Battle Harbour and Sandwich Bay' (Williams 1947).

The government rejected the loan request. Williams then scaled down his request to a temporary loan of $200 thousand. The government initially rejected Williams's request, then accepted it, but turned it down a month later. In so doing, Williams claimed that government left 250 Labrador loggers starving.[6]

Also in the autumn of 1947, the LDC entered a contract with the Amsterdam firm of Messrs Van Gelder Zonen to supply about twenty-two thousand cords. But again the LDC needed the $200 thousand Williams requested. The company's Newfoundland lawyer, Cook, wrote Commissioner of Natural Resources Flinn promising that the company would pay the $200 thousand loan back in 1948, and if this were not acceptable, would have to go into voluntary receivership, inflicting hardship on Newfoundlanders and Labradorians working for the company (Cook 1947). Cook's threat was for naught. The LDC went into voluntary liquidation on 15 November 1947, with J.O. Williams as liquidator (Governor of Newfoundland 1947). The LDC still owed the government $190,209 and Williams was given until 31 August 1948 to wind up the company's affairs. The company had only paid $4,433.33 on the $133 thousand mortgage taken out on 12 April 1946 (Russel 1949). In the months following liquidation, government commissioners became increasingly annoyed, believing that Williams was stalling. At least initially, the government decided against seizing timber the company had cut after liquidation, or cancelling company licences, even though both options were within its rights. Meanwhile, in the ten months after liquidation, Williams somehow managed to deliver the wood for the Dutch contract, and to travel to the United States and Canada, attempting (without success) to sell the company to firms such as K.C. Irving of New Brunswick, the Ontario Paper Company, and Bowaters of Newfoundland.

In his 8 September 1948 letter to his lawyer, Williams reported on his travels to the United States and Canada, his delivery of the Dutch wood, and his suit to the London Board of Trade. He also mentioned a report by surveyor Leif Holt that two sawmills were operating on LDC property in Sandwich Bay. Williams asked Cook to seek a delay of settlement until 31 December 1948 (Williams 1948). The government's response to Williams's request was that Williams had made insufficient progress on liquidation, and had 'gone outside his jurisdiction in embarking on new operations,' that the two sawmills (the one at Paradise Arm almost certainly being that of Fequet) were on Crown land, and that Williams's settlement date (which had already passed) must remain (Flinn 1948).

The LDC struggled for life during the final days of the commission of government. But finally, the company surrendered all its assets (excluding its interests in J.O. Williams and Company, Ltd of Cardiff) to the government on 31 March 1949, the day before April Fool's Day – the day Newfoundland joined the Canadian confederation (Cook 1949).

But J.O. Williams was not done yet. In a letter to newly elected Premier Smallwood dated 25 July 1949, with an enclosure outlining his version of the 'very raw deal' he maintained that the LDC had received, the ever-resilient Williams promised that if given half his Labrador land back (ca. three thousand square miles), plus $400 thousand (with £100 thousand deposited as collateral in London), he would continue operations (Williams 1949). Although the government rejected Williams's general proposal, it accepted his offer of a cargo of pit-props for $20 thousand worth of store goods sent to Port Hope Simpson in the fall of 1949 (Brookes 1949).

LIFE IN LABRADOR'S FIRST MODERN COMPANY TOWN

The Organization of Production

Southard writes that news of J.O. Williams's operation spread either by word of mouth or by notices posted in wireless stations in Newfoundland and along the Labrador coast (1982, 17). Most Newfoundlanders working for the LDC came from Newfoundland's northeast coast and northern peninsula (especially from the community of Griquit), and some had logging experience. Labrador Settlers came from as far south as Forteau, and as far north as Sandwich Bay, at least until 1941. After that, men from the northern part of southeastern Labrador preferred the better working and living conditions at the new Goose Bay Air Base to working for LDC. Partially because of its draconian working conditions and the nature of work performed, the labour force (numbering as high as six hundred, [Southard 1982, 18]) fluctuated considerably, both seasonally and annually. For example, as mentioned above, most Settlers quit LDC work in spring to fish during summer. Southard provides several reasons for this: a) there was less work in the woods in summer, b) Settlers wanted to maintain ownership of fishing berths and gear, and c) during the Second World War higher fish prices made fishing profitable (ibid., 19–20). Newfoundlanders, in contrast, tended to work for the company year-round, or returned to Newfoundland after a season or more with the company. Given the poor pay and spartan living conditions of the LDC, workers sometimes left Port Hope Simpson shortly after arriving, their home passage paid by the company or government. The commission of government and its local agents, the Newfoundland rangers, played key roles in recruiting and controlling the LDC labour force. A Battle Harbour ranger unsympathetic to LDC workers used the tactic of refusing to give out Able Bodied Relief, telling the men of his district that they could either go to work for LDC or go without cash (Noseworthy 1945, 1). This usually assured the company a labour force, albeit one 'not very anxious to work in the woods' (Noseworthy 1946, 1).

The production of mining pit-props, railway ties, and pulpwood – the main products of the LDC – followed a seasonal order. Most actual cutting of wood occurred in the fall (Coish 1982, 32). Workers used their own axes and buck saws to cut the spruce and fir trees. Port Hope Simpson residents also remember using an axe-like tool with a sharp hook facing the opposite side of the axe blade, a 'pick-a-roon,' to move logs. Loggers limbed felled trees and cut them into logs measuring four, six, or nine feet in length, with various minimum top diameters (Coish 1982, 36).

During winter, logs were hauled by horse-drawn sleds or piled on lakes where, when ice melted, they could be driven down the rivers flowing from these lakes (Coish 1982). The spring drives of hundreds of cords of logs down river were exciting but dangerous for the men stationed along the river banks, who used 'pick poles' (iron-pronged poles) to clear log-jams (Coish 1982, 36). (For a picture of a spring log drive, see Gillespie [1986, 111].) Logs transported to the bays were then towed by booms either to deeper water (Davis 1982, 37) or to Port Hope Simpson, where docking facilities existed. The labour-intensive tasks of loading ships, peeling bark, and milling logs were done in summer and early fall at the Port Hope Simpson plant and sawmill (Dwyer 1941b, 1).

Remuneration

Based on incomplete and often contradictory oral and written sources, there appear to have been two kinds of pay arrangements: full-time salaried work and contract work. Apparently describing salaried employees, Southard remarks that in the first years of the LDC operation, workers received 25 cents per hour for a ten-hour work day; boys received 12 cents (1982, 19). He adds that workers paid $5 per month to rent the company's stud houses during the second year of the company's tenure (i.e., 1935–6). Meanwhile, Coish, who teamstered logs by horse-drawn sled, received 20 cents per hour 'for years' and 25 cents per hour while performing the dangerous job of driving loaded sleds (Coish 1982, 30). Employees worked ten- to twelve- hour days, for six days a week. But contractual work emerged as an efficiency measure and was used in Newfoundland as early as 1934, coincidentally the LDC's first summer of operation. In Labrador, contracting for a certain number of cords of wood was especially common in the company's St Lewis Inlet branch. Clark notes that men received $3 per cord (eight by four by four feet) in December 1937. During the winter of 1941, several months prior to the strike of December 1941, the contracting situation is described as follows: 'Carl Peterson and Walter Cannings contractors in (St.) Lewis' Bay, cutting Pit-props for the Labrador Development Co. Ltd. have approximately one hundred men working in the woods and will give work to all men that apply for work. The men live in Camps and are charged sixty cents per day for Board and Lodgings. They work on contract and receive Two Dollars, at the stump, and Two Dollars Twenty Five cents, piled, per cord for the wood' (Christian 1941a, 1). By winter of 1945, loggers on contract received $5 per cord for wood piled on the bank of St Lewis Bay (Christian 1945b, 1).

Low wages and long hours of dangerous work were not the only problems experienced by LDC workers. As already mentioned above, loggers had to supply their woods tools, 'van' (clothing, blades, files, and so on), and their room and board out of their earnings (Dwyer 1942a). As with wages, these expenses increased during the company's tenure. By December 1941, workers received $35 per month in wages and out of that, paid $7 to rent 'shacks' from the company, and spent the rest on food, van, and the like (Dywer 1941c, 1). On many occasions, loggers complained of not being able to feed their families on what little remained of their wages after paying rent. And unlike loggers in Newfoundland, who formed the Newfoundland Lumbermen's Association in 1936 (Gillespie 1986, 58), southeastern Labrador loggers were not unionized.

At least two strikes sought to improve working and living conditions. Southard may have been referring to the strike of 1934 when he wrote: 'a few years after the (LDC) operation had begun, low wages prompted one man to organize a strike which lasted an entire summer and allegedly brought fifty Newfoundland Policemen to maintain order' (1982, 19). The December 1941 strike occurred among loggers cutting railway ties in St Lewis Bay. In principle, these men earned the flat rate of $35 per month just mentioned. However, because they were not paid for working days missed because of weather or illness, most earned only $15 to $20 a month, and after paying rent, they had little left to buy the exorbitantly priced food only available at the company store in Port Hope Simpson. Through Ranger Dwyer's mediation with the company manager, the manager agreed to go to Battle Harbour and wire headquarters for higher pay and a new pay policy which would pay per unit produced (Dwyer 1942a). Under the new policy, men were paid 8 cents per railway tie but were also required to pay 4 cents per railway tie for room and board. Consequently, by March 1942, workers complained (to Ranger Dwyer) that the new policy discriminated against the more productive workers by making them pay proportionally more per day for room and board than did less productive workers.

Food sold at the Company store was very expensive. Moreover, the Company store did not consistently permit sales on credit and, worse yet, as Ranger Dwyer writes, the store's 'prices for supplies are considerable [sic] higher than ordinary and although their (LDC) employees are paid cash they have to spend all their money at the Company's store, if they spend their money, elsewhere they get no further employment with the firm (1940a, 1).

Company nurse Dorothy Jupp (1971, 29) describes the variety of ailments and accidents customarily encountered, as well as more serious illnesses, including tuberculosis and, occasionally, diphtheria. Before venturing to Labrador, in 1938, Nurse Jupp had met the company's St John's manager and was instructed that when loggers hurt themselves, she was to administer 'a quick dressing and (send them) back to work' (ibid., 16).

The people of Port Hope Simpson also faced new and serious diseases. Disease struck early in 1942, when Ranger Dwyer noted that health in his district was improving but that there were 'a considerable amount of cases of gonorrhoea' at a logging camp near River Head, St Lewis Bay. He warned that three Port Hope Simpson men working in the woods there might bring the disease back 'to this area' (Dwyer 1942a). During February the Port Hope Simpson men left the infected camp and returned to their community, fearing the 'other sickness and sores in the camp' while worrying that they might bring 'the sickness' home (Dwyer 1942b). By late February Ranger Dwyer reported the sickness and 'other trouble at the camp' had been 'cleaned up' by St Mary's Hospital (ibid.).

Although clearly a difficult way to earn a living, working for J.O. Williams had its occasional high points. The company organized a St Patrick's Day sports day, a dance, and limited administration of relief to families suffering from desperate conditions (Jupp 1971, 38–42). Also, a company policy allowed workers to purchase surplus country foods harvested by nearby Settlers. During the winter of 1940–1, Battle Harbour area Settlers sold partridges for 15 cents, rabbits for 20 cents, and ducks for 25 cents to those working for the LDC (Christian 1941a, 1). The company, along with the Newfoundland rangers, also encouraged workers to produce some of their own foods, offering fencing for gardens. Goats and poultry were introduced for the first time in the fall of 1941 (Dwyer 1941c, 1). A fall fair was organized in 1940 and prizes were awarded for the best vegetables grown (Dwyer 1940b, 1). As elsewhere along the coast, workers at Port Hope Simpson also organized day-long 'times,' featuring dog-team races, soup suppers, and dances, which attracted Settlers from nearby communities (Whitaker 1954).

The founding of Port Hope Simpson was one of several crucial developments in this century that fundamentally changed the nature of community, work, and society in southeastern Labrador. The LDC offered wages for work, and the heterogeneity of Labrador's first modern company town was the antithesis of the Settlers' family-based homesteads. The lure of jobs proved irresistible to needy Settlers living near the new town; many abandoned their winter quarters and moved to the growing company town.

But while Port Hope Simpson meant the abandonment of many smaller winter settlements, many Settlers who moved to work at Port Hope Simpson continued to fish during summer, hedging their bets against an uncertain future. Settler workers often adopted a similar strategy towards work with the next intrusive wave to hit the coast – military bases.

WORK ON MILITARY INSTALLATIONS

The final centralizing development came with the construction of military bases. The massive air base at Goose Bay, central Labrador, was the most important of these, yet others built in conjunction with Goose Bay or after the Second World War also attracted Labrador people to work. The construction of Goose Bay irrevocably changed the entire Labrador territory, even though its direct impact on the southeastern Labrador region may have been lower than on other regions. This has not been the case with the short-lived coastal military installations built along the southeastern coast.

Goose Bay: The Background

Between Britain's entry into the Second World War on 3 September 1939 and the entry of the United States on 7 December 1941, an increasingly besieged Great Britain spent an extraordinary amount of its resources on the war effort. The situation eventually led to discussions between Great Britain, Canada, and the United States over sharing responsibility for the defence of North America and the continuation of the war in Europe. Because Britain's navy suffered extensive losses to German submarines, the United States and Britain announced a destroyer-for-bases deal on 4 September 1940. The United States would provide Britain with fifty First World War destroyers in exchange for rights (President Roosevelt considered these gifts – 'generously given and gladly received', [U.S. Army 1946, 1] to build eight military bases at strategic locations in North Atlantic and Caribbean Commonwealth countries (Straus 1975, 555; Miller 1967, 12). Newfoundland bases and related military installations ultimately built under this agreement include army bases at Pepperrell (St John's), Harmon Field (Stephenville), and Ft McAndrew (Argentia) and cost the United States about $67 million. Another base built under this agreement was the naval facility at Argentia; it cost some $45 million, more than any other American overseas base built during the Second World War. Shortly after the United States and Great Britain reached the destroyer-for-bases deal, on 15 January 1941, the Newfoundland Base Command was formed. Its mandate stipulated that 'regardless of any assistance which may be obtained from Canada, the defense of Newfoundland must be at all times assured by the United States' (quoted in Miller 1967, 13). War-strapped Britain required a second line of credit which the Lend-Lease Bill provided in 1941, allowing Britain to borrow and lease material from the United States (Miller 1967, 14).

   In Newfoundland, Gander airfield was operational by early 1938, and with the beginning of the Second World War, Gander replaced the recently upgraded seaplane base at Botwood as the terminus for transatlantic flights (Smallwood 1984, 469). But continued devastation of North Atlantic convoys by German submarines (and other reasons; see Carr 1944, 79–80) necessitated an 'Atlantic Bridge' (see Great Britain 1945) between North America and England. According to Dziuban (1959, 182)

American and Canadian authorities first considered an air bridge at a meeting in Ottawa on 20 March 1941.

Harvard professor and long-time Grenfell friend Alexander Forbes played an important role in locating a potential site for an airbase. Forbes had conducted aerial surveys of Labrador in 1931, 1935, and 1939; when he was summoned to Washington as an expert in May 1941 he learned of American plans for a chain of northern airfields. Initially, this northern chain of airfields would allow fighter planes to fly to England, thus avoiding losses by submarine attacks on convoys (Forbes 1953).

As early as June 1939 the Newfoundland government had given permission to Ottawa for the Royal Canadian Air Force (RCAF) to conduct an aerial photographic and mapping reconnaissance mission along the Labrador coast north of Battle Harbour. (I could not find evidence that this mission occurred.) However, on 5 January 1940, the Newfoundland government agreed to let the RCAF use 'unoccupied crown lands' at Red Bay (Labrador) as an advance base for seaplanes. These two requests apparently anticipated the Canadian survey which eventually chose Goose Bay.

The Americans entered the search for a northern airbase the following year when, on 24 June 1941, the U.S. State Department telegraphed its consul general in St John's ordering him to inform the Newfoundland government that under Article 10 of the 1940 Bases Agreement, the United States (in cooperation with Canadian Forces) would survey the east coast of Labrador. Four days earlier (20 June) Canadian External Affairs wrote the governor of Newfoundland for permission to allow American air forces to make the survey, admitting that Canada did not have seaplanes available.

The American survey for a suitable site occurred during July 1941. Dr Forbes accompanied President Roosevelt's son, Captain Elliot Roosevelt, to Labrador as technical adviser. About the same time, a Canadian survey party headed by Eric Fry (of the Dominion Geodetic Survey [Miller 1967, 14]) flew to Labrador to seek airbase locations near North West River and Hebron (Fry 1987, 5). The two expeditions independently examined a number of possible sites suggested by existing aerial surveys. On advice from local Settler Robert Michelin, Fry began surveying a large sandy terrace overlooking Goose Bay, which Forbes had photographed in 1939 (Carr 1944, 82–4; Fry 1987, 8; Forbes 1953). Fry informed the Americans of this site, and individuals from both countries visited the site on 4 July; in Fry's words, 'Robert's (Michelin) Berry Bank' was selected as the best available site (1987, 8–10).

Captain Roosevelt's report of 6 July 1941 was flown to Washington the next day (Forbes 1953). In it, he recommended the Lake Melville site 'as an alternate to the airports in Newfoundland for transoceanic flying' (Roosevelt [1941] 1987, 18). In a subsequent report (No. 4), dated 3 August 1941, Roosevelt again recommended the Goose Bay site and arctic sites near Ft Chimo, Frobisher Bay, and Padloping Island (Cumberland Sound). Miller states that these arctic sites became weather stations named Crystal I, II, and III (1967, 15).

Newfoundland's commissioner of justice and defence L.E. Emerson travelled to Ottawa for meetings of the Joint Defence Board on 30 July 1941 discussing, among other things, the possibility of an airport near North West River. In his report on this meeting, Emerson writes: 'it would appear that the desirability of creating this new port originated with the British Air Representatives in Washington. Two factors impelled them to promote this proposal, one being the variable weather conditions at the Newfoundland Airport (Gander) and the other the existing or impending congestion there' (1941). Two weeks after this meeting, on 14 August, the Canadian Committee of the Privy Council approved a report from the minister of national defence for air recommending immediate construction of two 150-by-5000-foot runways and other necessary facilities at Goose Bay. That month, the George McNamara Construction Company of Toronto was awarded the Goose Bay contract. The first materials reached Goose Bay on 17 September, and the first plane landed on a 7,000-foot-long temporary runway on 6 November 1941 (Miller 1967, 15). Liberator and other types of aircraft regularly used snow-packed runways as early as January 1942 (Great Britain 1945, 29). On 16 December 1942, the area within a five-mile radius of the Goose Aerodrome control tower was declared a 'restricted area,' as defined by the Defence Act of 1939 (Emerson 1942).

Goose Bay: The Lure of Jobs

As quickly as temporary airstrips were bulldozed out of the Labrador wilderness, news of the top-secret developments at Goose Bay reached Settlers on the coast. For example, in Cartwright in August 1941 Settler Clarice Hopkins was working at the Marconi telegraph station when a message for the local Anglican minister and Hudson's Bay Company factor arrived, seeking men to work at Goose Bay (Hopkins and Hopkins 1987, 50). It is not surprising that before long the rumour of work near North West River circulated throughout Cartwright, although it was initially thought that 'all labour was being imported' (Summers 1941a, 2; 1941b, 1). However, under the terms of the agreement between the United States and Canada, local labour was to be used. McNamara Construction hired two HBC coasters (the *Fort Cartwright* and *Fort Rigolet*), and their captains were ordered to travel to the coast and recruit all able-bodied labourers (Carr 1944, 105–6). The first groups of men from Sandwich Bay arrived at Goose Bay in September 1941, aboard the *Fort Cartwright*.

News of Goose Bay reached Port Hope Simpson by November 1941, but owing to 'transportation difficulties' no men went to work there that fall (Dwyer 1941b, 1). A Lodge Bay informant recalled that 1942 was the only year that work was available for them at the White Point radio station and that same year there was a man at White Point looking for workers for Goose Bay. Three Lodge Bay men (along with two men from Bay of Islands) went to Goose Bay in September 1942. The inform-ant recalled that he and the others were hired as carpenters, receiving 60 cents per hour, as opposed to the $1.10 per hour paid to Canadian carpenters, a discrepancy he believed existed 'so as to not inflate the Newfoundland economy with higher pay expectations.' My informant's recollection of wage differences is supported by Ranger J.J. Hogan's observation that: 'The scale of wages paid to Canadians ranges from 50 cents to one dollar and twenty five cents ... While the Natives are paid from thirty five to sixty cents an hour. All employees are fed and housed free of charge' (1942, 1). Others from southeastern Labrador, such as Gordon Acreman of Mary's Harbour (1987, 112–3), also worked at Goose Bay. Acreman worked in Goose Bay as a carpenter for about fifteen months, beginning in July 1943 (ibid.). Generally, however, most southeastern Labrador men working at Goose Bay were drawn from Sandwich Bay.

The status of Labrador workers at Goose Bay resembled that of New-foundlanders working on base construction in Newfoundland. There, 82 per cent of construction personnel were Newfoundlanders engaged as common labourers. Americans claimed that Newfoundlanders required more 'supervision' than their American counterparts. American bosses also complained that Newfoundlanders were not accustomed to continuing construction work during winter (U.S. Army 1946).

Labrador natives (including those from southeastern Labrador) were required to have registration cards to work at Goose Bay (Duff 1943, 1). These were issued by local ranger detachments throughout Labrador and were required for security checks. Similarly, rangers met and checked other civilians arriving by plane or by ship (the Montreal steamer) (Hogan 1942, 2). The largest proportion of Labrador people employed were Settlers, although some Inuit and Innu occasionally worked.

During their first several months at Goose Bay, Labrador workmen were housed in temporary canvas tents along the road leading inland from the landing place, presumably at Otter Creek. According to Davis, there was a North West River tent, a Rigolet tent, a Cartwright tent, and 'separate from them all,' a tent city for the mainlanders (1987, 77). Once completed, these male workers moved into housing provided by Mc-Namara Construction. During summer and fall of 1942, some couples and families moved to Goose Bay. Many of these settled at Otter Creek, living in small and rather modest houses or cabins. By April 1943, twenty-four families, totalling eighty-six people, lived in the twenty-three houses at Otter Creek (Hogan 1943d). My examination of the names of these families concludes that about thirteen (54 per cent) came from northern Labrador, nine (37.5 per cent) from central Labrador, and two (8.5 per cent) from southeastern Labrador (specifically Sandwich Bay). Both women and men worked, although the majority were men. Fifteen Otter Creek women (including seven whose husbands worked on the base) worked in the McNamara Company laundry (Hogan 1943d).

During 1942 ten 2.5-million-gallon fuel storage tanks were installed, and some of these were very near Otter Creek (Hogan 1942, 1). By the spring of 1943 civil and military authorities grew jittery about the possibility of fire starting in the Otter Creek houses and igniting these fuel tanks, one being as close as 150 feet. Acting on orders from St John's, Ranger Hogan visited all the houses in April 1943 and collected information about the owners' perceived house values, in anticipation of a planned relocation. Hogan also suggested a possible relocation site, although his incomplete description and the apparent typographical error in his report (i.e., 'boomo') make it impossible to credit him with selection of the site later called Hamilton Village (now Happy Valley). Hogan wrote, 'I believe a spot for this purpose could be located on the point of land between Hamilton River and the boomo [?] of Goose Bay. It would mean the clearing of a road for three or four miles, and hauling of the better houses there' (1943d). Official pressures, particularly from the RCAF, to relocate the eighty-six 'squatters' at Otter Creek continued through the summer of 1943 (Dunn 1943). The RCAF pressured Goose Airport ranger Morris, who in turn submitted reports on the Otter Creek 'problem' to the commissioner of justice and defence in St John's. Commissioners, Emerson of Justice and Defence and Wild of Finance, visited Goose Bay sometime in the fall of 1943. Emerson describes a 'shack town' on the periphery of the five-mile restricted zone. He writes:

Evils consequent upon having women near these encampments and having a shack town, have already arisen. Prostitution and shebeening [i.e., selling liquor illegally] are rife. Furthermore there are two other dangers to be apprehended, namely disease from lack of sanitation and forest fires. The houses are build [sic] in the trees and sparks from the fires will be an ever present and serious danger. Ranger Morris has informed us that several families from nearby places have announced their intention of coming and joining the new settlement. (1943)

How accurate Emerson's description of Otter Creek actually was is difficult to know, and his depiction of the settlement's depraved morality was probably intended to shock his audience into the need to close the shack town and relocate its inhabitants away from the threatened oil depot. However, assuming that even a fraction of the 'evils' Emerson described were true, his description is exceptional because it differs so completely from the romanticized versions of life in early Goose Bay (cf. Perrault 1976).

In any event, the eighty-six people living at Otter Creek in April 1943 constituted less than half of the Labrador people employed at the base. This number ranged between one and three hundred and, as explained below, fluctuated monthly. I mention this because the two Sandwich Bay families listed in Ranger Hogan's Otter Creek census were presumably not the only southeastern Labrador people working at Goose Bay in April 1943. Others would have been camped elsewhere or living in quarters provided by McNamara Construction. Happy Valley was finally established in September 1943, and populated by people from Otter Creek and additional coastal people drawn to Goose Bay (Perrault 1976).

At least initially, most Labrador people worked cutting wood, constructing the road to North West River (where sand and gravel were mined for use on the cement runways), in the laundry, at one of two sawmills, or at other unskilled labour. Settlers found working conditions and pay better than anything they had ever known. In the words of T.

Pardy: 'I worked for McNamara Construction, and I never worked for better people than them. We were well-fed and well-housed' (1981, 44). During the first year, unskilled Settler workmen received 35 cents per hour and room and board, wages more than twice the 15 cents offered by the Hudson's Bay Company or IGA for occasional labour in the years immediately preceding the building of Goose Bay (Rich 1981, 44). By January 1942, many workers had increased their salaries to 40 and 45 cents per hour, and those beginning to acquire trades such as carpentry or welding were earning 50 cents per hour (Summers 1942b, 2).

Generally, Labrador workers worked during winter, returning to the fishery each summer. Thus, 127 Labrador people were employed in September 1942 (Hogan 1942, 1), about 200 in December 1942 (Hogan 1943a, 1), 283 in February 1943 (Hogan 1943b, 1), 165 in March 1943 (Hogan 1943c), and so on. Over the next several years, a pattern emerged which saw coastal Settlers commute seasonally to Goose Bay for several months' work and then return to their home communities in winter to cut and haul essential firewood or, in summer, to fish. This seasonal adaptation to wage labour was compatible with the traditional Settler seasonal round and was acceptable to many. Outsiders, however, such as North West River ranger Duff, could not understand why Settlers refused to accept what he saw as the 'higher scale of living which the McNamara Construction Co.' was offering them permanently (Duff 1942, 1).

Goose Bay: Its Impact on Coastal Communities

The construction of Goose Aerodrome had major implications for communities throughout Labrador. Communities in the northern part of southeastern Labrador, principally in Sandwich Bay, were affected in several ways. First and most obviously, seasonal work at Goose Bay raised incomes for workers and their families. Some Cartwright workers, such as Lew Hopkins, sent money back to Cartwright. There, the money was banked in the Hudson's Bay Company bank books and accrued 6 per cent interest (Hopkins and Hopkins 1987, 50). If not unprecedented, such banking, particularly with the Hudson's Bay Company, was certainly unusual. The relatively high wages paid at Goose Bay, and the exodus of men to work there, meant that the Hudson's Bay Company and other occasional employers at Cartwright were forced to raise wages paid to local workers. By the spring of 1942, for example, the Hudson's Bay Company at Cartwright raised wages from 15 cents per hour to 20 to 25 cents per hour, a raise Ranger Summers attributed to 'the wages earned at Goose Bay' (1942d, 1). It is also clear that increased wage labour lowered the amount of relief issued (Summers 1942f, 1) and enabled some families to repay relief issued previously (Summers 1942d, 1). There is also some evidence that the exodus for work at Goose Bay created occasional labour shortages, such as the shortage Ranger Summers predicted for the summer fishery of 1942 (1942a, 2) and from 1942 onward at Port Hope Simpson.

Some of these implications might be expected, but others were less anticipated. There are indications that Goose Bay may have indirectly generated economic differentiation and discouraged the once adaptive, dispersed, and mobile Settler settlement pattern, a point that has not been made in the Labrador literature. I maintain that is exactly what was occurring.

In order for a man to go to work at Goose Bay he either had to have another man or older boy look after his home and family, or had to return home regularly to perform necessary tasks, such as stockpiling firewood. Men who either could not go to Goose Bay to work or could only stay there for short periods were not able to enjoy fully the economic benefits of construction work. In his description of five new families on relief, in January 1942, Ranger Summers gives some indication of how Goose Bay may have effectively left some men (and their families) behind. He writes: 'These five were men who had done well enough with last year's fishery to stay off relief until now, but who were unable to go to Goose Bay to work because they had no-one to leave with their families for the winter. In some cases they were already looking after some of the families of those who had gone to Goose Bay' (1942b, 1). The perpetuation of relative poverty appears to have particularly affected Settlers living in more 'isolated' locations and it is in this sense that I believe wage labour at Goose Bay encouraged centralization to places where a number of households could share in gathering firewood, hauling water, and so on. In March 1942, Ranger Summers provides more detail on families essentially left behind by not being able to work at Goose Bay. He observes:

Practically all able-bodied relief issues this winter have been made to families in one section of the coast, from Spotted Islands to Batteau. Most issues were to families with no-one to leave at home to attend to getting wood and water and getting next year's wood, as well as moving the family in and out of the bays [seasonal transhumance], if the head of the family went to Goose Bay to work. Even so some of the families combined resources, where possible and one member of one family went to work while the member of the other family remained at home to attend to the two families. This was not always possible, however, and accounts for the able-bodied relief when well paid work was available. (1942c, 1)

Now it must be acknowledged that the relative 'isolation' of settlements such as Spotted Island was probably diminished when the RCAF established an outpost there in 1943 and, later, built a radar base. But my point remains: the overwhelming *historic trend* set in motion by Goose Bay was towards centralization on the one hand and the emergence of economic differentiation on the other.

The emergence of new economic differences resembles that which I described some years ago, with respect to the northern Labrador community of Makkovik. There, the genesis of two categories of Settlers – 'Makkovik Settlers' living near an emerging mission centre, and the more dispersed 'Bay Settlers' – began during the first half of this century (Kennedy 1982, 78–81). However, I acknowledge that in the case of southeastern Labrador, the ability of only some men to work at Goose Bay was one of several 'causes' generating socio-economic differences. Cartwright ranger Hart commented on such differences in 1948 when asked to report on how people in his district felt about the confederation issue. He claimed that the decision 'hinged on a few people who may be termed as the higher class' and that by contrast, the vast majority of people in his district were not well educated and lived in small settlements along the coast. There, a lack of radios, among other things, limited access to information (Hart 1948, 1). Being free to work at Goose Bay was more possible where several families lived side-by-side and thus Goose Bay encouraged centralization. In the case of Cartwright, Goose Bay and other fortuitous events, such as the establishment of the Labrador Public School, the IGA Hospital, and the radar base in the 1950s (see below), were all links in a chain of events creating present-day Cartwright.

COASTAL MILITARY INSTALLATIONS

Like all three of Newfoundland's large military bases, Goose Bay had defensive outposts, searchlights, and related weather stations, both to prevent enemy attack and to facilitate communication. Information about these smaller military installations is limited, and even the handful of historical accounts concentrating on Newfoundland's bases, such as those of MacLeod (1986a, 1986b), make little reference to them. Yet, like Goose Bay, these smaller military installations were important: they both employed local people and served significant strategic functions.

The United States and Canada constructed several of these smaller installations in southeastern Labrador during and after the Second World War. For example, Lodge Bay informants recalled that in 1941 the Americans purchased land at White Point (near Battle Harbour) from local resident Jack Murphy for construction of a military installation. This appears to be the same base indirectly referred to by Carr, who cryptically observes that in the summer of 1942, the 'Americans wanted some work done' near Battle Harbour (1944, 124).

The White Point installation was one of two Long-Range Aid to Navigation (LORAN) stations (the other was at Bonavista, Newfoundland) agreed to in 1942 by the American and Canadian Joint Board of Defence and constructed with permission from the Newfoundland government. American and Canadian agreement to install such navigational aids apparently came on 18 June 1942. At that time, C.J. Burchell, high commissioner for Canada, wrote L.E. Emerson, Newfoundland commissioner of justice and defence, describing a recent meeting of the Permanent Joint Board of Defence. During the meeting, consideration was given to new and extended radio navigational aids in the eastern United States, Canada, and Newfoundland (Burchell 1942). Although White Point (or Battle Harbour) is not mentioned in Burchell's letter, mention is made of permission from the Newfoundland government for a radio site at Sandgirt Lake, Labrador (southeast of Lobstick Lake 53°55', 65°15'), presumably to improve radio transmission in western approaches to Goose Bay.

News arrived in Cartwright in May 1942 of a construction project at Rigolet, requiring some eighty to one hundred men (Summers 1942d, 1). In September 1942, Ranger Summers reported construction activity near Cartwright employing twenty to fifty local men, including some unable to work at Goose Bay because of their family commitments (Summers 1942e, 2). The new base Ranger Summers refers to may have been at Spotted Island, ninety kilometres south of Cartwright.

The LORAN stations became operational by United States Navy personnel about January 1943. Then in June 1943 the United States applied for permission to use about one acre at St Anthony and Twillingate to construct two more LORAN stations. The Newfoundland government soon gave permission.

By summer 1943 the RCAF sought permission from Newfoundland to build and occupy two Radio Direction Finding stations – one at Spotted Island and the other at Brig Harbour Island (east of Holton, about 54°33', 57°10') – for the duration of the war plus six months. Each would occupy about five hundred square feet and include an administration building, powerhouse, two barracks, mess and recreation building, three outdoor toilets, two warehouses, and wireless and emergency quarters (Britton 1943). Two officers and thirty-eight other ranks would be stationed at each.

However, in his report for October 1944, Ranger Clark writes that, 'The RCAF Base at Spotted Islands [sic], where over a hundred enlisted men, together with a small quantity of local labour, were rushing the project to completion, has been suddenly abandoned and is now being stripped of all movables, most of which will be transferred to the RCAF station at Brig Harbour' (1). Even though the RCAF base at Spotted Island appears to have been abandoned, a radar base was built there during the 1950s (see below).

During the Cold War, a chain of radar sites, the Mid-Canada Early Warning System – the southern arm of the better-known Distant Early Warning (DEW) line – was constructed along the Labrador coast. 'Radar and telecommunications installations were built in a string of sites between Frobisher Bay and St Anthony, linking DEW Line bases in the Arctic with NORAD headquarters in Colorado. Sites were erected at Cartwright, Spotted Islands and Fox Harbour' (Jackson 1982, 36). Initially, in August 1948, Ottawa informed St John's that radar stations were to be built at St Anthony, Hopedale, and Port Burwell (Cape Chidley). Additional Labrador stations were added at Cartwright, Saglek, Goose Bay (Miller 1967, 23), Fox Harbour, and Spotted Island and construction began as early as 1951. An agreement signed in 1955 between the United States and Canada explained the logistical details of coastal radar installations, including the instruction that American or Canadian contractors give preference to qualified Canadian labourers (U.S. Department of State 1955).

Schneider (1984, 412) writes that over two hundred people (50 per cent from Newfoundland and Quebec) worked on the two-year-long construction of the Cartwright radar base in the early 1950s. Once constructed, the workforce shrunk to about twenty, plus 150 American servicemen (ibid., 413). The Cartwright base operated until 1967, when it was taken over by the Newfoundland Telephone Company (ibid., 156). Significantly, the Cartwright base was still operating when the

Newfoundland government began its resettlement program, discussed in Chapter 10. Bureaucrats in distant centres linked the bases to the communities themselves, making them obvious destinations for a more centralized population.

The construction of military bases during and after the Second World War brought with it major cultural changes. In Labrador, as on the island of Newfoundland, military bases exposed residents to many new influences, ranging from the introduction of new foods and types of music to luxury goods and changing attitudes about the value of work and money (Straus 1975, 556–60). Coastal Labrador radar bases became symbols of change to a new way of life – huge radar domes were visible evidence that much that was unfathomable to local people was, indeed, real.

Military bases raised expectations – both locally and in St John's, the provincial capital – that communities near bases would be the centres of the future. Certainly at the time such a conclusion appeared warranted in the case of Cartwright and Fox Harbour. The radar station overlooking Cartwright advanced that community's growing status as a population centre while the one built at Fox Harbour accelerated that community's growth. Fox Harbour was only a small community when construction of the radar site begun in 1954. Many families had only began wintering at Fox Harbour in the 1940s, having wintered during the 1930s at Riverhead and other places in St Lewis Inlet while cutting pit-props for the Labrador Development Company.

However, base construction also brought consequences which, with hindsight, were unwelcome, such as sexual exploitation and alcohol abuse (Schneider 1984, 413). Bases may have left other, more invisible scars as well. During the years after the abandonment of the Cartwright base, locals pilfered the polychlorinated biphenyl (PCB) contaminated ruins looking for scrap metal and other useful things. Scavenging, or alternatively working at the base during its heyday, is now blamed for the occurrence of cancer, which locals believe is more common in Sandwich Bay than elsewhere and which they link to contamination with PCBs.

The three intrusive forces discussed in this chapter were important links in a chain starting with Labrador's dispersed and mobile lifestyle and ending in the eleven increasingly permanent communities found today. The often serendipitous nature of community evolution can briefly be summarized with reference to Cartwright. Early in the twentieth century, prior to the 1918 epidemic, the twelve families wintering at Paradise River made it the largest community in Sandwich Bay. Next, recall that the 1918 epidemic created the need for a boarding-school to house and educate the many orphans; the Grenfell Mission followed with a clinic, which evolved into a hospital, and a regional tuberculosis sanatorium. Then came the Second World War, confederation, military base construction and the convergence of outlying Settlers in Cartwright. Had this accidental chain of circumstances and events been broken, the fate of Cartwright, the second-largest community in the region today, would have been very different.

10

Resettlement

Soon after confederation, the new province entered the business of social engineering in the form of a major resettlement program which was to dramatically reshuffle the population of southeastern Labrador. If Newfoundland and Labrador's membership in the Canadian federation represents the birth of the modern era, resettlement was its baptism. Resettlement closed numerous little communities and relocated their inhabitants to places where the economic potential seemed more promising. This complicated and controversial saga in the history of modern Newfoundland still profoundly affects the communities to which people moved. But before examining the resettlement in southeastern Labrador, it is worthwhile to look at the background of what continues to be the most contentious of all Newfoundland government programs.[1]

Voluntary seasonal and permanent population movement has always been part of the socio-economic landscape of Newfoundland and Labrador. Perhaps the earliest government-initiated interest in resettlement dates to 1899, and followed a late nineteenth-century crisis in the fishery and a rapid growth in the rural population. At that time a report by Newfoundland's agricultural commissioners suggested that the government give assistance to resettle fishing settlements lacking good agricultural lands in places where a combined fishing and farming adaptation was possible (Anonymous 1985, 1–2).

Throughout the modern era, the costs of providing services to Newfoundland and Labrador's small and dispersed population have always been high. Stavely concludes that government subsidies to 'thinly patronized steamship and telegraph services' were a major reason for Newfoundland's bankruptcy in the 1930s (1981, 161). By the late 1940s and early 1950s people's expectations had soared after years of employment in military base construction and with the initial fruits of confederation with Canada. Yet as recently as the mid-1950s, Fraser estimates that 90 per cent of the province's 415,000 people lived in some three thousand small villages scattered along six thousand miles of rugged and often inaccessible coastline (1958, 273–4). The cost of providing an ever-expanding smorgasbord of services favoured some concentration of the new province's dispersed population.

Between 1945 and 1953 (or 1954), forty-one (Harnum 1973, 1) or forty-six (Copes 1971, 8) of Newfoundland's smallest villages were abandoned. People left their ancestral homes to obtain improved services, chiefly education, and apparently did so without help from government. Most moved only a few kilometres, settling in communities only slightly larger than those they left (Courtney 1973). In one such case, the people of Bragg's Island, Bonavista Bay, moved in the early 1950s, after repeatedly experiencing problems recruiting teachers. Around 1953 the new provincial government proposed a system of per capita cash grants which would become the template for subsequent government-assisted resettlement schemes (Stavely 1981, 162).

GOVERNMENT-ASSISTED RESETTLEMENT

In 1953 a Federal-Provincial Fisheries Development Committee recommended the centralization of Newfoundland's numerous fishing communities in places where fish-processing facilities were opening (Copes 1972, 25). As early as the first provincial government-assisted centralization program, drafted in 1953 (Copes 1971, 8), government sought to 'rationalize' population distribution, particularly in relation to the fishery, and to provide improved access to services and development opportunities.

The provincial Department of Welfare administered the first centralization program. One hundred per cent of a community's residents were required to sign a petition indicating their desire to resettle in order for each household to receive a maximum 'removal grant' of $150 (later increased to $600) (Harnum 1973, 1). Between 1954 and 1965, 115 communities, a total of about 7500 people, were centralized under this program (Lane 1967, 564).

The pace of change in the fishery intensified during the 1960s. In Newfoundland, a new fresh-frozen cod industry was replacing the ancient salt-cod fishery and new fish-processing plants opened in several larger outports. Emphasis shifted to middle-range and offshore fishing technologies requiring increasing numbers of workers for fish plants. New incentives were necessary to concentrate labour at these new centres of work. After 1965, the federal government took over the provincial government's role in fisheries development (Copes 1971, 12).

In 1964 the federal government agreed to assist the province in resettlement. On 16 July 1965, both governments signed the first federal-provincial agreement, which came into effect retroactively on 1 April 1965. The province administered the program but relied primarily on federal monies. Regulations stipulated that communities considering resettlement first hold a public meeting and decide whether or not to resettle. If residents chose to move, the community elected a three-person committee. Its job was to circulate a petition throughout the community and negotiate on behalf of the community with the director of resettlement. Initially, regulations required that 90 (then 80, and later 50) per cent of householders seeking to move sign this petition. A director initially operating within a division of a provincial department administered the program. A fifteen-member (ten representing the province and five Canada) federal-provincial committee reviewed resettlement applications and made recommendations regarding overall policy.

To be eligible for the larger federal grants provided under the 1965 program, householders could not move freely, but instead could only move to and from certain types of communities. Applicants traversed a labyrinth of bureaucracy, chief among which were several ambiguous definitions of 'community.' The intention of government was to ensure an orderly movement of people, both from and to specific kinds of places. Definitions of these types of communities follow, but they are, surprisingly, absent from the 1965 Newfoundland Household Resettlement Act and infrequently mentioned in academic studies on resettlement.

Several revisions to the program were made between 1965 and 1970, the most important being the 1966 amendment permitting *individual* householders to resettle (Canada [DREE] 1970a, 1). Individual householders eligible for resettlement included those moving to approved receiving communities with improved employment prospects, widows, the handicapped, and incapacitated persons (Canada [DREE] 1970b, 5–6). The inclusion of individual households opened the floodgates for resettlement in southeastern Labrador, and as we shall see, most resettlement there occurred between 1967 and 1970. Letters from southeastern Labrador residents to the director of resettlement reveal two main reasons why people wanted to move: a poor and uncertain fishery, and improved educational opportunities for their children.

In 1969 the federal government established the Department of Regional Economic Expansion (DREE) to foster regional development. In Newfoundland, one of DREE's strategies was to create 'special areas' for the concentration of people and development incentives. The economic assumption behind the special-area concept was that larger communities, so-called growth points, offered more economic diversity than smaller ones. Under terms of the Regional Economic Act (1969), the federal minister of DREE (with cooperation from the province) planned and approved special areas, including the St John's and Conception Bay area, Clarenville, and Corner Brook.

DREE took additional responsibility for resettlement at the beginning of the second federal-provincial agreement (Canada DREE 1970c, 1), signed on 17 July 1970 and covering the period from 1 April 1970 to 31 March 1975. The size of the federal-provincial resettlement committee decreased to eight, and its members were now equally divided between the federal and provincial governments. The proportionally larger federal representation indicates its growing financial contribution – up to $2.5 million yearly, by 1970–1 – to resettlement (Canada [DREE] 1970b). In 1970, the resettlement committee came under the direction of a federal-provincial joint planning committee and a DREE task force was established to assemble basic information relevant to resettlement. The province continued to administer the daily operations of the program, now through a division of the Department of Community and Social Development.

As mentioned, a householder's eligibility for assistance depended on the kind of community he or she moved to and from. To begin with, a person or family had to move from a 'designated outport.' As of 1970, a designated outport was any community where at least 80 per cent of householders signed the petition indicating their desire to move (Harnum 1970, 1). A similar, although more tentative classification was the 'sending community,' defined in 1971 as a community with fewer than three hundred people that had experienced at least 5 per cent population loss in the previous five years (Sametz and Miller 1971).

A 1973 report lists several characteristics of sending communities, chief among them that not less than 35 per cent of the householders living in the community five years before had moved (Canada [DREE] 1973, 1). A 'scoring team' (apparently a subcommittee of the resettlement committee) surveyed the province for potential sending communities, and some of these would later become 'designated outports.' All communities were potentially fair game for a visit by this team. 'Population rationalization' remained the committee's goal, and this was done on the basis of the level of unemployment, welfare, development possibilities, and the like in the communities (ibid.).

In order to receive financial assistance, people were required to move to 'receiving communities,' approved 'resettlement centres,' DREE 'special areas,' or major 'fishery growth centres' (Harnum 1970, 1). Receiving communities were designated according to their services and employment opportunities. Ideally, a receiving community needed to score at least sixty-five points but more generally had to be a place which the Joint Planning Committee assessed to be expanding (Canada [DREE] 1973, 1). After DREE became involved with the program, two types of receiving communities – DREE and non-DREE – emerged. I could find no explanation for this distinction.

The fact that few communities qualified for receiving community status restricted people's choice of destinations and, as seen below, created serious problems for the resettlement program. As of mid-January 1973, excluding DREE special areas, there were only 'approximately 22 approved Receiving Communities' in the whole province (Canada [DREE] 1973, 10; Harnum 1973, 3).

RESETTLEMENT IN SOUTHEASTERN LABRADOR

Since the Second World War, voluntary population movements, as well as the planned resettlement programs just described, have had a major impact on the communities of southeastern Labrador. We have seen that during the years of the Labrador Development Company and especially of military base construction at Goose Bay, a seasonal pattern of migratory labour developed, with men travelling to work sites for all or part of the winter. For some men and their families, this new pattern dovetailed with the customary seasonal cycle, and as we saw in the case of Goose Bay, winter wage labour replaced traditional winter pursuits such as trapping. I have no data on families moving permanently to Goose Bay during the period prior to the first Canada-Newfoundland resettlement agreement (1965), although some southeastern Labrador families undoubtedly did move. However, we do know about population moves within the region, such as Dyke's reference to the move of West Bay people to North River, Sandwich Bay, in the fall of 1963, under the Newfoundland government's centralization program (1969, 151). Another example of a community moving, en masse, is that involving the people currently wintering at Norman Bay. These families moved to Norman Bay from Otter Bay in 1956, to be nearer better sources of drinking-water and firewood. This move occurred independent of any government resettlement program. Similarly, Schneider (1984) gives a summary of specific details regarding centralization to Cartwright, some prior to the government resettlement program. For example, three people moved from Sandy Hill Bay in 1956, twelve families from Goose Cove in 1960, four families from Dove Brook in 1960, eleven people from Plant's Bight in 1962, and seven families from Spotted Island in 1965 (ibid., 126).

In southeastern Labrador, most government-assisted resettlement occurred between 1967 and 1970. The two Grenfell centres, Cartwright and Mary's Harbour, received most of the people who resettled within the region, while Happy Valley/Goose Bay and various Conception Bay and West Coast (Newfoundland) communities were the primary destinations of those moving outside the region. Cartwright, Mary's Harbour, and apparently Charlottetown were approved 'receiving communities' under the first federal-provincial program (1965–70) but after 1970 their status is more vague. The Minutes of the Newfoundland Resettlement Committee (hereafter RC) repeatedly claim that there were no receiving communities on the Labrador coast after 1970, whereas both Cartwright and Mary's Harbour appear in lists of non-Dree designated receiving communities in a 1973 report (Canada [DREE] 1973, unpaged appendix). I cannot resolve this discrepancy, but because of the frequent references to the absence of receiving communities after 1970, I accept that interpretation.

Table 2 presents government statistics about the communities that southeastern Labrador people moved to and from, and compares the incidence of resettlement under the first and second federal-provincial resettlement programs. Although incomplete, these statistics are the best available, and certain tentative conclusions may be drawn from them.

Most households (91 per cent, or sixty-seven out of seventy-three) moved between 1965 and 1970, more specifically between 1967 and 1970. Increased resettlement beginning in 1967 can be attributed to changes already described which permitted individual householders to relocate. However, in 1970 'receiving community' status for Mary's Harbour, Charlottetown, and Cartwright appears to have been withdrawn, removing nearby locations where southeast Labradorians could receive government assistance for moving. This withdrawal is an ironic and contradictory one, since the government had been encouraging people to move to communities near those they left so that they could

TABLE 2
Relocation of communities

Origin	Destination					
	1965–70			1970–5		
	Cwt	H.V.	M.H.	Cwt	H.V.	M.H.
Independ. Hr.	1 (5)					
North R.	1 (5)					
Paradise R.	3 (16)					
Spotted Is.	8 (63)	6 (58)		1 (5)		
Batteau	17 (115)	1 (4)				
Seal Is.	1 (3)			1 (10)		
Patridge Bay	5 (33)			1 (11)		
Square Is.			1 (3)			
Port Hope Simp.		1 (3)			1 (5)	
Fox Harbour					1 (2)	
Battle Hr.		1 (5)	14 (59)			
Indian Cove			5 (15)			1 (5)
White Point			1 (5)			
Henley Hr.			1 (4)			
Totals	36 (240)	9 (60)	22 (86)	2 (21)	3 (12)	1 (5)

SOURCE: compiled from Canada, Statistics Federal-Provincial Resettlement Program. CNS 1975
KEY: Cwt = Cartwright; H.V. = Happy Valley; M.H. = Mary's Harbour.
NOTES: The number preceding the parentheses is for household(s); that within parentheses represents number of persons. Thus, 3 (15) means three households totalling 15 people.

continue to use their old summer fishing premises. Local people favoured this idea. In the case of Charlottetown, withdrawal of 'receiving community' status appears to have caused tensions, as referred to in a letter dated 13 May 1970 from the Mary's Harbour welfare officer to the director of resettlement. It reads, in part: 'In connection with applicants for assistance to relocate to Charlottetown, I feel that this is a very touchy situation and I am very reluctant to have anything to do with it. It is a job for someone who knows the regulations and is qualified to coupe [sic] with such a situation' (Decker 1970).

Removal of receiving community status for Cartwright, Charlottetown, and Mary's Harbour produced a bureaucratic 'Catch 22' situation. The resettlement division could not consider requests from southeastern Labrador people for 'local consolidation' (i.e., resettlement within the region) because there were no receiving communities along the Labrador coast! The absence of receiving communities prompted the federal-provincial committee to invite the director of Northern Labrador Services Division (subsequently, LSD) to their November 1971 meeting, to seek his suggestions for potential coastal sending or receiving communities. The committee did not select any communities at the time but the director's testimony saved Paradise River from resettlement. The director explained that pulpwood was being harvested near Paradise River for a mill at Come By Chance, Newfoundland (RC 39th Meeting, 2), and that Paradise River could be the headquarters for pulpwood logging in the area (ibid.). By the fall of 1972, a subcommittee of the federal-provincial committee planned to visit Labrador to select one or more receiving communities. Then, the newly elected provincial government cancelled this visit and appointed a royal commission to investigate various Labrador problems; it was hoped the commission would gather information on potential receiving communities (RC 52nd Meeting).

Throughout the province, the slow-down in resettlement after 1970 was also related to the fact that fewer communities were being approved as sending communities. This slow-down eventually led the joint planning committee to request a report on the problem from the Newfoundland Resettlement Committee. Appendix IV of the Resettlement Committee's report lists 946 cases where resettlement was not permitted because of various technicalities. The Resettlement Committee denied resettlement in the majority of these cases (460) because the people applying did not live in approved sending communities (Canada [DREE] 1973, 19). The program had become entangled in its own bureaucracy.

Meanwhile, back in southeastern Labrador, the numbers of communities approved as 'designated outports' and 'sending communities' increased. Thus, at the 10 November 1970 meeting of the Newfoundland Resettlement Committee, Battle Harbour, Henley Harbour, and Spotted Island (communities from which many people had already moved) were approved as 'designated outports' while Fox Harbour, Hawke Harbour, Snug Harbour, Square Islands, and West Bay were approved as 'sending communities' (RC 14th Meeting, Appendix 1). By the autumn of 1971, Paradise River, Triangle, Indian Cove, Seal Island, and Cape Charles were listed as potential 'sending communities,' pending discussions in Labrador with the people of these communities (RC 37th Meeting and 38th Meeting). In March 1972, North River (Sandwich Bay) and Port Hope Simpson were approved by the Joint Committee as 'sending communities' (RC 52nd Meeting). In short, the slow-down in resettlement in southeastern Labrador was not caused by any shortage of communities from which people could move but by government's inability to decide which communities had enough of a future to be labelled 'receiving communities.'

Resettlement slowed after 1970 because most people who wanted government assistance for moving had already moved during the first federal-provincial program. Table 2 shows that the communities of Battle Harbour, Batteau, and Spotted Island provided approximately 70 per cent of all the people who moved to other communities within the region. The two most important destinations within the region were Cartwright and Mary's Harbour. Cartwright attracted people between Independent Island and Partridge Bay, while Mary's Harbour took people from Square Islands to Henley Harbour. If one examines these two districts, one discovers that there are more people per household in the northern (6.2 persons) than in the southern (3.6) district and that slightly more people relocated from communities in the northern district. I believe these differences are consistent with historic socio-economic differences between the northern and southern part of southeastern Labrador. Assuming household size may be inversely related to relative socio-economic conditions, we can infer from Table 2 that larger and poorer families from the northern district were more apt to move than were smaller and slightly more affluent southern families (see also Jackson 1982, 41–2).

COMMUNITIES WHICH MOVED AND THOSE WHICH DID NOT

During the resettlement era, especially between 1967 and 1970, roughly one-quarter of all the people in southeastern Labrador resettled. This migration swelled the size of destinations like Mary's Harbour and, especially, Cartwright. It produced new social divisions in these host communities, and reduced the traditional harvesting of winter resources at the former winter homes of those who moved (Jackson 1982). In order to understand how the resettlement program affected people, it is perhaps best to sharpen our focus and examine the case of one community that moved and one community that was not permitted to move. In order to do so, it is helpful to have some idea of the lifestyle and history of each community prior to the resettlement era.

Pitt's Arm/Henley Harbour

The winter community of Pitt's Arm and its summer fishing settlement,

Henley Harbour, were in some respects typical of seasonal southeastern Labrador communities. Until resettlement in 1970, the people of these seasonal communities practised a difficult, seasonally ordered and meaningful way of life.

Charles Stone (1803–88), the male progenitor of Henley Harbour, was a native of Dorsetshire, England, and began fishing at Henley Harbour around 1818. Informants told me (see also Dyke 1969, 42) that Stone initially wintered at Cape Norman, Newfoundland, commuting the approximately forty kilometres across the Strait of Belle Isle by bully boat each fall and spring. Stone and his family did so, their descendants surmise, because 'they weren't settled in here' yet. Most contemporary third- and fourth-generation Stones are descendants of Charles Stone and his second wife, Eliza (nee Lambert, 1834–97).

Today their descendants make a similar journey, not because they have not established a winter settlement, but because they were relocated from it in 1970 to several Newfoundland and Labrador villages. Most have a different lifestyle than they once practised at Pitt's Arm.

Throughout this century, people wintered at Pitt's Arm and then moved a few kilometres to Henley Harbour around mid-April. During May, people built or repaired boats, set seal nets around Castle Island, and hunted eider ducks at American Tickle, Antelope Tickle, and other locations. Salmon and cod fishing began in mid-June, followed by a herring fishery between August and early October. People moved back to Pitt's Arm in mid-October. Fur trapping on individually owned and inherited trap lines took place throughout the fall. Trap lines were located within an extensive area which other communities recognized as Henley Harbour land; this extended from St Peter's Bay inland to St Peter's Pond, thence to Chateau Pond, around Chateau Brook and Temple Bay.

Work repairing seal nets continued during long fall nights in preparation for the fall harp-seal fishery. Seal netting occurred around Seal Island and Bad Bay. People used seal meat for dog and human food and sold salted sealskins to Ayres and Sons, St Johns. People also used sealskins to make boots and dog-team traces and for filling snowshoe ('racket') bows. Much of the cutting of firewood and the sawing of logs occurred in December and January, before heavy snow accumulations. This was followed by sawmilling in March and April. During the 1960s, there were four individually owned sawmills at Pitt's Arm of six to ten horsepower. They produced sufficient rough lumber for local use and sold surplus two-by-fours and four-by-fours to Fishery Products, at Henley Harbour. Cooperative duck hunting occurred between late

December and early March. Bottled duck provided food for several months. Groups of from two to six men hunted caribou in March and April, covering a vast expanse of the interior from the St Lewis River south to Pinware. Older people told me that the closest place caribou were killed was in the Chateau Hills and remembered that the last caribou were killed about 1959. By mid-April Pitt's Arm people moved out to their summer homes at Henley Harbour.

During much of this century, the population of Pitt's Arm/Henley Harbour fluctuated between a low of thirty-seven and high of eighty-five (Dyke 1969, 42). Newfoundland stationers swelled the population of Henley Harbour each summer. Between the late 1930s (Smallwood 1984) and about 1974, the Newfoundland firm of Fishery Products purchased locally produced fish and sold supplies at Henley Harbour. Thus, even after the closure of Pitt's Arm in 1970, relocated Pitt's Arm Settlers still returned to Henley Harbour each summer to fish. A community stage was built for their use at Henley Harbour in 1977 and then leased to Central Diaries of Stephenville.

Before relocation Pitt's Arm and Henley Harbour had one-room schools which operated seasonally. For much of the administrative history of Battle Harbour and later Mary's Harbour, Henley Harbour and Pitt's Arm were the southernmost communities administered by the Anglican church and Grenfell Mission. These administrations linked Pitt's Arm and Henley Harbour to southeastern Labrador as did the marriage preferences of Pitt's Arm folk and the social ties created by marriage. Thus, most Pitt's Arm folk married north rather than south; marriages with Cape Charles spouses were especially common. Newfoundland stationer-fishing crews at nearby Chateau were often Roman Catholic, which diminished the possibility for marriage with the Anglican Settlers of Pitt's Arm/Henley Harbour.

According to Dyke's (1969) data, fifty-nine of the eighty people at Henley Harbour during the summer of 1965 spent the winter of 1965–6 at Pitt's Arm. Twenty-seven of the fifty-nine were under eighteen years of age, and of these, eighteen were students of Mr Davy, the British volunteer schoolteacher. Thirty-two of the fifty-nine were eighteen years or older, and of these, twenty were male and twelve female. As explained, the larger percentage of adult males to females is common in coastal communities, where men stay to fish while women leave to marry. In sum, on the eve of resettlement in 1965–6, Pitt's Arm and Henley Harbour were small, although viable, seasonal communities. By the fall of 1970, Pitt's Arm was abandoned.

Once the first federal-provincial resettlement program (1965-70) provided what people considered to be sufficient compensation, people chose to move, hoping to improve both educational and economic opportunities. Thus, in 1967, several months after the resettlement committee began subsidizing moves by individual families, Pitt's Arm people began writing Resettlement Director Harnum, inquiring about moving. In November of that year, for example, Allan (a pseudonym), a forty-eight-year-old father of five, wrote the director claiming that he could not afford to send his children away to school, and suggesting that if the whole family moved to a place like Churchill Falls (Labrador), there 'would be a good chance for them to get an education and good jobs when they grow up' (RF H 556, n.d.). In the autumn of 1969, Allan and his family moved to Manuels, Newfoundland, and later to nearby Seal Cove within the bounds of a DREE 'Special Area.' This destination made it possible for Allan to purchase a home with a mortgage jointly subsidized by the federal and provincial governments (75/25 per cent).

Similarly, in September 1968, John, a fifty-three-year-old father of four, wrote the director, claiming that he and his family planned to move permanently to Corner Brook, Newfoundland, the next month. John explained, 'I am moving there to work and I have a job awaiting my arrival. I have children of school age and I am interested in getting better schooling for them' (RF H 3475). As it turned out, John did not move at that time, and it is doubtful whether a job actually awaited his arrival. Quite possibly the welfare officer at Mary's Harbour, who helped people complete applications for resettlement, had advised John that his application stood a better chance if he claimed to have a job. When he and his family finally did move, in October 1969, he hoped to gain 'seasonal employment at a herring factory in Curling [Newfoundland]' (Cadigan 1969). John received a $2200 resettlement grant.

By 1969, the exodus of families such as those of Allan and John reduced the population of Pitt's Arm to thirty-five. Only nine students attended local schools that year. In addition to the loss of families, some informants place the blame for the school's shrinking enrolment also on new provincial school bursaries, which lured Pitt's Arm students to other, larger schools. In any event, Pitt's Arm residents learned that no teacher would be sent to Pitts Arm-Henley Harbour for the 1970–71 year. With obvious resentment, the same informants told me that, as they left Pitt's Arm forever in autumn 1970, a teacher, unbeknownst to them, was sailing on the coastal boat north to their community!

The fact that individual families vacated Pitt's Arm between 1967 and 1970 may be attributed to the changes made in 1967 which allowed individual families to move. People probably learned about the resettlement program from the welfare officer in Mary's Harbour, from other fishers, and from the radio. It may be noted that by 1965 all Henley Harbour households had radios (Dyke 1969, 44) and these received several Newfoundland stations.

In addition to their desire to improve educational opportunities for their children, Pitt's Arm/Henley Harbour people wanted to move also because of declining cod catches during the late 1960s. In his 15 November 1967 letter to the director of resettlement, Allan wrote: 'I have been fishing most of my life. I did very good for a few years, but the last four years was a complete blank, I had to go to the Welfare Department for help this year ... I don't see any future for my family if I stay here' (RF H, 556). Others like Bob, a sixty-three-year-old father of nine (only the two youngest still lived with him), wrote to the director of resettlement in October 1969 and mentioned the failure of that year's fishery. That same month, Bob and his family moved to Corner Brook 'temporarily' to look for work. They remained in Corner Brook, but because of the planned 'temporary' duration of their stay, were not able to receive resettlement assistance until 1970, when they received $1800 (RF H, 5107).

Some informants at Henley Harbour linked the traditional value placed on independence with the decision to close Pitt's Arm. They remembered that when the cod fishery began to fail in the late 1960s, some men brought their families to Corner Brook to work, rather than remain at Pitt's Arm on welfare. In one man's words, 'people were too independent to accept government relief when the fishery failed.' This decreased the population of Pitt's Arm and, they reasoned, encouraged government to close the village.

In the fall of 1970, the thirty-eight people remaining at Pitt's Arm moved elsewhere for the winter. News that some of these people had arrived in the Corner Brook/Curling area came on 17 September 1970, most ironically during a meeting of the Newfoundland Resettlement Committee. One of the Newfoundland committee members received a phone call from Corner Brook 'advising that a number of the residents from Henley Harbour had moved into Corner Brook and to some communities which had not been designated as receiving communities and this was presenting something of a problem' (RC 1st Meeting, 3).

Of the thirty-eight people who moved from Henley Harbour that fall, eighteen went to Corner Brook, eleven remained in Labrador communities, and nine moved to Kelligrews and Chamberlains, Newfoundland. Six of these nine included Allan and his family, who had returned that summer to fish at Henley Harbour.

While Pitt's Arm has been unoccupied since 1970, many former residents converge on Henley Harbour to fish each summer. During the summer of 1979, for example, thirty-four people (all but two named Stone) fished at Henley Harbour. Eighteen of these people now winter in Newfoundland, sixteen of them in four Labrador communities. Like their counterparts in other communities abandoned during the resettlement era, the former residents of Pitt's Arm/Henley Harbour remain divided about whether they should have moved. They argue about whether they relinquished their proprietary rights to Pitt's Arm or Henley Harbour, and about whether or not they are better off in their adopted communities.

One category of people who remain bitter about relocation is the ageing single men, many inveterate bachelors, who composed seven of the fifteen men over age twenty-five in my 1979 Henley Harbour census. Some of these men blame relocation on declining school attendance during the late 1960s. One of these bachelors angrily described the closing of Pitt's Arm by saying, 'it was just like taking a crowd of sheep off an island where there was plenty to eat and putting them where there's nothing to eat.' The same man described the Labrador community where he now lives as a 'starvation place' where all food consumed 'has to come out of the store.' Yet obviously these childless bachelors unintentionally helped to kill Pitt's Arm.

There can be little question that the quality of life for many who moved was diminished. Others, particularly those who wanted to move, are more acquiescent about resettlement. Whatever their views, however, the Pitt's Arm people with whom I spoke continue to express a strong primordial attachment to their former homeland.

Black Tickle: A Community Not Permitted to Move

The community of Black Tickle is located about 175 kilometres north of Henley Harbour, on the Island of Ponds, a low wetland interspersed with some 366 peat-coloured ponds. Given this profusion of ponds, it is ironic that access to potable drinking-water remains an elusive goal for Black Tickle today. Along with Black Tickle, three other communities on the Island of Ponds were once important fishing stations: Bat-

teau, Domino, and Salmon Bight, of which the last is considered to be
Black Tickle's twin settlement (Dyke 1969, 124). Although partially
based on confusing census materials, Dyke's population compilation
shows a combined figure of eighty-six for Black Tickle and Salmon
Bight, of whom forty-eight were stationers, primarily from Conception
Bay. The remaining thirty-eight people wintered at Porcupine Bay,
about fifteen kilometres from Black Tickle. Dyke also lists twenty-nine
and forty-two people as wintering during 1966 at Black Tickle and
Salmon Bight respectively; if they did so, then the combined population
wintering at either Porcupine Bay or Black Tickle/Salmon Bight was 109
(Dyke 1969, 125). As can be seen in Table 2, the people of Batteau and
nearby Spotted Island resettled between 1965 and 1970, most moving to
the growing centre of Cartwright.

Black Tickle is situated along a stretch of coast (between Seal Islands
and West Bay) where, as Jackson observes, more communities resettled
than anywhere else in Labrador (1982, 41–2). As early as the mid-1950s,
authorities had 'targeted' this area as 'special': 'In discussing the special
area comprising Batteau, Black Tickle, Seal Islands, etc. it was generally
agreed that, while the basic problems were economic, the circumstances
of the people might be improved by the services of a Travelling Public
Health Nurse and intensive Social Work. The real hope for the rehabilitation of these people, however, lies in resettlement in larger more
progressive communities, and they might be willing to move if proper
incentives were provided' (Labrador Conference 1956, 11).

Within southeastern Labrador, Black Tickle is unique in another
important respect: it is the only Roman Catholic community between
West St Modeste in the Labrador Strait and the Innu (Indian) community of Sheshatsheits, Lake Melville. Although the history of Black Tickle
is not well known, its Catholic origins likely lie in the last great Irish
immigration to Newfoundland. Irish settlement swelled the population
of Newfoundland's Avalon peninsula, and some Irish settled permanently in southeastern Labrador. Indeed, Black Tickle people told me
that some of the Dysons, a common Black Tickle surname along with
Keefe and Elson, came to Black Tickle from North River (Conception
Bay), Newfoundland.

Unlike Battle Harbour, where few traces of Roman Catholicism survive among the Irish Catholics who settled there, in Black Tickle Irish
Catholics have maintained their religion. In the Black Tickle case, maintenance of Catholicism or conversion to Anglicanism appears to have
followed family lines, possibly because of the personality of particular

family heads or, more likely, because of dominant links particular Labrador settlements had with Newfoundland Protestant or Catholic communities through the fishery (see for example, Hussey 1981, 80–3).

Black Tickle people declined to resettle under the 1965 program (McCarthy, personal communication, 13 Dec. 1978). And by 1970, we have seen that there were no approved 'receiving centres' along the Labrador coast and most resettlement had already occurred. During his invited testimony before the joint resettlement committee, in November 1971, the director of the Northern Labrador Services Division (LSD) was reported to have said the following about Black Tickle: 'Two families were assisted to move into this community and there is no indication that the householders will relocate. There are 35 families, all Roman Catholics, the only such community in the area. It is a desolate community that requires assistance. Electricity is now being installed. The community also has a good school and an I.G.A. Nursing station. It is heavily dependent upon Social Assistance' (RC 39th Meeting). A provincial member of the committee then asked the director if the people of Black Tickle might be moved into a subdivision of Cartwright. In his paraphrased response, the director is said to have responded that 'he did not think that this would work as it would be bringing a large new religious denominational bloc into the community, with the likelihood of having a separate enclave, but with careful planning and patience, an integral community could be achieved' (ibid.). The director had visited Black Tickle during the summer of 1971 and extended Northern Labrador Services Division help to improve local housing. In the winter of 1972 Black Tickle's new Local Improvement Committee accepted the LSD's offer and also that year, the Federal-Provincial Native Peoples Agreement (1970) was extended to Black Tickle (LSD 1973, 201). The inclusion of Black Tickle under Labrador's native peoples agreement was based more on the community's tarnished (although undeserved) reputation among bureaucrats and other outsiders as an inbred hell-hole than on the ethnicity of its people. After all, Black Tickle's English-speaking Settler population had no more (or less) 'native blood' than was present in such southeastern Labrador communities as Fox Harbour, Williams Harbour, and Cartwright. And while Black Tickle houses undoubtedly needed repairs, so did those of other fishing communities. Here it must be remembered that until the 1950s, Black Tickle had only been a summer fishing community. In short, the social isolation brought on by its regionally unique religion, economic depression, and geographic remoteness convinced visiting bureaucrats that Black Tickle needed help and that this was most easily provided under the native peoples agreement. By 1975, in an incredible example of bureaucratic imagination, the LSD director described the ethnic composition of Black Tickle's 170 people as 'two-thirds Eskimo and one-third Settler' (LSD 1975, 152). This outrageous claim would later raise the ire of other Labrador aboriginal peoples and ultimately lead to the community's removal from the Native Peoples Agreement.

In the summer of 1972, Labrador Services arranged for the construction of three homes, a new herring-packing shed, a wharf, and a boat slipway in Black Tickle. The LSD did not initiate any new projects the following year. Meanwhile the community debated whether it should, or should not, relocate (LSD 1974, 73).

In January 1972 a British-born storekeeper and his two brothers helped form a Local Improvement Committee (LIC). The storekeeper was elected chairman. The journalist Claire Hoy (1973) claims that the formation of the LIC and its campaign to move Black Tickle to Alex Cove, roughly twenty kilometres distant, split the village into two factions. Hoy writes: 'On one side of the issue stand the local storekeeper, two teachers, government officials and a few townspeople. On the other stand fishermen and their wives – poor, illiterate, unaccustomed to telling a government what they want' (ibid.). The fishers opposed the move for the understandable reason that the commute to the fishing grounds from Alex Cove would take two hours each way, rather than the twenty minutes from Black Tickle.

But the LIC persisted, and in March 1973 further discussions about relocating Black Tickle took place with LSD officials and with the Memorial University of Newfoundland extension worker stationed at Cartwright. The extension worker was summoned to the community by the LIC and interviewed local residents about resettlement. A meeting was held and attended by about eighty-four of Black Tickle's approximately one hundred and fifty people. While all but five or six are said to have supported relocation, it also appears that few really understood what the meeting was about (Hoy 1973). The university extension worker explained some of the failures of past cases of resettlement, perhaps having in mind that some of the people originally from Batteau, Spotted Island, and Seal Islands, now living in distinct neighbourhoods of Cartwright, were dissatisfied and contemplating leaving Cartwright.

By early May 1973, the Black Tickle LIC presented Resettlement Director Harnum with the required petition requesting assistance to resettle and build a new community (RC 63rd Meeting). Members of the Newfoundland Resettlement Committee vacillated; there were still no receiving communities on the Labrador coast. Designation of a receiving community would take time, and proper planning must precede any abandonment of Black Tickle. The people of Black Tickle were encouraged to stay put until further information was available. In the meantime, the resettlement director and officials from the provincial departments of Rural Development and Social Services and Rehabilitation would visit Black Tickle (RC 64th Meeting).

This visit occurred in late June or early July and produced conflicting findings. On the one hand, these officials concluded, during the previous three years Black Tickle had acquired a new four-room school, along with an apartment for two teachers, electrical power, a new wharf, and three new houses. Some were built in 1972 by the Labrador Services Division. On the other hand, excepting local merchants, nurses, and teachers, all residents received some seasonal social assistance (welfare). The value of Black Tickle's twenty-two modest houses hovered between $500 and $800, and villagers travelled forty-eight kilometres for firewood in winter and five kilometres for drinking-water (Hoy 1973). The three officials concluded that the people of Black Tickle were living under 'terrible conditions but were advised that they could not be assisted under the Federal-Provincial Resettlement Program to settle and build a new community' (RC 65th Meeting). At the next RC meeting, Resettlement Director Harnum seriously considered Black Tickle's request (RC 66th Meeting); however, by the end of that summer, the people of Black Tickle decided that they did not want to move to another organized community and instead requested support in developing services at Black Tickle (RC 67th Meeting).

RESETTLEMENT: CONCLUDING COMMENTS

The second federal-provincial resettlement program ended on 31 December 1976 (McGee 1976) and, with it, Newfoundland's last great experiment in social engineering. Whatever one thinks about resettlement (and I applaud only its daring), it cannot be denied that in the years since resettlement, the state has increasingly shouldered the economic burden of rural Newfoundland and Labrador. Of course, state support for the rural economy began during (and in some instances before) the resettlement era, and appeared in forms such as the extension of unemployment insurance (UI) benefits to fishers in 1956 and, more recently, a succession of variously named make-work schemes, aimed mainly at qualifying those with insufficient 'stamps' for unemployment insurance. While resettlement was an attack on the core of the rural economy and society (Canning 1985, 10), the programs that followed it were little better than 'development palliatives,' creating a situation in which 'hundreds of communities and thousands of people are locked into a dependency situation they cannot break' (ibid., 13).

Perhaps as noteworthy as the communities in southeastern Labrador that relocated are those that chose not to – such as the winter villages of Lodge Bay and Norman Bay. Although these villages were no larger than other settlements which people abandoned, Norman Bay and Lodge Bay people opposed moving. Even though Lodge Bay still complain about the navigational problems endemic to the shallow- water conditions along the St Charles River and acknowledge that such problems would have been solved had they moved to the nearby deep waters of Simms Bay (Horn Bay), they preferred remaining in Lodge Bay to moving to Mary's Harbour, as favoured by government. And as the Black Tickle case shows, after about 1970, establishing new communities was difficult because of the bureaucratic tangle of the resettlement program. Lodge Bay people are deeply attached to their community, and although they can now drive to Mary's Harbour, most prefer the occasional inconvenience of low-water conditions to living in Mary's Harbour. Similarly, the people of Norman Bay people resisted resettlement, living without community-wide electricity until 1988. As Brox (1968) argued, people in communities which chose not to move concluded that the continued value of place and kin was preferable to moving.

Resettlement also had a significant social impact on the communities where people moved. Cartwright became even more divided, and now includes several distinct neighbourhoods of people from various abandoned Sandwich Bay communities and, more recently, from Batteau and Spotted Island (Jackson 1982, 43–4). Indeed, in Schneider's words, 'Cartwright is less a community than a collection of families' (1984, 136). Still strangers in a strange land, those resettled are reluctant to hunt or trap near their new communities because they might be encroaching on lands customarily used by locals (Schneider 1984, 145). At Mary's Harbour, the St Mary's River divides the community, separating the older, north side from a newer neighbourhood originally composed of families which relocated to Mary's Harbour from the Battle Harbour/Indian Cove area. Even though a bridge has spanned the river since 1963

(Acreman n.d., 8), some residents on the older side view those 'across the harbour' as 'poor' countrymen.

Resettlement is another example of the enormous role external forces, here the state, have played in shaping the very existence of southeastern Labrador communities. Although some people resisted resettlement, most moved, and except for Black Tickle, this was particularly true of people who lived on the long stretch of coast north of Fox Harbour, where poverty has long been the rule.

My interviews with locals who moved to other communities within the region were often emotional, and I sensed that people had confronted the state with a sense of desperation. Resettlement has removed people from the land, increasing their dependency on government, and with that, their vulnerability.

11

An Institutional Umbrella

Resettlement decreased the total number of winter communities in southeastern Labrador to eleven. Resettlement served the needs of administrators, not those moved (Jackson and Jackson 1971, 94). Centralizing people may have 'rationalized' southeastern Labrador in the minds of bureaucrats from St John's and Ottawa, but it removed people from the land they once had known intimately, and made them strangers in their new communities. People who once garnered a fragile living became by necessity increasingly dependent on the state. Resettled people were crowded like refugees into enclaves set in undeveloped sections of host communities. Resettlement was a cruel and poorly conceived scheme; there were very few beneficiaries and many victims.

Even more tragic than resettlement itself is the fact that shortly after most people were moved, the expanding economy predicted for the growth centres foundered. This phenomenon is seen most clearly at Cartwright, where the radar base was expected to provide long-term benefits. Elsewhere, the alternative economies envisioned by planners simply never materialized. Now in saying all this, I fully realize that Settlers continued to return to their old summer stations to fish. But resettlement concentrated more people into less space, and in the absence of economic alternatives to a declining fishery, increased dependence was in many ways inevitable.

Along with increased dependence came a plethora of new organizations which provide an institutional framework – an umbrella covering and occasionally uniting communities along the southeastern coast. At least in theory, this institutional umbrella also ties communities to various departments of the provincial or federal government. New municipal and regional institutions, as well as three organizations based primarily in Happy Valley/Goose Bay but extended to the region, have, to varying degrees generated regional consciousness.

COMMUNITY COUNCILS, LOCAL SERVICE DISTRICTS, AND OTHER MUNICIPAL BODIES

Unlike in northern Labrador, where the provincial government encouraged all municipalities to incorporate in the late 1960s and early 1970s, most southeastern Labrador communities remained unincorporated until the early 1980s. Incorporation governs communities according to the provincial Municipalities Act, requiring that they periodically elect community or town councils, collect taxes, and administer local services.

The provincial Department of Municipal Affairs initiated a flurry of incorporations during the early 1980s. Several smaller communities were incorporated as local service districts, a designation replacing their previous status as local improvement committees. As matters now stand, only three permanent winter communities in the region are unincorporated: Williams Harbour, Norman Bay, and Paradise River.

Development Associations

Although regional development associations (RDA) did not emerge in Newfoundland and Labrador until the 1960s, the Amulree Royal Commission (1933) and, later, the British Commission of Government Commissioner John H. Gorvin identified the need to diversify and stimulate rural socio-economic conditions (Anonymous 1985), both goals of today's regional development associations. Among the recommendations of Gorvin's 1938 report on 'rural reconstruction' was one calling for community-based regional development strategies, coordinated by a Regional Development Council, a body intended to stimulate local development in the fishery, forestry, agriculture, and so on (Anonymous 1985, 3).

The emergence of regional development associations in the 1960s can be interpreted in different ways. On the one hand, it may be seen to represent a shift away from 'costly and often unsuccessful capital intensive industrial projects' to small-scale, resource-based developments (Anonymous 1985, 6). On the other hand, government support for development associations may have been either an implicit acknowledgment of the failure of the resettlement program (Snowden 1975, 14) or, more cynically, a 'holding operation' for rural Newfoundland (Cashin 1976, 6).

The Newfoundland and Labrador Rural Development Council (NLRDC) was founded in 1969 and formally incorporated on 3 September 1976. It serves as an umbrella organization for regional development associations. As of 1989, administrative funding for each of the province's fifty-six development associations is about $36,500 and enables the hiring of a development coordinator who 'assists people who are interested in development projects in the region, prepares applications, supervises projects and maintains contact with various government agencies and departments' (Newfoundland 1986, 366). Eligibility for administrative grants requires that a development association be incorporated, hold training seminars for members, and represent 75 per cent of the communities within its area. Each member community or local development committee elects one or more persons to the association's board of directors and/or executive.

RDA's hold ordinary, extraordinary, and annual meetings. At these meetings, the board of directors and executive decide which projects will be sought, usually from one or more government (federal) departments. Most projects are related to the fishery but others are in agriculture, tourism, and forestry (Anonymous 1985). Projects are usually short-term and intended to qualify people for unemployment insurance benefits (ibid., 17). The House commission provides some quantitative evidence for this: 'RAND research staff estimated that in the 1982/1983 fiscal year, projects valued at nearly $12 million created only 12 full-time jobs and 78 seasonal jobs, but gave short-term employment to 2,307 people' (Newfoundland 1986, 370). The royal commission concludes that the original purpose of RDAs has been subverted; they have become 'conduits' to the 'Unemployment Insurance (UI) make-work system' upon which rural Newfoundland and Labrador has become increasingly dependent. Consequently, their potential role as the 'main vehicles' for development has largely been removed (ibid., 369–70).

Why has this occurred? I believe that following resettlement and the resulting population centralization, diminishing cod stocks, and soaring demands for social services during the late 1950s and 1960s, both levels of government essentially gave up on rural Newfoundland, or, to put it more charitably, were unable to envisage locally meaningful economic alternatives. Government was also reluctant to surrender significant decision-making authority to rural communities, where relevant solutions to local problems might be found. Increasingly, governments began exploiting this new rural vulnerability to their advantage, with a 'pork barrel' system of dispensing 'job creation programmes' in return for political support. Since the 1970s, rural development associations have become the regional organizations through which such largesse is dispensed.

Given that rural development associations represent groups of communities, discord often occurs between communities competing for the few projects available. Also, in the context of chronic unemployment, a development project may promote competition for available work within communities, between community factions, and/or between families. Development associations now take extraordinary measures to prevent accusations of nepotism, either community- or family-based. These and other problems, as well as the many accomplishments of development associations, may be illustrated by reference to southeastern Labrador.

The roots of what is now the Eagle River Development Association can be traced to the Sandwich Bay Development Committee. In 1972 and 1973 this committee received several federal Local Initiatives Program (LIP) projects. One was to fence Cartwright's old cemetery, another to cut winter snowmobile trails from Cartwright to both Paradise River and Frenchman's Islands, while still another was to build emergency cabins along the trail leading to Frenchman's Islands. The snowmobile route to Frenchman's Islands was intended to provide access to good hunting areas for people who had been relocated to Cartwright.

Also in 1972, discussions took place between the Black Tickle Local Improvement Committee (mentioned in Chapter 10) and the Sandwich Bay Development Committee, concerning Black Tickle's possible involvement with the Sandwich Bay group. The Black Tickle people suggested that the Sandwich Bay committee would need to change its name, and the Cartwright people responded by questioning whether Black Tickle should be allowed to vote or merely to attend committee meetings. Nothing came out of these discussions.

While both Black Tickle and Cartwright are now included in the Eagle River Development Association, old squabbles persist between the two communities. For example, for several years after the establishment of the Eagle River Development Association in 1979, the Black Tickle people criticized the fact that most Eagle River directors and members of its executive resided at Cartwright, the site of the association's office and home to approximately two-thirds of its members. A 1986 amendment to the association's Articles of Association attempts to resolve this issue by decentralizing power. The amendment states:

Three Directors shall be elected from each local Development Committee of Association members in the region represented by the Association (Black Tickle, Cartwright and Paradise River). In addition, one Director shall be elected from each of the six fishing communities – Seal Islands, Batteau, Domino, Spotted Islands, Pack's Harbour and Fish Cove. A fishing community is to be defined as a place consisting of 5 or more bona-fide full-time fishermen ... This makes a total of 15 directors, plus the immediate Past President, to constitute the Board of Directors of the Association. (Eagle River Development Association 1988)

Between 1979 and 1983, the ERDA sponsored eleven projects. During 1980–1, for example, these included a $44,244 winter snowmobile trail linking Paradise River with Charlottetown and $61,917 of Canada Works money to build a log cabin youth camp at Muddy Bay (NLRDC 1983, 211). As so often occurs with government-funded 'make work' projects, the selection of particular projects has been questioned (Southard 1982, 85). In one of countless examples, in 1980 and 1981, the ERDA received some $105,362 from Canada Works and CEIC to build a greenhouse at Cartwright. By 1983, we learn that the 'greenhouse receives limited use during the summer months so the association (ERDA) is looking into the possibility of using it as a rink during the winter' (NLRDC 1983, 211). During my stay in Cartwright that fall, the greenhouse lay dormant. Unused (or underused) greenhouses, poorly situated 'twine lofts' (buildings for working on fishing nets), or other inadequately conceived projects may be one reason why provincial civil servants resist giving development associations greater discretionary powers over spending. But it must also be said that the fact that development projects have devolved into politically motivated 'make work' schemes is not the fault of rural development associations. So long as development projects are intended primarily to meet the short-term 'job creation' objectives of politicians, it is unlikely that they will serve long-term community needs.

One trend common to the regional development association movement is the tendency for some associations to subdivide into two or more smaller development associations, representing fewer communities. This fissioning process is often motivated by the very real frustrations of serving many communities scattered over a large geographic space. And, as noted in Chapter 1, such splits may also say something about locally perceived regional boundaries.

Prior to the formation of the Eagle River Development Association, between 1975 and 1979, the area between Paradise River and Mary's Harbour was served by the Eastern Labrador Development Association (ELDA), sometimes referred to as the Labrador East Development Association. However, the territory covered by the ELDA was considered 'too large. Problems of size led to discussions about subdividing ELDA during 1978. At an ELDA meeting on 13 January 1979, it was resolved to divide ELDA into two new development associations. The East Shore Labrador Development Association (ESLDA) and Eagle River Development Association (ERDA) were formed that winter. The ESLDA included communities from Lodge Bay to Norman Bay and the ERDA included the communities of Black Tickle, Paradise River, and Cartwright. Mary's Harbour native and long-time regional activist Claude Rumbolt, then Memorial University's extension worker with headquarters in Port Hope Simpson, helped orchestrate the split.

Incorporated on 5 October 1979, the East Shore Labrador Development Association (ESLDA) had its headquarters at Port Hope Simpson, the northern centre of the large territory stretching from Lodge Bay to Norman Bay. According to the association's articles of association, two persons from each community development committee in the eight winter communities were to comprise the association's Board of Directors and elect the executive. Between 1979 and 1983, the ESLDA completed seventeen projects (NLRDC 1983, 209–10). A sample of these include a $10,135 slipway constructed at the fishing village of Triangle in 1982, a $2278 floating dock built at Cape Charles in 1981, and a $8765 above-ground water system installed at Cape Charles in 1980. In 1983 the ESLDA appropriated $362,902 for projects ranging from the construction of fish-holding units and wharfs at George's Cove and Snug Harbour to a ski-slope at Port Hope Simpson (ESLDA 1983). The association's 'most successful project ever' is a network of groomed two-lane intercommunity snowmobile trails, funded by the provincial Department of Transportation (ibid., 1). These trails and others like them within the region have greatly increased communication between winter communities which once had limited contacts. In 1985, the ESLDA compiled a regional development strategy. The main recommendation was to improve the region's infrastructure by extending the Labrador Strait highway north to the region. This highway remains a goal of many people, who believe that it could help develop forestry and tourism (ESLDA 1985).

There have been other projects since 1985. However, in March 1989, the ESLDA informed government that it wished to be dissolved and would temporarily surrender its assets to the Rural Development Council. It would then subdivide into two new development associations (Burden 1989). The main reason for splitting the ESLDA was that its territory was too large, making it difficult to hold regular meetings. The two new associations were formed in 1989. The Battle Harbour Area Development Association has its headquarters in Mary's Harbour and serves the communities of Lodge Bay, Mary's Harbour, and St Lewis (Fox Harbour), and the White Bear Arm Development Association has its headquarters in Charlottetown and serves the communities of Port Hope Simpson, Norman Bay, Charlottetown, Pinsent's Arm, and Williams Harbour.

THE LABRADOR RESOURCE ADVISORY COUNCIL (LRAC)

A plethora of new organizations emerged in Labrador during the 1970s. These produced an endless, and exciting, series of meetings, conferences, and resolutions. Debatably the most significant of these new organizations was the Labrador Resource Advisory Council (LRAC). Between 1976 and 1982 this advisory group profoundly changed Labrador's social and political landscape. To an unprecedented extent, the LRAC temporarily unified Labrador's diverse regions and peoples, bridging previously distinct cultural and regional chasms. The LRAC's 'people first' small-scale renewable-resource development philosophy contrasted sharply with Newfoundland's historic preference for large-scale development projects. By the early 1980s, however, the quagmire of political condemnation which the LRAC had successfully managed to sidestep finally ensnared it, enabling the provincial government to cease funding the council in 1982, without suffering significant political fallout.

LRAC Origins

The LRAC has several roots, some deeper and more directly related to the body of the organization than others. Most of these roots ultimately stem from chronic problems of underdevelopment and high unemployment in Newfoundland and Labrador. Others, more unique to Labrador, embody the way that Labrador people believe insular Newfoundland has treated them.

After joining Canada in 1949, Newfoundland and Labrador elected a liberal government headed by J.R. Smallwood, which remained in office for twenty-three years. In addition to bringing Newfoundland and Labrador into Confederation, Smallwood is perhaps best remembered for his partiality for large-scale industrial developments, few of which produced the promised socio-economic benefits. By the late 1960s, criticism of Smallwood's policies had grown, even among the normally staid students of Memorial University of Newfoundland, the provincial university. It should be noted that some persons later active in the LRAC (as well as in provincial politics) attended the university during this time and were undoubtedly influenced by the anti-Smallwood movement.

The published academic critique of large-scale development was contained in studies on 'intermediate adaptation' and 'intermediate technology' conducted by Memorial University's Institute of Social and Economic Research (ISER). Intermediate adaptation espoused small-scale, decentralized and locally meaningful economies (cf., for example, Freeman 1969; Brox 1972, 90–2), similar to those proposed by Schumacher in his influential book *Small Is Beautiful* (1973). The handful of Labrador students then attending Memorial, along with field workers of the university's Extension Service, carried the message of intermediate adaptation to Labrador.

Back in Labrador, antipathy towards what Labrador people believed was Newfoundland's historic exploitation of Labrador was growing. Alienation and resentment fuelled suggestions that Labrador should separate from insular Newfoundland. Though primarily a ruse intended to place Labrador on the public agenda, separatist rhetoric made island Newfoundlanders nervous. Such rhetoric was most common wherever Labrador people had most contact with Newfoundland and/or Newfoundlanders, particularly the Labrador Strait, the Lake Melville area, and western Labrador. A political party promoting these and other 'Labrador first' concerns was formed in January 1969 and was eventually called the New Labrador Party (NLP) (Fowler 1976, 40). The provincial house of assembly eventually elected two NLP members; one, a Cartwright Settler, represented the old Labrador South district between 1972 and 1975.

In October 1972, the newly elected government of Premier Frank Moores appointed a royal commission to investigate a broad range of Labrador concerns. The publicity associated with the commission's sixteen months of research raised the expectations of Labrador people, and media coverage of the commission's work increased Labrador's profile in kitchens and living-rooms across Newfoundland. One of the commission's 287 recommendations called for the establishment of a 'planning and advisory committee' for the development of the Labrador fishery which would facilitate 'liaison between different agencies and fishermen' and advise on 'jurisdictional responsibilities' (Newfoundland 1974, 3: 576). The proposed advisory committee would include representatives from the federal, provincial, and local levels. Years later, in the provincial government's 1979 and 1985 'progress reports' on the implementation of the commission's recommendations, the LRAC is listed as the government's response to the call for a fishery advisory committee.

Yet another of the LRAC's roots also provided an appropriate model for regional consultation. This was the Combined Councils of Labrador North. By 1969 and 1970 all northern Labrador communities (except Postville) were incorporated as 'community councils' under the provincial Community Councils Act (1962). In the spring of 1972, the combined councils held their first annual meeting at Hopedale, Labrador. The 1972 (and subsequent) annual meetings enabled the expression of common municipal and regional concerns, ranging from the collection of local taxes to the protection of 'territorial rights' (an early reference to aboriginal 'land claims'). Since 1979 the combined councils have included all Labrador communities, but by then the LRAC had borrowed and perfected the regional model.

A final and very important generating influence for the LRAC was the Company of Young Canadians (CYC). Between 1972 and 1976, this federally funded youth employment strategy initiated some thirty-eight community development projects throughout Labrador (CYC 1976, 2). The CYC's decentralized philosophy stipulated that individuals or communities could submit project proposals, that projects be directed at community problems, and that projects be evaluated yearly. Projects ranged from research on offshore gas and oil to organizing groups such as the Labrador Heritage Society. Several CYC projects produced important long-term results – for example, *Them Days* magazine, which began in 1975 as a quarterly jointly published by the Labrador Heritage Society and the Old Timers League (an organization funded by the federal New Horizons Program). The philosophy and personnel associated with the CYC also played a key role in the creation of two regional organizations: the Labrador Resource Advisory Council (LRAC) and the Labrador Craft Producers Association (LCPA).

The Founding of the LRAC

Although the 'advisory committee' recommended by the Royal Commission on Labrador was to focus on the fisheries, scarcely one year after the royal commission released its report the mandate of the proposed council changed from fish to oil. The catalyst for this change was the 1973 'energy crisis,' which increased petroleum prices and encouraged exploration in marginal areas, such as Labrador. Petroleum exploration had occurred off Labrador since the 1960s and one company, the French-owned consortium Eastcan Exploration, is said to have spent $100 million on Labrador exploration between 1968 and 1977 (LRAC AR 1976–7, 24).

Just why Labrador replaced Newfoundland's Grand Banks as the locus of offshore petroleum exploration is unknown. While promising geological evidence from the Labrador shelf obviously attracted multinational oil companies (Scarlett 1977, v), Newfoundland officials undoubtedly encouraged their enthusiasm. After all, Newfoundland had always considered Labrador its resource pantry and thus the appropriate place for oil. Until the discovery of the Hybernia oilfield 350 kilometres east of St John's in 1979, the popular notion was that any oil in the area *must* be off Labrador. Increased petroleum exploration off Labrador concerned groups such as the Company of Young Canadians, who worried about the ecological and social consequences. By 1974 and 1975, even provincial officials acknowledged that the people of coastal Labrador deserved some role in planning for petroleum development. This was probably more a political strategy calculated to undermine the alleged separatist threat than evidence of a new consultative approach towards Labrador. Even so, by 1974, the provincial Department of Mines and Energy sponsored the visit by a delegation from coastal Labrador to a symposium on oil at Memorial University of Newfoundland (Scarlett 1977, xiii).

In 1975, the CYC conducted a survey along the Labrador coast entitled 'Oil and Gas: Labrador,' which presented the concerns of coastal residents about petroleum development. The same year, the provincial Department of Mines and Energy circulated the paper 'The Background Paper ... ' (Martin 1975) in coastal Labrador communities. This document claimed that 'government earnestly wishes the people of coastal Labrador to become engaged in the process of planning and preparing for these (oil) developments,' and recommended that 'an Advisory Council could be established' with fifteen members from coastal communities (22). The council would periodically meet and report to the Department of Mines and Energy, and would serve as a government-funded conduit between coastal people and the government (23).

Further discussion about an advisory council took place in November 1975, and the Labrador Resource Advisory Council (LRAC) was formed at Cartwright on 9 January 1976 (LRAC AR 1976–7). The council's Articles and Memoranda of Association are dated 24 February 1977 and incorporation occurred on 1 April of that year. The council's first objective, as stated in its Memoranda of Association, was 'to develop an organization which will represent and articulate the feelings, opinions and beliefs of all the people of Labrador concerning all the renewable, non-renewable and human resources of Labrador.' This would be accomplished by an executive composed of one member from each of the following regional or ethnic constituencies: L'Anse au Clair to Red Bay; Lodge Bay to Paradise River (i.e., southeastern Labrador); Rigolet to Nain, Happy Valley, North West River, and Mud Lake; Churchill Falls and Wabush; the Indian (presumably Sheshatsheit) Band Council; and the Labrador Inuit Association. The massive territory represented by the council, and the regularity of executive meetings (normally four times per year), confirm that support for the LRAC remained strong, particularly during the period from 1976 to about 1980. The executive elected a chairperson for a two-year, potentially renewable, term. After about one year of operation, it was obvious that the council's heavy workload required more permanent, paid staff and at its October 1977 annual general meeting, delegates voted to create a salaried position of executive director. A Rigolet man filled this position. At the same meeting a Makkovik resident replaced the founding chairperson, an Ontario man who had worked with the Company of Young Canadians from about 1972 to 1975.

From the outset, the LRAC struggled with two weighty realities. First, it was dependent on provincial funding, and second, it was attempting to juggle the conflicting, often antithetical interests of Labrador's many regional, economic, and ethnic groups. Regarding the first of these, the council's political course lay along the minefield between criticizing government policies too vociferously, and thus having government cut its funding, or being interpreted by one or more Labrador groups as being little more than a provincially financed intelligence service (see LRAC AR 1977–8, 16). The Council's major accomplishment may lie in its transitory and fragile consolidation of Labrador's diverse groups. However incomplete, this was most apparent during the first couple of years of the LRAC's existence.

It is hardly coincidental that the Newfoundland delusion that Labrador people wanted to separate was most common during 1976–7, the period of the 'separatist' Parti Québécois government in Quebec. As noted, long-standing Labrador discontent about mistreatment by Newfoundland was most apparent wherever contacts between residents of the two parts of the province were greatest. And Newfoundlanders regularly and erroneously equated pro-Labrador sentiments with separatism. However, while many involved with the LRAC were Labrador nationalists, the LRAC never advocated separatism and even when mentioned it was always more rhetoric than policy. In fact, among the people of Labrador, such as those in southeastern or northern Labrador, separatism meant little. Labrador separatism was always more important in Newfoundland than in Labrador, and interpretations of the 'separatist threat' depended on one's political stripe. In Newfoundland, ignorance of Labrador abounded. Thus among politicians and the media alike, talk of separatism persisted; it made good political fodder and the widespread neo-colonial view continued that Labrador's primary importance was to bolster Newfoundland's economic position.

Two debates about separatism occurred in the provincial House of Assembly, and they help illustrate both the diversity of the political uses of separatism and the attempts to identify LRAC with separatism. The first began in February 1977, when a Liberal opposition member representing the former Labrador district of Eagle River called for a 'Select Committee' of the House to investigate the 'state and sentiment of public opinion in Labrador,' especially regarding separatism (*ET* 3 Feb. 1977, 4). In the course of nearly eight weeks of bizarre debate, the premier attributed separatist sentiments to 'outside agitators' in one case, and in another to 'sociologists' going to Labrador communities and accepting local leadership roles (*ET* 3 Mar. 1977, 4) (in point of fact there has been practically no research conducted in Labrador by sociologists). A government minister declared that the select committee proposed by the opposition might even spread separatist beliefs (*ET* 17 Feb. 1977, 4), while an opposition member, in a probable reference to the LRAC, suggested that both levels of government were funding Labrador alienation (ibid.). The spectre of Quebec was never far from this debate, causing the opposition Liberal leader to remind members that only a few years before the separatist movement in Quebec had been but a splinter group, whereas by 1977, separatists formed the government (*ET* 10 Mar. 1977, 4). When the call for a select committee was defeated in late March, the government member for central Labrador, a Labrador native and former New Labrador Party activist, absented himself from the House (*ET* 31 Mar. 1977, 4).

Although the LRAC was mentioned during the select committee debate, it was to be the centrepiece of a similar, though shorter, debate three years later. In 1980, the opposition Liberal MHA for the Eagle River riding claimed that the LRAC was advocating pro-separatist ideas and urged that the $120 thousand (1980) provincial grant be given instead to the Combined Councils of Labrador. The MHA made these allegations only days after the LRAC had convened a gathering of various Labrador organizations to discuss possible forms of regional control for Labrador (LRAC NL June 1980, 11). Although the government member responsible for funding the LRAC (the same MHA who absented himself from the House on the 1977 'select committee' vote) defended government funding to LRAC, it is apparent that throughout the LRAC's tenure, the unproven association with separatism clouded provincial government views of the council, and ultimately played some role in its demise.

Before we examine the LRAC's work in southeastern Labrador, a summary of several of its major campaigns and accomplishments is needed. Even though government may have initially envisioned the council as a means of garnering intelligence on various non-renewable resource developments planned for Labrador, council made it clear from the beginning that it favoured renewable resource development, especially in the fishery (LRAC AR 1976-7, 4-5; 1977-8, 16). These two conflicting development priorities repeatedly clashed, but it must also be noted, somewhat ironically, that the LRAC admired (publicly and, I believe, rhetorically) the (Progressive Conservative) provincial government's stance on offshore development and claimed to have its most 'meaningful and satisfactory' relations with the province on oil-related issues (LRAC AR 1977-8, 16). The council's relations with the (Liberal) federal government were even better, although I believe that this was related less to partisan politics than to the different structural relationships the LRAC had with the two levels of government. The LRAC often explained its pro-Labrador philosophy by analogy to Newfoundland's efforts to gain provincial control over offshore oil and the fisheries from the federal government (see LRAC NL June 1980, 11). The LRAC rather impudently attributed its better relationship with federal officials to their 'ignorance of Labrador' and, consequently, their desire for local input (LRAC AR 1977-8, 3). This, the council claimed, contrasted with Newfoundland's 'colonial' attitude towards Labrador – its 'deep-rooted habit of looking upon Labrador's resources as Newfoundland's salvation' (ibid.).

The issues of federal jurisdiction in which the LRAC was involved included a large DREE agreement for Labrador, plans for two national parks in Labrador, the Labrador component of a federal environmental assessment on East Arctic petroleum exploitation (the so-called OLABS study), and fishery allocations for northern codfish stocks.

Even in matters primarily federal, such as the DREE Community Development Subsidiary Agreement for Coastal Labrador (1981–7), the LRAC complained about the attitudes, assumptions, and actions of the provincial government. In the case of this agreement, a draft proposal was made public in December 1977, based primarily on the recommendations of the Report of the Royal Commission on Labrador (Newfoundland 1974). The LRAC argued that this report was outdated (LRAC AR 1977–8, 4), that the province's 'consultation' (a commonly used word of the era) with it about the proposal consisted of a letter from the deputy minister of Rural Development in August 1977, five months before LRAC had seen the proposed agreement (LRAC AR 1977–8, 1), and that the province had hastily drafted its proposal to DREE and had deliberately ignored the council's recommendations. Consequently, between June and November 1978, the LRAC executive conducted meetings in all Labrador communities and solicited written statements from various community organizations. The council presented this information in a report entitled *Community Priorities for Development in Labrador* (LRAC n.d.).

Two main suggestions emerge from the many recommendations of this exceptional report: that various Labrador organizations (such as its development associations) form a working committee which, along with relevant government departments, would formulate development plans, and that a $2 million Resource Development Fund be established to provide venture capital for small-business development. Although the final DREE agreement included a number of the specific recommendations of 'Community Priorities,' such as construction of a $1.5 million road between Lodge Bay and Mary's Harbour, neither of these two main points were implemented at the time; consequently, another opportunity for development was lost.

The LRAC in Southeastern Labrador

From the beginning, the LRAC recognized that government had ignored southeastern Labrador and that resource development there must take into consideration the continued importance of seasonal transhumance.

The LRAC either initiated or supported several studies, two of which concentrated on the fishery. One, a brief overview of the Labrador fishery, recommended diversification and the development of an 'integrated multispecies' fishery (Williamson 1976, 5). Claude Rumbolt, long-time Labrador nationalist and the LRAC's most ardent supporter in southeastern Labrador, conducted the other study. During the winter of 1976–7, Rumbolt investigated the technological needs of the southeastern Labrador fishery for the provincial Department of Fisheries (Rumbolt n.d.). The government accepted Rumbolt's recommendation for new fish-processing plants at Mary's Harbour and Cartwright. Once built, however, the new plants initially received little use, as they were far away from the cod-fishing grounds, but they were later more sucessfully converted to process snow crab.

The Cartwright plant entangled the LRAC in an unfortunate clash with locals. This dispute began in June 1978 when the Federal Department of Fisheries reserved three new offshore shrimp licences for Labrador fishers. An initial agreement was reached for the pilot project at Cartwright, but this required installation of shrimp-processing equipment worth $750 thousand, an expenditure that both the province and the LRAC hoped the federal government would cover. Such equipment would have secured a shrimp licence for the LRAC, which planned to contract the United Maritime Fishermen (UMF), an Atlantic Canada fishing cooperative, to catch the shrimp during the trial period. In 1979, people from Cartwright accused the LRAC of failing to communicate its plans to use their community's new, but as yet unused, fish plant for the shrimp pilot project. Though the LRAC explained its actions (LRAC NL June 1979, 2 (5): 6–7), the federal fisheries department backed off, and the pilot project was cancelled. Later, the federal government awarded two of the three Labrador shrimp-processing licences to the new Union Shrimp Company in the Strait of Belle Isle, and the two plants became important local employers.[1]

The 1970s marked the beginning of land-claim research in Labrador and in 1978–9, the LRAC (along with *Them Days* magazine and the Extension Department of Memorial University) organized research on traditional land use and resource harvesting among the Settlers of southeastern Labrador. Long-time Labrador resident and writer Lawrence Jackson later presented some of the data collected (1982).

As with all organizations, the LRAC encountered its share of problems. Briefly, the council's main problem in southeastern Labrador was the criticism that 'ordinary' people did not understand the council or its work, and that the council needed to spend more of its time in local communities, learning about problems and encouraging local development. This criticism could be heard in kitchens throughout the region and was even occasionally voiced in public meetings. At a LRAC meeting held in October 1976, for example, an outspoken former Spotted Island man condemned the council for not getting out among the people (LRAC 1976, 12). The council's executive director responded by reminding the man that each community could elect a delegate to voice community concerns at LRAC forums (ibid., 18).

In these and other problems, the LRAC faced the 'no win' task of balancing a plethora of distinct community and regional priorities against the major development needs of Labrador. Executive council members were acutely sensitive to allusions that their consultation with local people was incomplete. Although not unique to LRAC, a major part of the problem here was the tendency for council executive members to rely primarily on a handful of 'contact people' in each community, and to assume that these individuals shared the information they garnered. A more radical democratizing structure in which new representatives would be elected periodically to non-renewable terms, along with a requirement to conduct regular public information meetings, may have helped. Such a procedure could have broadened the community leadership base and more effectively promoted 'bottom-up' development.

In 1980 the LRAC relocated its Goose Bay fieldworker to Port Hope Simpson, in a move designed to 'improve the rapport and working relationship between the communities and the council' (LRAC NL Sept. 1980). The placement was on a one-year trial basis and served the vast coast between Cartwright and L'Anse au Clair. However, the fieldworker seldom left Port Hope Simpson and failed to improve relations between the council and local communities. The fieldworker was withdrawn from Port Hope Simpson in 1981 but another LRAC fieldworker was stationed at Red Bay (LRAC NL Sept. 1981, 2).

The Demise of LRAC

In a special resolution passed at its 6 May 1981 meeting, the LRAC amended Article V(1) of its 1977 membership eligibility criteria which had read 'membership in the Council shall be open to all Community Council and Indian Band Councils in Labrador and to the Labrador Inuit Association' to read: 'Membership in the Council shall be open to all town councils, Indian Band Councils, the LIA, the Chambers of

Commerce, Labrador West District Labour Council, the Development Associations of Labrador, the Women's Institute, and an aggregate from the Fishermen's Committees in each region of Labrador' (LRAC 1982). At the same time, amendments to the council's executive enlarged the number of executive members to thirteen and increased the number of 'non-native' executives to be in proportion to those permitted to be drawn from the Labrador Inuit Association and Innu band councils.

These changes belatedly acknowledged the LRAC's failure to secure Innu (Indian) involvement on the council's executive and, as well, acknowledged the decreased interest of the Labrador Inuit Association. Innu involvement in the LRAC had always been limited. Innu occasionally attended LRAC meetings, especially during the council's first two years, and less frequently offered support on particular issues (see, for example, LRAC NL Oct./Nov. 1977, 9). But Innu never took their seat on the LRAC executive, and I could find little evidence of Innu involvement with LRAC after its October 1977 annual general meeting, during which Innu unsuccessfully sought to amend the LRAC constitution allowing Innu veto powers over all council decisions (ibid., 15). The Labrador Inuit Association relinquished its seat on the LRAC executive in October 1981 because it no longer believed the council's decisions were acceptable to LIA members (ET 4 Dec. 1981, 2).

The early 1980s also signalled a change in development issues and the political climate of Labrador. Although not dead, two herculean LRAC struggles of the 1970s – offshore oil and the proposed Brinex uranium mine – had been pushed to the back burner and replaced by vexatious new issues, such as allocations of northern cod stocks and plans for a year-round seaport ('Port Labrador') in Lake Melville. As the state's Labrador development emphasis shifted towards various federal-provincial agreements, such as the DREE Subsidiary Agreement, LRAC ceased (in November 1978) being responsible to the influential Resource Policy Committee of Cabinet and began reporting only to the provincial Department of Rural Development (LRAC NL June 1979, 2). Following the provincial election of June 1979, there were indications that the new government led by Brian Peckford wished to change LRAC's mandate (See, for example, LRAC NL Oct. 1979, 3). Lastly, but significantly, Newfoundland's anxiety about Labrador separatism waned.

By September 1981 only five of the thirteen seats on the LRAC's expanded executive were filled; two more seats were filled by January 1982 (LRAC NL Jan. 1982, 2). Representatives of the most developed and populous parts of Labrador – the west, the Strait, and central

Labrador – dominated these seven executive seats. The six vacant seats awaited aboriginal and coastal representatives. In its commendable goal of speaking for all of Labrador, the LRAC had opened its doors to the interests of developed Labrador, and these soon overshadowed the very different needs of aboriginal and coastal Labrador people. Finally, in 1982 the provincial government cut funding to the LRAC, arguing that other organizations, particularly aboriginal organizations, made the LRAC redundant. More likely, however, the government stopped the LRAC funding because the possibility that Labrador might seek to separate from Newfoundland had lessened and because the provincial government had grown tired of LRAC opposition to the kinds of development proposals it favoured.

LABRADOR CRAFT PRODUCERS ASSOCIATION

Handicraft production plays an important role in the domestic economy of southeastern Labrador. The making and selling of locally crafted items has been going on since the late nineteenth century. Today the Labrador Craft Producers Association organizes this production. During the Grenfell era, the commercial production of handicrafts occurred under the direction of the IGA Industrial Department. In southeastern Labrador, the foremost individual associated with Grenfell craft production was K.M. ('Kitty') Keddie, who worked for the Grenfell Mission between 1930 and 1958 (Curtis 1958, 69; TD 1994).

Even though the craft movement today is not formally linked to the Grenfell organization, some older craftspeople may be considered Mrs Keddie's protégés (McGrath 1985, 8). Like so much of the Grenfell movement, the Grenfell-organized craft development disintegrated by degrees, first during the Second World War and later in the years following confederation. By the 1960s and early 1970s, little remained of the once-flourishing craft industry, even though individuals continued to sew, knit, hook rugs, or carve for home consumption. By the early 1970s a new restlessness reverberated across Labrador, and a part of this would ultimately be expressed in the contemporary craft movement.

Like the LRAC, the roots of the craft movement may be traced to a federal Company of Young Canadians (CYC) project in the early 1970s. In 1972, a young British schoolteacher organized a craft council as a CYC project in the northern Labrador community of Makkovik. Similar councils were soon formed in other northern Labrador communities and at Cartwright. In May 1975, a $2000 grant from the provincial Department of Rural Development funded a meeting at Happy Valley at which the Labrador Craft Producers Association (LCPA) was formed (LCPA n.d., 1). Further organization of the LCPA occurred during the next five years, and the association was incorporated as a local company on 22 November 1979. The association's Articles and Memoranda of Association are dated 13 August 1979. The articles outline membership and organizational criteria while the memoranda lists the association's objectives, such as to 'promote and encourage the continuation, advancement, appreciation and use of traditional crafts among the people of Labrador.'

The LCPA has always been a very political organization, especially during its early years. This is surprising, especially when one juxtaposes notions of political activity with the individualistic and seemingly apolitical craft-producing activities of craftspersons, most of whom are women. The political activities of the LCPA range from preparing conventional position papers to making relatively radical pro-Labrador 'nationalist' resolutions. Exemplifying the former is the LCPA submission to DREE in 1978, made with reference to the proposed DREE Comprehensive Agreement for Labrador. The association criticized the fact that the DREE draft proposal (the so-called Red Book) largely ignored craft development. Instead, the association urged that craft production be viewed as economic development rather than as leisure activity and that the association be recognized as the sole coordinating body for Labrador crafts. One of the contentious issues debated by association members in 1979 was whether 'outsiders' or only 'Labradorians' should lead the association. The resolution appears in the LCPA's Articles of association (1979), stating that only those born in Labrador are eligible for the association's presidency.

The association's articles permit five categories of members, although of these, 'ordinary' and 'constituent members' are most important. Ordinary members are typically individual Labrador craftspersons while constituent members are community-based craft councils. Both types are eligible to attend the association's annual general meeting, normally held during February at locations throughout Labrador.

A board of directors, which meets twice a year, governs the association. Each community craft council sends a delegate to the annual general meeting and together delegates from each of Labrador's regions elect a regional executive member. The association's president is elected for a two-year, potentially renewable term, while remaining executive members are elected for one year.

While board and executive members serve on a voluntary basis, the association employs several salaried persons, including a secretary, travelling coordinator, and field instructors. Money for salaries and office and other expenses comes from various government sources. Until 1979, the LCPA received part of its core funding from the federal-provincial agreement for native peoples and the remainder from the provincial Department of Rural Development. Between 1984 and 1988 the association received $45 thousand in core funding from the Rural Development Subsidiary Agreement (LCPA Newsletter Summer 1987, 2), which was often supplemented from other sources. The same amount of core funding was awarded to the Newfoundland and Labrador Craft Development Association, the LPCA's older 'sister organization in Newfoundland' (LCPA Newsletter Fall 1983, 1). As the umbrella group for Labrador craftspersons, the LCPA attempts to maintain contacts between craft producers and the world beyond Labrador.

The LCPA is sensitive to criticism and cautious about its public image, perhaps because of scars from the xenophobic debates over the association's constitution in 1979. In 1981, in a Happy Valley newspaper, an anonymous columnist ('Homebrew') criticized the LCPA for its crafts display at the 1981 festival in the community. One of several responses to this criticism, published in the LCPA newsletter, referred to 'trouble areas' in the association's history, perhaps a veiled reference to the aforementioned constitutional debates (LCPA NL Summer 1981, 10).

Yet the LCPA practices democracy to an extent exceeding many other Labrador organizations. The association has twice reviewed and revised its 1979 constitution, once in 1982 and again in 1989, in response to changes both within the LCPA and in government legislation. In July 1986, the association asked all constituent and individual members whether or not they should adopt a new method of electing regional members of the board of directors. The result was the establishment of a method by which regional representatives are elected through mail-in ballots. Each region elected one director until 1987, when delegates to the annual general meeting voted to elect two directors from each region (LCPA NL Spring 1987, 4).

In June 1985, the LCPA began experimental use of Labrador's newly installed teleconferencing network, enabling monthly contact between the executive and board members (LCPA NL Winter 1985, 5). When reviewed one and one-half years later, the procedure was judged to be 'extremely beneficial'; by then, such meetings occurred on the last Thursday of every month except July, August, and December (LCPA NL Spring 1986, 6).

A final example of the Association's flexibility was evident in 1988. The association held a workshop in February of that year and redefined its 1975 objectives. The 1988 objective emphasized the production and marketing of contemporary crafts, rather than the organization of the craft movement's infrastructure (LCPA NL Spring 1988, 8).

The priority that the LCPA places on communication with its widely dispersed membership is quite remarkable in the Labrador context and is facilitated through its quarterly newsletter. The newsletter began around 1981 and is distributed to all members. It contains information on the LCPA business, on past and future workshops, on craft books members may borrow, on alternative sources of supplies, on patterns and markets, and on small business and taxation, as relevant to craft producers. The newsletter also presents candid information on the association's sources of funding and on the responsibilities of regional board members to their regions.

LCPA Involvement in Southeastern Labrador

As noted previously, prior to the founding of the LCPA, Cartwright was the first southeastern Labrador community to establish a craft council. By 1983, the communities of Lodge Bay, Mary's Harbour, St Lewis, Port Hope Simpson, Norman Bay, Black Tickle, and Cartwright had each established craft councils and were constituent members of the LCPA (LCPA NL Autumn 1982, 2; Spring 1983, 5).

Local craft councils that maintain their status as constituent members of the LRAC are eligible to hold workshops in their communities. Most of these travelling LRAC workshops receive funding from the provincial government and disseminate unique regional craft traditions throughout the Labrador territory. For example, in March 1985, a central Labrador woman taught the central Labrador practice of making grass baskets in industrialized Churchill Falls, while a northern Labrador woman taught the Innu technique of making beaded moccasins at Mary's Harbour (LCPA NL Spring 1985, 7). Such workshops are popular, probably because they offer craftspeople the opportunity to congregate during winter at the local craft shop or community hall and learn something new.

Many Labrador craft councils have craft shops which councils use for holding meetings and workshops and for selling crafts. Craft shops are often built as 'make work' projects and later maintained through federal employment incentives. One example is the five-room Mary's Harbour craft shop, constructed as a Canada Works Project and opened in 1985. The use of craft shops as retail stores works well in communities regularly visited during summer by coastal boats. Craft shops are obviously less effective in communities where seasonal transhumance removes most of the population during summer or when located too far from the dock to enable tourists to shop in a leisurely way during coastal boat stops.

Finally, four implications of the LCPA-organized craft movement deserve comment; these relate to all regions of coastal Labrador, instead of simply the region discussed here. The first concerns the sexual and ethnic make-up of the contemporary craft movement. Although there are some male craft producers in Labrador, the vast majority of them are women. Women dominate the organization of the craft movement, at both the local and regional level. So far as I know, only one man has ever been elected to the LCPA executive or board of directors. He is a Strait of Belle Isle man, elected as LCPA president for one term (1985–7) and as a board member (1987–8). Consequently, the contemporary craft movement provides political training primarily for women, some of whom later participate in other political arenas. Public awareness of the significance of women in the craft movement has begun to reverse the historic male monopoly on leadership. Although no causal connection can be proved, during the 1980s increased numbers of women became involved in municipal councils and development associations. In southeastern Labrador, for example, a woman was elected as mayor of Cartwright and as president of a development association.

The second point concerns the decreased involvement of Inuit and Innu in the LCPA. Put differently, as in the case of the LRAC, the LCPA has seen the increased 'settlerization' of its ethnic composition. Although Innu and Inuit continue to work as craftspeople and to sell their crafts at local craft shops, their members have been noticeably absent from the LCPA board or executive for many years. Even in northern Labrador, Settlers or outsiders are commonly elected as regional board members.

A third point involves the homogenization of formerly distinct and localized craft idioms. In Labrador, dissemination of craft idioms once associated with a single cultural group finds historical precedent in the Grenfell Industrial Department practice of encouraging Labrador Settlers and Newfoundlanders to produce crafts with 'Eskimo' motifs (such as carved dog teams or embroidered mats depicting Eskimos harpooning seals). These 'genuine' Labrador handicrafts were readily identifiable and thus commercially viable in the United States, Britain, and Canada.

Today the LCPA travelling workshops teach craft techniques from various parts of Labrador to community craft councils in other parts with the aim of increasing production and sales.

The state, rather than Grenfell handicrafts, encourages today's production. Let us consider the example of Labrador grass work. Labrador Inuit grass work is related to Alaskan Inuit woven grass work, and consists of continuous coils of local sea grass, exquisitely sewn into baskets and other containers. Functional, often waterproof, and strong, grass containers probably once enjoyed widespread use by Labrador Inuit, but by historic times they were primarily made only by Inuit and the Settlers of the Rigolet/Groswater Bay area. What happens then when Rigolet grass workers disseminate this idiom throughout Labrador? The provincial government department sponsoring LCPA workshops requires such a dissemination. These rules specify that: 'Skills learned in Rural Development sponsored workshops should be further utilized by workshop participants for economic gain (i.e., if a group receives a workshop in grasswork, members of that group will be expected to produce and sell grasswork in future in order to qualify for future Rural Development sponsored workshops)' (LCPA NL Fall 1988, 13). However, the question remains: at what point does the grass basket made by a recently trained Black Tickle or Mary's Harbour craft producer deserve the label of 'genuine' Labrador grass work? And how does this affect the quality and value of all Labrador grass work? Although the extent to which anyone or any group 'owns' a craft idiom may be debated, the LCPA and the government risk sacrificing the reputation and long-term economic viability of Labrador's several unique and localized craft idioms by stipulating that increased commercial production must result from travelling workshops.

Finally, perhaps more than any other exogenous type of economic development seen in this book, the craft movement is a cottage industry which allows people to remain at home and produce according to their own schedules. The Settler way of life has undergone many changes during this century, especially since confederation. However, the contemporary craft movement perpetuates memories of a vanished life, even though the cultural meaning of handicrafts produced for sale is undoubtedly different than when the same items (be they knitted or sewn articles) were made for domestic consumption. Thus, the modern handicraft movement resembles the developments discussed in Chapter 8, which dovetailed with the historic Settler way of life rather than transformed it.

THE LABRADOR METIS ASSOCIATION (LMA)

When Newfoundland and Labrador joined Canada in 1949, Newfoundland did not seek application of the federal Indian Act, meaning that, unlike the rest of Canada, aboriginal peoples initially became the responsibility of the new province. Newfoundland had never signed treaties with its indigenous peoples, and by ignoring aboriginal status, or leaving it undefined, the new province left natives ineligible for various federally funded programs provided by the Crown as a matter of right to other native Canadians. To rectify this situation, between 1951 and 1953, discussions between federal and provincial officials resulted in the first of a series of federal-provincial agreements. Under these agreements, Ottawa was to provide most of the housing, education, municipal, and economic development funding for *designated* Labrador Inuit (including Settlers) and Innu communities. The provincial government administers these funds. The designated community system emerged because of Labrador's particular colonial history and complex ethnic mosaic; it qualifies communities rather than individuals. Consequently, many northern Labrador Settlers displaying varying degrees of native ancestry and culture are eligible for native funding because they live in communities once served by Newfoundland's Northern Labrador Trading Operation, the predecessor to today's Labrador Services Division (Kennedy 1977, 1987).

By the early 1970s, a number of developments across Canada led to the emergence of aboriginal organizations in Newfoundland and Labrador (Kennedy 1987). The first such organization, the Native Association of Newfoundland and Labrador (NANL), was founded in Newfoundland in February 1973, and in September 1973, the second aboriginal organization, the Labrador Inuit Association (LIA), was formed.

The period between 1973 and 1975 was marked by much confusion, rivalry, and distrust between supporters of NANL and LIA. NANL primarily included (in descending order) Newfoundland Micmacs, northern Labrador Settlers, Labrador Innu, and some Labrador Inuit. The LIA was primarily composed of Labrador Inuit, in addition to a few Settlers, initially from the community of Nain. To the extent to which both organizations competed for members, northern Labrador Settlers enjoyed some influence, because the mixed physical and cultural characteristics of some Settlers made them theoretically able to join either organization. But LIA's national organization, the Inuit Tapirisat of Canada (ITC), opposed the inclusion of Settler members, advocating instead an all-Inuit organization. Yet even when LIA ignored ITC concerns, in October 1974, and offered northern Labrador Settlers full membership, few initially joined. Northern Labrador Settler vacillation probably sought to determine whether NANL or LIA would offer them the most benefits.

By June 1975, the ambiguities inherent in the use of the term 'native' in its title prompted NANL to change its name to the Indian and Metis Association of Newfoundland and Labrador (IMANL),[2] and to open an office in Goose Bay, Labrador. By the fall of 1975, however, Labrador Innu were increasingly concerned about the Newfoundland Micmac dominance of IMANL and separated from that organization to form their own native organization, the Naskapi-Montagnais Innu Association (NMIA). The IMANL struggled to retain its northern Labrador Settler members but, by then, both LIA (Brantenberg 1977, 399) and federal officials considered northern Labrador Settlers to be full members of the LIA. IMANL eventually retreated to insular Newfoundland and by 1978 became the Federation of Newfoundland Indians (Kennedy 1988b). In short, by the mid-1970s, Labrador had two relatively stable aboriginal organizations: LIA, whose members were northern Labrador Inuit and Settlers, and NMIA, whose members were Labrador Innu. Settlers from other parts of Labrador were not involved with aboriginal organizations, although by the 1980s this too would change.

The Founding of the Labrador Metis Association

Beginning in 1979, several North Atlantic Treaty Organization (NATO) countries expanded low-level military air combat training exercises from Goose Bay airport, flying over much of the Quebec-Labrador peninsula. Since then, the number of these noisy low-level flights has increased exponentially, and this has generated a vitriolic public debate as to whether the flights should continue (Armitage and Kennedy 1989). Proponents of military low-level training, including many Goose Bay business-people and most elected politicians, believe militarization is Goose Bay's ticket to prosperity. Opponents, primarily Labrador Innu and their supporters (as well as some Settlers and Inuit), argue that increased low-level flying makes the interior of Labrador uninhabitable and that alternative economic strategies must be found. Significantly, the debate over low-level flying has occurred mainly in central and to some extent western Labrador, but far less in southeastern Labrador. Evidence for this statement comes from attendance and participation at the public meetings leading to a federal environmental review of low-level flying, and from the revised Environmental Impact Statement itself. Southeastern Labrador people do not believe their region is or will be affected by low-level military flying.

In central Labrador, however, debate over militarization polarized public opinion. In Goose Bay the debate generated several new organizations supporting military development. One organization partially rooted in the military debate is the Labrador Metis Association (LMA). As mentioned above, the term 'Metis' was used in Labrador in 1975 in the title of the defunct Indian and Metis Association of Newfoundland and Labrador (IMANL), and Plaice (1990) claims that discussion of a 'Metis Association' to represent central Labrador Settlers occurred in 1983. However, the actual formation of the LMA occurred in 1985 when an influential white civil servant who actively promoted military expansion in Labrador and was then posted in Goose Bay, encouraged formation of a new native organization to subvert Innu opposition to low-level flying. Once formed, however, other historical currents sustained LMA, and many of these pertained directly to southeastern Labrador Settlers.

From a legal perspective, the emergence of the LMA finds justification in Section 35 of the Canadian Constitution Act of 1982, which includes Metis (along with Inuit and Indians) as 'aboriginal peoples.' The legitimacy offered various ethnically mixed Canadians through this constitutional change, coupled with the Constitution's failure to define 'Metis,' has split the established national Metis organization (Bolsvert and Turnbull 1985; Sawchuck 1985) and generated new 'Metis' regional organizations like the LMA across Canada.

The LMA attracts mixed-blood Settlers from southeastern and central Labrador. In the latter area, for example, some Settlers were unable to join LIA, because they do not come from within the Labrador Inuit Settlement Area (LISA), the area claimed by LIA. Many of these Metis, rightly, felt 'dispossessed' (Plaice 1990) and envied the generous health and educational benefits available to LIA members. Significantly, many of these central Labrador Metis have just as much aboriginal 'blood' as northern Labrador Settler (Kablunangajuit) members of LIA; they just come from the 'wrong' part of Labrador.

The LMA was registered under the provincial Companies Act on 4 September 1986 and by then enjoyed the support of a number of what might be called 'middle class' (permanently employed and relatively affluent) central Labrador Settlers. One reason for the growth of the

LMA during its first two years was its critique of the then thirty-five-year-old federal-provincial system of funding native peoples living in designated communities. The LMA correctly argues that this system funds northern Labrador Settlers (as well as Inuit and Innu) according to the historical circumstances of where they live, as much as to their degree of 'native blood' or expression of aboriginal culture.

How many Metis are there and how has the organization fared in southeastern Labrador? Various estimates of the LMA's membership have been given (Kennedy 1987, 23), but as of 1993, the association claims around 2600 members. Eligibility criteria are sweeping, defining a Metis as 'A Person with Indian (Naskapi, Montagnais) and white ancestry, and a person of Inuit and white ancestry and their descendants who are recognized by the Association as Metis or to a person called an 'Original Labradorian,' that is, who settled in Labrador North of the Pinware River prior to 1940, who has remained there since, and their descendants' (LMA 1986). It is clear then that 'Metis' falling within the category of 'original Labradorians' need not have any 'native blood.'

The LMA's objectives include the protection of the Metis' traditional, constitutional, and aboriginal rights. The Metis claim to aboriginality is rejected by the provincial government, which apparently misunderstands the Metis claim to mixed blood and thinks Labrador Metis are claiming to be Red River Metis. Similarly, although progress has been slow, the LMA continues to seek recognition by the federal government, which funded the LMA to conduct genealogical and land-use research. LMA members have also obtained development funding through national 'status blind' programs such as the Native Economic Development Program (NEDP) and its successor, the Canadian Aboriginal Economic Development Strategy (CAEDS). For example, as of 1988, seven privately owned Labrador Metis companies have obtained a total of $1.5 million in grants and interest-free loans from the NEDP (CBC 1988). Some of these grants have gone to southeastern Labrador Metis. One southeastern Labrador businessman secured $289 thousand in grants and interest-free loans from NEDP (ibid.) and in another instance, NEDP officials telephoned me asking whether persons from a particular southeastern Labrador community had native ancestry. (I would not, for ethical reasons, answer).

Today, obtaining one's 'Metis card' is an important goal for those southeastern Labrador people who believe they have aboriginal ancestry. This represents a remarkable change from the situation I encountered between 1979 and 1983. Then, whenever I discussed the issue of social background with persons of obvious 'native' phenotype, they usually skirted the issue of native ancestry, conveying the impression that they were ashamed of their aboriginal ancestry. Since then, assertions of aboriginality have replaced stigma and shame, a process of ethnic liberation similar to that occurring in much of the former colonial world (Cohen 1985, 79).

The story of the LMA is unfolding and could become more contentious within small communities, particularly if the LMA becomes more exclusive about membership criteria and if, as appears likely in 1994, Ottawa recognizes the aboriginal right of Labrador Metis to harvest certain species of wildlife. In short, while the LMA's call for equity for the mixed Settlers of southeastern Labrador rests on solid historical footing, emergence of the LMA could divide small communities, where some qualify and others do not.

In the years since relocation, the organizations discussed in this chapter, and others, have created an institutional umbrella linking southeastern Labrador communities to each other and to the world beyond the region. Many of these organizations entered the region from afar and have required that southeastern Labrador people adopt modes of interaction based on meetings, reports, and budgets, practices quite unlike the spontaneous face-to-face interaction of the past. It remains to ask whether the fate of these southeastern Labrador communities rests with local Settlers or with forces beyond their control.

12

Conclusions

This book has examined the long-term developmental history of communities in a little-known region of eastern Canada, focusing, in Mintz's words (1977, 260), on the 'maturation, apogee and decline' of Labrador communities. Among other things, we have seen how Mary's Harbour developed as a mission station, how Port Hope Simpson began as a logging town, and how the expansion of St Lewis began with erection of a radar installation. Concurrently and related to this development was the abandonment of many obscure winter settlements: New York (St Michael's Bay), Riverhead, Sandy Hill Bay, Dove Brook, Pitt's Arm, and many more. These and other examples of growth and decline resulted from transitions in the Settlers' economy. Since the beginning of permanent European settlement in the early nineteenth century, the Settler economy has changed, first from a difficult subsistence economy, next to a periodic wage labour and/or subsistence economy, to the present, and unprecedented, dependence on the state – from a fragile independence to an equally fragile (although more comfortable and less meaningful) dependence. These economic transformations entailed changes in the use of space: from highly dispersed, seasonal, family-based homesteads to modern communities that are increasingly populated all year round. Meanwhile, while these economic and community changes were occurring in the bays and inlets of the inner coast, the summer fishing stations on the barren headlands and islands survived until very recently, as did the maritime economy that sustained them. As we approach the present era, this demanding, seasonally ordered, and meaningful lifestyle becomes increasingly under assault – first from intrusive (although sometimes well-intentioned) institutions, next by an increasing dependence on a more affluent state, and finally by depletion of the resource base.

My purpose has been largely descriptive – to discover the unknown Labrador. I also have advocated the combined use of both field and archival methods, emphasizing (though not for the first time) that the two approaches complement each other and generate new questions.[1] As my research revealed linkages between the southeastern Labrador region and influences from afar, such as the American fishery, I began to question the extent to which the people of the bays and headlands actually shaped their own history. Most of the recent theoretical literature on this topic I examined, indeed the primary theoretical current, emphasized how individual actors and groups affected change and stood their ground, often against formidable odds. Yet the Labrador case did not seem to show this, at least not over the long haul. This final chapter relates the current discussion of agency and structure to the descriptive materials presented above.

THE FATE OF COMMUNITIES

What shapes the fate of isolated, marginal communities such as those discussed above? Do peoples, such as the Settlers, play a determining role in shaping their own fate or are they moved by larger, structural events and forces over which they have limited control?

There appear to be two answers to these questions, commonly labelled 'agency' and 'structure.'[2] The theory of agency concludes that individuals or groups, regardless of their structural placement in society, play a conscious, knowledgeable, and effective role in shaping their histories. The term 'structure,' in contrast, is shorthand for arguments concluding that unified, global structures and events play the determinant role. It is also important to mention that a middle ground exists between agency and structure. Bourdieu (1977) and Giddens (1984, and elsewhere), for example, seek to bridge the structure/agency abyss, and their growing influence is reflected in recent empirical studies by Comaroff (1985) and Keesing (1992) showing how agency is affected by structural conditions.[3] I leave to others the task of applying such a middle-ground position to Labrador and instead present the agency and structure positions as if they were irreconcilable. I then briefly sketch possible applications of the two approaches to the Labrador materials.

Agency

The modern agency perspective begins with Vico (Said 1978, 5) and

later Marx's observation that 'men make their own history,' albeit not
under circumstances they choose. More recently, agency theory ex-
presses itself through the efforts of historians or historically minded
social scientists to rewrite history to include peoples previously ignored.
E.P. Thompson, for example, rescues the eighteenth- and nineteenth-
century English working-class from the 'enormous concession of poster-
ity' ([1963] 1984, 12).

Similarly, yet with a different empirical focus, is Ranajit Guha's subaltern (subordinate) studies.[4] Guha and his colleagues attempt to restore
the suppressed histories of the dispossessed – agricultural workers,
peasants, tribals – of South Asia. Subaltern studies make a compelling
critique of the conventional historiography of élite classes, which dis-
counts the potential for agency and consciousness among structurally
subordinate peoples. Instead, subalternists show that the real 'history
from below' often involves resistance, and that beliefs, symbols, and
traditions mobilizing resistance are of local rather than élite origins.[5]
Thus rural Indian peasants, some as socially and ideologically marginal
to the centre as Labrador Settlers, use their own rather than foreign
cultural experience to mobilize and resist domination.

The political expression of agency is exemplified by Scott's work
(1985) on 'everyday forms of resistance,' describing hitherto ignored
local responses to oppression. Scott presents an empirical study based
on two years of research in a small (360 people), rural, rice-growing,
Islamic, Malaysian village he calls Sedaka. The 'green revolution'
entered Sedaka with double-cropping in 1972 and combine-harvesters
in 1976. Sedaka's landowning class benefited at the expense of poorer
peasants, engendering a tacit class war in which poorer peasants resist
their wealthier neighbours by everyday forms of resistance: by foot-
dragging, false compliance, pilfering, slander, and arson. Yet such
resistance, a veritable 'cold war of symbols' (22), does not develop into
open rebellion because both parties have important shared interests
and because poor villagers are aware they would lose in any outright
confrontation (22). However, there are a number of obstacles to collective resistance (242–6), leading Scott to question the consequences of
everyday forms of resistance. Citing Genovese, Scott discusses real and
token resistance, but he then cites evidence to contest the view that
token resistance (unorganized, individual, accommodative, and so on),
such as in Sedaka, is inconsequential (292). Thus, Scott appears to
vacillate on the issue of consequence, first likening token resistance to
events leading to the Russian and Mexican revolutions and then admit-

ting that peasant resistance designed to stop the introduction of the combine-harvester, and other acts including sabotage, ultimately failed (248–9).

Scott's work has attracted considerable attention (cf. Colburn 1989). And drawing on Scott, Guha, and others, Roger Keesing promotes a dynamic, metaphoric, and conscious conceptualization of Kwaio (Solomon Islands) resistance to British colonial rule. Keesing also makes an important methodological point: that we view historical cases of potential political resistance in their context, and not through the retrospective lucidity of today.

Structure

Marxist and dependency theories (sometimes called political economy; see Roseberry 1988) are two theories advancing the view that structures beyond the control of individuals ultimately shape their lives. Stripped to its essentials and detached from recent problems of communist regimes, Marx's 'materialist conception of history' offers a comprehensive set of relatively 'flexible structural concepts' with which to interpret the historical development of any area (McLellan 1975, 42). Most important for Marx, the economic base (or substructure), that is, the relationship to the means of production, conditioned or determined a society's social, political, intellectual, and religious superstructure (ibid., 40–1).

Marx (and his colleague, Engels) supported Irish attempts at self-determination (cf., for example, Marx 1972, 145–8) and viewed Ireland as a colonial example of English economic and political domination. Marx uses the Irish case as an example of his general law of capitalist accumulation, in *Capital* ([1867] 1977, 854–70). He explains that the depopulation of Ireland during the twenty years following the famine of 1846 did not improve conditions for the 80 per cent of the population still working on small-sized farms. Instead, emigration and the 'agricultural revolution' (e.g., turning arable land into pasture, concentrating farms, evicting small cultivators) placed the remaining small and medium-sized farms in competition with increased numbers of large, cattle-breeding farms, financed and managed by capital. Lacking alternative sources of employment, many former agricultural labourers and small farmers were forced either to emigrate or to become labourers in English industries. Marx considered both the agricultural revolution and the 'thinning' of the rural population to be deliberate policies enacted by Irish landlords and the English legislature to serve their interests.[6] Just as Irish staples produced English capital, the codfish of southeastern Labrador have long been extracted chiefly to benefit the small capitalist classes of England, and later Newfoundland.[7]

Contingent on the Marxist approach and also favouring the role of exogenous forces in local development is dependency theory. This developed from the Marxist interest in imperialism and the world-wide penetration of European capitalism. Dependency theory provides a method for explaining specific cases of underdevelopment (Palma 1978). This theory, pioneered by A.G. Frank and greatly advanced by I. Wallerstein, focuses on the unequal economic relations between different geographic and economic zones – specifically, on how metropolitan centres exploit geographically peripheral satellites. Frank's (1967) example of underdevelopment in Chile concludes that powerful urban Chilean interest groups often accept or tolerate international economic and political structures which subordinate them because these same structures enable powerful Chileans to exploit people in the Chilean periphery (95). This hierarchic system of exploitation and dependence resembles Marx's Irish case and, I believe, the Labrador case, insofar as metropolitan interest groups in Newfoundland (i.e., the 'fishocracy' of Water Street merchants) were both exploited by the Canadian metropolis and, in turn, exploited the hinterland of Labrador.[8]

Wallerstein's (1989) interpretation of dependency theory and the determining role of external forces is even more extreme than Frank's. Wallerstein claims that not even the three great revolutions – industrial, French, and decolonization of the Americas – 'represented fundamental challenges to the world capitalist system' (256). Although resistance and revolution figure in Wallerstein's account, such action is either suppressed by state forces (cf. 238) or inconsequential to the world capitalist system. Whether we are talking about the expropriation of fish from Labrador peripheries or nitrates, copper, or wheat from the Chilean hinterland, dependency theory emphasizes the ever-changing exploitation of the periphery by metropolitan market forces.

Marxist and dependency theory offer complementary ways to interpret regional and community development, even though each emphasizes the articulation between local regions and global forces in a slightly different manner. Both are historical arguments and compatible with my contention that much of what determines change in rural communities originates beyond the communities themselves.

Agency and Structure in Southeastern Labrador

Some measure of agency and structure probably figures in all human contexts, and the mere fact that Settlers have survived for nearly two hundred years is an indication that they are not entirely overpowered by structural forces beyond their control.

What has been the *consequence* of Settler agency and what is its effect on the long-term development of the region? As explained in Chapter 1, I have used 'community' in its older, morphological sense, but of course individuals, not communities, are the acting units. Regrettably, in the case of southeastern Labrador, we often lack the ethnographic or historical evidence necessary to clearly evaluate the extent and consequence of the agency of historic actors. Thus, while we know about specific historical events in which Settlers covertly 'resisted' the dictatorial policies of the Grenfell Mission or refused to sell their salted codfish for low prices, in most cases individual action is lost to time, unrecorded and forgotten. As we move closer to the present, we have better examples of individual action, such as in the case of resettlement. There, Settlers acted individually or collectively to request or oppose relocation from their ancestral winter communities. Yet the broader context in which such agency occurred was drafted by bureaucrats in St John's, with the approval of those in Ottawa. The resettlement programs themselves, with their financial compensation packages and bureaucratic procedures, were part of a larger plan to 'rationalize' the economies of rural Newfoundland and Labrador, and thus to trim the number of communities in Canada's newest province. Thus Settlers acted out a script written by others.

Another problem I have with the agency position centres on the notion of consequences. As noted above, even Scott hesitates to claim that Sedaka resistance, important as resistance may be in allowing oppressed peoples to endure, actually changed anything. When applied to southeastern Labrador, the consequences of individual and collective agency appear to have been repeatedly undermined by the kinds of structural conditions Settlers faced. I have in mind here conditions such as the Settlers' dispersed settlement pattern – which impeded possible Settler coalitions and encouraged the subordinate position Settlers occupied in relation to virtually every external institution. Certainly several examples of Settler resistance have been noted above, including the looting of the burning Battle Harbour IGA hospital and stealing food from merchant stores. That such an oral tradition persists will be considered sufficient proof to some, yet these covert acts failed to remove the source of exploitation. Merchants and Newfoundland fishers continued to dominate Settlers; the Grenfell Mission barely noticed Settler resistance, yet continues to be revered both within and outside Newfoundland for improving the health conditions of Labrador folk. Even the kind of overt resistance made possible by the congregation of people at Port Hope Simpson, such as the two strikes against the Labrador Development Company, changed little and is only remembered by a few. Thus, while agency occurred, Settler society, like that of the 'classless' peasants described by Marx (cited in Wolf 1966, 91–2), lacked the organizational means to make agency effectual. Certainly the history of southeastern Labrador has no dearth of examples of agency and resistance. My argument has been simply that they failed to affect the fate of their communities.

Moreover, I maintain that the extent to which agency affects a people's history varies with structural and socio-economic circumstances. We should not take a 'one size fits all' approach to agency. I am reminded here of Callinicos (1985), who writes that the 'scope for agency (and hence for resistance, a political expression of agency) in history varies according to the specific circumstances in which people find themselves' (140). He continues, 'the scope for resistance of ... a slave in the Athenian silver mines at Laureion, while no doubt real enough, was surely much narrower than that of, say, the auto-workers at Ford Halewood' (141).

Thus, my application of the agency position to the Labrador data produces a conclusion similar to that of Sider in *Culture and Class* (1986). Sider maintains that Newfoundland values such as individualism and self-sufficiency (102–3) undermine agency and its expression, effectual resistance. The paired, dyadic relations each fisher had with his supplying merchant, and the dispersed, family-based settlement pattern undermined inter-family political coalescence. Consequently, even when locals opposed the government resettlement of their communities they were unable to stop it (183). Sider grapples with the question of how indebted fishers react to exploitative merchants, and his conclusions resemble my own.

My contention that structure plays a greater role than does agency in the rise and fall of southeastern Labrador communities raises the question of what explains such structural forces themselves. With Wolf (1982, 304–5) and Marshall (1987), I believe that a starting point for answers lies in theories which acknowledge 'the existence of alternating long-term phases of relative expansion and contraction in the historical development of industrial capitalism' (Marshall 1987, 19). Marshall's overview of long-wave theory presents the following cycles of British expansion: the Industrial Revolution (1790–1825/6), the Victorian boom (1847/8–1873/4), the Imperialist boom (1893/4–1913/14), the Postwar boom (1940/5–1966/7), and intervening periods of contraction such as the Victorian Depression or the Great Depression (1873/4–1893/4) and the Interwar Depression (1913/14 to 1940–5) (99). While clearly a topic for further research, at least some specifics of Labrador regional development appear linked to these long waves. For example, in Labrador the consequence of the European Industrial Revolution is the arrival of the earliest permanent Settlers, many of whom were craftsmen from the English interior displaced by agricultural enclosure and the mechanization characteristic of the revolution. Likewise, the onset of the Victorian depression coincides with and partially explains the economic slow-down along the southeastern Labrador coast during the 1870s. As suggested, this slow-down was also caused by natural factors (such as long-term cold-water cycles). In addition, the slow-down reflected the culmination of maximal levels of economic growth, both in Newfoundland (Alexander 1976, 61) and in England. Finally, the phase Marshall calls the Interwar Depression produced, in Newfoundland, the depressed economic conditions leading to the commission of government during the 1930s. As I explained in Chapter 9, this resulted in attempts to diversify the economy, illustrated by the founding of the logging community at Port Hope Simpson. And while regional development cannot be entirely explained by long-wave theory, the theory does provide a useful starting point for questions about growth and decline, and is compatible with the view that regional and global histories need to be integrated.

A LOOK TO THE FUTURE

The northern cod moratorium hangs over Newfoundland and Labrador like the pall on a coffin. It is an understatement to say that the moratorium has fundamentally distressed Newfoundland society. Unemployed fishers and plant workers are rightly bitter because they had warned of such a collapse for many years and now are its victims, suggesting again the limits of agency among peoples on the periphery. Yet outright rebellion is obviated by the ironic fact that some former fishers and plant workers are actually economically better-off on federal subsidies (the so-called package) than during the fishery – the moratorium's guaranteed weekly payments are greater than their previous earnings. Many doubt that the cod fishery will ever return and, if it does, that it will ever employ as many as it did.

The increased dependence on Ottawa epitomized by the cod moratorium has fuelled the mistaken belief among some Canadians that Newfoundland is an economic drain, with misfortunes that are, like its appalling climate, endemic and irreparable. Of course, improving the economic position will not be easy: the province of Newfoundland and Labrador has a rigorous natural setting and a finite number of economic alternatives to its traditional industries. Yet let us apportion blame appropriately. As the fishery crisis shows, the residents of Canada's tenth province have been no better served by Canada than they were by the local 'fishocracy' of historic times. The Dominion of Newfoundland's entry into the Canadian federation carried a very high price. Term 3 of the 1948 Terms of Union placed the new province under the British North America Act (1867), which surrendered jurisdiction of the offshore, and with it, the cod fishery, the raison d'être of the dominion. Ottawa and the rest of Canada benefited substantially, using federal control of Newfoundland's rich fishing grounds as a new card to be dealt in the international poker game with European fishing nations. Rural Newfoundlanders and the Settlers described in this book (most of whom, ironically, supported confederation) enjoyed short-term universal benefits for a very high price: the cod fishery.

Even before the moratorium, the provincial government sought alternatives to the cod fishery and increasingly settled on three: high-tech industries, aquaculture, and tourism. One tourist development in southeastern Labrador is the restoration of historic Battle Harbour. In 1991, after a couple of years of planning – much of it by the Battle Harbour Area Development Association – the restoration of Battle Harbour began, under the supervision of a non-profit historic trust composed of distant business-people. The Atlantic Canada Opportunities Agency (ACOA) provided $1.585 million dollars over five years, and the Canada Employment and Immigration Commission (CEIC) and the Labrador Rural Development Agreement also contributed to the project. The plan sounds millenarian: to restore this once-prominent fishing centre, to recreate the old salt-cod fishery, and to thereby attract tourists. The concept is appealing, especially given the proximity of three other tourist attractions – the Norse site at L'Anse au Meadows, the Maritime Archaic site at Port au Choix, and the Basque whaling site at Red Bay. Certainly local people – roughly twenty each summer since 1991 –

welcome the restoration jobs. Yet the locals I interviewed in 1992 emphasized that the success of the project depends entirely on extension of the
road from Red Bay north to Mary's Harbour, and beyond to Goose Bay.
Whether such a road (approximately 475 kilometres in length and estimated to cost $2222 million dollars) will be built remains to be seen
(Fiander-Good Associates 1993). But even if it is built and if it attracts
tourists, two points seem inescapable. Tourism can only augment but
never replace former labour-intensive economies such as the fishery,
and roads run two ways; they may bring tourists in, but they also
provide Settlers an easy and appealing way out.

Aquaculture, the provincial government's second alternative to fishing, appears difficult in the subarctic waters off southeastern Labrador,
and so far there has been little discussion of placing high-tech industries
there. More promising alternatives are rooted in the region's history,
and include logging (in Sandwich Bay), an expanded handicraft industry, and alternative fisheries. For example, since the mid-1980s, a snow-
crab fishery has enjoyed considerable success. The Labrador Fishermen's
Union Shrimp Company converted its Mary's Harbour and Cartwright
fish plants to process crab and another plant began at St Lewis. By 1993,
a total of around three hundred men and women were hired to fish and
process crab. Here again, the location of crab plants in the three communities bolstered their status as population centres; many former cod
fishers and their families left their outside fishing settlements and
moved near one of these crab plants. Wages and unemployment insurance earnings have been high, yet there are signs that the future of this
new fishery is problematic. An oversupply of crab has caused prices to
drop steadily since the late 1980s. Moreover, aggressive Newfoundland-
based crab buyers came to Labrador in 1993 to buy the raw crab necessary to employ Settlers at Labrador plants, offering better prices, free
bait, and other incentives. Such purchases illustrate the economics of
scale and the recurrent effects of exogenous structural forces in the
underdevelopment of marginal regions.

Readers who have followed me this far deserve to know what I think
about the future of southeastern Labrador communities, however risky
making such predictions is. Recently, and especially since the cod moratorium, the debate over Newfoundland's future has consolidated into
two alternative viewpoints; the two occasionally collide but more often
pass each other by. The first, from 'mainland' editorialists and conservative economists (including Newfoundlander Michael Walker, of Vancou-
ver's Frazer Institute), lambastes recipients of the moratorium subsidy

and restates the need for the rationalization of rural Newfoundland. The second is more 'politically correct' but is also made far from the hinterland. This second view encourages sustainable economies and is the view of academics and government planners (cf. House 1989).

While my heart warms to many components of the second view, my mind questions its message and its relevance to the real hinterland. What does 'sustainable' mean and what is being asked of those who are to become sustainable? It seems *as if* after discouraging the dispersed way of life that had sustained the people of the bays and headlands for two hundred years, and offering them the rewards of Canadian citizenship whilst simultaneously destroying their resource base, we metropolitans are expecting those at the periphery to reclaim the precarious independence they once enjoyed. It seems to me more likely that the economic forces now crashing against the Labrador coast will be too powerful to withstand. And I doubt that the alternatives described above can provide for the present population, and foresee instead the death of some communities by attrition, the young emigrating and their elders remaining. While I fervently hope I am wrong, my guess is that the years to come will prove very difficult for the people of the bays and headlands.

Notes

CHAPTER 1 Introduction

1 Minor discrepancies exist in southeastern Labrador census data, as may be seen by comparing the Statistics Canada data presented in my text with Brice-Bennett (1992, 23, 173) and CLTEAC (1992, 9). The decreasing population figures from southeastern Labrador contrast with the increasing population of Labrador as a whole, from 28,741 (1986) to 30,375 (1991). This increase is attributable to the military expansion at Happy Valley/Goose Bay, where the population grew a whopping 18.8 per cent. Between 1986 and 1991, the population of island Newfoundland remained stable. More generally, historic inaccuracies in Labrador census data, especially those from southeastern Labrador, make such data difficult to work with.

2 My historical focus fits within the renewed anthropological interest in history, although it is beyond my intent to make a theoretical contribution to this growing literature. The recent dialogue between anthropologists and historians has exposed anthropologists to an alternative way of conceptualizing change, based more on concepts such as colonialism and imperialism than on acculturation and modernization. The growing and complex literature on 'historical anthropology' views all peoples according to the dictates of processual theory. It questions, as did Evans-Pritchard in 1950, the notion of a static ethnographic present, suggesting instead that what we observe at any point in time is the culmination of events and processes preceding it. A good example is Brody's ([1973] 1982, 5–6) observation that Irish 'familism' (inter-family reciprocity), focal to Arensberg's ([1937] 1968) functional analysis, has not been part of Irish culture since time immemorial but developed no earlier than 1840. Thus, historical anthropology examines the 'ethnographic present in longitudinal perspective'

(Biersack 1991, 25) and, by so doing, raises new questions. Work published from this approach, such as that of Wolf (1982), Sahlins (1985, 1994), and Hasrup (1990), illustrates a shift away from the study of single communities or peoples in isolation.

3 While problematic, the term *Settler* (capitalized for a people) remains the best ethnic name for the descendants of English or Irish emigrants and their Inuit, Settler, or Newfoundland spouses. Other terms used by Settlers and referring to them include liveyers, Labradormen, natives, Labradorians, Kablunangajuit, and Metis. Along with Plaice (1990, 113–14) and most others, I use Settler because of its common (albeit problematic) usage and because it lacks the imprecision or political implications associated with alternatives like Labradorians.

4 Four very different examples of Canadian regional studies are: a study of an ethnically heterogeneous region of Nova Scotia (Hughes et al. 1960); a project on identity and modernity in the East Arctic carried out by Memorial University's Institute of Social and Economic Research, between 1968 and 1971; a multidisciplinary study of the Quebec county of Bellechasse carried out by Laval University researchers in the 1970s; and a popular and insightful history of the Kingston peninsula of New Brunswick (Calder 1984).

5 In his 1887 classic *Community and Society*, sociologist Ferdinand Tonnies argues that *Gemeinschaft* or community is intimate, familial, and sacred; whereas *Gesellschaft* or society is distant, contractual, and profane. At any point in time, gesellschaft is the negation of gemeinschaft, while over time, gemeinschaft may develop into gesellschaft. Tonnies's analysis ultimately influenced the typological theories of Durkheim, Weber, Redfield, and others. Today we apply the term 'community' to organizations such as the 'European economic community' or the 'academic community.'

CHAPTER 2   Environment, Prehistory, and European Exploitation to 1763

1 This essential interdependence formed the logic underlying the evidence collected by the Newfoundland side of the Labrador boundary dispute, settled in 1927. Newfoundland officials asked Settlers (principally in central and northern Labrador) summering on the coast about their use of the interior.

2 Labrador Innu are the easternmost branch of Algonquian-speaking Cree peoples. Archaeological interpretations of the antiquity of Innu origins range from William Fitzhugh's (1972) belief that modern Innu represent the culmination of an evolutionary process beginning with the Maritime

Archaic to Loring's (1992) estimation that their arrival dates from at least 2000 BP.

3 Controversy will likely always surround the location of Cabot's New World landfall. As with the Vikings and other early European explorers, Cabot's descriptions of the lands he encountered are general enough to prevent positive identification. In any event, Cabot and his son Sebastian carried English discovery patents, thereby establishing English sovereignty over the Atlantic seaboard (Gosling 1910, 112).

4 Following the Portuguese expeditions of Gaspar and Miguel Cort Real, in the early sixteenth century, early maps such as the Kuntsman III map, dating from around 1503, began to include such places as 'Ilha de Frey Luis,' near present-day St Lewis Inlet and 'Cabo de San Antoine' (St Anthony). By the time of Jacques Cartier's first voyage in 1534, places such as Bay of Chatteaux (Chateau Bay), Hable de Balleine (Red Bay), and Blanc Sablon were named, even though certain place-names were not included on earlier maps or were later changed.

5 In 1977, the remains of a shore whaling station were discovered at Red Bay, and the following year divers discovered the submerged wreck of a Basque cargo ship in Red Bay harbour. The story of Basque whaling at Red Bay is presented by Tuck and Grenier (1989). Red Bay was one in a chain of Basque stations, including some within the study area (Stage Island [Henley Harbour], Pleasure Harbour, and Cape Charles).

CHAPTER 3 An Early British Adventure

1 On my visit to Labrador in May and June 1992, I discovered at Lodge Bay what is probably the remains of Cartwright's Ranger Lodge.

2 The remains of this house were known by local people. They were 'discovered' by Charles Townsend (1907) and later by me in August 1980. On my recommendation, the Stage Cove site was excavated by a Memorial University graduate student in archaeology, Kevin McAleese, in 1986 (see McAleese 1991).

3 Perhaps it was named after the HMS *Merlin*.

CHAPTER 4 Visiting Fishers

1 Following older historical usage and Labrador informants, I use *trawls* to refer to baited longlines, not as it is used today, to refer to net bags towed behind offshore fishing vessels.

2 A few American traders continued to visit the coast after this time. In the

last decade of the century, Dr Grenfell observes, 'We met in another harbour an American vessel exchanging "strong water" for fish – by which at
once the merchant is robbed and the fisherman ruined' (1893, 280).
3 On other occasions, Labrador Settlers accused Newfoundland fishers of
destroying their property (see Hamilton 1863, 399).
4 This may be the earliest published use of the recent political term 'Labradorians.'

CHAPTER 5 A New World

1 Since my research, the Labrador Metis Association has assembled impressive geneological data, showing as argued here, the many Aboriginal-Euro-
pean unions which occurred historically.
2 Tory may have been buying fish at Chateau but Cartwright visited a cod-
fishing room belonging to a Mr Tory at Square Islands, in the summer of
1786 (1792, 3: 197).
3 The curiosity southeastern Labrador people have about the past is part of a
larger phenomenon occurring throughout the Labrador territory. The
ever-increasing pace of change which has transformed the region since the
Second World War has also spurred considerable nostalgic reminiscence
about the past, a time when life seemed less complicated, even if more
physically challenging. One manifestation of this renaissance is *Them Days*
magazine, an oral history quarterly published since 1975. Its transcribed
stories contain entertaining and often valuable information about Labrador
history; a few touch on early settlement.
4 William, the earliest Acreman (Akerman) to whom my data refer, was
born about 1826. William may have fathered John (born about 1849), who
definitely fathered Samuel (1878–1953), father of the oldest Mary's
Harbour Acremans. But John's paternity is indefinite and, significantly,
Acremans today claim that some of their ancestors came from Bay Roberts
(Newfoundland) and only summered in Battle Harbour. Even so, one
Acreman showed me a deed, dating from 12 November 1844, in which a
William Acreman purchased property at Battle Harbour. The informant did
not know who this William Acreman was. If this is the same William who
is recorded in my computer data, and if he is the father of John, then this
would show both a continuity at Battle Harbour dating to the early nineteenth century and the limitations of attempting to reconstruct social
history based solely on either archival or ethnographic methods. In sum,
although Whitely (1977) is probably correct in concluding that a continuity
of surnames exists in many cases, there are also situations where

apparent continuity is illusory, and where the real story may never be known.

CHAPTER 6 Life in the Bays and on the Headlands

1 Both the date of Packard's interview (1864) and his observation that Stone had ten children leave no doubt that the man referred to in this account was Charles Stone, the founder of modern Henley Harbour/Pitt's Arm (Packard 1891). Stone was born in Dorsetshire in 1805. He wintered for unknown periods at Summerside, Bay of Islands, Newfoundland, during the 1850s, on the French Shore (Pye et al. n.d.), at Carbonear, and presumably at Pitt's Arm. Stone died at Henley Harbour in 1888.

2 Informants recalled that during the 1920s, a Cape Charles merchant stored the little money he had in several small canvas bags. Each contained either five-cent, ten-cent or twenty-five-cent pieces, from which a few dollars might be returned to fishers who actually made money that year.

3 During the late nineteenth century there was also a short-lived tinned salmon industry. Problems also occasionally arose when salmon nets were set in harbours and bays, as is now required by law. Thus, Commissioner March describes disputes between salmon fishers and cod fishers at Chateau Bay. March writes: 'At Henley, the whole of their principal fishing grounds and hauling Coves are occupied by salmon nets, as far as York Point, to the West of Chateau. Parties from Halifax do a large business in manufacturing salmon. Some of the oldest residents of this place complained most bitterly that their cod fishery had been completely destroyed by the setting of salmon nets. Shoals of [cod] fish have been seen coming in, but their coves being blocked by salmon nets, the fish would shy off and go to some coves where it could have free access' (1866, 181–2). The importance of frozen salmon to the southeastern Labrador economy is suggested by the fact that the 829,803 pounds shipped from Battle Harbour in 1945 represented 82 per cent of all goods shipped from Battle Harbour that year (Christian 1945a).

CHAPTER 7 The Impact of the State: 1832–1949

1 Examples in this unsigned review include systematic differences in law enforcement for transient Newfoundlanders and Labrador Settlers. The author notes cases of collusion between judges (said to have been appointed through patronage) and unsavoury local traders, often victimizing local Settlers; he describes a police constable who was 'energetic after

Labradormen, but could not be got to move against his fellow countrymen on Labradormen's behalf'; and he cites cases of economic and sexual exploitation against Labrador people. My conjecture that Dr Paddon is the author is based on content, style, and the report's resemblance to material presented in Paddon's emotional defence of the IGA (1917).

CHAPTER 8 Compatible Developments

1 In an unpublished paper, Laracy (1973) claims that Grady was opened in 1924. However, former Cartwright resident Willis Bird dates it to 1927, the same summer his sister Hazel was born (1977, 8).

2 Environmental impacts may not have been the only reason for McRae's suit. Noseworthy (1977, 12) claims that McRae first unsuccessfully attempted to sell Grady Island to the whaling company for $30 thousand and sued only as a recourse. It is also quite possible that some complaints about pollution from fishers may have been red herrings to conceal competition over space. Yet Judge Kent accepted most of McRae's complaints. Finally, Grenfell's opinion of the episode is most interesting, revealing his bias towards a large-scale development. His aversion towards either McRae and/or the Labrador fishery is obvious in his observation: 'Whaling made great strides for a few years when a Norwegian company brought to Gready Islands, Labrador, huge portable buildings and a big "mother" steamer ... They were bitterly attacked, however, and subjected to much hostility by moribund vested interests, and their activities so restricted that they were forced to abandon the enterprise' (Grenfell, quoted in Smallwood 1984, 676).

CHAPTER 9 From Homestands to Centres

1 In one of innumerable examples of his many connections, Mr and Mrs William G. Gosling met Grenfell during his first visit to Newfoundland in 1892, and as Mrs Gosling recorded, 'we both like[d] and admire[d] him immensely' (A.N. Gosling 1935, 35). A decade or so later, Grenfell proposed that William Gosling contribute a chapter on Labrador history to a forthcoming Grenfell collection. The impossibility of condensing this history (ibid., 49–50) led to Gosling's classic history of Labrador, published in the autumn of 1910 and still nonpareil.

2 The non-spitting anti-tuberculosis campaign included payment of bonuses to rug-hookers whose rugs read 'Don't spit' instead of the customary 'God

bless our home' (Grenfell 1934, 310). Even so, tuberculosis continued, and it wasn't until portable X-ray equipment became available during the Second World War that the incidence of the disease in Labrador began to be controlled (W.A. Paddon 1981, 12).

3 Blanchard's unintentional role in the IGA's selection of Mary's Harbour requires brief mention. The reclusive Blanchard came from St Andrew's, Newfoundland (near the Codroy Valley), by way of the United States, leaving behind three sons and, perhaps, a broken marriage. 'Uncle Peter' (as he was known) lived by trapping, gardening, and selling watches and perfumes. His gardens were located at 'Old Petes,' near the western end of the Mary's Harbour airstrip. He grew a variety of crops, including strawberries. Blanchard died about 1938, at the age of sixty-five, and is buried in the Roman Catholic cemetery at Trap Cove.

4 The British Privy Council ruled against the Newfoundland government's attempt to sue holders of undeveloped timber leases, a move by which Newfoundland probably sought to keep Labrador primed for sale or attractive to future speculators (Simpson 1934).

5 A local account of Eric Williams's death, gleaned from an older Port Hope Simpson resident, claims that the wily J.O. Williams sent his twenty-seven-year-old son to Labrador to avoid military service; that Eric's wife (called only 'Mrs Williams' in all published accounts but referred to as the 'white Russian' by my informant) began a love affair with the LDC paymaster and intended to kill Eric; that she escaped unharmed from the early-morning inferno that consumed their 'palatial' home and killed Eric and two-year-old Erica Annatol; and that she married the paymaster in the fall of 1940. The accounts published in the St John's *Evening Telegram* (3 and 5 February 1940 and in the Grenfell publication *Among the Deep Sea Fishers*) differ as to the fire's cause and the extent of Mrs Williams's injuries, and on a number of less significant details. If nothing more, the irreconcilable discrepancies between these accounts illustrate how 'official' and local versions of history conflict, complicating efforts to reconstruct local history. Whatever really happened early in the morning of 30 January 1940 at this isolated company town will probably never be known. My informant could have been simply entertaining the anthropologist or, less charitably, generating vicious gossip in a belated attempt to right a perceived or real injustice.

6 In a reference to Williams's unsuccessful request for the $200 thousand loan, Major Peter Cashin claimed during the national convention on 8 January 1948 that the effect of the loan rejection was to raise Labrador

relief expenditures from the regular amount of $10 thousand annually to
$50 thousand.

CHAPTER 10 Resettlement

1 The resettlement of Newfoundland and Labrador communities in the 1960s
resembles the evacuation of the ancient 'bird people' of St Kilda in 1930 as
described in Steel's (1975) fascinating account. Barren St Kilda island,
located off Scotland's west coast, would (by the early twentieth century) be
seen by planners as increasingly isolated from modern services and so the
need for resettlement. Similar arguments, also made by well-intended
nurses, teachers, the clergy, and government planners, would justify Newfoundland resettlement.

CHAPTER 11 An Institutional Umbrella

1 Like the LRAC, the Labrador Fishermen's Union Shrimp Company Limited
(the Shrimp Company) represents a regional institution with its headquarters located outside southeastern Labrador, but with a substantial presence
in the region. The Shrimp Company was formed in 1979 (albeit with a
different name), during intense competition over three licences to catch
shrimp. With strong and controversial backing from the Newfoundland
Fishermen, Food and Allied Workers Union, the Shrimp Company eventually won control of two of these lucrative licences. Since then the shrimp
fishery has been profitable, funding other sectors of the Shrimp Company's
operations in southern Labrador. Initially, the Labrador Inuit Association
held the remaining shrimp licence in trust, but eventually the Torngat
Fisheries Producers Cooperative Society (the Torngat Co-op) and its members along the northern Labrador coast used the licence. Some Labrador
people (and the author) question the 'real' motives of the Newfoundland-
based union, pointing out that the union's interest in Labrador coincided
with the announcement of three shrimp licences. Union representatives
counter such accusations by explaining that their only interest in originally
backing the Strait Co-op's application for the two shrimp licences was to
get the shrimp fishery started, not in profiting from it.
2 There are two definitions of the word 'Metis' in Canada; one specifically
refers to the descendants of French fur traders and Indian women in western Canada, and the other, more generic definition refers to descendants of
Europeans and aboriginal Canadians. The LMA employs the latter meaning
of Metis.

CHAPTER 12 Conclusions

1 Historian Sean Cadigan's (1990) study of merchant-fisher relations in the
  Battle Harbour district during the 1930s exemplifies the limitation of depending solely on archival data. These data lead him to conclude that
  fisher folk could and did effectively oppose local fish merchants. He uses
  the 1935 census to show the near-total dependence of families on
  merchants Baine Johnston and Company and concludes that 'there existed
  almost no way for most of the coast's residents to subsist without resorting
  to the fish trade and dealing with merchants' (130). Cadigan is only partially correct; the economy was actually more open, although seemingly without advantage to local Settlers. Surprisingly, Cadigan ignored the region's
  whaling and pit-prop timber industries, then offering some seasonal or
  year-round labour to Settlers. And had he travelled to the Battle Harbour
  area, older informants would have told him how they often journeyed to
  Blanc Sablon (Quebec) in the fall and spring to acquire cheaper provisions
  (especially flour) at the Hudson's Bay Company store. For example, my
  fieldwork revealed that an army (a minimum of sixteen men and their
  families, from the communities between Battle Harbour and George's
  Cove) of Battle Harbour area people moved to work at Port Hope Simpson
  in 1934, a very different picture than Cadigan found in the archives. Similarly, Cadigan's conclusion assumes that Baine Johnston and Company.
  was the only source of local supplies – again as if in isolation. A two-
  pronged methodology would have shown the Battle Harbour economy to
  be a more diversified one than that presented by Cadigan, although (contra
  Cadigan) this does not appear to have increased the effect of Settler
  agency.
2 Consideration of the various philosophical arguments for agency and structure (necessity) is beyond my range although I refer interested readers to
  Flew and Vesey (1987). Other social scientists use different terms to talk
  about local or global causality. For example, in her introduction to a book
  on the historical anthropology of Oceania, Biersack (1991) identifies two
  theoretical approaches. First, the culturalist or 'islands of history' approach
  of Marshall Sahlins and others maintains that local histories are culturally
  variable and that small-scale societies effectively mediate and accommodate
  global forces, albeit in locally meaningful ways. And second, there is the
  political economy or world-systems approach, which, at its extreme, concludes that world history is unified and that local (or regional) history is
  subordinated to global forces (cf. Roseberry 1988). Generally, these two are
  compatible with what I am calling 'agency' and 'structure,' respectively.

3 Anthony Giddens's theory of 'structuration' attempts to bridge and thereby replace the dualism between agency and structure. Giddens introduced structuration (not to be equated with structuralism or structural-functionalism) in 1976 but I draw my examples of it from his more recent *The Constitution of Society* (1984). First, Giddens's *structure* differs from standard sociological usage (were it refers to relations of interaction) and instead refers to generative rules and resources used and changed by individuals in their reproduction of society. Giddens criticizes the tendency of structural-functionalist theory to separate the reproduction of society from the individual actors whose conduct constitutes that society. Instead, structuration and its theorem, 'duality of structure,' propose a continuous interaction between the actions of knowledgeable individuals and the social structures that they both influence and are influenced by (1984, 25–6). Individual social action and structure are thus linked by a mutually interdependent causal loop (27); individuals both affect the social structure and are affected by it. The human agency Giddens identifies is bounded and often produces 'unintended consequences,' which in turn, feed back to the social structure itself. Giddens illustrates structuration with Willis's (1977) study of English working-class children ('the lads'). Knowledgeable about the school environment and authority system, 'the lads' rebel against the school through banter and aggressive sarcasm. Unlike their accommodating and conformist peers, the incorrigible 'lads' have the power (in Giddens's terms, the 'transformative capacity' of human agency) to make others 'laff' and use that power to encourage incidents that amuse, subvert, and incite (Giddens, 290). The oppositional behaviour of 'the lads' leads them to quit school and take factory jobs, where, coincidentally, their aggressive, joking culture 'strongly resembles that of the shop-floor' (293) and enables an easy adjustment to the working world they tolerate for the rest of their lives.

4 The restoration of subaltern history is important and overdue. Its mission appears philosophically (if not methodologically) similar to Urgent Anthropology's campaign to press the case of threatened peoples (see any of the documents from *Cultural Survival Quarterly* or the *International Work Group for Indigenous Affairs*). However, the tendency in subaltern studies to discount the importance of external influences in peasant consciousness strikes me as questionable and inimical to over a century of anthropological research on culture contact.

5 In her review of subaltern studies, O'Hanlon (1988) notes a tendency toward 'essentialism,' the philosophical notion that at least some objects have essence.

6 Brody's ([1973] 1982) and Scheper-Hughes's (1979) examinations of rural west Ireland provide two excellent non-marxist confirmations of the role of English colonization in community decline.

7 Another approach to regional development is staples theory. This theory originates in the extensive work of Canadian economic historian Harold Innis and focuses on the extraction of staples (commodities) and the institutions that emerge in conjunction with their production. We have seen that during the nineteenth century, the Anglican and Grenfell missions, and the Newfoundland government, came to Labrador primarily to serve transient Newfoundland fishers. We have also seen how these institutions brought about the emergence of new Settler communities and the death of others.

8 Newfoundland sociologist J.D. House (1981) applies a 'moderate' dependency perspective to the problems of unemployment and underdevelopment in Newfoundland and Labrador. House discusses the future impact of offshore oil development on coastal Labrador communities. He concedes that offshore oil development threatens Labrador's environment, fishery, and communities, yet confidently predicts that if oil were responsibly developed, the Labrador coast could move from 'a situation of underdevelopment and chronic undevelopment to one of dynamic dependent development' (449).

A Note on Documentation

An explanation is needed regarding the referencing and bibliographical format used. I have followed, with minor exceptions, the author-date system recommended by the 1982 *Chicago Manual of Style*. My aim has been to provide a 'user friendly' referencing system, which allows the reader to immediately see the author or organization responsible for the information cited, the actual date (supplied in the text, so as to furnish historical context) in which the information was created or published, and the page reference. This system allows the citation of both primary sources (such as the original and often hand-written letters, journals, and telegraphs I examined in the field or archive) and secondary sources in the text. Authors and their works are then listed alphabetically and chronologically in the reference section.

Where particular sources are difficult to locate, such as at the Provincial Archives of Newfoundland and Labrador (PANL), my bibliographical entries also provide the archive's actual catalogue and file numbers (which are sometimes inconsistent, as in the Newfoundland Ranger reports), allowing the retrieval and reinterpretation of sources discussed. I also supply the location of rare or otherwise inaccessible sources, such as diaries I copied in Labrador, using the following abbreviations: Author's Collection, meaning copy with author; *ADSF, Among the Deep Sea Fishers*; CNS, Centre for Newfoundland Studies; ESLDA, East Shore Labrador Development Association; *JHA, Journal of the House of Assembly*; ISER, Institute of Social and Economic Research; LCPA, Labrador Craft Producers Association; LINS, Labrador Institute of Northern Studies; LMA, Labrador Metis Association; LSD, Labrador Services Division; LRAC, Labrador Resources Advisory Council; MUN, Memorial University of Newfoundland; PANL, Provincial Archives of Newfoundland and Labrador; PC, Privy Council [British]; RAND, Rural, Agricultural and Northern Development, Department of; *TD, Them Days*.

I diverge from the author date system insofar as I use the category 'anonymous' to acknowledge unknown authorship and in that all of my text references to historic sources assembled for and published in the 1927 Privy Council (PC) boundary case provide the date the document was written and not the 1927 PC date of publication. Endnotes containing relevant information not essential to the text appear at the end of the book.

References

Abbott, J. 1990. Report on Labrador – 1923. *TD* 16 (1): 2–21.

Abbott, L. 1988. *The coast way: A portrait of the English on the Lower North Shore of the St. Lawrence.* Montreal and Kingston: McGill-Queen's University Press

Acreman, C. 1987. A big help. *TD* 12 (4): 112–13

– N.d. *Mary's Harbour Labrador 1930–1985.* Printed pamphlet, Author's Collection

Alexander, D. 1976. Newfoundland's traditional economy and development to 1934. *Acadiensis* 5 (2): 56–78

– 1977. *The decay of trade: An economic history of the Newfoundland saltfish trade, 1935–1965.* Newfoundland Social and Economic Studies, no. 19. St John's: ISER

Amulree, Lord. 1933. See Great Britain 1933.

Anderson, D. 1984. The development of settlement in southern coastal Labrador with particular reference to Sandwich Bay. *Bulletin of Canadian Studies* 8 (1): 23–49.

Anonymous. 1773. Remarks etc. made in obedience to His Majesty's instructions to Governor Shuldham. PC 3 [280]: 1083–9

– 1857. Diary from Cape Charles. Author's Collection

– 1888. Untitled Diary from Lodge Bay/Cape Charles. Author's Collection.

– 1920a. The mission stations through the eyes of a London director. *ADSF* Oct.: 133–6

– 1920b. Battle Harbour 1920. *ADSF* Oct.: 111–14

– 1920c. A brief review of administrative methods employed on the Labrador coast, with special reference to justice, charity and industry. GN 1/3A. Governor's Miscellaneous and Local Correspondence. no. 87 (498). PANL [Unsigned although probably written by H.L. Paddon in June 1920]

- 1939. Memorandum re earnings of Esquimaux at Nain, Labrador, season 1937–1938. GN 13/2/A. Box 5, File 2. PANL Justice Department
- 1985. The role of regional development associations and their contribution to rural planning in Newfoundland and Labrador – Some preliminary findings. Paper presented at the Seminar on the Atlantic Provinces, Edinburgh University, March 1985. CNS.
Arensberg, C.M. [1937] 1968. *The Irish countryman.* Garden City, NY: Natural History Press
Arensberg, C.M., and S.T. Kimball. 1965. *Culture and community.* New York: Harcourt, Brace and World
Armitage, P., and J.C. Kennedy. 1989. Redbaiting and racism on our frontier: Military expansion in Labrador and Quebec. *Canadian Review of Sociology and Anthropology* 26 (5): 798–817
Assistant Secretary for Justice (unsigned). 1942. Letter from Assistant Secretary for Justice to Secretary for Natural Resources, 30 Oct. 1942. GN 13/2/A. Box 123, File 18 'Labrador Development Company'. Justice Department, PANL
Auger, R. 1991. *Labrador Inuit and Europeans in the Strait of Belle Isle: From the written sources to the archaeological evidence.* Collection Nordicana, no. 55. Quebec: Laval University
Baikie, M. 1976. *Labrador memories: Reflections at Mulligan.* Happy Valley, Labrador: *TD*
Bear, J.C. 1984. The genetic structure of the Newfoundland population: A descriptive inquiry. Unpublished final report to the National Health Research and Development Program, Health Services and Promotion Branch, Health and Welfare Canada. Author's Collection
Beare, G. 1983. A chilling experience. *TD* 8 (3): 22–5
Beauharnois, C. Marquis de, and G. Hocquart. 1735. Concession, 27 Sept. 1735, of Cap. Charles to Sieur Marsal for nine years, 1735–44. PC 7 [1405]: 3662
- 1743. Extension of concession, 7 Sept. 1743, to Marsal for 6 years, 1744–1750. PC 7 [1406]: 3663
Bell, C., and H. Newby. 1978. *Community studies.* London: George Allen and Unwin
Bemister, J. 1867. Letter to Thomas E. Gaden, Esq. 5 Aug. 1867. PC 3 [649]: 1604.
Berthelsen, Nurse. 1933. From a letter from Nurse Berthelsen. *ADSF* July: 88
Berton, P. 1978. The adventures of Wilfred Grenfell. In *The wild frontier,* edited by P. Berton. Toronto: McClelland and Stewart
Biersack, A. 1991. Introduction: History and theory in anthropology. In *Clio*

in Oceania: Toward a historical anthropology, edited by A. Biersack. Washington: Smithsonian Institution Press

Bird, M. 1980. Fishin' in them days. *TD* 6 (1): 44–8.

Bird, W. 1977. Big, big furnace!! *TD* 3 (2): 8–9

Black, W.A. 1960. The Labrador floater codfishery. *Annals of the Association of American Geographers* 50 (3): 267–95

Bolsvert, D., and K. Turnbull. 1985. Who are the Metis? *Studies in Political Economy* 18: 107–47

Boston Board of Selectmen. 1756. Report filed by the selectmen of Boston to the Governor, the Council and House of Representatives. Vol. 117: 55–7. Massachusetts Archives

Bordieu, P. 1977. *Outline of a theory of practice.* Translated by Richard Nice. Cambridge: Cambridge University Press

Bourque, B. 1975. Feature: S.B.F. Fequet & Son. *TD* 1 (2): 2–8

Bowen, N.H. 1854. The social conditions of the coast of Labrador. *Transactions of Quebec Literary and Historical Society* 2: 329–41

Bowring Brothers. 1903. Whale fishery: Application for licence. GN 2/5. Box 6, 'Whale fishery: Application for Licences'. PANL

Brantenberg, T. 1977. Ethnic commitments and local government in Nain, 1969–1976. In *The White Arctic,* edited by R. Paine. Newfoundland Social and Economic Papers, no. 7. St John's: ISER

Brice-Bennett, C. 1992. Obituary on the Labrador Coast Fishery. Final report of the Industrial Adjustment Service Committee on the Labrador Coast Fishery. CNS.

British Secretary of State for Dominion Affairs. 1947. Telegram to Newfoundland Governor, 15 May 1947. GN 13/2/A. File 19, LDC 1945–8. PANL

Britton, J.C. 1943. Letter to L.E. Emerson, 23 July 1943. GN 13/2/A. Box 390, Labrador Radio Finding Stations. PANL

Brody, H. [1973] 1982. *Inishkillane: Change and decline in the west of Ireland.* Boston: Faber and Faber

Brookes, H.R. 1949. Letter to ?, 17 Oct. 1949. in GN 13/2/A. Box 123, File 24. PANL

Brown, Turner, Compton Carr, Co. 1945. Letter to British Under-Secretary of State, 26 June 1945. GN 13/2/A. Box 123, File 19, 'LDC 1945–8' (1980). Justice Department, PANL

Brown, W. (Captain). 1872. Second cruise. *JHA* 661–71

Browne, P.W. 1909. *Where the fishers go: The story of Labrador.* New York: Cochrane Publishing

Brox, O. 1968. Resettlement in Newfoundland: Some sociological comments.

In *Viewpoints on communities in crisis,* edited by M.L. Skolnik. Newfoundland Social and Economic Papers, no. 1. St John's: ISER

– 1972. *Newfoundland fishermen in the age of industry: A sociology of economic
dualism.* Newfoundland Social and Economic Studies, no. 9. St John's:
ISER

Budgel, R., and M. Stavely. 1987. *The Labrador boundary.* Happy Valley–Goose
Bay: Labrador Institute of Northern Studies

Burchell, C.J. 1942. Letter to L.E. Emerson, 18 June 1942. GN 38. Box S 4-1-2,
File 4, Justice and Defence. No. 64, 1942. PANL

Burden, M. 1989. Letter to Department of Justice, 24 Mar. 1989. ESLDA
Articles of Association, Registry of Deeds and Local Companies, Confederation Building St John's

Burns, W.N. 1921. A ten-mile dam across the Strait of Belle Isle. *ADSF* Oct.:
82–4

Cadigan, D.A. 1969. Letter to K.M. Harnum, 20 Oct. 1969. GN 39/1. File H
3475. In Newfoundland (Resettlement Files) PANL RAND

Cadigan, S. 1990. Battle Harbour in transition: Merchants, fishermen, and the
state in the struggle for relief in a Labrador community during the 1930s.
Labour/Le Travail 26: 125–50

Calder, D. 1984. *All our born days.* Sackville, NB: Percheron Press

Callinicos, A. 1985. Anthony Giddens: A contemporary critique. *Theory and
Society* 14 (2): 133–66

Campbell, S. 1984. John Campbell. *TD* 9 (3): 54–5

Canada (DREE). 1970a. Status-progress report on the Newfoundland Resettlement Program. 19 Mar. 1970. Task Force Newfoundland, no. 43. CNS

– 1970b. Review of Newfoundland Fisheries Resettlement Program 1965–70.
June 1970. CNS

– 1970c. Second Newfoundland Resettlement Agreement. 17 July 1970. CNS.

– 1973. Newfoundland Resettlement Program. Report to Joint Planning Committee from Newfoundland Resettlement Committee. Ottawa. CNS

– 1975. Statistics Federal-Provincial Resettlement Program. CNS

Canadian Broadcasting Company (CBC). 1988. On Camera. CBC Television,
St John's, 15 Nov. 1988

Canning, S. 1985. 'Existence rationality' and rural development policy in
Newfoundland. CNS

Carr, W.G. 1944. *Checkmate in the North: The axis planned to invade America.*
Toronto: Macmillan

Cartwright, G. 1773. Memorial of Geo. Cartwright. PC 3 [268]: 1059–66

– 1792. *A journal of transactions and events during a residence of nearly sixteen
years on the coast of Labrador.* 3 vols. Newark, England: Allin and Ridge

Cashin, R. 1976. A rural development policy for Newfoundland. *Rounder* 1 (9): 6

Chappell, E. 1818. *Voyage of His Majesty's ship 'Rosamond' to Newfoundland and the southern coast of Labrador.* London: J. Mawman

Christian, S.M. 1941a. Report of the Newfoundland Ranger Force, Mary's Harbour, 3 Feb. 1941. GN 13/4. Loose Ranger Reports, 1941–2, File: Monthly Condition Reports, PANL

– 1941b. The report of the Newfoundland Ranger Force, Battle Harbour, 1 Aug. 1941. GN 13/4. Loose Ranger Reports, 1941–2. PANL

– 1941c. The report of the Newfoundland Ranger Force, Battle Harbour, 8 Sept. 1941. GN 13/4. Loose Ranger Reports, 1941–2. File: Monthly Condition Reports. PANL

– 1942. The report of the Newfoundland Ranger Force, Battle Harbour, 4 Feb. 1942. GN 13/4. Loose Ranger Reports, 1941–2, File: Miscellaneous Condition Reports, 2. PANL

– 1945a. The report of the Newfoundland Ranger Force, Battle Harbour, 31 Jan. 1945. GN 38 S2-5-2. File 2. PANL

– 1945b. The report of the Newfoundland Ranger Force, Battle Harbour, 12 May 1945. GN 38 S2-5-2, File 2. PANL

Clark, D. 1981. More extracts from the diary of a doctor stationed at Mary's Harbour, Labrador, 1937–8. *ADSF* July: 16–19

Clark, D.B. 1973. The concept of community: A re-examination. *Sociological Review* 21 (3): 397–416

Clark, E.G. 1944. The report of the Newfoundland Ranger Force, Cartwright, 31 Oct. 1944. GN S2-5-2. File 2. PANL

Clutterbuck, P.A. 1945. Letter to Brain, 10 Sept. 1945. GN 13/2/A. Box 397, Justice Department, Labrador Railway 6/01/6. PANL

Coastal Labrador Training and Education Advisory Committee (CLTEAC). 1992. A training needs assessment of Labrador coast communities, vol. II, (B) District Analysis: Southeast Labrador. Happy Valley–Goose Bay, Labrador. Mimeographed

Coghlan, J. 1777. Correspondence between Jeremiah Coghlan of Fogo and Governor Montagu, about the interference with Coghlan's fisheries on Labrador. PC 3 [392]: 1269–72

Cohen, A.P. 1980. The anthropology of proximate cultures: The Newfoundland School, and Scotland. *Scottish Journal of Sociology* 4 (2): 213–26

– 1985. *The symbolic construction of community.* New York: Tavistock Publications

Coish, A. 1982. The Labrador Development Corporation [sic], Port Hope Simpson. *TD* 8 (2): 30–7.

Colburn, F.D., ed. 1989. *Everyday forms of peasant resistance.* New York: M.E. Sharpe, Inc.

Collingham, W. 1922. Voluntary statement, 27 Mar. 1922. *PC* 3 [618]: 1568–70

Comaroff, J. 1985. *Body of power, spirit of resistance: the culture and history of a South African people.* Chicago: University of Chicago Press

Company of Young Canadians (CYC). 1976. Proposal for Labrador Community development project. Feb. 1976. Mimeographed.

Cook, E. 1944. J.O. Williams's submission [written by Cook] to Judge Dunfield. GN 13/2/A. Box 123, File 20 'LDC Ldt. Briefs' (1980). PANL

– 1947. Letter to Flinn, Commission of Natural Resources, 8 Nov. 1947. GN 13/2/A. File 19. PANL

– 1949. Letter to R.L.M. James, 26 Mar. 1949. GN 13/2/A. Box 123, File 24 (1980). Justice Department, PANL

Copes, P. 1971. Community resettlement and rationalization of the fishing industry in Newfoundland. Discussion Paper 71-3-1, Deptartment of Economics and Commerce: Discussion Paper Series, Simon Fraser University, Burnaby, BC

– 1972. The resettlement of fishing communities in Newfoundland. Canadian Council on Rural Development, Apr. 1972. CNS

Courtney, D.S. 1973. The Newfoundland Household Resettlement Programs: A case study in spatial reorganization and growth centre strategy. MA thesis, Memorial University, St John's

Curtis, C.S. 1958. Mrs. Keddie showed the way. *ADSF* Oct.: 69

Davidson, W.E. (Governor). 1916. Visit by the governor to Labrador and northern Newfoundland August 1916. GN 1/3A. 1920, File 79, Labrador Reports. PANL

Davis, J. 1981. Davis' of Sandwich Bay. *TD* 6 (4): 4–23

Davis, J.C. 1976. Building the Cora May. *TD* 2 (1): 14–16

– 1977. Grady Whale Factory Smoke and Steam. *TD* 3 (2): 4–8

Davis, K.G. 1974. *The North Atlantic world in the seventeenth century.* Vol. 4 of *Europe and the world in the age of expansion.* Minneapolis: University of Minnesota Press

Davis, R. 1980. The way we did it. *TD* 6 (1): 59–62

– 1982. Bert Coish. *TD* 8 (2): 37

– 1987. 42 years on the Goose. *TD* 12 (4): 76–85

Davis, R.H. 1976. Boat building. *TD* 2 (1): 11–13

Dawe, E. 1906. Annual report of the Department of Marine and Fisheries, Newfoundland, for the year 1905. *JHA* 140–70

De Boilieu, L. [1861] 1969. *Recollections of Labrador life.* Edited by Thomas F. Bredin. Toronto: Ryerson Press

Decker, H.A. 1970. Letter to Harnum, 13 May 1970. GN 39/1. File H 3920. Newfoundland (Resettlement Files), PANL RAND

Delaney, E. 1945. Report on Grave Newfoundland problems at Labrador-Quebec border. GN 13/4. File 7. Newfoundland Rangers. PANL

Department of Education. 1884. Reports on schools in Labrador. PC 3 [665]: 1620–2

Disney, H.P. 1851. Letter to the Reverend Mr Ernest Hawkins. In E. Feild, *Church in the colonies no. 21, Journal of the Bishop of Newfoundland's voyage of visitation and discovery on the South and West coasts of Newfoundland and on the Labrador, in the church ship 'Hawk,' in the year 1848.* London: Society for the Propagation of the Gospel

Dohme, D. 1921. Nurse Dohme's letter to Dr. Grenfell. *ADSF* July: 59–60

Duff, V.P. 1942. Report of the Newfoundland Ranger Force, North West River, 6 Mar. 1942. GN 13/4. Loose Ranger Reports, 1941–2, File: Miscellaneous Condition Reports, no. 1. PANL

– 1943. The report of the Newfoundland Ranger Force, North West River, 10 Mar. 1943. GN 13/4. File 7. Newfoundland Rangers, PANL

Dunbar, M.J. 1951. *Eastern arctic waters.* Bulletin no. 88. Ottawa: Fisheries Research Board of Canada

Dunfield, B. 1945. Report on the affairs of the LDC, Ltd 1934–44 (12 May 1945). GN 13/2/A. Box 123, File 21. PANL

Dunn, P.D.H. 1943. Memo to L.E. Emerson, 15 July 1943, Ref. no W/G3. GN 13/2/A. Box 390, 1943, Justice Department. File: Goose Airport Prohibited Places. PANL

Duquesne, M., and F. Bigot. 1753. Cancellation of grant to Baune and regrant to Marsal, 24 Sept. 1735, for 9 years, 1754–63. PC 7 [1408]: 3667

Durgin, G.F. 1908. *Letters from Labrador.* Concord, NH: Rumford Printing

Dwyer, C.G. 1940a. Report of the Newfoundland Ranger Force, Port Hope Simpson, 30 Sept. 1940. GN 13/4. File: Monthly Condition Reports. PANL

– 1940b. Report of the Newfoundland Ranger Force, Port Hope Simpson, 31 Oct. 1940. GN 13/4. High Commission – Rangers/1940, File: Monthly Condition Reports. PANL

– 1941a. The report of the Newfoundland Ranger Force, Port Hope Simpson, 30 June 1941. GN 13/4. Loose Ranger Reports, 1941–2, File: Monthly Condition Reports. PANL

– 1941b. The report of the Newfoundland Ranger Force, Port Hope Simpson, 3 Nov. 1941. GN 13/4. Loose Ranger Reports, 1941–2, File: Monthly Condition Reports. PANL

– 1941c. Report of the Newfoundland Ranger Force, Port Hope Simpson, 30

Sept. 1941. GN 13/4. High Commission, Rangers 1940, File: Monthly Conditions. PANL

- 1942a. Report of the Newfoundland Ranger Force, Port Hope Simpson, 31 Jan. 1942. GN 13/4. Loose Ranger Reports, 1941–2, File: Miscellaneous Condition Reports, No 2. PANL

- 1942b. Report of the Newfoundland Ranger Force, Port Hope Simpson, 28 Feb. 1942. GN 13/4. Loose Ranger Reports, 1941–2, File: Monthly Condition Reports. PANL

Dyke, A.P. 1969. Community inventory of Coastal Labrador. St John's, Department of Labrador Affairs. CNS

Dyson, A. 1980. Fishin' at Batteau. *TD* 6 (1): 54–8

Dyson, W. 1982. I was born to Mussel Brook. *TD* 8 (1): 52–3

Dziuban, S.W. 1959. *Military relations between the United States and Canada 1939–1945*. Washington, DC: Office of the Chief of Military History, Department of the Army

Eagle River Development Association (ERDA). 1988. By-laws to Articles of Association. Registry of Deeds and Local Companies, Confederation Building, St John's

East Shore Labrador Development Association (ESLDA). 1983. Annual Report, year 1983. Author's Collection

- 1985. Development strategy for eastern Labrador, 5 Jan. Author's Collection

Elson, W. 1981. Off to the 'gold rush.' *TD* 7 (1): 36–42

Elton, C.S. 1942. *Voles, mice and lemmings: Problems in population dynamics*. Oxford: Clarendon Press

Emerson, L.E. 1938. Memorandum on need for magistrate in Labrador, 27 June 1938. GN 38, Box S-4-1-5. File 4, Justice Department, PANL

- 1941. Report on visit of Commissioner for Justice and Defence to meeting of Permanent Joint Defence Board held at Windsor Hotel, Montreal, on Wednesday, 30 July 1941. GN 38. S-4-1-6. File 4, Justice and Defence. 1938–41. PANL

- 1942. Memorandum on Goose as prohibited area, n.d. GN 38S. 4-1-7. File 16, Justice and Defence, 108 – 1942. PANL

- 1943. Memorandum for Commission. 10 Nov. 1943. GN 13/2/A. Box 390, 1943, Goose Airport – Prohibited Places J and D 70 – 1943. PANL

Evans, A.R. 1954. *Wilfred Grenfell*. London: Oliphants

Evening Telegram (*ET*). 1940. Father and child burned to death. 3 Feb.: 4

- 1940. Mr. Eric Williams lost life attempting rescue. 5 Feb.: 4

- 1977. Wide variety of topics covered as MHAs present their resolutions. 3 Feb.: 4

- 1977. Committee would fan fires of separatist group says Hickey. 17 Feb.: 4

- 1977. Quick visits by committee won't solve problem – Moores. 3 Mar.: 4
- 1977. Feelings, needs of Labrador being ignored says Roberts. 10 Mar.: 4
- 1977. Legislature defeats resolution on select committee for Labrador. 31 Mar.: 4
- 1981. Labrador Inuit Association breaks with Advisory Council. 4 Dec.: 2

Feild, E. (Bishop). 1849. *Church in the colonies no. 19. A visit to Labrador*. London: Society for the Propagation of the Gospel
- 1851. *Church in the colonies no. 21. Journal of the Bishop of Newfoundland's voyage of visitation and discovery on the South and West coasts of Newfoundland and on the Labrador, in the church ship 'Hawk', in the year 1848*. London: Society for the Propagation of the Gospel

Fiander-Good Associates. 1993. Trans Labrador Highway: Social and Economic Project Feasibility Analysis. Report for Department of Works, Services and Transportation, Government of Newfoundland

Findlay, D.K. 1943. Goose: Key air base. *Maclean's Magazine* 15 July: 1943: 12–13, 42–4.

Finlay, J. 1853. Report of proceedings on protection of the fisheries at Belle Isle, the Straits, and coast of Labrador. *JHA* 134–40

Fitzhugh, W. 1972. *Environmental archaeology and cultural systems in Hamilton Inlet, Labrador*. Smithsonian Contributions to Anthropology, no. 16. Washington: Smithsonian Institution Press
- 1982. Smithsonian surveys in central and southern Labrador in 1981. In *Archaeology in Newfoundland and Labrador, 1981*, edited by J.S. Thomson and C. Thomson. St John's: Government of Newfoundland and Labrador, Historic Resources Division, Department of Culture, Recreation and Youth, Annual Report No. 2
- 1985. Early contacts north of Newfoundland before A.D. 1600: A review. In *Cultures in contact*, edited by W. Fitzhugh. Washington: Smithsonian Institution Press

Flew, A., and G. Vesey 1987. *Agency and necessity*. Oxford: Basil Blackwell.

Flinn, W.H. 1946. Memo for Commission of Government Labrador Development Co. Application for release of dollars, 10 Apr. 1946. GN 13/2/A. Box 123 (1980), File 19, Justice Department, LDC 1945–8, N.R. 31 – '46. PANL
- 1948. Memo on Labrador Development Co., 22 Sept. 1948. GN 13/2/A. Box 123, File 19 (1980), NR 70/48. PANL

Forbes, A. 1953. *Quest for a northern route*. Cambridge: Harvard University Press

Fornel, L. 1742. Report re: Baye des Chateaux and application for authority to explore Bay des Esquimaux, 27 Oct. 1742. PC 7 [1402]: 3656

Forsyth, C.H. 1936. First impressions (as recorded by a new district head). *ADSF* July: 60–3

– 1937. St Mary's River in 1936. *ADSF* Apr.: 12–13

Fowler, W.A. 1976. The growth of political conscience in Labrador. *Newfoundland Quarterly* 72 (4): 38–44

Frank, A.G. 1967. *Capitalism and underdevelopment in Latin America*. New York: Monthly Review Press

Fraser, A.M. 1958. Newfoundland. In *Encyclopedia Americana*, Canadian edition. Toronto: Americana Corporation of Canada

Freeman, M., ed. 1969. *Intermediate adaptation in Newfoundland and the Arctic: A strategy of social and economic development*. Newfoundland Social and Economic Studies no. 4. St John's: MUN Institute of Social and Economic Research

Fry, E. 1987. Search for the Goose. *TD* 12 (4): 5–11

Furlong, P. 1871. Report of P. Furlong, mail officer on board the steamer, Walrus, on her trip to Labrador. *JHA* 706–9

Giddens, A. 1984. *The constitution of society*. Cambridge: Polity Press

Gillespie, B. 1986. *A class act*. St John's: Creative Printers and Publishers

Gilmour, M.T. 1931. St. Mary's River. *ADSF* Jan.: 175–8

Goldthwait, J. 1932. An experiment in agriculture. *ADSF* Apr.: 36–7

Goode, G.B. 1887. *Fisheries and Fishery Industries of the U.S.*, section V, vol. 1. Washington: Government Printing Office

Gordon, H. 1972. *The Labrador parson*. St John's. PANL

Gordon, W., et al. 1845. Journal of the general assembly, Thursday, 3 April 1845. *JHA* 100–1

Gosling, A.N. 1935. *William Gilbert Gosling: A tribute*. New York: Guild Press

Gosling, W.G. 1910. *Labrador: Its discovery, exploration, and development*. London: Alston Rivers

– 1911. The Anglo-American fishery case before the Hague Tribunal. Typescript. CNS

Goudie, E. 1973. *Woman of Labrador*. Toronto: Peter Martin Associates

Governor of Newfoundland. 1947. Telegram to Secretary of State for Commonwealth Relations, 22 Nov. 1947. GN 13/2/A. File 19: LDC 1945–8. PANL

Great Britain. 1933. Newfoundland Royal Commission. *Report presented by the Secretary of State for Dominion Affairs to Parliament by command of His Majesty, Nov. 1933*. London: HMSO

Great Britain (Air Ministry). 1945. *Atlantic Bridge* (official account of RAF Transport Command's ocean ferry). London: HMSO

Grenfell, W.T. 1893. Our work in Labrador. *Toilers of the Deep*. Aug.–Sept.: 280–6
- 1902. Labrador jottings. *Toilers of the Deep*. 16: 18–19
- 1904. The log of the S.S. *Strathcona*. *ADSF* Oct.: 10–19
- 1905a. Grenfell lectures on his Labrador labours. *Evening Telegram* 12 Dec. 1905. Copy in P.T. McGrath, Collection, Box 13, Folder 9, 78. PANL
- 1905b. The log of the SS *Strathcona*. *ADSF* Jan.: 5–11
- 1906. Grenfell's log. *ADSF* Apr.: 12
- 1913. The people of the coast. In *Labrador: The country and the people*, edited by W.T. Grenfell (and others). New York: Macmillan
- 1914. Dr. Grenfell's log. *ADSF* Oct.: 88–96
- 1917. Report of the Superintendent, year 1916. *ADSF*, July: 62–8
- 1918. Report of the Superintendent, year 1917. *ADSF* Oct.: 121–9
- 1920. Report of the Superintendent, year 1919. *ADSF* July: 78–82
- 1921a. The nursing stations: St. Lewis Bay, Labrador. *ADSF* July: 58–9
- 1921b. Dr. Grenfell's log. *ADSF* Oct.: 76
- 1927. The log of the *Strathcona*. *ADSF* Apr.: 36
- 1929. A fireproof hospital for Labrador. *ADSF* Apr.: 36–7
- 1930. A happy New Year to all. *ADSF* Jan.: 150
- 1931. Sir Wilfred's Christmas letter. *ADSF* Apr.: 40–2
- 1932. *Forty years for Labrador*. Boston: Houghton Mifflin
- 1934. *The Romance of Labrador*. New York: Macmillan Co.
- 1935. The progress of a year. *ADSF* July: 46–51
Grieve, J. 1911. Battle Harbour items. *ADSF* July: 35–6
Guzzwell, G.C. 1941a. The report of the Newfoundland Ranger Force, Forteau, 31 July 1941. GN 13/4. Loose Ranger Reports, 1941–2, File: Monthly condition reports. PANL
- 1941b. The report of the Newfoundland Ranger Force, Forteau, 31 Aug. 1941. GN 13/4. Loose Ranger Reports, 1941–2, File: Monthly condition reports. PANL
Hamilton, R.V. 1863. Report of Captain Hamilton, of her Majesty's ship 'Vesuvius,' of his cruize [sic] on the Labrador and west coast of Newfoundland, in charge of the service of protecting the fisheries, etc. *JHA*, 398–401
Handcock, W.G. 1989. *Soe longe as there comes noe women: Origins of English settlement in Newfoundland*. Newfoundland History Series, no 6. St John's: Breakwater Books
Harnum, K.M. 1970. Basic outline of the Fisheries Household Resettlement Program in Newfoundland. CNS
- 1973. Resettlement Program. Letter to Federal/Provincial Resettlement

Committee. GN 59/7/A. Minutes of Resettlement Committee, 61st meeting, 7 Mar. 1973. PANL RAND

Harris, C.A. (Governor). 1920. (Untitled) Report on trip to Labrador. GN 1/3A. File 79. Labrador Reports, 1920. PANL

Harris, L. 1990. *Independent review of the state of the northern cod stock.* Ottawa: Fisheries and Oceans

Hart, E. 1948. The report of the Newfoundland Ranger Force, Cartwright, 15 Jan. 1948. GN 38 S2-5-2. File 8. PANL

Hasrup, K. 1990. *Island of anthropology.* Odense: Odense University Press

Head, C.G. 1976. *Eighteenth century Newfoundland.* Toronto: McClelland & Stewart

Hickson, T. 1824. Extracts from his journal, in N. Windsor, n.d., *Building on a firm foundation: A history of Methodism in Newfoundland, 1825–1855,* vol. 2. Economy Printing Ltd. CNS.

Hillary, G.A. 1955. Definitions of community: Areas of agreement. *Rural Sociology* 20: 111–23

Hine, J., and R. Slade 1793. Untitled truce, dated 21 Sept. 1793, at Temple Bay. MG 460, Box 23. Slade Ledgers, Battle Harbour, 1793, New System. PANL

Hogan, J.J. 1942. The report of the Newfoundland Ranger Force, 7 Oct. 1942. GN 13/4. File 7. Newfoundland Rangers, PANL

– 1943a. The report of the Newfoundland Ranger Force, 11 Jan. 1943. GN 13/4. File No. 7. Newfoundland Rangers, PANL

– 1943b. The report of the Newfoundland Ranger Force, 8 Mar. 1943. GN 13/4. File 7. Newfoundland Rangers, PANL

– 1943c. Report of the Newfoundland Ranger Force, 12 Apr. 1943. GN 13/4. High Commission Rangers/1940, File: Miscellaneous Condition Reports, 2, 1941–3. PANL

– 1943d. List of families at Otter Creek, 29 Apr. 1943 (unsigned but compiled by Ranger J.J. Hogan). GN 13/2/A. Justice, Box 390, 1943, File: Goose Airport – Prohibited Places. PANL

Hood, A.W.A. 1865. Continuation of Report on the information obtained by me whilst performing the duties of senior officer on the coasts of Newfoundland and Labrador. *Journal of Legislative Council of the Island of Newfoundland.* St. John's: J.C. Withers, Printer to the Queen's Most Excellent Majesty

– 1866. Report of Captain Hood, R.N., of H.M. Ship *Pylades. JHA* 504–11

Hopkins, L., and C. Hopkins. 1987. Not a bite of meat. *TD* 12 (4): 50–2

Horwood, H. 1986. *A history of the Newfoundland Ranger Force.* St John's: Breakwater Books

Hosmer, H.R. 1941. At St Mary's River. *ADSF* Apr.: 9–10

Houghton, F.L. 1966. The Strathcona line. *ADSF* July: 34–7

House, J.D. 1981. Big oil and small communities in coastal Labrador: The local dynamics of dependency. *Canadian Review of Sociology and Anthropology* 18: 433–52

– 1986. See Newfoundland 1986.

– 1989. The sustainable outport: A model for community development? *Canadian Journal of Community Mental Health* 8 (2): 25–40

Hoy, C. 1973. Deep roots vs. progress: A tiny village must choose. *Toronto Star*, 11 Aug.

Hughes, C.C., et al. 1960. *People of the cove and woodlot: Communities from the viewpoint of social psychiatry*. New York: Basic Books

Hussey, G. 1981. *Our life on Lear's Room Labrador*. St John's: Robinson-Blackmore Printing and Publishing

Innis, H.A. [1940] 1978. *The cod fisheries*. Revised edition. Toronto: University of Toronto Press

Jackson, L. 1982. *Bounty of a barren coast*. Happy Valley/Goose Bay: Memorial University of Newfoundland, Labrador Institute of Northern Studies

Jackson, L. and L. Jackson. 1971. *Labrador*. Ottawa: Information Canada.

Jillett, W. 1935. Untitled letter to Chief of Police, St John's. Box 166 (1980) GN 13/2/A. Justice Department, File 72: Relief conditions on Labrador. PANL

Jolin, P. 1965. Processus et principes d'organisation d'un village insulaire du Labrador méridional. *Anthropologica* 7: 59–79

Jones, A. 1921. Two experiments at Battle Harbour. *ADSF* Jan.: 161–2

Journal of the House of Assembly (JHA). 1857. Monday, 16 March 1857, 118

– 1863. A bill to regulate the fisheries of the island of Newfoundland and its dependencies, 627–9

– 1875. Labrador school return, 930–42

Jupp, D. 1971. *A journey of wonder and other writings*. New York: Vantage Press

Kaufman, H.F. 1959. Toward an interactional conception of community. Social Forces 38: 8–17

Keesing, R.M. 1992. *Custom and confrontation*. Chicago: University of Chicago Press

Kennedy, J.C. 1977. Northern Labrador: An ethnohistorical account. In *The White Arctic*, edited by R. Paine. Newfoundland Social and Economic Studies, no. 7. St John's: ISER

– 1982. *Holding the line: Ethnic boundaries in a northern Labrador community*. Social and Economic Studies, no. 27. St John's: MUN Institute of Social and Economic Research

- 1987. Aboriginal organizations and their claims: The case of Newfoundland and Labrador. *Canadian Ethnic Studies* 19 (2): 13–25
- 1988a. The impact of the Grenfell Mission on southeastern Labrador communities. *Polar Record* 24 (149): 199–206
- 1988b. The changing significance of Labrador Settler ethnicity. *Canadian Ethnic Studies* 20 (3): 94–111
- N.d. *Labrador village.* Prospect Heights, Ill.: Waveland Press (forthcoming)
Kent, J. 1928. Judgment of Mr Justice Kent in the Supreme Court of Newfoundland, 26 Apr. 1928. GN 13/2/A. Justice, Box 284, File 33. 'R.D. McRae and Sons vs. British Norwegian Whaling Company'. PANL
Kerr, J.L. 1959. *Wilfred Grenfell: His life and work.* New York: Dodd, Mead
Kerr, W.B. 1941. Newfoundland in the period before the American Revolution. *Pennsylvania Magazine* 65 (1): 56–78
Kleivan, H. 1966. *The Eskimos of northeast Labrador: A history of Eskimo-white relations, 1771–1955.* Oslo: Norsk Polarinstitutt
Knapp, C.S. 1924. Battle Harbour Hospital. *ADSF* Apr.: 6–8
Kober, C.J. 1979. Wilfred Grenfell (1865–1940): Portrait of a medical missionary and his work in Newfoundland and Labrador. PhD thesis, Albert-Ludwigs-Universität, Freiburg
Kottak, C., and E. Colson. 1994. Multilevel linkages: Longitudinal and comparative studies. In *Assessing cultural anthropology*, edited by R. Borofsky. New York: McGraw-Hill
Labrador Conference. 1956. *Proceedings of the conference on Labrador affairs held Feb. 13–16, 1956.* St John's: Guardian
Labrador Craft Producers Association Newsletters (LCPA NL). Various issues from 1981 to 1988. Mimeographed
- N.d. History of the Labrador Craft Producers Association. CNS
Labrador Metis Association (LMA). 1986. Articles of Association. Registry of Deeds (and Companies), Confederation Building, St John's
Labrador Resource Advisory Council (LRAC). 1976. Meeting of the LRAC held in Happy Valley, Labrador, Oct. 18, 19, 1976, and Fisheries Conference held in Goose Bay, 20 Oct. 1976. MUN Extension. Mimeographed
- 1977. Annual Report (AR) 1976–7. Mimeographed
- 1978. Annual Report (AR) 1977–8. Mimeographed
- 1982. Amendment to article V (1) of 1977 membership criteria, Jan. 1982. Registry of Local Companies, Drawer 64, Confederation Building, St John's
- N.d. Community priorities for development in Labrador. Mimeographed
Labrador Resource Advisory Council (LRAC). Newsletters (NL) Various numbers. Mimeographed.
Labrador Services Division (LSD). 1973. Annual Report for the year ending

31 March 1973. Department of Social Services and Rehabilitation, Government of Newfoundland
– 1974. Annual Report for the year ending 31 March 1974. Department of Rehabilitation and Recreation, Government of Newfoundland
– 1975. Annual Report for the year ending 31 March 1975. Department of Rehabilitation and Recreation, Government of Newfoundland
Labrador Syndicate. 1909–30. Correspondence on Labrador Syndicate. GN 2/5, 40. April 1909–April 1930. PANL
Lajonquiere, Marquis de, and F. Bigot. 1749. Grant, 1 Nov. 1749, of Cap Charles to Capt. Baune (deBonne) for 9 years, 1750–9. PC 7 [1407]: 3665
Lane, C.M. 1967. Centralizing our population. In *The book of Newfoundland*, vol. 3, edited by J.R. Smallwood. St John's: Newfoundland Book Publishers
Laracy, P. 1973. A report on the historical geography of whaling in Newfoundland 1900–1939. Unpublished paper. CNS.
Lethbridge, C. 1979. We followed the fur. *TD* 4 (3): 35
Lewis, D.G. 1940. From Indiana to George's Cove. *ADSF* Oct.: 82
Lodge, T. 1939. *Dictatorship in Newfoundland.* London: Cassell
Loring, S.G. 1992. Princes and princesses of ragged fame: Innu archaeology and ethnohistory in Labrador. PhD thesis, University of Massachusetts
Lucas, R.A. 1971. *Minetown, milltown, railtown: Life in Canadian communities of single industry.* Toronto: University of Toronto Press
Luther, J. 1915. The industrial work. *ADSF* Apr.: 8
Lyon, L. 1987. *The community in urban society.* Philadelphia: Temple University Press
Macdonald, D. 1988. Really no merchant: An ethnohistorical account of Newman and Company and the supplying system in the Newfoundland fishery at Harbour Breton, 1850–1900. PhD thesis, Simon Fraser University
– 1989. They cannot pay us in money: Newman and Company and the supplying system in the Newfoundland fishery, 1850–1884. *Acadiensis* 19 (1): 140–56
MacGregor, W. 1909. Reports of official visits to Labrador, 1905 and 1908. CNS
MacKay, R.A. 1946. *Newfoundland: Economic, diplomatic, and strategic studies.* Toronto: Oxford University Press
MacLeod, M. 1986a. Peace of the continent, Part I: Economic and political impact. *Newfoundland Quarterly* 81 (3): 21–30
– 1986b. Peace of the continent, Part II: Social impact. *Newfoundland Quarterly* 81 (4): 21–8
Mallalieu, W.S. 1929. Whaling. *ADSF* Apr.: 26
Mannion, J.J., ed. 1977. *The peopling of Newfoundland.* Social and Economic

Papers, no 8. St John's: Institute of Social and Economic Research

March, S. 1866. Copy of report of general superintendent of fisheries, of his proceedings in the Straits of Belle Isle, and upon the coast of Labrador, during the summer of 1865, etc. *JHA*, 177–83.

Marshall, M. 1987. *Long waves of regional development*. New York: St Martin's Press

Martin, C. 1975. *Background paper on the social and economic impacts of offshore petroleum developments*. St John's: Department of Mines and Energy, Government of Newfoundland

Martin, E.L. 1936. Low morale in Cartwright district south, Labrador, contrasted higher morale in Sandwich Bay. From a report entitled 'Relief from November 1935 to May 31, 1936, Cartwright.' GN 31/3C. Department of Natural Resources. PANL

Marx, K. [1867] 1977. *Capital: A critique of political economy*. New York: Vintage Books

– 1972. *Ireland and the Irish question: A collection of writings by Karl Marx and Frederick Engels*. New York: International Publishers

Matthews, K. 1968. A history of the West of England–Newfoundland fishery. DPhil thesis, Oxford University

– 1988. *Lectures on the history of Newfoundland 1500–1830*. Newfoundland History Series, no. 4. St John's: Breakwater

Matthews, R. 1983. *The creation of regional dependency*. Toronto: University of Toronto Press

Mayou, E. 1910. Harrington items. *ADSF* July: 26–8

Maxwell, W.F. 1887. *The Newfoundland and Labrador pilot*. 2nd ed. London: Printed for the Hydrographic Office

McAleese, K. 1991. The archaeology of a late 18th century sealing post in southern Labrador: George Cartwright's 'Stage Cove.' MA thesis, Memorial University of Newfoundland

McCloskey, W.B. 1990. *Fish decks*. New York: Paragon House

McClure, E. 1975. Clarence Birdseye: The Labrador years. *ADSF* 72 (2): 1–7

McGee, R.H. 1976. Letter to G.J. O'Reilly, 13 April, 1976. GN 59/7/A. 94th Resettlement Committee meeting, 24 Aug. 1976. PANL RAND

McGrath, J. 1985. *Labrador crafts past and present*. St John's: Memorial University of Newfoundland Art Gallery

McLellan, D. 1975. *Marx*. Glasgow: William Collins

McNeill, H.W. 1956. The Jessie Goldthwait diary. *ADSF* Apr.: 19

Meredith, R.S. 1934. Letter to J.H. Thomas, 22 May 1934. GN 13/2/A. Box 397, Justice Department, Labrador Railway 6/01/6. PANL

Mews, A. 1922. Census figures on Labrador, from 1857 to 1884. PC 3 [646]: 159–60

Miller, M.A. 1967. *A brief history of the 95th strategic wing and Goose Air Base.* Goose Air Base. CNS.

Mintz, S.W. 1977. The so-called World System: Local initiative and local response. *Dialectical Anthropology,* 2 (4): 260

Moody, W.R. 1906. With Dr. Grenfell on the Labrador. *ADSF* Apr.: 5–11

Moore, J. 1890. Report – Inspector pickled fish. *JHA.* (1891): 436–43

Moore, T. 1980. *Wilfred Grenfell.* Don Mills, Ont.: Fitzhenry and Whiteside

Morris, F.J. (Judge). 1909. Untitled report on Circuit Court. *JHA* (1910): 464–70

Moss diary. 1832. Remarks at Battle Habour from 9 Feb. 1832 to 7 Sept. 1832. GN P3/B/3. PANL

Muir, E.G. 1910. The people of Labrador and their needs. *ADSF* July: 38–9

Murphy, T.J. 1903. Annual Report of the Newfoundland Department of Fisheries for the year 1903 *JHA* (1904): 130–90

Neary, P. 1980. The French and American shore questions as factors in Newfoundland history. In *Newfoundland in the nineteenth and twentieth centuries,* edited by J. Hiller and P. Neary. Toronto: University of Toronto Press

Newfoundland. 1876. Census and return of the population of Newfoundland and Labrador, 1874. St John's: J.C. Withers, Queen's Printer

– 1974. Department of Provincial Affairs. Report of the Royal Commission on Labrador. 6 vols. St. John's

– 1986. Royal Commission on Employment and Unemployment. Building on our strengths: Final Report of the Royal Commission on Employment and Unemployment (RCEU)

Newfoundland and Labrador Rural Development Council (NLRDC). 1983. Development associations in Newfoundland and Labrador: A project inventory. Mimeographed

Noble, J., and A. Pinson. 1773. Petition of Noble and Pinson to Lords of Trade. *PC 3* [270]: 1068–9

Noble, L.L. (Reverend). 1861. *After iceberg with a painter: A summer voyage to Labrador and around Newfoundland.* New York: D. Appleton

Noel, S.J.R. 1971. *Politics in Newfoundland.* Toronto: University of Toronto Press

Noseworthy, E.L. 1945. The report of the Newfoundland Ranger Force, Battle Harbour, 4 Dec. 1945. GN 38. S2-5-2. File 2. PANL

– 1946. The report of the Newfoundland Ranger Force, Battle Harbour, 8 Jan. 1946. GN 38. S2-5-2. File 2. PANL

Noseworthy, F. 1977. Forty-five dollars and found. *TD* 1977: 11–12

Noseworthy, J. 1911. Letter to Mr Pickett, Minister of Fisheries. Original in possession of Mr Ken Green, Mt Pearl, Newfoundland

O'Hanlon, R. 1988. Recovering the subject: Subaltern studies and histories of resistance in colonial South Asia. *Modern Asian Studies* 22 (1): 189–224

Owen, C.W. 1911. Letter to E. Morris, Prime Minister, 10 Feb. 1911. GN 2/5, 48. Correspondence Labrador Syndicate, Ltd April 1909 – April 1930. PANL

Packard, A.S. 1891. *The Labrador coast: A journal of two summer cruises to that region.* New York: N.D.C. Hodges

Paddon, H.L. 1917. Letter of 23 Aug. 1917 to Mr R.A. Squires, Colonial Secretary. GN 2/5. 225–8. PANL

– 1929. Vale, Indian harbour *ADSF* July: 108–10

– 1930. Ye Goode Olde Days. *ADSF* Jan.: 155–63

– 1933. Change without decay and the darkest hour. *ADSF* July: 68–72

– 1939. Dr. Paddon views the situation. *ADSF* Oct.: 85

Paddon, W.A. 1947. Log of the *Marval. ADSF* July: 50–2

– 1981. The forgotten years – 1912–1945. *ADSF* July: 12

Palma, G. 1978. Dependency: A formal theory of underdevelopment or a methodology for the analysis of concrete situations of underdevelopment? *World Development* 6 (7/8): 881–924

Pardy, E. 1977. Big excitement. *TD* 3 (2): 10–11

Pardy, T. 1981. Experience the best Teacher. *TD* 7(1): 42–4

PC. See Privy Council.

Pendergast, B. 1981. Whaling at Hawke's Harbour. *TD* 7 (1): 5–12

Perrault, A. 1976. History of Happy Valley. *TD* 1 (4): 21–5

Piccott, A.W. 1913. Report of the Department of Marine and Fisheries for the year 1912: Labrador. *JHA* 570–1

Pike, J. 1869. Report of the school at Venison Tickle, Labrador, week day school, 1868. *JHA* 776

Pinhorn, A.T. 1976. Marine resources of Newfoundland and Labrador. Bulletin of the Fisheries Research Board of Canada, no. 194. Ottawa: Environment Canada

Pinsent, R.J. (Judge). 1868. [20 Dec. 1867] Report of R.J. Pinsent, Esq., Judge of the Court of Labrador. *JHA* 549A–549H

– 1869. [31 Dec. 1868] Report of R.J. Pinsent, Esq., Judge of the Court of Labrador. *JHA* 658–62

– 1870. [28 Nov. 1869] Report of R.J. Pinsent, Esq., Judge of the Court of Labrador. *JHA* 501–7

– 1871. [31 Dec. 1870] Report of R.J. Pinsent, Esq., Judge of the Court of Labrador. *JHA* 701–5

- 1872. [30 Dec. 1871] Report of R.J. Pinsent, Esq., Judge of the Court of Labrador, 1871. *JHA* 872–5

- 1874. [31 Dec. 1873 Report] To His Excellency Colonel Stephen J. Hill, C.B., Governor of Newfoundland, ? & c., & c. *JHA* 866–70

Plaice, E. 1990. *The native game*. Social and Economic Studies, no. 40. St John's: MUN Institute of Social and Economic Research

Pomphrey, B. 1932. Experiences of 2 outdoor workers: 1931 illustrated. *ADSF* Jan.: 166–75

Poole, G. 1987. *A lifetime listening to the waves*. St John's: Harry Cuff

Porter, V.R. 1975. Dr. Wilfred Grenfell and the founding of the Grenfell Mission, 1892–1914. BA Honours thesis, Memorial University of Newfoundland

Powell, B.W. 1979. *Labrador by choice*. Toronto: Testimony Press

Pownall, J. 1773. Letter to A. Pinson, inviting observation upon Cartwright's Memorial. PC 3 [269]: 1067

Prendergast, J.L. 1875. Labrador postal service. *JHA* 949–53.

- 1877. Report of Mail Officer, Labrador Service for 1876. *JHA* 1112–14

Preston, D. 1865. Report of Commander Preston, of HMS 'Medea' to his Excellency the Governor, on the protection of the Labrador coast, from Battle Harbour to Cape Harrison. *JHA* 630–2

Privy Council (Great Britain) Judicial Committee (PC). 1927. *In the matter of the boundary between the Dominion of Canada and the colony Newfoundland in the Labrador peninsula, between the Dominion of Canada of the one part and the colony of Newfoundland of the other*. 12 vols. London: W. Clodwes & Sons

- Baye-des-Chateaux concession. vol. 7 [1234]: 3187–8

- Grant, 26 April 1763, of Cape Charles to Bryner for 4 years, 1763–67. Vol. 7 [1410]: 3671

- The particulars of the case of Nicholas Darby, merchant. Vol. 3 [310]: 1166–8

Prowse, D.W. [1895] 1972. *A history of Newfoundland*. Canadiana Reprint Series, no. 33. Belleville, Ont.: Mika Studio

Pye, F., M. Graham, and L. Stone. N.d. The Stone heritage. Author's Collection. Mimeographed

Rendell, E. 1841. Of Mr. Rendell's proceedings on the coast of Labrador. *JHA* 42–3

Resettlement Committee, The Newfoundland (RC). 1970. 1st Meeting of Resettlement Committee, 17 Sept. 1970. GN 59/7/A. PANL RAND

- 1970. 14th Meeting of Resettlement Committee, 10 Nov. 1970, Appendix 1. GN59/7/A. PANL RAND

- 1971. 37th and 38th meetings of Resettlement Committee, 1, 3 Nov. 1971. GN 59/7/A. PANL RAND

- 1971. 39th Resettlement Committee Meeting, 18 Nov. 1971. GN 59/7/A. PANL RAND
- 1972. 52nd Resettlement Committee Meeting, 3 Oct. 1972. GN 59/7/A. PANL RAND
- 1973. 63rd Resettlement Committee Meeting, 2 May 1973. GN 59/7/A. PANL RAND
- 1973. 64th Resettlement Committee Meeting, 6 June 1973. GN 59/7/A. PANL RAND
- 1973. 65th Resettlement Committee Meeting, 4 July 1973. GN 59/7/A. PANL RAND
- 1973. 66th Resettlement Committee Meeting, 8 Aug. 1973. GN 59/7/A. PANL RAND
- 1973. 67th Resettlement Committee Meeting, 5 Sept. 1973. GN 59/7/A. PANL RAND
- 1976. 94th Resettlement Committee Meeting, 24 Aug 1976. GN 59/7/A. PANL RAND

Resettlement Files, The Newfoundland (RF). 1967. GN 39/1. Resettlement File H 556. PANL RAND
- 1968. GN 39/1. Resettlement File H 3475. PANL RAND
- 1969/70. GN 39/1. Resettlement File H 5107. PANL RAND

Rich, I. 1981. Goose Bay meant good pay. *TD* 7 (1): 44

Robbins, M.A. 1949. George's Cove station reopened. *ADSF* Oct.: 73–5

Rompkey, R. 1991. *Grenfell of Labrador: A biography*. Toronto: University of Toronto Press

Roosevelt, E. [1941] 1987. Report number 1. *TD* 12 (4): 16–19

Roseberry, W. 1988. Political economy. *Annual Review of Anthropology* 17: 161–85.

Rothney, G.O. 1934. The case of Bayne and Brymer: An incident in the early history of Labrador. *Canadian Historical Review* 40: 264–75

Rowe, F.W. 1980. *History of Newfoundland and Labrador*. Toronto: McGraw-Hill Ryerson,

Rumbolt, C. N.d. Eastern Labrador fisheries report. Author's Collection. Mimeographed

Russel, E. 1949. Memorandum for Executive Council on the Labrador Development Company, Ltd 27 July 1949. GN 13/2/A. Box 123, File 24 (1980). Justice Department, PANL

Ryan, S. 1983. Fishery to colony: A Newfoundland watershed, 1793–1815. *Acadiensis* 12 (2): 34–52

Sabine, L. 1853. *Report on the principal fisheries of the American seas*. Washington: Robert Armstrong, Printer

Sahlins, M. 1985. *Islands of history*. Chicago: University of Chicago Press

– [1993] 1994. Goodbye to Tristes Tropes: Ethnography in the context of modern world history. In *Assessing cultural anthropology*, edited by R. Borofsky. New York: McGraw-Hill

Said, E.W. 1978. *Orientalism.* New York: Pantheon Books

Sametz, Z.W. and J.L. Miller 1971. Letter to J.P. Francis, dated 23 Sept. 1971. GN 59/7/A. Minutes of Resettlement Committee, 35th meeting, 15 Dec. 1971. PANL Rand

Sawchuck, J. 1985. The Metis, non-status Indians and the new aboriginality: Government influences on native political alliances and identity. *Canadian Ethnic Studies* 17 (2): 135–46

Scarlett, M.J. ed. 1977. Consequences of offshore oil and gas – Norway, Scotland, and Newfoundland. Newfoundland Social and Economic Papers, no. 6. St John's: MUN Institute of Social and Economic Research

Scheper-Hughes, N. 1979. *Saints, scholars, and schizophrenics: Mental illness in rural Ireland*. Berkeley: University of California Press

Schneider, R.H. 1984. The formation of attitudes toward development in southern Labrador. PhD thesis, McGill University

Schomberg, I. 1777. Lieut. Schomberg's order. *PC* 3 [395]: 1274–5

Schumacher, E.F. 1973. *Small is beautiful: A study of economics as if people mattered*. New York: Harper & Row

Scott, J.C. 1985. *Weapons of the weak: Everyday forms of peasant resistance*. New Haven: Yale University Press

Sears, F.C. 1929. The agricultural possibilities in Labrador. *ADSF* Jan.: 144–7.

Sergeant, D.E. 1953. Whaling in Newfoundland and Labrador waters. *Norwegian Whaling Gazette* 12: 687–95

Shea, E.D. 1869. Financial Secretary's office: Detailed statement [31 Dec. 1867]. *JHA*, 128.

Shea, T. 1777. Correspondence between J. Coghlan of Fogo and Governor Montagu. PC 3 [392]: 1271

Sider, G.M. 1986. *Culture and class in anthropology and history: A Newfoundland illustration*. New York: Cambridge University Press

Simpson, J.H. 1934. Letter to Howley, 15 Sept. 1934. GN 38. Box S 4-1-1, File 6, J. 122–'34. PANL

– 1935. Formulation of policy regarding timber limits and water powers on the Labrador which are held undeveloped by speculators, 23 Mar. 1935. GN 38. Box S 4-1-1, File 6, J–122–'34. PANL

Slade Ledgers (Battle Harbour). 1793. (Untitled) Truce between Noble and Pinson and John Slade. MG 460. Box 23. PANL

– 1798. Indian account. MG 460. Box 23. PANL

Smallwood, J.R., ed. 1981. *Encyclopedia of Newfoundland and Labrador*, Vol. 1. St John's: Newfoundland Book Publishers
– 1984. *Encyclopedia of Newfoundland and Labrador*, vol. 2, St John's: Newfoundland Book Publishers
Smith, I. 1988. Interview with Cathy Porter. CBC Radio Fisheries Broadcast, 5 and 6 Jan.
Smith, P.E.L. 1987. In winter quarters. *Newfoundland Studies* 3 (1): 1–36
Snowden, D. 1974. See Newfoundland 1974.
– 1975. Speech to 5th Annual Meeting of Newfoundland and Labrador Rural Development Council, Gander, Newfoundland, Dec. 1974. *Rounder* 1 (1): 14
Southard, F.E. 1982. Salt cod and God: An ethnography of socio-economic conditions affecting status in a southern Labrador community. MA thesis, Memorial University of Newfoundland
Stavely, M. 1981. Resettlement and centralization in Newfoundland. In *Policies of population redistribution*, edited by J.W. Webb, A. Naukkarinen, and L.A. Kosinski. Oulu, Finland: Geographical Society of Northern Finland for the IGU Commission on Population Geography
Stearns, W.A. 1884. *Labrador: A sketch of its peoples, its industries and its natural history*. Boston: Lee and Shepard
Steel, T. 1975. *The life and death of St. Kilda*. Glasgow: Collins
Steffler, J. 1992. *The afterlife of George Cartwright*. Toronto: McClelland & Stewart
Stevenson, R.L. 1950–1. Untitled diary from Hawke Harbour. Author's Collection
Stopp, M.P., and K. Reynolds. 1992. Preliminary report of the 1992 Labrador south coastal survey. St John's. CNS
Stopp, M.P, and D. Rutherford. 1991. Preliminary report of the 1991 south Labrador coastal archaeological survey. St John's.
Story, G.M. 1981. Old Labrador: George Cartwright 1738–1819. *Newfoundland Quarterly* 77 (1): 23–30, 35
– 1983. George Cartwright. In *Dictionary of Canadian Biography*, vol. 5. Toronto: University of Toronto Press
Story, G.M., W.J. Kirwin, and J.D.A. Widdowson, eds. 1982. *Dictionary of Newfoundland English*. Toronto: University of Toronto Press
Straus, R. 1975. The Americans come to Newfoundland. In *The book of Newfoundland*, vol. 6, edited by J.R. Smallwood. St John's: Newfoundland Book Publishers
Strauss, S. 1993. The mystery of the missing cod. *Globe and Mail*, 10 July 1993, sec. D, 8

Summers, C.L. 1941a. Report of the Newfoundland Ranger Force, Cartwright, 3 Sept. 1941. GN 13/4. Loose Ranger Reports, 1941–2. File: Monthly Condition Reports. PANL

– 1941b. Report of the Newfoundland Ranger Force, Cartwright, 4 Oct. 1941. GN 13/4. Loose Ranger Reports, 1941–2. File: Miscellaneous Condition Reports, no. 2. PANL

– 1942a. Report of the Newfoundland Ranger Force, Cartwright, 3 Jan. 1942. GN 13/4. Loose Ranger Reports 1941–2. File: Miscellaneous Condition Reports, no. 1. PANL

– 1942b. Report of the Newfoundland Ranger Force, Cartwright, 3 Feb. 1942. GN 13/4. High Commission Rangers/1940, File: Monthly Condition Reports. PANL

– 1942c. Report of the Newfoundland Ranger Force, Cartwright, 8 Apr. 1942. GN 13/4. Loose Ranger Reports, 1941–2. File: Monthly Condition Reports. PANL

– 1942d. Report of the Newfoundland Ranger Force, Cartwright, 3 June 1942. GN 13/4. Loose Ranger Reports 1941–2. File: Miscellaneous Condition Reports, no. 1. PANL

– 1942e. Report of the Newfoundland Ranger Force, Cartwright, 2 Oct. 1942. GN 13/4. Loose Ranger Reports, 1941–2. File: Miscellaneous Condition Reports, no. 2. PANL

– 1942f. Report of the Newfoundland Ranger Force, Cartwright, 3 Dec. 1942. GN 13/4. Newfoundland Rangers, File no. 7. PANL

Summers, G.B. 1935. Abstract of title of Labrador property. Enclosure in memo to J.H. Simpson, 29 Apr. 1935. GN 13/2/A. Box 123, File 17 (1980). Justice Department, PANL

Swaffield, W.E. 1926. Sworn affidavit. PC 2 [88]: 384–485

Sweetland, B. 1865. Report of Judge Sweetland, of proceedings of Labrador court, during the summer of 1864, &., Together with census returns of resident population, from Blanc Sablon to Indian Harbour. *JHA* 707–12

– 1866. Report of Judge Sweetland, of his visit upon the Labrador circuit, during the summer of 1865. *JHA* 196–7

Tachet et al. 1758. Authorization, 20 Mar. 1758, by Vaudrevil to creditors of Marsal to operate Cap Charles to expiration of concession in 1763. PC 7 [1409]: 3669

Tanner, V. 1944. *Outlines of the geography, life and customs of Newfoundland-Labrador*. Helsinki: Acta Geographica, 8

Taylor, J.G. 1977. *Moravian mission influence on Labrador Innuit subsistence, 1776–1830*. Ottawa: National Museum of Man

- 1979. Indian-Inuit relations in eastern Labrador, 1600–1976. *Arctic Anthropology* 16 (2): 49–58
- 1980. The Inuit of Southern Quebec-Labrador: Reviewing the Evidence. *Inuit Studies* 4 (nos. 1–2): 185–93
- 1983. The two worlds of Mikak, Part I. *The Beaver Outfit* 314 (3): 4–13
- 1984. The two worlds of Mikak, Part II. *The Beaver Outfit* 314 (4): 18–25

Templeman, W. 1966. *Marine resources of Newfoundland.* Ottawa: Fisheries Research Board of Canada, Bulletin No. 154

Them Days. (*TD*). [1975] 1982. *Alluring Labrador.* Happy Valley, Labrador
- 1994. K.M. Keddie (1887–1966). *TD* 19 (3): 4–5

Thompson, E.P. [1963] 1984. *The making of the English working class.* Harmondsworth: Penguin Books

Thornton, P.A. 1977. The demographic and mercantile bases of initial permanent settlement in the Strait of Belle Isle. In *The peopling of Newfoundland,* edited by J.J. Mannion. Newfoundland Social and Economic Papers, no. 8. St John's: ISER
- 1979. Dynamic equilibrium: Settlement, population and ecology in the Strait of Belle Isle, Newfoundland 1840–1940. 2 vols. PhD dissertation, University of Aberdeen
- 1990. The transition from the migratory to the resistant fishery in the Strait of Belle Isle. *Acadiensis* 19 (2): 92–120

Tobin, J. 1853. Letter to C. Ayre, on the protection of the fisheries at Belle Isle and Labrador. *JHA* 1953: 131–2

Tonnies, F. [1887] 1957. *Community and society.* East Lansing: Michigan State University Press

Townsend, C.W. 1907. *Along the Labrador coast.* Boston: Dana Estes

Trudel, F. 1978. The Inuit of southern Labrador and the development of French sedentary fisheries (1700–1760). In *Canadian Ethnology Society, Papers from the Fourth Annual Congress, 1977,* edited by R.J. Preston. Mercury Series, Canadian Ethnology Service, Paper no. 40. Ottawa: National Museum of Manitoba

Tuck, J.A. 1975. *Prehistory of Saglek Bay, Labrador: Archaic and Palaeo-Eskimo occupations.* Archaeological Survey of Canada, Paper no. 32. Ottawa: National Museums of Canada
- 1982. Prehistoric archaeology in Atlantic Canada since 1975. *Canadian Journal of Archaeology* 6: 201–23

Tuck, J.A., and R. Grenier. 1989. *Red Bay, Labrador: World whaling capital AD 1550–1600.* St John's: Atlantic Archaeology

Tucker, E.W. 1839. *Five months in Labrador and Newfoundland.* Concord, NH: I.S. Boyd and W. White

U.S Army. Corps of Engineers. 1946. Historical monograph on U.S. Army
    bases in Newfoundland. Office of Division Engineer, North Atlantic
    Region. CNS
U.S. Department of State. 1955. Defense: Radar stations in Newfoundland-
    Labrador area. Agreement between the U.S.A. and Canada. CNS
Vibe, C. 1967. *Arctic animals in relation to climatic fluctuations.* Copenhagen:
    Meddelelser om Gronland, vol. 170, no. 5
von B. Neuhauser, D. 1959. Along the way by Maraval. *ADSF* Oct.:
    72–3
Wallerstein, I. 1989. *Modern world–system III.* San Diego: Academic Press
Walsh, H.C. 1896. *The last cruise of the Miranda: A record of arctic adventure.*
    New York: Transatlantic Publishing
Warren, M.H. 1851. Evidence taken before select committee on the French
    encroachments on this island and Labrador. *JHA* 157–8
Watson, R. 1910. Letter from R. Watson (Col. Secret.) to R.S. Fulton, Chm.
    Lab. Syndicate, 5 Apr. 1910. GN 2/5, 48. Correspondence Labrador Syndi-
    cate, April 1909–April 1930. PANL
Whitaker, I. 1988. Core values among Newfoundland fishermen in the 1960s.
    Anthropologica 30 (1): 75–86
Whitaker, J.S. 1954. A day at the races. *ADSF* Apr.: 11–14
White, E. 1852. Documents from his Excellency the Governor, in reference to
    the encroachments of the French on the Labrador. *JHA* 112–13
White, F.J. 1887. Medical report of Dr. White, Labrador, 1886. *JHA* 875–80
Whitely, W.H. 1969. Governor Hugh Palliser and the Newfoundland and
    Labrador fishery, 1764–8. *Canadian Historical Review* 50 (2): 141–63
– 1976. Newfoundland, Quebec, and the Labrador merchants, and the admin-
    istration of the coast of Labrador, 1774–1783. *Acadiensis* 6 (1): 92–112
– 1977. Newfoundland, Quebec, and the Labrador merchants, 1783–1809.
    Newfoundland Quarterly 73 (4): 18–26
Whiting, L.R. ed. 1974. *Communities left behind.* Ames: Iowa State University
    Press
Williams, C. 1964. Spotted Island, Summer 1963. *ADSF* Jan.: 106–8
Williams, J.O. 1934. Letter to W.R. Howley, 21 Oct. 1934. GN 13/2/A. Box
    123, File 17 (1980), Justice Department, PANL
– 1945. Letter to W.H. Flinn, 27 Nov. 1945. GN 13/2/A. Box 123, File 19
    (1980), Justice Department. PANL
– 1947. Letter to Flinn, Comm. of Nat'l Res., 6 Sept. 1947. GN 13/2/A. File
    19, LDC, 1945–8. PANL
– 1948. Letter to E. Cook, 8 Sept. 1948. GN 13/2/A. Box 123, File 19 (1980).
    PANL

– 1949. Letter and enclosure to J.R. Smallwood, 25 July 1949. GN 12/2/A. Box 123, File 24, LDC, 1949 (1980). PANL

Williamson, H.A. 1976. The shore-based fishery on the Labrador coast. Paper presented to Labrador Fisheries Conference, Happy Valley, 24–5 April. Author's Collection.

Willis, P. 1977. *Learning to labour*. Farnborough: Saxon House

Willway, F. 1898. The mission at work in Labrador. *Toilers of the Deep* 13: 330

Wilson, W.E. (Reverend). 1869. Report on school at Battle Harbour, Labrador. *JHA* 775

Winsor, N. N.d. *Building on a firm foundation: A history of Methodism in Newfoundland, 1825–1855*, vol. 2. Economy Printing Ltd. CNS.

Winter, J. 1864. Reports. *JHA* 618–24

– 1865. Reports. *JHA* 697–706

Winterbotham, W. 1795. *An historical, geographical, commercial and philosophical view of the American United States, and of the European settlements in America and the West-Indies*, vol. 4. London: J. Ridgway

Wolf, E. 1966. *Peasants*. Englewood Cliffs, NJ: Prentice Hall

– 1982. *Europe and the people without history*. Berkeley: University of California Press

Woods, H.J.B. 1907. Report of the postmaster general for the year ending 30 June 1906. *JHA* 141–8

– 1912. Report of the postmaster general for the year 1910–1911. *JHA* 544–58

– 1913. Report of the postmaster general for the year 1911–1912. *JHA* 320–31

Woodwell, J. 1809. Journal of voyage from Newburyport to Labrador. Kept by John Woodwell, of Newburyport, 1809 aboard schooner Phenix. Phillips Library, Peabody Museum of Salem, Salem, Mass.

Young, C. 1869. Report from Miss Catherine Young, 1868. *JHA* 774,

Zimmerly, D.W. 1975. *Cain's land revisited*. Newfoundland Social and Economic Studies, no. 16. St John's: MUN Institute of Social and Economic Research

Index